THE BRONT

C000296567

Very few families produce oɪ
family produced three. The wɪ
remain immensely popular, an   _ ...
relation to the surroundings anᴜ ...ᴜᴄɪ context that formed them.
The forty-two new essays in this book tell 'the Brontë story' as it has
never been told before, drawing on the latest research and the best
available scholarship while offering new perspectives on the writings
of the sisters. A section on Brontë criticism traces their reception to
the present day. The works of the sisters are explored in the context
of social, political and cultural developments in early nineteenth-
century Britain, with attention given to religion, education, art,
print culture, agriculture, law and medicine. Crammed with information, *The Brontës in Context* shows how the Brontës' fiction
interacts with the spirit of the time, suggesting reasons for its
enduring fascination.

MARIANNE THORMÄHLEN is Professor of English Literature and
Dean of Research in the Humanities and Theology at Lund Univer-
sity, Sweden. The author of books and articles on T. S. Eliot and on
John Wilmot, Earl of Rochester, she has published two books on the
Brontës, both with Cambridge University Press: *The Brontës and
Religion* (1999) and *The Brontës and Education* (2007).

THE BRONTËS IN CONTEXT

EDITED BY
MARIANNE THORMÄHLEN

CAMBRIDGE
UNIVERSITY PRESS

CAMBRIDGE
UNIVERSITY PRESS

University Printing House, Cambridge CB2 8BS, United Kingdom

Cambridge University Press is part of the University of Cambridge.

It furthers the University's mission by disseminating knowledge in the pursuit of education, learning and research at the highest international levels of excellence.

www.cambridge.org
Information on this title: www.cambridge.org/9781107479951

© Cambridge University Press 2012

First published 2012
First paperback edition 2014

A catalogue record for this publication is available from the British Library

Library of Congress Cataloguing in Publication data

The Brontës in context / edited by Marianne Thormählen.
pages   cm. – (Literature in context)
Includes bibliographical references and index.
ISBN 978-0-521-76186-4
1. Brontë family.   2. Authors, English–19th century–Biography.
3. English literature–19th century–History and criticism.   I. Thormählen, Marianne, 1949–
PR4168.B775 2012
823'.809–dc23
2012015673

ISBN 978-0-521-76186-4 Hardback
ISBN 978-1-107-47995-1 Paperback

Contents

v

Illustrations

For kind permission to reproduce the illustrations listed above, and for supplying photographs, the editor wishes to thank Mr Simon Warner (Figure 2), the National Portrait Gallery, London (Figures 13–15), and the Brontë Parsonage Museum, Haworth (all remaining pictures).

Notes on contributors

CHRISTINE ALEXANDER is Scientia Professor of English at the University of New South Wales, a Fellow of the Australian Academy of the Humanities and Director and General Editor of the Juvenilia Press. She has written and edited many publications on the Brontës, including *The Early Writings of Charlotte Brontë* (1983), the co-authored books *The Art of the Brontës* (Cambridge University Press, 1995) and *The Oxford Companion to the Brontës* (2003), and most recently the Brontës' *Tales of Glass Town, Angria and Gondal: Selected Writings* (2010).

SIMON AVERY is Principal Lecturer in English Literature at the University of Westminster, London. His publications include *Elizabeth Barrett Browning* (2011), *Mary Coleridge: Selected Poems* (2010) and *Thomas Hardy: A Reader's Guide* (2009).

MICHAEL BAUMBER has an MA in history from the University of Manchester and was Head of History at Greenhead Grammar School in Keighley for many years. He has written extensively on local history, both in book form – most recently *A History of Haworth* (2009) – and in the form of articles in various journals, including *History Today* and *Brontë Society Transactions/Brontë Studies*.

BIRGITTA BERGLUND is a senior lecturer in English at Lund University, Sweden. Her PhD thesis dealt with the novels of Ann Radcliffe, Jane Austen and Mary Wollstonecraft. She has published articles on Daphne du Maurier and Ann Radcliffe, on children and childhood in Jane Austen's novels, on women detectives in fiction and on Charlotte Brontë's *Villette*.

DINAH BIRCH is Pro-Vice-Chancellor (Research) at Liverpool University. She is the general editor of the *Oxford Companion to English Literature* (2009). Her publications include *Our Victorian Education* (2008), editions of Elizabeth Gaskell's *Cranford* (2011) and *John Ruskin:*

Selected Writings (2004), and she is co-editor of *Conflict and Difference in Nineteenth-Century Literature* (2010) and *Ruskin and Gender* (2002).

MIRIAM ELIZABETH BURSTEIN is Associate Professor of English at the College at Brockport, State University of New York. She is the author of *Narrating Women's History in Britain, 1770–1902* (2004) and of articles on historical fiction and nineteenth-century religious literature. She recently completed a second book manuscript, 'Victorian Reformations'.

JANIS MCLARREN CALDWELL is a former physician and now an associate professor of English at the University of California, Santa Barbara. The author of *Literature and Medicine in Nineteenth-Century Britain: From Mary Shelley to George Eliot* (Cambridge University Press, 2004), she is now at work on a project on the interrelationship of psychology and poetry in the Victorian period.

EDWARD CHITHAM has taught at the Universities of Wolverhampton and Warwick, at Newman College and at the Open University. He has written a number of books on the Brontës, including biographies of Anne and Emily Brontë, *The Birth of* Wuthering Heights (1998) and *A Brontë Family Chronology* (2003). His edition of Anne Brontë's poems was published in 1979.

STEPHEN COLCLOUGH is Lecturer in Nineteenth-Century Literature in the School of English at Bangor University. He is the author of *Consuming Texts: Readers and Reading Communities, 1695–1870* (2007), co-editor with Alexis Weedon of *The History of the Book in the West: 1800–1914* (2010) and a contributor to the *Cambridge History of the Book in Britain*, vol. VI: *1830–1914* (Cambridge University Press, 2009).

ANN DINSDALE is Collections Manager at the Brontë Parsonage Museum, Haworth, where she is involved in organizing exhibitions and caring for the collections. She lectures and writes on aspects of the Brontës' lives and social conditions in mid-nineteenth-century Haworth. She is the author of *The Brontës at Haworth* (2006).

BOB DUCKETT is a retired reference librarian and former editor of *Brontë Studies*. As Publication Secretary of the Brontë Society, he was responsible for the society's publications programme and organized two conferences. For his published output on professional library and information issues he was recently awarded a doctorate. He has edited several books on local history.

MARIA FRAWLEY is Professor of English at George Washington University. Her books include *Invalidism and Identity in Nineteenth-Century Britain* (2004), an edition of Harriet Martineau's *Life in the Sick-Room* (2003), *A Wider Range: Travel Writing by Women in Victorian England* (1994) and the Twayne volume on Anne Brontë's life and works (1996).

BARBARA T. GATES is Alumni Distinguished Professor of English and Women's Studies Emerita at the University of Delaware. She is the author of *Victorian Suicide: Mad Crimes and Sad Histories* (1988), *Kindred Nature: Victorian and Edwardian Women Embrace the Living World* (1998) and numerous essays, including essays on the Brontë novels. In addition, she has edited a number of books, among them a volume of critical essays on Charlotte Brontë.

JANET GEZARI is Lucretia L. Allyn Professor of Literature in English at Connecticut College. She is the author of *Charlotte Brontë and Defensive Conduct* (1992) and *Last Things: Emily Brontë's Poems* (2007), as well as the editor of the Penguin edition of Emily's poems. She is currently working on an annotated edition of *Wuthering Heights*, forthcoming in 2012.

DUDLEY GREEN took a degree in classics at Oxford and then embarked on a career in teaching. Particularly interested in the father of the Brontë family, he is the editor of *The Letters of the Reverend Patrick Brontë* (2005) and the author of *Patrick Brontë: Father of Genius* (2008).

DAVID JASPER is Professor of Literature and Theology in the University of Glasgow and Changjiang Chair Professor at Renmin University in Beijing. His earliest research was in Victorian fiction and religion, and he has recently completed editing a volume of nineteenth-century religious biographies by Margaret Oliphant. His most recent book is *The Sacred Body* (2009), and he was an editor of the *Oxford Handbook of English Literature and Theology* (2007).

DREW LAMONICA ARMS is Professional-in-Residence and Director of Fellowship Advising at the Louisiana State University Honors College in Baton Rouge, and a Rhodes Scholar. She is the author of *'We Are Three Sisters': Self and Family in the Writing of the Brontës* (2003).

ELIZABETH LANGLAND is Foundation Professor and Dean of New College of Interdisciplinary Arts and Sciences at Arizona State University.

She is the author of numerous articles and books, including *Society in the Novel* (1984), *Nobody's Angels* (1995), *Telling Tales* (2002) and *Anne Brontë: The Other One* (1989).

ALEXANDRA LEWIS is a lecturer in English at the University of Aberdeen. She holds a PhD from Trinity College, Cambridge, and is editor of the *British Association for Victorian Studies Newsletter*. Her publications include a chapter in *Acts of Memory* (ed. Ryan Barnett and Serena Trowbridge, 2010) and reviews for the *Times Literary Supplement* and *Women: A Cultural Review*. She is currently completing a monograph on trauma in nineteenth-century literature and psychology.

SARA J. LODGE is a senior lecturer in English at the University of St Andrews. She is the author of Jane Eyre: *A Reader's Guide to Essential Criticism* (2009), *Thomas Hood and Nineteenth-Century Poetry: Work, Play and Politics* (2007) and numerous articles on nineteenth-century writing and print culture.

SUE LONOFF retired from the Harvard Extension School Faculty in 2011. Her Brontë publications include *Approaches to Teaching Emily Brontë's 'Wuthering Heights'* (co-edited with Terri A. Hasseler, 2006), *Charlotte Brontë and Emily Brontë, the Belgian Essays: A Critical Edition* (1996) and the Penguin enriched e-book edition of *Wuthering Heights*. She also edited a recent special issue of *Brontë Studies*, 'Men in the Brontës' Lives' (vol. 36.1, January 2011).

JILL L. MATUS is Professor of English and Vice Provost, Students, at the University of Toronto. A Fellow of the Royal Society of Canada, she is the author of numerous articles on the Brontës, Dickens, Gaskell and George Eliot. Her publications include *Unstable Bodies: Victorian Representations of Sexuality and Maternity* (1995), the *Cambridge Companion to Elizabeth Gaskell* (2007) and, most recently, *Shock, Memory and the Unconscious in Victorian Fiction* (Cambridge University Press, 2009).

VICTOR A. NEUFELDT is a professor emeritus of English at the University of Victoria. His publications include editions of the poems of Charlotte Brontë (1985) and *The Works of Patrick Branwell Brontë* (1997–9), as well as the entries for Branwell in *The Oxford Companion to the Brontës* (2003), *The Child Writer from Austen to Woolf*, edited by Christine Alexander and Juliet McMaster (Cambridge University Press, 2005), and the *Oxford Dictionary of National Biography*.

LINDA H. PETERSON is Niel Gray, Jr. Professor of English at Yale University and the author of *Becoming a Woman of Letters: Myths of Authorship and Facts of the Victorian Market* (2009). She has edited Elizabeth Gaskell's *Life of Charlotte Brontë* (2006) and Emily Brontë's *Wuthering Heights* (2003) and published on the Brontës in *Dickens Studies Annual, Studies in English Literature 1500–1900* and *The Cambridge Companion to Elizabeth Gaskell* (2007).

STEPHEN PRICKETT is an honorary professor of English at the University of Kent in Canterbury and Regius Professor Emeritus of English at the University of Glasgow. In addition to his seven scholarly monographs he has published one novel, seven edited volumes and over ninety articles on Romanticism, Victorian studies and literature and theology. His latest book, *Modernity and the Reinvention of Tradition*, was published by Cambridge University Press in 2009.

LYN PYKETT is an emeritus professor at Aberystwyth University. Her books include full-length studies of Emily Brontë (1989), Charles Dickens and Wilkie Collins; *The Improper Feminine: The Women's Sensation Novel and the New Woman Writing* (1992); and *Engendering Fictions: The English Novel in the Early Twentieth Century* (1995). A revised and expanded edition of her book on the sensation novel in the series Writers and their Work appeared in 2012.

HERBERT ROSENGARTEN taught for many years in the English Department at the University of British Columbia (Vancouver), specializing in nineteenth-century fiction. He was one of the team assembled by Ian Jack to produce the Clarendon edition of the novels of the Brontës, on which the Oxford World's Classics editions referred to in this volume are based, and he was a contributor to *The Oxford Companion to the Brontës* (2003).

JANE SELLARS is Curator of the Mercer Art Gallery, Harrogate, and a former trustee of the Brontë Society. She was formerly Education Officer at the Walker Art Gallery, Liverpool, Director of the Brontë Parsonage Museum at Haworth and Principal Curator of Harewood House, Leeds. Her writing on the Brontës includes co-authorship of *The Art of the Brontës* (Cambridge University Press, 1995) and *Writing Lives: Charlotte Brontë* (1997).

JOANNE SHATTOCK is Emeritus Professor of Victorian Literature at the University of Leicester. She edited *The Cambridge Companion to*

English Literature 1830–1914 (2010); a volume of Margaret Oliphant's literary criticism for the *Selected Works of Margaret Oliphant*, edited by Joanne Shattock and Elisabeth Jay (2011); and Elizabeth Gaskell's journalism for *The Works of Elizabeth Gaskell* (2005). She is the author of *The Oxford Guide to British Women Writers* (1993).

MARGARET SMITH was born in Yorkshire. She gained her BA and MA degrees at the University of London and was then, under Ian Jack's guidance, textual editor of the Clarendon editions of Charlotte Brontë's major novels and of the subsequent Oxford World's Classics editions. She edited the three-volume *Letters of Charlotte Brontë* (1995–2004), as well as Charlotte Brontë's *Selected Letters* (2007).

PATSY STONEMAN is Emeritus Reader in English at the University of Hull and the author of *Brontë Transformations: The Cultural Dissemination of* Jane Eyre *and* Wuthering Heights (1996) and *Jane Eyre on Stage, 1848–1898: An Illustrated Edition of Eight Plays with Contextual Notes* (2007). She has contributed essays to both the *Cambridge Companion to the Brontës* (Cambridge University Press, 2002) and the *Oxford Companion to the Brontës* (2003).

MARIANNE THORMÄHLEN is Professor of English Literature and Dean of Research in the Humanities and Theology at Lund University, Sweden. The author of books and articles on T. S. Eliot and on John Wilmot, Earl of Rochester, she has published two books on the Brontës, both with Cambridge University Press: *The Brontës and Religion* (1999) and *The Brontës and Education* (2007).

IAN WARD is Professor of Law at Newcastle Law School. He is the author of a number of studies in the field of law and literature, including *Law and Literature: Possibilities and Perspectives* (1995) and *Law, Text, Terror* (2009), both published by Cambridge University Press, and *Law and the Brontës* (2011).

STEPHEN WHITEHEAD is a former trustee of the Brontë Society and Chair of the Parsonage Museum Committee, having worked on the museum's front-of-house staff for thirteen years. He has had a number of essays published in *Brontë Studies*, and his book *The Brontës' Haworth: The Place and the People the Brontës Knew* appeared in 2006.

T. J. WINNIFRITH taught at Eton College and the University of Warwick from 1961 to 1998. He has written *The Brontës and their Background* (1973), *The Brontës* (1977), *Brontë Facts and Brontë Problems* (with Edward Chitham; 1983) and *A New Life of Charlotte Brontë* (1988). He has also written a number of articles for the *Brontë Society Transactions/Brontë Studies* and continues to lecture on the Brontës.

STEVEN WOOD has been researching the history of Haworth for over twenty years. He has made transcriptions and studies of many of the principal nineteenth-century sources. His publications include *Haworth: 'a strange uncivilized little place'* (2005), *Haworth through Time* and *Oxenhope and Stanbury through Time* (both 2009) and two more books of old photographs from the area (2011).

Acknowledgements

Editing a volume with contributions by thirty-six authors is a time-consuming enterprise, and most of that time was the gift of the Swedish Research Council. I will always remain enormously grateful for its munificence – which included a liberal travel allowance – for six years altogether, the most fruitful research period of my life.

Another kind of generosity was provided by Ann Dinsdale, Collections Manager of the Brontë Parsonage Museum, with whom I have been discussing this project from its inception and whose wisdom and enthusiasm have been invaluable at every stage. Additional Haworth-based support came from Steven Wood, who, among other things, gave swift and sterling assistance over the provision of maps.

For the second time in less than a decade, Dr Linda Bree, my editor at Cambridge University Press, recalled me to the nineteenth century by commissioning a Brontë book from me just as I was about to immerse myself in modern poetry. I am very grateful to her, not only for all the enjoyment this project has given me, but also for immensely helpful hands-on scrutiny and advice.

My greatest debt is to the thirty-five colleagues from all over the world whose contributions make up this book. Every one of them has been a pleasure to work with from start to finish. They made what I feared would be a stressful if worthwhile endeavour into a privilege, and my heartfelt thanks go out to them all.

Marianne Thormählen
Lund, Sweden

Chronology

Compiled by Marianne Thormählen, with frequent recourse to Edward Chitham, *A Brontë Family Chronology* (Basingstoke: Palgrave Macmillan, 2003). The comprehensive chronology in Christine Alexander and Margaret Smith's *Oxford Companion to the Brontës* (Oxford University Press, 2003) also assisted. Except where special reasons make such information useful, no precise dates are given for the historical and literary events entered under relevant years.

1777	
17 March	Patrick Brunty/Branty/Prunty born at Imdel (Emdale), County Down, Ireland.
1783	
15 April	Maria Branwell born at Penzance, Cornwall.
1802	Peace of Amiens creates a brief lull in the war between Britain and France (broken by Britain's declaration of war on France in May 1803).
September	Patrick Brontë enters St John's College, Cambridge, as a sizar. Changes his name from 'Branty' to 'Brontë'.
1804	Napoleon becomes Emperor of the French. William Pitt is made Prime Minister.
	William Blake's *Jerusalem* and *Milton* published.
1805	Napoleon defeats the Austrians and Russians at Austerlitz. Battle of Trafalgar. Death of Lord Nelson.
1806	Napoleon closes Continental ports to British trade. Death of William Pitt.
April	Patrick Brontë takes his bachelor's degree.
Summer	Patrick Brontë ordained. First curacy, at Wethersfield, Essex (until 1809).
1807	Abolition of the slave trade throughout the British Empire.
1808	Sir Walter Scott's *Marmion* published.

1812	Britain at war with the USA. Napoleon retreats from Russia.
	First two cantos of Lord Byron's *Childe Harold's Pilgrimage* published. Charles Dickens born.
Spring	Luddite riots in Yorkshire, near Hartshead where Patrick Brontë is curate. Attempted murder of a mill-owner (William Cartwright).
29 December	Marriage of Patrick Brontë and Maria Branwell.
1814	Napoleon abdicates and is exiled to Elba. War with the USA ends.
	Lord Byron's *Lara* and *The Corsair* published, also Scott's *Waverley*.
January	Maria Brontë born.
1815	Napoleon defeated at Waterloo and exiled to St Helena. Congress of Vienna redraws map of Europe; restoration of the Bourbon monarchy in France. Corn Laws introduced in the UK, forbidding the importation of cheaper grain from abroad.
	Patrick Brontë's *The Cottage in the Wood* published.
February	Elizabeth Brontë born.
May	Brontë family move to Thornton, where Patrick Brontë has been appointed curate.
1816	Jane Austen's *Emma* and S. T. Coleridge's *Christabel* and *Kubla Khan* published.
21 April	Charlotte Brontë born.
1817	Death of Princess Charlotte, the Prince Regent's daughter.
	Byron's *Manfred*, Coleridge's *Biographia literaria* and Scott's *Rob Roy* published. *Blackwood's Edinburgh Magazine* founded.
	Mary Taylor and Ellen Nussey born.
26 June	Patrick Branwell Brontë born.
1818	Austen's *Northanger Abbey* and *Persuasion* published, also Byron's *Beppo*, Mary Shelley's *Frankenstein*, Scott's *Heart of Midlothian* and John Keats' *Endymion*.
	Patrick Brontë's prose tale *The Maid of Killarney* published. Advertised in *Blackwood's* (April).
6 January	Arthur Bell Nicholls born.
30 July	Emily Jane Brontë born.

1819	'Peterloo Massacre': troops shoot at a mass meeting of workers. The Poor Relief Act passed. Queen Victoria, Mary Ann Evans (George Eliot) and John Ruskin born.
	Byron's *Don Juan*, cantos I–II, published, also Scott's *The Bride of Lammermoor* and *Ivanhoe*.
	Chapelry of Haworth resists appointment of Patrick Brontë as perpetual curate.
1820	Death of King George III and accession of the Prince Regent as George IV. Trial of Queen Caroline.
	Keats' best-known poems published, also Charles Maturin's *Melmoth the Wanderer*, P. B. Shelley's *Prometheus Unbound* and Thomas Malthus' *Principles of Political Economy*.
17 January	Anne Brontë born.
April	Brontë family move to Haworth following Patrick Brontë's appointment as perpetual curate.
1821	Death of Napoleon on St Helena. Greek War of Independence begins.
	Byron's *Cain* and *Don Juan*, cantos III–V, published, also Thomas De Quincey's *Confessions of an English Opium Eater*, Scott's *Kenilworth* and Shelley's *Epipsychidion* and 'Adonais' (the latter following the death of Keats).
Spring	Miss Elizabeth Branwell arrives in Haworth to help look after Mrs Brontë, who fell ill in late January, and the family.
15 September	Death of Mrs Brontë, probably from uterine cancer.
1824	George Birkbeck founds first Mechanics' Institute (later Birkbeck College) in London.
	Death of Byron. Publication of Thomas Carlyle's translation of J. W. von Goethe's *Wilhelm Meister's Apprenticeship*, and of James Hogg's *Private Memoirs and Confessions of a Justified Sinner*. The Grimm brothers' *Fairy Tales* translated into English.
July	Maria and Elizabeth Brontë go to the Clergy Daughters' School at Cowan Bridge.
10 August	Charlotte Brontë goes to Cowan Bridge.
25 November	Emily Brontë goes to Cowan Bridge.

1825   First railway passengers transported. A crisis year in the
            economy.
            William Hazlitt's *The Spirit of the Age* published.
            Founding of the Keighley Mechanics' Institute.
            Tabitha Aykroyd ('Tabby') starts working as a servant
            at the parsonage.

6 May   Maria Brontë dies of pulmonary tuberculosis, having
            been brought home from Cowan Bridge by her father
            in February.

1 June   Patrick Brontë takes Charlotte and Emily home from
            Cowan Bridge. They are taught at home by their father
            and aunt until 1830.

15 June   Elizabeth Brontë dies, also of pulmonary tuberculosis,
            after just over two weeks at home.

1826   Power-looms destroyed by unemployed weavers.

5 June   Patrick Brontë brings back toys for the children from
            Leeds, including the toy soldiers for Branwell which
            inspire the 'Young Men's Plays', the inception of the
            Brontë juvenilia.

1827   University College London founded. Death of
            Beethoven.
            John Keble's *The Christian Year* published, also Scott's
            Life of Napoleon; Scott acknowledges his authorship of
            the Waverley novels.
            Brontë children's writing takes off. Branwell's 'Battell
            Book', his first manuscript, dates from this year.

1828   Test Act repealed. Wellington Prime Minister. Mad-
            house Act passed, a result of growing concern over
            mental health. Thomas Arnold becomes headmaster
            of Rugby School.
            George Combe publishes *The Constitution of Man*.
            Brontë children busy writing and drawing.

1829   The passing of the Catholic Emancipation Act, sup-
            ported by Patrick Brontë, enables Roman Catholics to
            hold public office and own property. John Peel sets up
            the Metropolitan Police in London.
            Thomas Carlyle publishes *Signs of the Times* in the
            Edinburgh Review. James Mill publishes *Analysis of
            the Phenomenon of the Human Mind*.

	Brontë children productive, 'Branwell's Blackwood's Magazine' testifying to the influence of *Blackwood's* on the children at least from this point. The children are given art lessons by John Bradley of Keighley.
1830	Death of George IV and accession of his brother William IV. 'July Revolution' in France leads to the accession of Louis Philippe. Pressure for parliamentary and social reform in the UK; a resisting Wellington resigns as Prime Minister and is replaced by the Whig Lord Grey. Stephenson's 'Rocket' wins speed contest. Greek independence achieved. Cholera epidemic (1830–2).

Fraser's Magazine begins. Carlyle's *On History* published, also William Cobbett's *Rural Rides* and Thomas Moore's *Letters and Journals of Lord Byron, with Notices of his Life*. Publication of Auguste Comte's *Cours de philosophie positive* begins, also of Sir Charles Lyell's *Principles of Geology*.

1831	Charles Darwin sets off on his *Beagle* expedition. 'Swing Riots' against the mechanization of agriculture and resulting job losses. House of Commons passes Reform Bill, but Lords veto it. Sir James Clark Ross locates the magnetic North Pole.
17 January	Charlotte Brontë goes to the Misses Wooler's school at Roe Head, near Mirfield.
May	Aunt Branwell subscribes to *Fraser's Magazine*.
1832	The Reform Bill is passed, extending franchise and improving representation in Parliament (abolition of 'rotten boroughs').

Deaths of Scott and Goethe.

| Summer | Charlotte Brontë returns to Haworth from Roe Head. |
| 1833 | Factory Act limits child labour. The Oxford Movement in the Church of England begins with John Henry Newman's *Tracts for the Times*. |

Carlyle's *Sartor Resartus* published (1833–4), also Hartley Coleridge's *Poems* and Charles Lamb's *Last Essays of Elia*. Patrick Brontë joins the Mechanics' Institute at Keighley.

1834	Melbourne has brief spell as Whig Prime Minister; Robert Peel's Tory government takes over. New Poor Law leads to the establishment of workhouses. 'Tolpuddle Martyrs' sentenced to seven years' transportation. Houses of Parliament destroyed by fire. Slavery abolished throughout the British Empire.
	Deaths of S. T. Coleridge and Charles Lamb. Harriet Martineau's *Illustrations of Political Economy* published.
1835	Melbourne Prime Minister again.
	Robert Browning's *Paracelsus* published.
	Branwell Brontë's ambition to join the Royal Academy of Arts remains unrealized; he also writes to *Blackwood's* proposing that he be taken on to replace James Hogg.
29 July	Charlotte Brontë goes to Roe Head to teach, Emily accompanying her as a pupil.
Autumn	Emily returns to Haworth and is replaced at Roe Head by Anne.
1836	Chartist movement begins.
	Dickens' *Sketches by Boz* published, also A. W. N. Pugin's *Contrasts*.
	Charlotte Brontë teaches at Roe Head, unhappily. Writes to Robert Southey telling him of her ambition to become a famous poet.
1837	Death of William IV; accession of Victoria. Benjamin Disraeli elected to Parliament.
	Carlyle's *The French Revolution* published; serial publication of Dickens' *Oliver Twist* begins.
	Southey replies to Charlotte Brontë encouraging her to write poetry for its own sake.
December	After an illness, Anne Brontë leaves Roe Head School.
1838	Great Western Railway opens. Isambard Kingdom Brunel designs the *Great Western*, the first steamship built to cross the Atlantic. First Afghan War breaks out. People's Charter set up by the Chartists. The Anti-Corn Law League created, to promote free trade.
	Dickens' *Nicholas Nickleby* published. Johann Strauss and his orchestra perform in Halifax.

	Roe Head School moves to Dewsbury Moor; Charlotte continues to teach. Branwell sets up as a portrait painter in Bradford (until February 1839).
Autumn	Emily Brontë teaches for a couple of months at Law Hill, near Halifax.
1839	Chartist rising at Newport repulsed by soldiers with loss of life. First Opium War between Britain and China. Custody of Infants Act allows separated wives to petition for custody of children under the age of seven. Carlyle's *Chartism* published, also Harriet Martineau's *Deerbrook*. J. M. W. Turner paints *The Fighting Téméraire*. Charlotte and Anne Brontë have short-lived posts (lasting a couple of months) as governesses.
1840	Queen Victoria marries Prince Albert. The Penny Post is introduced. Construction of the new Houses of Parliament begun. Browning's *Sordello* and Dickens' *Old Curiosity Shop* published. Branwell Brontë has a short-lived post as tutor (January–June). Subsequently starts working as a clerk at Sowerby Bridge railway station.
May	Anne Brontë takes up post as governess to the Robinson family at Thorp Green.
1841	Sir Robert Peel (Conservative) becomes Prime Minister and begins fiscal and budgetary reform work. Carlyle's *On Heroes and Hero-Worship* and Newman's *Tract xc* published. *Punch* founded. Charlotte Brontë spends most of the year working as governess to the White family in Rawdon.
April	Branwell Brontë is transferred to Luddenden Foot station.
5 June	Branwell's poem 'Heaven and Earth' published in the *Halifax Guardian*.
1842	Mines Act bans underground work by women and children. Chartist riots. Copyright Act. Edwin Chadwick's *Report on the Sanitary Condition of the Labouring Population* submitted. Mudie's Lending Library starts operations. Two volumes of Alfred Tennyson's poems published. *Illustrated London News* begins.

February	Charlotte and Emily Brontë go to Brussels, to learn and teach at the Pensionnat Heger.
March	Branwell Brontë dismissed from railway post.
September	William Weightman, the Haworth curate, dies of cholera.
29 October	Aunt Branwell dies aged sixty-six, leaving legacies to her nieces.
8 November	Charlotte and Emily return to Haworth.
1843	Governesses' Benevolent Institution founded. Sir Marc Isambard Brunel's Thames Tunnel completed.
	William Wordsworth succeeds Robert Southey as Poet Laureate. Dickens' *A Christmas Carol* published, also the first volume of Ruskin's *Modern Painters* and Carlyle's *Past and Present.* Thomas Babington Macaulay's collected *Essays* published.
January	Charlotte Brontë returns to Brussels alone. Branwell Brontë joins his sister Anne at Thorp Green, as tutor to the Robinsons' son.
1844	Factory Act limits working hours of women and children. Massive expansion of the railways. Rochdale pioneers open first co-operative retail shop. Bank Charter Act regulates issue of bank notes. First telegraph line opens.
	Elizabeth Barrett's *Poems* published, also Dickens' *Martin Chuzzlewit.* Turner paints *Rain, Steam and Speed.*
January	Charlotte leaves Brussels and returns to Haworth.
	Charlotte plans to start a school at the parsonage, but fails to attract pupils. Patrick Brontë's eyesight poor. Family acquires *The Musical Library*, an eight-volume anthology.
1845	'Potato blight' in Ireland; Great Famine begins. Newman converts to Roman Catholicism. Much speculation in railways.
	Disraeli's *Sybil* published, also Edgar Allan Poe's *Tales of Mystery and Imagination*, John Stuart Mill's *Principles of Political Economy* and Friedrich Engels' *The Condition of the Working Class in England.*
March	Mary Taylor leaves for New Zealand.

May	Arthur Bell Nicholls comes to Haworth as curate under Mr Brontë.
June	Anne Brontë ends five years of work as a governess at Thorp Green.
July	Branwell Brontë dismissed from his post as tutor at Thorp Green. Drinks heavily.
October	Charlotte Brontë discovers her sister Emily's poetry.
1846	Famine in Ireland continues. Corn Laws repealed in May. Peel's ministry falls, succeeded by John Russell's Whig government. Attempt made to introduce compulsory national education, a scheme supported by Patrick Brontë. Serial publication of Dickens' *Dombey and Son* begins. George Eliot's translation of D. F. Strauss' *Das Leben Jesu* published, also Edward Lear's *Book of Nonsense*.
January	Emily Brontë writes 'No Coward Soul Is Mine'.
28 January	Charlotte Brontë contacts the publishing firm Aylott and Jones about the publication of a book of poems by all three 'Bells'.
Spring	Branwell Brontë's condition deteriorating, according to Charlotte's letters.
May	*Poems* by Currer, Ellis and Acton Bell published.
July	Favourable reviews of the *Poems* in *The Athenaeum* and *The Critic*.
August	Patrick Brontë is operated on for cataracts in Manchester, accompanied by Charlotte, who begins to write *Jane Eyre* while attending him. Attempts to place *Agnes Grey*, *Wuthering Heights* and *The Professor* with publishers made over a period of several months.
1847	Attempt to introduce national education fails. Factory Act limits working hours for women and children to ten. 'Gorham controversy' over the doctrine of baptismal regeneration in the Church of England. First use of chloroform. Tennyson's *The Princess* published. W. M. Thackeray's *Vanity Fair* begins to appear in serial form.
Spring	Anne Brontë works on *The Tenant of Wildfell Hall*.

July	T. C. Newby agrees to publish *Wuthering Heights* and *Agnes Grey.*
August	Smith, Elder & Co. refuse to publish *The Professor* but encourage Charlotte Brontë to submit a three-decker novel. Charlotte sends them the just-completed *Jane Eyre.*
October	*Jane Eyre: An Autobiography* published by Smith, Elder & Co. as 'edited by' Currer Bell.
December	Newby publishes *Wuthering Heights* and *Agnes Grey* under the pseudonyms Ellis and Acton Bell.
1848	Year of revolutions in Europe (France, Prussia and the Habsburg Empire, where the young Franz Joseph becomes Emperor). Louis Napoléon President of France. Roman Republic declared.
	Queen's College for Women founded in London. Chartist demonstrations; unsuccessful presentation of Charter to Parliament, whereupon Chartism gradually becomes a spent force. Outbreak of cholera in London. Public Health Act, inspired by Chadwick's *Report* of 1842. Karl Marx and Friedrich Engels' *The Communist Manifesto.* Pre-Raphaelite Brotherhood formed.
	Elizabeth Gaskell's *Mary Barton* published, also G. H. Lewes' *Rose, Blanche and Violet.* Thackeray's *Vanity Fair* and Dickens' *Dombey and Son* published as books. Serial publication of Thackeray's *Pendennis* begins. J. A. Froude publishes *The Nemesis of Faith.*
June	Publication of *The Tenant of Wildfell Hall.*
July	Charlotte and Anne Brontë visit London to prove the existence of separate 'Bells' to their publishers.
24 September	Death of Branwell Brontë from 'chronic bronchitis – Marasmus' (doctor's certificate).
19 December	Death of Emily Brontë from pulmonary tuberculosis.
1849	Disraeli becomes Conservative leader. New cholera outbreak. F. D. Maurice and Charles Kingsley advocate 'Christian Socialism'. *The Morning Chronicle* begins to publish Henry Mayhew's *London Labour and the London Poor.*

	Dickens' *David Copperfield* begins serial publication. Matthew Arnold's *The Strayed Reveller and Other Poems* published, also Kingsley's *The Saint's Tragedy*, volumes I–II of Macaulay's *History of England* and Ruskin's *The Seven Lamps of Architecture*.
January	Anne Brontë's decline in health confirmed by surgeon's examination.
25 May	Anne and Charlotte Brontë, with Ellen Nussey, arrive in Scarborough, hoping for a beneficial effect on Anne's health.
28 May	Death of Anne Brontë in Scarborough. Funeral two days later.
8 September	James Taylor of Smith, Elder & Co. comes to Haworth to collect the manuscript of *Shirley*, which was completed in August.
26 October	*Shirley: A Tale* published by Smith, Elder & Co.
December	Charlotte Brontë spends first half of the month in London, meeting Thackeray, Harriet Martineau and various people connected with the literary scene.
1850	Appointment of N. P. S. Wiseman as Roman Catholic Archbishop of Westminster launches much indignation against this Roman Catholic 'Papal Aggression' in England. Death of Peel in a riding accident. Frances Mary Buss, aged twenty-three, founds the North London Collegiate School for Girls. Public Libraries Act establishes lending libraries. J. E. Millais paints *Christ in the House of his Parents* and D. G. Rossetti exhibits *'Ecce ancilla Domini'*. Pre-Raphaelite journal *The Germ* launched. Tennyson made Poet Laureate after Wordsworth's death. Dickens begins the periodical *Household Words*. Elizabeth Barrett Browning's *Sonnets from the Portuguese* published, also Kingsley's *Alton Locke* and Tennyson's *In memoriam*. Wordsworth's *The Prelude* posthumously published.
March	Charlotte Brontë spends time with the educationist Sir James Kay-Shuttleworth and his wife.
June	Charlotte spends most of this month in London. Portrait drawn by Richmond.

August	Charlotte meets Elizabeth Gaskell while staying with the Kay-Shuttleworths.
December	Smith, Elder & Co. reissue *Wuthering Heights, Agnes Grey* and poems by Emily and Anne, with a 'Biographical Notice' by Charlotte Brontë. Charlotte spends a week with Harriet Martineau.
1851	Great Exhibition in London from May to October. Louis Napoléon's *coup d'état*, in which he dissolved the Constitution of France, subsequently approved by plebiscite. William Thompson (later Lord Kelvin) publishes first and second laws of thermodynamics. Gaskell starts publication of *Cranford*. In the USA, Herman Melville's *Moby-Dick* appears. Part I of Ruskin's *The Stones of Venice* published. Turner dies.
April	Charlotte Brontë considers possibility of marrying James Taylor but decides against it.
June	Charlotte spends most of the month in London, meeting Thackeray, hearing F. D. Maurice and Cardinal Wiseman preach and visiting the Great Exhibition. Also sees 'Rachel' act and visits phrenologist (with George Smith) for a character reading.
1852	Death of the Duke of Wellington. Conservative government under Derby followed by coalition under Aberdeen. New Houses of Parliament open. Louis Napoléon crowned Emperor Napoleon III. Publication of Harriet Beecher Stowe's *Uncle Tom's Cabin*. Serial publication of Dickens' *Bleak House* begins. Matthew Arnold's *Empedocles on Etna and Other Poems* published, also Thackeray's *Henry Esmond*. Millais paints *Ophelia*.
March	Charlotte Brontë finishes the first volume of *Villette*.
Summer	Patrick Brontë in poor health, suffering from, among other things, a minor stroke.
November	Charlotte finishes *Villette*.
December	Arthur Bell Nicholls proposes to Charlotte. Patrick Brontë violently opposed.
1853	Another cholera epidemic. Inept diplomacy has Britain 'drifting' towards war with Russia. Much popular feeling against Prince Albert.

	Gaskell's *Ruth* published, also F. D. Maurice's *Theological Essays* and Thackeray's *The Newcomes*.
January	Charlotte Brontë's last visit to London. *Villette* published.
Spring	Much tension in Haworth Parsonage owing to Mr Nicholls' proposal. Nicholls leaves in May.
April	Charlotte Brontë visits Gaskell in Manchester. Gaskell returns visit in September.
November	Charlotte Brontë dismayed at news of George Smith's engagement.
1854	Crimean War breaks out under much popular enthusiasm. 'Charge of the Light Brigade' one of several disasters. Tennyson's poem published the same year. Coventry Patmore begins publication of *The Angel in the House*. Dickens' *Hard Times* published. Gaskell's *North and South* begins serial publication.
January	Strikes and civil unrest in Haworth.
Spring	Patrick Brontë gradually relents towards Nicholls.
29 June	Charlotte Brontë marries Arthur Bell Nicholls. Honeymoon in Ireland.
August	Charlotte Nicholls begins her new life as a married woman. Finds it hard to find time to write, but begins a novel called 'Emma'.
1855	Stamp Tax abolished, making newspapers more affordable. Palmerston Prime Minister. Fall of Sebastopol. Dickens begins serial publication of *Little Dorrit*. Browning's *Men and Women* published, also Anthony Trollope's *The Warden*, Kingsley's *Westward Ho!* and Tennyson's *Maud*.
January	Charlotte Brontë in poor health, probably due to early pregnancy.
February	Death of 'Tabby'.
31 March	Death of Charlotte Nicholls, *née* Brontë. Death certified as due to 'phtisis', but severe nausea owing to pregnancy ('hyperemesis gravidarum') has been mentioned as a contributing factor.
4 April	Charlotte's funeral.
16 June	Patrick Brontë suggests to Gaskell that she should write a memoir of his daughter; she agrees.

1857   Matrimonial Causes Act makes divorce available to both men and women without special Act of Parliament. Indian Mutiny.

Gaskell's *Life of Charlotte Brontë* published by Smith, Elder & Co. in May, in a two-volume edition. The same year sees the publication of Barrett Browning's *Aurora Leigh* and George Eliot's *Scenes of Clerical Life*. Charlotte Brontë's *The Professor* published, with a preface by Nicholls.

1861   Death of Prince Albert. Louis Pasteur publishes theory that disease is spread by germs. Duty on paper abolished, lowering the price of printed matter. American Civil War breaks out.

Dickens' *Great Expectations* published, also Eliot's *Silas Marner*, Mrs Henry (Ellen) Wood's *East Lynne* and *Palgrave's Golden Treasury*.

7 June   Patrick Brontë dies, aged eighty-four.

October   Arthur Bell Nicholls, not having been offered his father-in-law's post, leaves for Ireland and becomes a farmer at Banagher. Marries a cousin in 1864.

Abbreviations and editions

ABBREVIATIONS

Barker: Juliet Barker, *The Brontës*. London: Weidenfeld & Nicolson, 1994. (As Barker's biography is a reliable and convenient source for the Brontës' diary and birthday papers, these documents are quoted from Barker throughout the volume.)

BST: *Brontë Society Transactions*.

Gaskell, *Life*: Elizabeth Gaskell, *The Life of Charlotte Brontë*, ed. Angus Easson. Oxford World's Classics. Oxford University Press, 1996, subsequently reissued. (First published in 1857.)

Smith, *Letters*: Margaret Smith, ed., *The Letters of Charlotte Brontë with a Selection of Letters by Family and Friends*. Oxford: Clarendon Press, vol. I: *1829–1847*, 1995, with corrections 1996; vol. II: *1848–1851*, 2000; vol. III: *1852–1855*, 2004. (As appendices to volumes I and II respectively, Smith reprints Ellen Nussey's 'Reminiscences of Charlotte Brontë' as well as Charlotte Brontë's 'Biographical Notice of Ellis and Acton Bell' and her prefaces to her sisters' works. These texts are quoted from Smith throughout.)

EDITIONS

References to the seven Brontë novels are made parenthetically in the running text. Small upper-case Roman numerals refer to volume numbers (wherever appropriate), lower-case ones to chapter numbers and Arabic figures to page numbers in the Oxford World's Classics editions published by Oxford University Press – whose texts are based on the Clarendon editions of the Brontë novels – listed below.

Anne Brontë

Agnes Grey, ed. Robert Inglesfield and Hilda Marsden with an introduction and additional notes by Sally Shuttleworth. 2010. (The Clarendon edition appeared in 1988.)

The Tenant of Wildfell Hall, ed. Herbert Rosengarten with an introduction and additional notes by Josephine McDonagh. 2008. (Clarendon edition 1992.)

Charlotte Brontë

The Professor, ed. Margaret Smith and Herbert Rosengarten with an introduction by Margaret Smith. 1991. (Clarendon edition 1987.)

Jane Eyre, ed. Margaret Smith with an introduction and revised notes by Sally Shuttleworth. 2000. (Clarendon edition 1975.)

Shirley, ed. Herbert Rosengarten and Margaret Smith with an introduction and additional notes by Janet Gezari. 2007. (Clarendon edition 1979.)

Villette, ed. Margaret Smith and Herbert Rosengarten with an introduction and notes by Tim Dolin. 2000. (Clarendon edition 1984.)

Emily Brontë

Wuthering Heights, ed. Ian Jack with an introduction and additional notes by Helen Small. 2009. (Clarendon edition 1976.)

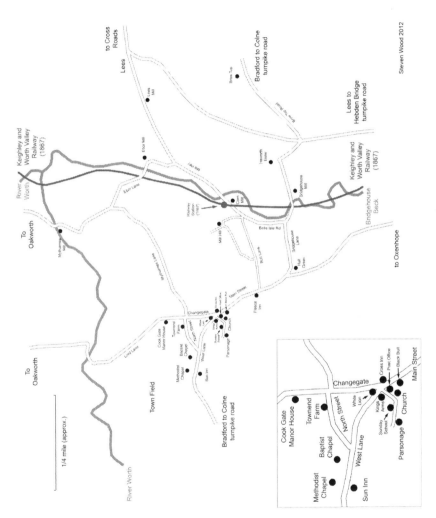

1 Haworth and its surroundings

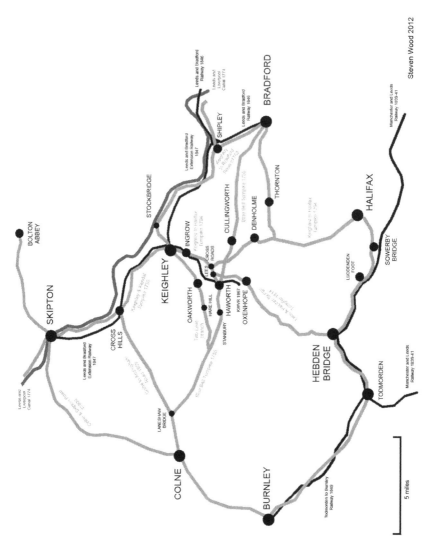

2 The Brontës' region of Yorkshire and Lancashire

Steven Wood 2012

5 miles

BOLTON
ABBEY

SKIPTON

Leeds and
Liverpool
Canal 1774

Leeds and Bradford
Extension Railway
1847

CROSS
HILLS

Keighley & Kendal
Turnpike 1753

Colne & Broughton
Road 1755

Blue Bell Turnpike 1755

LANESHAW
BRIDGE

COLNE

BURNLEY

Todmorden to Burnley
Railway 1849

STOCKBRIDGE

Leeds and Bradford
Extension Railway
1847

Keighley to Hebden
Turnpike 1825

INGROW

KEIGHLEY

LEES CROSS
ROADS

OAKWORTH

HARE HILL

STANBURY

HAWORTH

KWVR 1867

OXENHOPE

Lancs & Yorks Railway 1847

HEBDEN
BRIDGE

TODMORDEN

Manchester and Leeds
Railway 1839-41

SHIPLEY

Leeds and Bradford
Railway 1846

Leeds and
Liverpool
Canal 1774

Keighley to Bradford
Road 1714

CULLINGWORTH

Brig a 1847 Turnpike 1755

DENHOLME

THORNTON

Keighley to Halifax
Turnpike 1754

LUDDENDEN
FOOT

HALIFAX

SOWERBY
BRIDGE

Manchester and Leeds
Railway 1839-41

BRADFORD

Leeds and Bradford
Railway 1846

Introduction

Marianne Thormählen

Like the other volumes in the Literature in Context series, *The Brontës in Context* is intended for present-day readers, academic and general, who want to find out more about the forces and circumstances that shaped literary works which have captivated generations of readers across the globe. The book resembles its fellows in the series in having a tripartite structure organized along the following lines: the initial section focuses on biographical matters; the middle section deals with reception and critical fortunes; and the final section discusses historical and cultural phenomena of particular relevance to the authors and their works.

This volume is a special case, however. First, it deals with three authors, not one; second, the lives of those authors have exerted a peculiar fascination for a century and a half. Outwardly uneventful, these lives are the stuff of legend: three young women, daughters of an impecunious clergyman in a Yorkshire village, developed extraordinary literary talents that gave the world some of the best-loved classics of the modern era – whereupon they all died young, leaving their aged father the sole survivor of a family of eight. With little leisure in which to foster those talents, and no material or cultural advantages to speak of, the Brontë sisters lived far from the intellectual circles of London and other large cities in the British Isles. 'How could it happen?' is a question that has been asked by millions over the years.

Without prescribing any one formula, *The Brontës in Context* helps its readers to perceive at least partial answers to that question. Within the covers of one book, a large number of experts form a league of guides to the Brontës in their time. The reader gains insights into the concerns that filled the days of these remarkable young women and found expression in their writing, from household chores to preoccupation with the fortunes of their country and with the ultimate destiny of their own souls. Familiarity with the circumstances that shaped their lives, and with the stuff that nourished their minds and fired their imaginations, brings modern readers closer to the realities of 'the Brontë story'. At the same time, such knowledge adds powerful layers of meaning to the experience of reading what they wrote.

To a twenty-first-century academic, the idea that learning about an author's life makes for a richer understanding of his or her work is far from self-evident. Indeed, the content of the preceding paragraph goes against the grain of much that has come from the field of academic literary study for a long time. Ever since the 1940s, literary criticism as practised in the academy has attempted to demarcate between authorial biography and scholarly discussion of texts; and throughout this time, the uniqueness of the Brontë phenomenon has formed a stubborn challenge against those endeavours. Whatever the topic of a scholarly text on a Brontë-related matter, some aspect or aspects of the Brontës' lives will be woven into it, in ways and on a scale that does not happen with other writers.[1]

Even so, accepting the ubiquitousness of 'the Brontë story' and the desirability of factual knowledge about the Brontës in the context of their time does not amount to arguing that any worthwhile critical engagement with their works must rely on such knowledge. First of all, of course, it is important to remember that the Brontë novels are creations of the imagination. As such, they belong to a timeless sphere from which no lively mind, however uninformed, is ever debarred. The fact that most of us who work with the Brontës in the academy today came to their works as adolescents or teenagers, totally ignorant of the books' historical context, and were 'hooked' for life testifies to the imaginative power of the Brontë fiction. Second, every generation will apply its own distinctive perspectives to readings of classic works of literature, seeing them through the lenses of ideological concerns and debates of their own time: that is partly what literature is for, and what keeps the classics alive. General readers have always felt free to do this; and the second half of the twentieth century liberated academic critics from the obligation to prove that a certain critical approach to a literary text was not at odds with what the author might have meant. It was a real liberation which invigorated academic criticism across the board, including the field of Brontë studies.

Nevertheless, freedom – at least in the academic sphere – needs to be exercised with responsibility. *The Brontës in Context* will, it is hoped, help readers steer clear of anachronistic views of the kind that might infringe the integrity of works and writers, for instance by imputing certain values and opinions to them without being in full command of the historical picture. The more people know about the lives and times of the Brontë sisters, the less inclined they will be to distort these authors' work by approaching it from the moral high ground of a supposedly more enlightened age. Anybody who has devoted serious work to Brontë material in its historical context will have discovered that he or she has little reason to adopt a censorious attitude to the people of the early nineteenth century, of which the Brontë sisters were part.[2]

Young scholars who turn to Brontë studies today are in a much better position to do justice to the lives and works of the Brontës than their predecessors, thanks to the fine scholarly work in the field that has appeared during the last few decades. Juliet Barker's splendid biography of the family did away with many old misconceptions, showing the men – including Charlotte's husband Arthur Bell Nicholls – in a more favourable light than had been customary before; Margaret Smith's definitive edition of the Brontë correspondence not only established reliable texts for the first time but provided a wealth of initiated commentary; and Christine Alexander and Margaret Smith's *Oxford Companion to the Brontës* supplied masses of updated and expertly compiled information on all kinds of topics germane to the Brontës and their works.[3] Between them, and aided by other excellent studies with a historically contextualizing orientation, they ensured that the ground was cleared of many erroneous notions.

The debunking of myths is a satisfying pastime, but those who indulge in it should be wary of laying the foundations of new ones. An idea which has the potential of becoming a new 'Brontë myth' is the notion that Charlotte Brontë deliberately concocted misleading images of her sisters and their work for selfish purposes, and that Elizabeth Gaskell later became an accomplice in a project whose fundamental object was to glorify Charlotte Brontë, partly at her sisters' expense. It is easy to see how this idea could take root: important works on the Brontës published in the 1990s and 2000s showed that both Charlotte and Gaskell were at pains to mitigate the feeling that Emily's and Anne's work, especially *Wuthering Heights* and *The Tenant of Wildfell Hall*, was tainted by 'coarseness'.[4] By romanticizing Emily as an unschooled creature of the wild moors and representing Anne as the victim of an earnest but misguided ambition to turn vulnerable youth away from sin and error, both women certainly made the younger Brontë sisters look less complex and serious in their artistry than present-day scholars can see that they were.

Making Charlotte into some kind of villain owing to her desire to make the Brontë phenomenon acceptable to the reading public of the mid nineteenth century seems unwarranted, however. Most solitary victims of repeated bereavement would want posterity to think kindly of their dead loved ones; and if that excuse is felt to be insufficient, another circumstance may give Charlotte's critics pause: if it had not been for her iron determination to 'get on', the world would never have known anything about the Brontës of Haworth. Being the 'doer' of the family is sometimes an ungrateful role. Alone among the siblings, Charlotte Brontë had inherited her father's dogged ambition, and it carried her through difficulties and disappointments which would have caused lesser spirits to despair. This was the woman to whom Elizabeth Gaskell paid tribute in ways that secured a prominent place for the name of Brontë in the literary landscape of the mid nineteenth century. Whatever strictures anyone might wish to subject them to in a very different age, admiration for Charlotte Brontë's indomitable courage and what it enabled her to do for generations of enthusiastic readers prompts a desire to see her name 'free from soil'.[5]

Another misleading notion which has attained semi-mythical status over the decades is the belief, often encountered in popular writing on the Brontës, that the works of the Brontë sisters are expressions of a rebellious attitude to Victorian values. There is plenty of rebelliousness in them, to be sure; but to begin with, not every rebel in the Brontë fiction is valorized, and then, the main action in every single Brontë novel is set in a pre-Victorian historical period. Anne Brontë's *The Tenant of Wildfell Hall* may serve to illustrate both points: Arthur Huntingdon rebels against the domestic atmosphere whose tone is set by his wife Helen's moral superiority, with terrible results for all concerned; and Anne set the action of that novel in the time before the first Infant Custody Act, thus precluding even a hint of possible mitigation as regards Helen's dreadful position in the eyes of the law (see Chapters 35 and 38 below).

What successful rebels in the Brontë novels turn against is tyranny, not social convention as such. Young Jane Eyre challenges the Reeds, mother and son, because they oppress her, and later Jane refuses to yield to pressure from Mr Rochester as well as from her cousin St John; in all contexts she is motivated by a longing for freedom from improper personal restraint, not by ideological disapproval of notions prevalent in her time. Even Caroline Helstone's impassioned plea to the 'fathers of England' to allow their daughters the fulfilment of useful occupation (*Shirley*, II.xi.330) is, first and foremost, the expression of a yearning for freedom to improve oneself while carving out a life of one's own. In promoting the desire to accomplish something worthwhile, for women as well as for men, the Brontë novels are in fact in tune with, rather than oppositional to, strong social and political currents in early Victorian Britain.

The Brontës in Context appears at a point in time when Brontë experts have long tried to correct the impression that the three surviving Brontë sisters were dreamy geniuses isolated on their faraway moors. Instead, scholars have endeavoured to present them as early nineteenth-century intellectuals with a keen interest in what was happening in the world, in the arts, in politics at home and abroad, in philosophy and religion, and at all levels of society – and with very decided professional ambitions. Charlotte, Emily and Anne Brontë were women of their time, and readers of this volume will become aware of the degree to which their writings show it. Those writings were themselves part of that time, tapping into its concerns and generally contributing to the mid-nineteenth-century *Zeitgeist.*

A consecutive reading of the volume will go some distance towards clarifying the extent to which the Brontë works were part of the period in which they were written, but not all readers will wish to undertake such a reading. For those who consult the book in pursuit of information on a particular topic or topics, it is inconvenient to have to look up chapters which are not of immediate relevance. With the interests of such readers in mind, a limited element of repetition has been allowed; for instance, Charlotte Brontë's account of her discovery of her sister Emily's poems is quoted more than once. For similar reasons, the section called 'Further reading' mentions some critical works on several occasions: the reader interested in a particular chapter will hence find bibliographical guidance under the corresponding chapter number and not have to scour the entire section in pursuit of pertinent works.

Whatever impulse sends a reader to this book, the editor and contributors hope that he or she will find it both stimulating and helpful. If it inspires further scholarly efforts to elucidate ways in which the Brontës' life stories and works interact with their time – and there is plenty of work still to be done along those lines – that will be the happiest of outcomes.

NOTES

1 For that reason, the first section of this book, unlike other volumes in the Literature in Context series, is not called 'Lives and works'. It would have been misleading to suggest that the second and third sections do not constantly engage with the lives and works of the Brontës, although the topics were not chosen with biographical elucidation in mind.

2 On the dangers of patronizing the people of the past, see the introduction to my *The Brontës and Education* (Cambridge University Press, 2007), esp. pp. 2–3.

3 See the beginning of the 'Further reading' section at the back of this book. Robert and Louise Barnard's *A Brontë Encyclopedia* (Oxford: Blackwell, 2007) is a useful and readable complement to the *Oxford Companion*.

4 See, for instance, Lucasta Miller's *The Brontë Myth* (London: Jonathan Cape, 2001).

5 The last sentence of Charlotte's 'Biographical Notice of Ellis and Acton Bell' runs, 'This notice has been written, because I felt it a sacred duty to wipe the dust off their gravestones, and leave their dear names free from soil.' Quoted from Smith, *Letters*, vol. II, p. 747.

PART I

Places, persons and publishing

CHAPTER I

Haworth in the time of the Brontës

Michael Baumber

Haworth is a moorland village in the hills known as the Pennines, in the West Riding of Yorkshire in northern England, about nine miles west of Bradford and eight miles north of Halifax. The Halifax area has a long history as a major centre for the production of textiles even before the Industrial Revolution. Haworth belongs to that area, and both before and after the forty years that the Revd Patrick Brontë spent there as its parish priest, the manufacture of worsted cloth played a vital role in the lives of its people.[1]

When Patrick Brontë first became perpetual curate of Haworth in 1820, the village was nowhere near as extensive as it is today.[2] If you had approached it from Keighley, the road would have left the Halifax turnpike (a toll road) at Cross Roads and plunged down the hill to the Bridgehouse beck through fields with a scattering of farmhouses.[3] The Worth valley railway was not built until after Brontë's death. What we call Haworth Brow, with its rows of late nineteenth-century terraces, did not exist, nor did the housing down the present Mytholmes Lane. As the road crossed the beck near the present railway station, you would have seen a corn mill. Your route would then have followed the present Belle Isle road, and you would not have come to the village proper until you had laboured up the other side of the valley to Hall Green at the bottom of the present Main Street. Main Street itself was cobbled, as it still is, and was another stiff climb. Today the lower part is flanked by houses of various styles, but then there would have been seventeenth-century stone cottages on the left-hand side, some of them still farms. On the other side, where the school and park are now, you would have seen fields, because there were no houses at all below Butt Lane. At the top were the church and the parsonage (see Figure 1), the Wesleyan Methodist and Baptist chapels and Townend Farm. There were more cottages in and around the triangle formed by West Lane, Changegate and North Street, one or two general shops and five inns – the Black Bull, the King's Arms, the White

1 Haworth Old Church, Sunday School and Parsonage, photographed before 1878

Lion, the Cross and the Fleece – with a sixth, the Sun, in West Lane. Much of the old open fields had been enclosed, but on the Worth valley side of West Lane the old town field still remained with its separate strips.

It was therefore quite possible for incurious visitors to see 1820s Haworth as an isolated rural village, and what they thought of it might well have depended on the weather, as the houses were made of millstone grit which water turned black. Ellen Nussey cherished memories of delightful summer rambles on the moors with the Brontë sisters; but Bessie Parkes remembered a 'dreary, black-looking village' and a parsonage 'without a single tree to shield it from the chill wind', and Mrs Gaskell, who painted a picture of a dismal backwater, came on 'a dull, drizzly, India-inky day' with a leaden sky.[4]

Yet sharp eyes would have noticed that many of the upper storeys of the cottages were occupied by handlooms. Those energetic enough to walk out of the village into the countryside would have found farmhouses (often with attached cottages) at frequent intervals, all of which contained handlooms, as few of the inhabitants could do more than scratch a living from agriculture. The cloth being made was worsted, so they would have contained combers as well as weavers.

Formerly women would have been found spinning the yarn as well, but by 1820 most spinning was done in factories. They were powered by water

2 Ebor Mill. Photograph by Simon Warner

wheels, so they were down in the valleys; if you lived in the old village you had to look hard to see them, but whichever road down the hill you chose to take, you would stumble across the reality. If you went back down Main Street to the beck, you would find on the right-hand side a pleasant Georgian house with an attached barn, but behind it was the Bridgehouse mill, the biggest in the area. If you took Mytholmes Lane and then turned into Ebor Lane, you would find Ebor Mill at the bottom (see Figure 2). Alternatively, if you continued down Mytholmes Lane itself, you would reach the Mytholmes mill. Even if you ventured onto the hillside at the back of the church around Upper Marsh, the Old Oxenhope mill would be nestling in the trees below you; and beyond, on the upper reaches of the Bridgehouse beck, you would see small textile mills at every convenient fall of water.

These mills marked the first stage of an upheaval which had changed Haworth out of all recognition by the time of Patrick Brontë's death. Originally the mills had spun cotton, the first textile to be spun in factories; but by the time the Brontës arrived in Haworth, worsted had also entered the era of mechanization, and most of the local mills were converted to the manufacture of this material, so characteristic of the area. The early years of Brontë's incumbency were generally prosperous ones, but already the unscrupulous use of child labour was causing social problems. More followed as one crisis after another gripped the worsted industry. The first, between 1839 and 1842, was accompanied by serious disturbances. The next, in 1848, was worse, because it was exacerbated by further structural changes within the textile industry, as power looms multiplied rapidly.

Most handloom weavers were men, but mid-nineteenth-century census figures for power-loom weavers show roughly equal numbers of men and women. Alternative employment in the expanding factories was limited, so many redundant weavers turned to combing. Combing proved only a temporary refuge, however. The first combing machines came to Haworth in 1852; usually operated by men, they required only a few, putting the rest out of work. The 1850s was a decade of volatile textile markets, and Haworth was badly affected, with especially severe job losses in 1854–5. As a result, many textile workers – especially among the combers – gave up and left the district. Haworth suffered worse than most of the worsted industry because it was on the periphery and had no workable coal when steam power replaced water. The terrain was not suitable for canals, so goods had to be moved by turnpike roads, which were still charging tolls as late as 1860. The failure of a project to build a railway up the Worth valley in 1845 also left the township at a disadvantage in relation to its larger neighbour Keighley.

Similar strains were evident in the religious life of Haworth. In the mid eighteenth century, a religious revival had been sparked by William Grimshaw, perpetual curate in the years 1742–63. He was an enthusiastic supporter of John Wesley's Methodist movement, which was then part of the Church of England. Later, strains between Methodists and more traditional supporters of the Church led to the Bradford and Halifax Wesleyan Methodist circuit organizing rival services from 1812. The competition was intense. In 1817 the perpetual curate of the time, the Revd James Charnock, fell ill, with the result that by his death in 1820 a large part of the congregation had been lost, and Patrick Brontë was only partially successful in reclaiming it. Paradoxically, too, Grimshaw's efforts also provided a shot in the arm for the rival Particular Baptist movement when some of his followers defected to it. Although both Baptists and Methodists endured splits, Brontë could do little to halt their growing supremacy. He was not helped by the internal row, between 1835 and 1842, over the church rate, which was levied on all ratepayers for the repair and maintenance of the church. Dissenters who no longer used Haworth Church were not the only ones who objected to paying it. Haworth was a chapelry of the parish of Bradford, so the legal church rate went to support Bradford Parish Church, with the result that Anglicans found themselves paying for two churches. After 1842 Brontë stopped trying to levy it.[5]

Yet the real root cause of his difficulties was the insistence of the Church of England (with which he fully agreed) that all its activities should be clergy-led. The chapelry of Haworth covered the hamlets of Near and Far Oxenhope and Stanbury as well as Haworth itself. The Methodists had a chapel in Oxenhope as early as 1806 and another in Stanbury by 1831, served by lay preachers on a circuit system, and they were soon followed by the Baptists. As Patrick Brontë was the only beneficed clergyman, Stanbury did not get an Anglican church until 1848, and Oxenhope received one only in 1849, after the formation of a separate parish.[6] The position with Sunday schools was even worse. When Brontë arrived, there was a joint Sunday school in the Methodist chapel. In 1831 there was a split, each of the denominations going its own separate way. The result was that Brontë was able to organize only one school under his own direction, while the Wesleyan Methodists had six in different parts of the chapelry run by lay superintendents, the Baptists three and the Primitive Methodists one.[7] Brontë did not get an assistant curate until 1835, so it was fortunate that day schools did not make their appearance until later, a Church of England National School in 1844 and a British and Foreign non-denominational one in 1845. The figures in the 1851 religious census should be treated with care, but when all the caveats have been considered, the census shows that at this time the Church of England commanded the allegiance of only between a third and a quarter of the church- and chapel-going population.

After 1840, Haworth grew in size because the changes described above effectively destroyed the old domestic system of production. A minority of men found employment in the stone quarries, but most of the outlying farms were progressively abandoned, their inhabitants relocating in the triangle formed by Haworth village, Lees and Cross Roads and Oakworth. In 1841 there were forty-four tradespeople in Haworth village, of whom fifteen described themselves as grocers, six as innkeepers, spirit merchants or beer sellers, five as bread-bakers, four as butchers and one as a druggist. There were sixty artisans, among them twenty shoemakers, ten tailors, six dressmakers and seven blacksmiths, and there were two surgeons, two clockmakers and a barber, Jack Toothill, who regularly shaved Patrick Brontë.[8] A post office opened in 1843, close to the church steps, and street gas lighting was introduced in 1845. By 1851 there were ninety tradespeople and ninety artisans. Despite the fall in the chapelry's population as a whole after 1851, there had been a further rise to 105 tradespeople and 103 artisans by the time of Brontë's death. William Scruton commented with surprise in 1858:

We had supposed Haworth to be a scattered and straggling hamlet with a desolate vicarage and a dilapidated church surrounded and shut out from the world by a wilderness of barren heath. Instead of that we found it transformed into a large and flourishing village – a not very enlightened or poetical place certainly but quaint, compact and progressive.[9]

Unfortunately the increase also put an intolerable pressure on the village's resources because most of the housing now contained not handloom weavers but mill employees, many of them out of work, squashed together in slum tenements or cellar dwellings. In consequence of Benjamin Herschel Babbage's 1850 report (see also Chapter 2), a Local Board of Health was set up to deal with the problems of sanitation – a board which, in time, collected other functions and proved to be a precursor of the later Urban District Council. Yet we should beware of placing too much emphasis on sanitary problems. They were certainly the cause of the spike in infant mortality, which Babbage noted, but the real problem was poverty.

The problem of the poor was universal. It led to the passage in 1834 of the Poor Law Amendment Act, which was opposed in the textile areas by manufacturers – to whom Haworth's chief attraction was its abundant supply of cheap labour – and workers alike. The transformation into an industrial village brought other problems. Drunkenness was present, as elsewhere; but Haworth seems to have been less affected by it than were larger towns. Patrick Brontë did form 'an Association for the Suppression of Vice', which kept a close watch on unlicensed beer houses, but this was largely because they were thought to be centres of crime.[10] Haworth did not have a police officer until 1860.

The minor clergy of the Church of England and their families were always a race apart. Their education in the liberal arts separated them from the working classes, and their lack of income caused their children to be looked down on both by the landed gentry and by the *nouveaux riches* among the manufacturers, so the daughters usually ended up marrying other minor clergy, as Charlotte Brontë eventually did. There were few openings for those who remained single except teaching. For Patrick Brontë himself, this isolation was mitigated by the way in which his profession took him out into the chapelry at large, and men generally had more freedom than women, so Branwell could create a circle of friends for himself at the Black Bull. The female world was far more circumscribed, especially when, as with the Brontë sisters, their mother died early, their father never remarried and the place where they lived was almost totally devoid of the families of professional classes, which were most likely to treat them as social equals. Indicative of this lack of sophistication was the fate of the old free grammar school. Founded in 1636 to educate suitable boys in the Latin, Greek and English languages, it had long since ceased teaching the Classics, and an attempt to revive their study in 1844 failed abysmally.[11]

Haworth was not entirely devoid of culture; but it was largely music-based, as it was centred on the churches and chapels and, to a lesser extent, on the festive side of the benefit societies such as the Freemasons and the Oddfellows. In the early nineteenth century, the benefit societies had more members in relation to the total population in Haworth than anywhere else in the vicinity.[12] Branwell was a Freemason.[13] Church services were usually accompanied by wind bands, but some had stringed instruments by this time, creating small orchestras.[14] There was a Haworth orchestral society as early as 1780, and by the 1830s it was giving quarterly concerts, supplemented by soloists from Halifax. The abandonment of religious bands and orchestras in favour of organs seems to have killed it off, however, in conjunction with the industrial turmoil. Choral music, particularly of the sacred variety, was more durable, and in Thomas Parker Haworth produced a tenor of national stature. Domestic music-making was popular among the farmers and weavers as well as among the better-off, but literature was a different matter. Vernacular stories were popular, and poetry was written by Branwell, Joseph Hardaker the apothecary, Abraham Wildman the assistant Poor Law overseer and others;[15] but there was no market for it, except odd corners in the Halifax papers. Haworth did not get a Mechanics' Institute until 1849. Its reading room provided the national newspapers, but it could rarely afford visiting lecturers. It had a library, but the hasty way in which copies of *Jane Eyre* and *Shirley* had to be purchased for it when the identity of Currer Bell was revealed suggests that novels were not on its shopping list.[16]

The Brontë sisters were not as isolated as this review might suggest, but with the exception of their father, the influences that operated on them came from outside Haworth. Halifax, Bradford and Keighley all had circulating libraries, and by 1820 turnpike roads had made them easily accessible to wheeled vehicles. Looking back in 1850, Charlotte could write quite truthfully: 'Resident in a remote district where education had made little progress, and where, consequently, there was no inducement to seek social intercourse beyond our own domestic circle, we were wholly dependent on ourselves and each other, on books and study, for the enjoyments and occupations of life.'[17] Together with a potentially hostile intellectual environment and the escalating industrial unrest around them, this lack of social contact was instrumental in the creation of the Brontë novels. In summer the sisters could contrive to ignore their surroundings by leaving the village and its problems and roaming the moors; but when winter came they had no other recourse than to shut their doors and, feeding off one another, wander in worlds of their own imagining.

NOTES

1 I am indebted to Steven Wood for correcting a number of inaccuracies in the original draft of this chapter.

2 A perpetual curate (the title was abolished in the late 1960s) was a clergyman in the Church of England who officiated as parish priest in an ecclesiastical district which did not have a vicar or rector. He could be removed from his post only by the person who had licensed him for the appointment, usually the bishop. A perpetual curate could have 'ordinary' temporary curates serving under him, as Patrick Brontë did.

3 'Beck' is a northern word for 'brook' or 'stream'.

4 Charles Lemon (ed.), *Early Visitors to Haworth* (Haworth: Brontë Society, 1996), pp. 4–5, 16 and 19, and J. Horsfall Turner, *Haworth, Past and Present* (1879; Otley: Olicana, 1973), pp. 149–52.

5 Michael Baumber, 'The Haworth Church Rate Controversy', *Yorkshire Archaeological Journal*, 75 (2003), 115–28.

6 John Lock and W. T. Dixon, *A Man of Sorrow: The Life, Letters and Times of the Rev. Patrick Brontë 1777–1861* (London: Nelson, 1965), p. 328.

7 Michael Baumber, 'Patrick Brontë and the Development of Primary Education in Haworth', *BST*, 24.1 (1999), 66–81.

8 1841 census for the village of Haworth. These are individuals, not businesses. The same is true of the figures quoted for 1851 and 1861.

9 Lemon, *Early Visitors to Haworth*, p. 45.

10 Lock and Dixon, *A Man of Sorrow*, pp. 318–19.

11 Baumber, 'Patrick Brontë', 66–81.

12 J. M. Hagerty, 'Bradford Friendly Societies in the 1790s', *Bradford Antiquary*, n.s. 46 (1976), 64.

13 A 7 Sept. 1833 sermon by 'Rev. Brother Bronte' suggests that Patrick was a Freemason as well as Branwell, though he is not mentioned in the lodge records. On Branwell's membership, see Barker, pp. 230 and 247.

14 Dudley Green, *Patrick Brontë: Father of Genius* (Stroud: Nonsuch, 2008), p. 75, lists Thornton chapel as owning two violins and a cello.

15 Kenneth Emsley, *Historic Haworth Today* (Bradford Libraries, 1995), pp. 36 and 43.

16 Juliet Barker, *The Brontës: A Life in Letters* (London: Viking, 1997), p. 263.

17 'Biographical Notice of Ellis and Acton Bell', quoted from Smith, *Letters*, vol. II, p. 742.

Domestic life at Haworth Parsonage

Ann Dinsdale

Some of the most frequently asked questions about the Brontës relate not to their novels but to the minutiae of their everyday lives. Fortunately a great deal of material evidence has survived, and the collection held at the Brontë Parsonage Museum in Haworth can tell us much about the Brontës' domestic life, which in turn played an important role in their writing. In addition to the parsonage building itself, the collection includes letters and manuscripts, drawings and paintings, sewing boxes and tools, samplers, fancy work, costume items, furniture, china and other household items. All these artefacts possess a certain fascination – not merely as relics, but also because of their ability to bring the members of this remarkable family to life by virtue of their very ordinariness.

HAWORTH PARSONAGE

Haworth Parsonage became home to the Brontë family in 1820. The house is set above the village and separated from it by the church and a square plot of garden, given over to rough grass and a few stunted bushes in the Brontës' time. The front door leads into a flagged entrance hall, 'always beautifully clean as everything about the house was', as Ellen Nussey recalled.[1] Flagstone floors extended to all the ground-floor rooms; and when Ellen first visited in 1833, there was 'not much carpet anywhere except in the sitting room, and on the centre of the study floor'. The room to the right of the hall was Mr Brontë's study, sparsely furnished but housing a well-thumbed library and with walls covered in engravings of works by John Martin – fantastic visions which stirred his children's imaginations. Across the hall is the dining room, with its 'hair-seated chairs and mahogany tables' (see Figure 3). The windows are fitted with wooden shutters, and Ellen described how Mr Brontë's fear of fire meant that 'the interior lacked drapery of all kinds'. After the deaths of her sisters, Charlotte took some pleasure in making the house more comfortable. The income from

3 Emily Brontë's diary paper of 26 June 1837, with a sketch of herself and Anne
writing at the dining-room table

her writing allowed her to assert her independence and carry out alterations
to the parsonage interior. In 1850 she enlarged and refurbished the rooms
she herself used – the dining room and main bedroom above – and the cold,
grey outlook from the dining-room windows was softened by the addition

of new crimson-coloured curtains. Ellen describes the walls as 'not papered
but coloured in a pretty dove-coloured tint'. Clearly papers were used at a later
date, for a sample which ended up in the New York Public Library was
authenticated by Mrs Gaskell as the paper chosen by Charlotte to decorate the
study for her husband-to-be, Arthur Bell Nicholls, in 1854. Formerly, this
room had served as 'a sort of flagged store-room' (Gaskell, *Life*, p. 41).

Behind Mr Brontë's study is the kitchen, the warm heart of the
household where the Brontë children would gather on winter nights.
A vaulted cellar used for storage extends beneath it. A detailed plan of
Haworth dating from 1853 shows a back kitchen to the parsonage containing a stone sink, where the washing and heavier household work
would have been carried out.[2] The back kitchen was demolished during
alterations made to the house by Mr Brontë's successor in the late 1870s.

The stone staircase in the hallway leads to five bedrooms, occupied by
different members of the family depending on who was living at home at
the time. After Mrs Brontë's death the main bedroom was taken over by
Aunt Branwell, and it was here that she taught her nieces the arts of
sewing and household management. Mr Brontë had moved into the
bedroom across the landing, and a small room squeezed in between the
two, known as 'the children's study', served as a nursery in the early days.
Later it became Emily's room, and her diary paper for 1845 includes a
sketch she made of herself seated here with her portable writing desk on
her lap and her dog Keeper at her feet. Of the remaining rooms, one was
allocated to the servants. The other served as Branwell's studio in the late
1830s, but it was usually a bedroom occupied by one or more of his sisters.

Ellen, coming from a more affluent background, found the parsonage's
rooms '[s]cant and bare indeed' (another quotation from her reminiscences;
Smith, *Letters*, vol. 1, p. 599). Twenty years later, Mrs Gaskell noted how
'[e]verything fits into, and is in harmony with, the idea of a country parsonage,
possessed by people of very moderate means' (Gaskell, *Life*, p. 439). By this
time Charlotte had completed her alterations, and clearly other comforts had
been added; the sale of the parsonage's contents, held after Mr Brontë's death
in 1861, included 'Damask and Muslin Window Hangings', 'Stairs Carpets
and Rods' and 'Kidderminster Carpets and Rugs'.[3]

DAILY ROUTINE

Sarah Garrs, a young servant in the Brontë household who accompanied
the family from Thornton, has provided a picture of the family's daily
routine at the parsonage during their first year there. After the children

had been washed and dressed, they went to their father's study for prayers. Prayers being over, Patrick would join his children for breakfast in the dining room. This meal was described by Sarah as being 'plain but abundant', consisting of 'porridge and milk, bread and butter'.[4] The children, with the exception of baby Anne, would then return to their father's study for lessons. The girls spent the interval between morning lessons and the lunch hour with Sarah, who taught them the rudiments of sewing. Lunch was usually a simple meal of roast or boiled meat and potatoes, followed by sweets such as bread and rice puddings, custards and 'other preparations of eggs and milk, slightly sweetened'. In the afternoons, while their father's time was taken up with parish business, the children, accompanied by Sarah, would walk on the moors. On their return they would take tea in the kitchen, Mr Brontë taking his meal later in the study. After tea he gave his children 'oral lessons in history, biography or travel' while the girls worked at their sewing. When their mother was still alive, the children would say their evening prayers at her bedside before seeking their own 'warm, clean beds'.

The first extant accounts of life at the parsonage written by Charlotte herself date from 1829. By this time Mrs Brontë and her two eldest daughters were dead, and Aunt Elizabeth Branwell had stayed on at the parsonage to look after the remaining children. Aunt Branwell instilled a keen sense of order and routine into the lives of her nieces. Mrs Gaskell claimed that '[p]eople in Haworth have assured me that, according to the hour of day – nay, the very minute – could they have told what the inhabitants of the parsonage were about' (*Life*, p. 148). Charlotte was beginning to chronicle the fantasy world she was developing with her brother Branwell, and her accounts contain details of their everyday lives:

While I write this I am in the kitchin of the parsonage house Hawarth [*sic*] Taby the servent is washing up after Breakfast and Anne my youngest Sister (Maria was my eldest) is kneeling on a chair looking at some cakes whiche Tabby has been Baking for us. Emily is in the parlour brushing it papa and Branwell are gone to Keighly Aunt is up stairs in her Room and I am sitting by the table writing this in the kitchen.[5]

One of the interesting things about the accounts of life at the parsonage are the items which remain constant throughout the years, including meal-times and the periods set aside for walking and writing. In 1832, after Charlotte returned from Roe Head School, she wrote to her new friend Ellen Nussey:

You ask me to give you a description of the manner in which I have passed every day since I have left School: this is soon done as an account of one day is an account of all. In the morning from nine o'clock till half past twelve I instruct my Sisters & draw, then we walk till dinner after dinner I sew till tea-time, and after tea I either read, write, do a little fancy work or draw, as I please. Thus in one delightful, though somewhat monotonous course my life is passed. (Smith, *Letters*, vol. I, p. 114)

What is hidden behind this conventional, lady-like account is the fervid creativity that was going on within the parsonage's walls as the Brontës developed their fantasy worlds. The sheer volume of writing produced by Charlotte in this period is astonishing when her drawings and other duties are taken into account. Emily and Anne wrote a series of diary papers which are well known for the way in which the sisters slip between the worlds of their imagination and the real events taking place at Haworth Parsonage: 'The Gondals are discovering the interior of Gaaldine Sally mosley is washing in the back Kitchin.'[6]

It is clear from Mrs Gaskell's accounts of her visit to the parsonage in 1853 that following the deaths of her brother and sisters, Charlotte kept to the routines of earlier times, and the structure of her day changed very little. Gaskell's account is also clear in showing how deeply the loss of her sisters affected Charlotte. Martha Brown told Mrs Gaskell of the sisters' nightly habit of walking around the dining-room table, discussing their plans and projects into the night. After Emily's death Charlotte and Anne continued the ritual, and now Martha's heart ached to 'hear Miss Brontë walking, walking, on alone'.[7]

FOOD

Fiona Lucraft has drawn attention to the significance of food in the Brontë novels and compiled a glossary listing the surprisingly high number of references to food and drink they contain.[8] The Brontë sisters were expected to carry out a share of the household chores, and Emily in particular was often to be found in the kitchen, assisting Tabby and acting as housekeeper after Aunt Branwell's death in 1842. In her diary paper for 1834, Emily writes: 'It is past Twelve o'clock Anne and I have not tid[i]ed ourselves, done our bed work or done our lessons and we want to go out to play We are going to have for Dinner Boiled Beef Turnips potato's and applepudding' (Barker, p. 221). Baking the bread and working in the kitchen allowed Emily the mental freedom to focus on her writing. Although her early prose works have not survived, clearly domestic routine figured largely in her writing. An article written by Charlotte for the 'Young Men's Magazine' of October 1830 describes a visit by her character Lord Charles Wellesley to Sir Edward Parry's Land, Emily's imaginary kingdom. Charlotte revelled in written descriptions of lavish settings, and her account of Parry's Land pokes fun at her younger sister's more homely creation. Parry's Palace, square and stone-built, has a garden of 'moderate dimensions' containing 'rows of peas, gooseberry bushes, black, red and white currant trees, some few common flowering shrubs, and a grass place to dry clothes on'.[9] The palace clearly bears a close resemblance to Haworth Parsonage, and the meals served up within its walls are also examples of parsonage fare: 'roast-beef, Yorkshire pudding, mashed potatoes, apple pie and preserved cucumbers'.[10] Emily used domestic detail to great effect in *Wuthering Heights*, a point made by David Daiches in his introduction to the novel:

All this concrete domestic detail [in *Wuthering Heights*] helps to steady it, as it were. Here is the world that the author has lived in and carefully observed. The fire, the hearth, the dishes, the porridge, are a guarantee of authenticity ... throughout the novel the homely and familiar and the wild and extravagant go together, the former providing a setting for the latter, with the result that the simplest domestic detail can, in virtue of being made the scene of such monstrous conflicts of passion, become symbolic. Conversely, passion set in such scenes becomes credible.[11]

NEEDLEWORK

The novels of Charlotte and Anne also include many references to needlework. 'Plain' sewing, including the making and repairing of house-hold linen and clothing, was often delegated to servants while 'fancy' work, including embroidery, was one of the accomplishments expected of a gentlewoman. In their writing the sisters demonstrate familiarity with both branches of needlework. Plain sewing was an essential skill in a household where money was not plentiful, and it was also considered to be something of a discipline. In a letter to Elizabeth Gaskell, Mary Taylor recalled how 'Miss Branwell ... made her nieces sew, with purpose or without, and as far as possible discouraged any other culture. She used to keep the girls sewing charity clothing, and maintained to me that it was not for the good of the recipients, but of the sewers. "It was proper for them to do it", she said' (Gaskell, *Life*, p. 95). Two faded samplers are the only surviving relics of Maria and Elizabeth Brontë. The parsonage collection also includes samplers worked by their younger sisters, all attesting to the years spent stitching under Aunt Branwell's supervision.

HEATING AND LIGHTING

Its stone floors and exposed situation make the parsonage a cold house, and Aunt Branwell is said to have rarely left her over-heated bedroom (Gaskell, *Life*, p. 49). During her last illness Mrs Brontë would request to be raised up in her bed in this same room so that she could watch the servant cleaning the grate, 'because she did it as it was done in Cornwall' (Gaskell, *Life*, p. 43). A mixture of coal and peat was burnt for heat, and Mrs Gaskell recalled how fires burning in the grates made a 'pretty warm dancing light all over the house' (*Life*, p. 439). Lighting would have been provided by candles and oil lamps.

WASHING

All water for washing would have to be pumped from the well and then heated in the fireside boiler in the kitchen range. Cans of water would be carried to the bedrooms, where washstands with a ewer and basin were provided for the occupants. In a letter written to Ellen Nussey in the summer of 1849, Charlotte requests that Ellen buy her a 'patent shower-bath', which was supplied by Nelsons of Leeds and arrived at the parsonage in late September (Smith, *Letters*, vol. II, p. 233). In a letter written the following day, Charlotte promised Ellen 'a thorough drenching in [her] own shower-bath' whenever she next visited Haworth (Smith, *Letters*, vol. II, p. 265). The household linen was washed in tubs in the back kitchen. The sisters often shared the hard work of putting the wet washing through a mangle and doing the ironing.

SANITATION

Although the parsonage was kept scrupulously clean, the Brontës had little control over their outside environment. We know a great deal about the filthy and unhealthy state of Haworth because Mr Brontë, who always took a keen interest in public health, petitioned the General Board of Health to investigate the township's sanitation and water provision. The commissioned inspector, Benjamin Herschel Babbage, arrived in 1850 and spent three days in Haworth carrying out a thorough investigation. His report paints a grim picture of a village littered with stinking midden heaps and overflowing cesspits.[12] Haworth was served by only a small number of privies (small outhouses used as toilets), in some instances only one to a dozen households. Although sanitary arrangements at the parsonage were primitive, the Brontës fared slightly better than many of their neighbours, having their own privy in the back yard with seats for adults and children (the 1861 bill of sale also lists two night commodes among their household effects). The parsonage was also one of only five houses in Haworth to have a private well. Mr Brontë noted in his account book that in 1847 the well was cleaned for the first time in twenty years, and that eight decomposing tin cans, which had tinged the water yellow, were removed.[13]

Babbage's report provides a contrast to the romanticized image of Haworth which emerges from many a Brontë biography. He concluded that despite Haworth's hilltop setting and bracing moorland air, the village's average life expectancy of 25.8 years corresponded with that of some of the unhealthiest districts of London. In the years following Babbage's report, health improvements came about slowly in Haworth – too late to benefit Patrick Brontë's family. In Haworth terms, their early deaths were unremarkable.

NOTES

1 The quotation is from an account written by Ellen Nussey, a shorter version of which appeared in *Scribner's Monthly* in May 1871 (pp. 24–31). In the present volume, these 'Reminiscences of Charlotte Brontë' are quoted from Smith, *Letters*, vol. 1, where the details contained in this paragraph appear on p. 599.

2 Haworth Local Board of Health, detailed plan, 1853, Keighley Local Studies Library.

3 Bill of sale: sale by auction at Haworth Parsonage, 1 and 2 Oct. 1861, Brontë Parsonage Museum, BS X.

4 Marion Harland, *Charlotte Brontë at Home* (New York: G. P. Putnam's Sons, 1899), p. 17. The remaining quotations in this paragraph are from pp. 22 and 24.

5 Charlotte Brontë, 'The History of the Year', 12 Mar. 1829; see Juliet Barker, *Sixty Treasures* (Haworth: Brontë Society, 1988).

6 Emily and Anne Brontë's diary paper of 24 Nov. 1834; quoted from Barker, p. 221.

7 J. A. V. Chapple and Arthur Pollard (eds.), *The Letters of Mrs Gaskell* (Manchester: Mandolin, 1997), p. 247.

8 Fiona Lucraft, 'Food and Eating in the Brontë Novels', *Petits propos culinaires: Essays and Notes on Food, Cookery and Cookery Books*, 62 (1999), 29–52.

9 Christine Alexander (ed.), *An Edition of the Early Writings of Charlotte Brontë*, vol. 1 (Oxford: Blackwell, for the Shakespeare Head Press, 1987), p. 230.

10 *Ibid.*, p. 232.

11 David Daiches, introduction to *Wuthering Heights* (Harmondsworth: Penguin, 1985), p. 12.

12 Benjamin Herschel Babbage, *Report to the General Board of Health on a Preliminary Inquiry into the Sewerage, Drainage, and Supply of Water, and the Sanitary Condition of the Inhabitants of the Hamlet of Haworth* (London: HMSO, 1850).

13 Patrick Brontë, account book, *c.* 1847–1861, Brontë Parsonage Museum, BS 173.

CHAPTER 3

Locations in northern England associated with the Brontës' lives and works

Ann Dinsdale

The first illustrated edition of the Brontë novels, published by Smith, Elder & Co., appeared in 1872 – twenty-five years after the publication of *Jane Eyre, Wuthering Heights* and *Agnes Grey*. The commissioned artist, E. M. Wimperis, had been supplied with a list of original locations provided by Charlotte's school-friend Ellen Nussey, and it was announced in the advertisement for the new edition that the places described by the Brontës in their works of fiction were actual places. This idea had been reinforced by *Jane Eyre*'s being subtitled 'an autobiography'; and as far back as 1850, Charlotte told Ellen how visitors were arriving in Haworth 'on the wise errand of seeing the scenery described in *Jane Eyre* and *Shirley*' (Smith, *Letters*, vol. II, p. 353). Neither novel has a Haworth setting, but it became an established idea from early on that the geographical settings of the Brontë novels did have real-life counterparts.

JANE EYRE

The schools and private houses where Charlotte had taught suggested the settings for her novels. In writing the Lowood chapters of *Jane Eyre*, Charlotte recreated the charity school which she and her sisters had attended over twenty years before. The Clergy Daughters' School at Cowan Bridge, near Kirkby Lonsdale, offered the daughters of impoverished clergymen an education that would equip them to become teachers and governesses, and must have seemed like the answer to a prayer for Patrick Brontë, faced with six children to educate on a limited income. In 1824 the four elder daughters went to Cowan Bridge. Charlotte's fictional account of the school, clearly rooted in fact, strikes an ominous note: 'Have I not described a pleasant site for a dwelling, when I speak of it as bosomed in hill and wood, and rising from the verge of a stream? Assuredly pleasant enough: but whether healthy or not is another question' (1.ix.76).[1]

Armed with her Lowood education and accomplishments, Jane goes on to become a governess in the household of Mr Rochester at Thornfield Hall, Millcote, —shire. Ellen Nussey believed that her own old home, Rydings, in the parish of Birstall, six miles south-east of Bradford, had provided the inspiration for Thornfield, and Wimperis used it as the basis for his illustration. When Ellen came to describe Rydings in her reminiscences, she was careful to emphasize those features which corresponded most closely to Thornfield: 'the old turret roofed house, the fine chesnut [sic] trees on the lawn (one of which was iron "garthed" having been split by storms ...) a large rookery gave a good background to the house' (Smith, *Letters*, vol. 1, p. 596). Externally, Rydings has been preserved, although the lawns and chestnut trees have made way for the Leeds and Huddersfield road. The house itself is hemmed in on all sides by industrial units, and the internal features have long since been swept away. We can no longer see Rydings as it would have looked when Charlotte first visited in 1832, although Erskine Stuart, writing in the late 1880s, could still claim the house to be 'a beautifully situated residence in the castellated style, standing on an eminence outside Birstall. In Charlotte Brontë's word-picture of Thornfield in *Jane Eyre*, we have the description of this building given to the life.'[2] Stuart goes on to say: 'Although many persons are of the opinion that The Rydings is the Thornfield Hall of *Jane Eyre*, another party leans to the belief that Norton Conyers, near Ripon, the seat of Sir Reginald Graham, Bart., is the original.'[3] It is possible that during her time as governess to the Sidgwick family of Stonegappe, in 1839, Charlotte visited Norton Conyers, which was rented for a time by Mrs Sidgwick's brother, Frederick Greenwood. Although there are no references to Norton Conyers in Charlotte's surviving letters, Ellen Nussey remembered 'receiving from Charlotte a verbal description of the place, and recalled also the impression made on the mind of Charlotte by the story of the mad woman' confined to the attic.[4]

Another contender for Thornfield is North Lees Hall near Hathersage, close to where Charlotte stayed with Ellen Nussey in the summer of 1845. Ellen's brother Henry was vicar of Hathersage, and the two friends went to prepare the vicarage before Henry's return with his new bride. Henry (often viewed as the inspiration for St John Rivers) had been casting around for a suitable wife for some time and had once proposed marriage to Charlotte. During their stay at Hathersage, Charlotte and Ellen visited North Lees, which was home to the Eyre family, and where

Charlotte observed the 'great cabinet . . . whose front, divided into twelve panels, bore in grim design, the heads of the twelve apostles, each inclosed in its separate panel as in a frame' (*Jane Eyre*, II.v.210), which she transplanted to the Thornfield attics.

Following her flight from Thornfield, Jane finds a temporary refuge at Moor House (also called Marsh End), home of the Rivers family. Moorseats, an old house just outside Hathersage, fits Charlotte's description and is claimed as its inspiration (although bay windows and an extension have been added since Charlotte's time). It is said that the vicarage people were on visiting terms with the occupants of Moorseats, and that Charlotte went there with Ellen Nussey.

Ferndean Manor, the house to which Rochester retreats following the fire at Thornfield, was depicted by Wimperis as Kirklees Hall near Huddersfield. Ferndean is described as 'a building of considerable antiquity, moderate size . . . deep buried in a wood', a description which is more applicable to Wycoller Hall near Colne, the house which has become established in the popular imagination as Ferndean. We do not know for certain that the Brontës ever visited Wycoller, although in her biography of Charlotte, Mrs Gaskell recounts tales concerning the eccentric squire of Wycoller, Henry Owen Cunliffe, which Charlotte herself may have told her. After Cunliffe's death in 1818 the house remained uninhabited, and today it survives as a picturesque ruin.

SHIRLEY

Charlotte's second published novel, *Shirley* (1849), was set at the time of the Luddite risings in west Yorkshire. Charlotte would have heard her father's accounts of Luddite violence from his days as minister at Hartshead, and her own schooldays had been mainly spent at Roe Head, Mirfield, in the heart of Luddite country. Charlotte's friends Ellen Nussey and Mary Taylor lived in the Birstall area, and the Taylors' family home, the Red House at Gomersal, became Briarmains in the novel, home of the Yorke family (see Figure 4). So detailed was Charlotte's description of the Red House, even down to the pictures on the walls, that Mary, writing from New Zealand, informed Charlotte she had 'not seen the matted hall and the painted parlour windows so plain these 5 years'.[5] It is also well established that Oakwell Hall at Birstall, a seventeenth-century yeoman's house, was the inspiration for Shirley Keeldar's home, Field-head. Both houses are proud of their Brontë association and are open to the public.

4 The windows at the Red House, Gomersal, which are graphically described in
Charlotte Brontë's novel *Shirley*

'You asked me in one of your letters lately whether I thought I should escape identification in Yorkshire', Charlotte wrote to W. S. Williams in September 1849, shortly before the novel's publication, adding, 'I am so little known, that I think I shall. Besides the book is far less founded on the Real – than perhaps appears' (Smith, *Letters*, vol. II, p. 260). Charlotte had underestimated the degree of interest in her sources. A host of people from the Birstall area recognized themselves and their neighbours in the novel, and the closely guarded secret of Charlotte's identity as an author was soon found out.

WUTHERING HEIGHTS

The houses in the novels of Charlotte and Emily are as memorable as the characters. Emily's *Wuthering Heights*, as the title implies, is a book which focuses on property and ownership as well as on elemental passion and extremes of experience. In a persuasive article, Hilda Marsden expresses the following belief:

Emily Brontë clearly [had] some particular locality in mind [when writing the novel], and when Lockwood describes Heathcliff's dwelling, or Ellen Dean the valley of Gimmerden Sough on an evening in late summer, they are describing what Emily herself saw, not once but many times, for the detail is too exact to have been gathered from a single impression.[6]

Perhaps surprisingly, the locality Marsden believes to have inspired the landscape of *Wuthering Heights* is not Emily's home environment at Haworth, but the bleak hilltop parish of Southowram, near Halifax, where she went as a teacher to Law Hill in 1838. What sets Wuthering Heights apart from the farmhouses Emily would have seen dotting the moors at Haworth is its air of decayed grandeur and the singular stone carving covering the façade: 'Before passing the threshold, I paused to admire a quantity of grotesque carving lavished over the front, and especially about the principal door, above which, among a wilderness of crumbling griffins and shameless little boys, I detected the date "1500" and the name "Hareton Earnshaw"' (1.i.2). It seems likely that the detail of Wuthering Heights came from High Sunderland Hall at Southowram – a seventeenth-century mansion standing on an exposed hillside just two miles from Law Hill (see Figure 5). The impressive gateway to the hall, which appeared to be a part of the house and could easily have been mistaken for the principal door, was decorated with a quantity of carving consisting of a nude man and leering faces, with two griffins on the reverse side of the gateway. Similar carvings, interspersed with Latin inscriptions and armorial bearings, stood out from every corner of the building.

Emily would have been able to learn about the hall and its history by consulting John Horner's *Buildings in the Town and Parish of Halifax*, a copy of which was held in the library at Law Hill. High Sunderland was one of the West Riding's great houses, but by the late 1830s it was occupied by tenant farmers and falling into a state of decay. Mining in the area weakened the building's foundations, and after years of dereliction it was demolished in 1950.

Looking down the valley from High Sunderland is Shibden Hall, now a museum and frequently claimed as the model for Thrushcross Grange, home of the Lintons. Shibden is a fifteenth-century timbered house which was inherited by Anne Lister in 1826. Emily's time at Law Hill coincided with extensive alterations taking place there. Despite Lister's gentrification, however, Shibden Hall remains a far more modest house than the Grange.

Law Hill has also been suggested as the original of Wuthering Heights. Although the building bears little resemblance to the house she described, Emily is likely to have heard the story of its builder, Jack Sharp, a cuckoo

5 High Sunderland Hall at Southowram, Halifax. It is likely that features of the house came into Emily Brontë's mind when she began to write *Wuthering Heights*

in the nest who was adopted by his uncle, John Walker, and who attempted to usurp the family fortunes and displace the rightful heir. After his ejection from the Walker family home, Walterclough Hall, Sharp built Law Hill and lived a life of debauchery there until mounting debts forced him to flee the area.

For many, Haworth remains the presumed landscape of *Wuthering Heights*. Ellen Nussey suggested that Top Withens, an isolated farmhouse about four miles from Haworth Parsonage, was the model for Wuthering Heights. Ellen's long friendship and correspondence with Charlotte lent authority to her suggestions regarding original locations, but when it came to Emily's and Anne's sources, Ellen was on less certain ground. We do not know why she suggested Top Withens, for although Emily may have had the old farmhouse's dramatic moorland setting in mind when she wrote her novel, the building bears little resemblance to the house she described. Clearly Wimperis thought so too; although the image he produced is recognizable as Top Withens, he enlarged the house and added another storey.

Another Haworth candidate for the Heights is Sowdens, home of William Grimshaw, which carries the initials 'HE' and the date '1659' above the entrance. Grimshaw was a leading light in the eighteenth-century

Evangelical revival, and minister at Haworth almost a hundred years before the Brontës arrived in the village. Colourful tales abound of him haranguing sinners and driving his parishioners from public house to church, brandishing a horsewhip. The story of Grimshaw's children must have struck a chord with the young Brontës – Jane who, like the eldest Brontë sisters, died after being sent away to school, and John, his wild alcoholic son, who died as a result of his excesses at the age of thirty.

AGNES GREY AND *THE TENANT OF WILDFELL HALL*

Anne Brontë's first novel, *Agnes Grey*, was coloured by her experience of working as a governess – first to the Ingham family of Blake Hall at Mirfield, and then to the Robinson family of Thorp Green Hall near York. It is usually claimed that the Bloomfield family in *Agnes Grey* are based on the Inghams, and that Blake Hall provided a model for their home, Wellwood House. Similarly, the Robinsons are said to have inspired the Murrays of Horton Lodge. The final chapters, where Agnes is reunited with the young curate whom she eventually marries, are set at a seaside resort, usually identified as Scarborough on the Yorkshire coast, a place to which Anne became attached during summers spent there with the Robinson family.

The locations and houses in Anne's novels lack recognizable originals. Although she relied on her own experience, she appears to have been less inspired than her sisters by a sense of houses and their histories. In her second novel, *The Tenant of Wildfell Hall*, the action of the story can be divided into two types of setting: the small rural community at Linden-Car, to which Helen escapes, and the more sophisticated and corrupt world represented by Grassdale, Huntingdon's country seat. Linden-Car is clearly located in Yorkshire, 'car' being a northern dialect word for pool or boggy ground, although the characters speak in standard English rather than dialect. Wildfell Hall is situated in the vicinity of Linden-Car, and early in the novel we are given a description of the house:

Near the top of this hill, about two miles from Linden-car, stood Wildfell Hall, a superannuated mansion of the Elizabethan era, built of dark grey stone, – venerable and picturesque to look at, but doubtless, cold and gloomy enough to inhabit, with its thick stone mullions and little latticed panes, its time-eaten air-holes, and its too lonely, too unsheltered situation, – only shielded from the war of wind and weather by a group of Scotch firs, themselves half blighted with storms, and looking as stern and gloomy as the Hall itself. (i.20)

The phrasing echoes Lockwood's description of Wuthering Heights in the opening chapter of Emily's novel:

Wuthering Heights is the name of Mr Heathcliff's dwelling, "Wuthering" being a significant provincial adjective, descriptive of the atmospheric tumult to which its station is exposed in stormy weather. Pure, bracing ventilation they must have up there, at all times, indeed: one may guess the power of the north wind, blowing over the edge, by the excessive slant of a few, stunted firs at the end of the house; and by a range of gaunt thorns all stretching their limbs one way, as if craving alms of the sun. Happily, the architect had foresight to build it strong: the narrow windows are deeply set in the wall, and the corners defended with large jutting stones. (1.i.2)

We know that the young Brontës vied with one another in the creation and development of the characters and events taking place in their fantasy worlds, and that they would sometimes adapt situations and settings borrowed from one another. The striking similarity between the two houses was noted by an anonymous critic who reviewed *The Tenant* for the *Examiner* in July 1848: 'Here is a description ... of Wildfell Hall, which is not very unlike the house inhabited by the wild people of *Wuthering Heights*.'[7]

It is not clear whether Ellen suggested originals for *The Tenant* or Wimperis was left to improvise. The illustration of Wildfell Hall which he produced has never been identified with a real house. Anne includes a generalized picture of Grassdale, the other main house in *The Tenant*, which Wimperis based on Blake Hall. Although neither Blake Hall nor Thorp Green corresponds with what we know of Grassdale, we do know that Anne's time at Thorp Green provided what she describes as 'some very unpleasant and undreamt of experience of human nature',[8] which found its way into the book.

In the writing of their novels, Charlotte, Emily and Anne Brontë did, to varying degrees, make use of memories of places they had known. Charlotte's letters indicate that she would often take real people and places as a starting-point for her fiction – to invest her work with what, in a letter to George Smith dated 6 December 1852, she called 'the germ of the *real*' (Smith, *Letters*, vol. III, p. 88; Charlotte underlined the last word). This is not to deny the Brontës' powers of creativity, however; writing to Ellen Nussey on 16 November 1849, Charlotte also insisted that 'we only suffer Reality to *suggest* – never to *dictate*' (Smith, *Letters*, vol. II, p. 285).

The idea that the literary tourist can physically travel through the landscapes of the Brontës' imaginations has proved persistent. Fact and fiction have merged, drawing thousands of visitors every year to explore both the real and the imaginary landscape which has become known as 'Brontë Country'.

NOTES

1 On the school-related deaths of the eldest sisters Brontë, see Chapter 41.

2 J. A. Erskine Stuart, *The Brontë Country: Its Topography, Antiquities, and History* (London: Longmans, Green & Co., 1888), p. 114.

3 *Ibid.*, p. 121.

4 Herbert E. Wroot, 'Sources of Charlotte Brontë's Novels: Persons and Places', *BST*, 8.45 (1935), 20.

5 Joan Stevens (ed.), *Mary Taylor, Friend of Charlotte Brontë: Letters from New Zealand and Elsewhere* (Auckland University Press, 1972), p. 97.

6 Hilda Marsden, 'The Scenic Background of *Wuthering Heights*', *BST*, 13.67 (1957), 111.

7 Miriam Allott (ed.), *The Brontës: The Critical Heritage* (London: Routledge & Kegan Paul, 1974), p. 256.

8 Anne Brontë's diary paper of 31 July 1845; quoted from Barker, p. 455.

CHAPTER 4

The father of the Brontës

Dudley Green

The Revd Patrick Brontë was born on St Patrick's Day, 17 March 1777, in Drumballyroney, a rural parish of County Down in Ireland. He was the eldest of the ten children of Hugh and Alice Brunty. His father was a farmer of limited means, who had a considerable local reputation as a storyteller. Details of Patrick's upbringing are difficult to establish with any certainty, but he clearly showed early intellectual promise. After running his own school for a short time, he attracted the attention of his local rector, through whose patronage he gained a place at St John's College, Cambridge. Here, while managing to maintain himself on slender financial resources, he devoted himself to his studies to such an extent that he was placed in the first class for each year of his residence and was awarded several university scholarships.

Patrick Brontë's remarkable emergence from a background of rural poverty in Ireland reveals the firm determination which he was to display throughout his long clerical ministry. This certainly made an impression on his daughter Charlotte, who, when seeking her aunt's financial support for her Brussels plan in September 1841, wrote, 'Papa will perhaps think it a wild and ambitious scheme; but who ever rose in the world without ambition? When he left Ireland to go to Cambridge University, he was as ambitious as I am now' (Smith, *Letters*, vol. 1, p. 269).

Although we only know of one return to his Irish homeland, Patrick kept in regular touch with his family there. It is clear that he spoke with a strong Irish accent, so much so that his name was mistakenly entered in the St John's Admissions Register as 'Branty'. It is perhaps not surprising that his daughter Charlotte was described by her school-friend Mary Taylor as speaking 'with a strong Irish accent' (in a letter to Elizabeth Gaskell; *Life*, p. 80).

After his ordination in 1806, Patrick served his first curacy at Wethersfield in Essex. Here he fell in love with Mary Burder, his land-lady's niece, and they became engaged. Fearing, however, that her strong

6 A portrait of Patrick Brontë as a young man, by an unknown artist

nonconformist background might impede his ministry in the Church of England, Patrick later broke off the engagement. After a second curacy at Wellington in Shropshire, he moved north to the parish of Dewsbury in Yorkshire, where he was appointed perpetual curate of Hartshead. In his first year there he experienced the Luddite risings, which were mainly centred in the parish. It was here that he met Maria Branwell, and after a short courtship (during which she addressed her letters to him 'My dear saucy Pat') they were married on 29 December 1812. Their first two children were born at Hartshead, and it was here that Patrick produced his first books, volumes of poetry designed for the education of the poor. In 1815 he moved to Thornton near Bradford, where the remaining members of his family were born.

In 1820 Patrick Brontë was nominated to the perpetual curacy of Haworth. His joy at this appointment, however, was soon dimmed by the death from cancer of his wife Maria within eighteen months of his arrival. Realizing that it was necessary for him to provide a secure home background for his six motherless children, he made some abortive attempts to marry again. He first thought of Elizabeth Firth, who had been a close family friend in Thornton, but she gave him a firm refusal. He then turned to his first love, Mary Burder, but his approach met with a bitter rejection. In the summer of 1825 Patrick suffered the further sorrow of the deaths from tuberculosis of his two elder children, Maria and Elizabeth. He himself was destined to outlive all his other children. Branwell, Emily and Anne died in a sad succession between September 1848 and May 1849 and Charlotte in March 1855. Patrick remained in Haworth until his own death in June 1861, thus completing a ministry in the township of over forty years.

For over a century and a half, the picture of the father of the Brontës in the public mind has been that of a strange, obstinate old man who did not like children and who was subject to fits of bad temper during which he performed actions of extreme eccentricity. This is due to the unfavourable portrait of him given by Mrs Gaskell in her famous biography of Charlotte Brontë. In an attempt to explain the powerful and violent nature of the novels written by the Brontë sisters, Mrs Gaskell sought to attribute their lack of sensitivity to the isolation of Haworth from all civilized influences and also to the strange, eccentric nature of their family life under the influence of their widowed father.

It is unfortunate that for much of her information about the early life of the children Mrs Gaskell relied on the evidence of Martha Wright, a nurse from Burnley whom Patrick had engaged to assist in the care of his wife during her last illness and whom he had later dismissed. Martha Wright clearly bore a grudge against Mr Brontë, and after Charlotte's death she gave Mrs Gaskell a distorted view of the children's family life. It may be significant that in her obituary she was described as possessing 'a large fund of anecdote and folk-lore'.[1] She was the source of the stories told by Mrs Gaskell of Patrick in fits of fury cutting up his wife's silk dress, burning a hearth-rug in the grate and sawing the backs off chairs, all of which allegations Patrick vehemently denied. In recent years, more detailed study of Patrick's life and correspondence has revealed a strikingly different picture of him. He is seen to have been a loving father with a deep concern for his children's education, a dedicated clergyman who took a keen interest in the affairs of his parishioners and an intelligent observer of political and religious affairs, making frequent observations in the local press on matters of contemporary interest.

Although it was natural that during their mother's illness the young Brontë children should have been quiet and subdued, there is evidence to show that they generally lived normal, happy and boisterous lives. A detailed picture of the children's home life after their mother's death was given many years later by their nursemaid, Sarah Garrs. She stated that they were given plain but abundant food and, after lessons with their father in the morning, revelled in walks on the moors when 'their fun knew no bounds' and 'they enjoyed a game of romps, and played with zest'.[2] It is also clear that, far from being the remote father depicted by Mrs Gaskell, Patrick took an active part in his children's upbringing. William Dearden, a schoolmaster friend of the family, later recorded that the Brontë children frequently accompanied Patrick on his moorland walks and that 'he took a lively interest in all their innocent amusements'.[3] The truth of this latter assertion may be seen from Patrick's statement to Mrs Gaskell that he was occasionally asked to intervene in the children's disputes over the relative merits of the Duke of Wellington, Napoleon, Hannibal and Caesar. Indeed it was Patrick's gift of toy soldiers for Branwell which was responsible for sparking off his children's vivid imagination in their juvenile writings, thus providing the seedbed for their later novels.

Patrick made careful provision for his children's education. For a short time he sent his two eldest daughters to a school near Wakefield, an expense which he could barely afford. He then sent all his daughters except the youngest, Anne, to the Clergy Daughters' School at Cowan Bridge. When all the family were at home after the tragic deaths of Maria and Elizabeth, Patrick taught them himself. Later he arranged for Charlotte, Emily and Anne to be educated at Roe Head School, Mirfield. He kept Branwell at home and read a wide range of classical literature with him. The children were all given lessons by a local artist named John Bradley, and Branwell was taught by the Leeds portrait painter William Robinson. They had music lessons from Abraham Sunderland, the

Keighley organist, and Patrick bought a piano for the parsonage so that the children could play at home. He had a deep love of music and regularly took his family to the concerts of the Haworth Philharmonic Society. He also, unusually, taught Emily to shoot when they were alone together in the parsonage during a time of civil unrest.

Patrick had a deep sense of his vocation as a clergyman. When, in 1819, he was considering his move to Haworth, he summed up his views on the Christian ministry in a letter to Stephen Taylor, a church trustee: 'I do humbly trust that it is my unvarying practice to preach Christ faithfully, as the only Way, the Truth, and the Life.' When the trustees responded by inviting him to Haworth to preach a trial sermon, he replied: 'My conscience does not altogether approve to a circumstance of exposing myself to the temptation of preaching in order to please, through divine grace my aim has been, and I trust, always will be, to preach Christ and not myself.'[4] It is clear that of all the varied responsibilities of a clergyman, Patrick always considered preaching to be the chief of his clerical duties, and he continued to perform this function virtually to the end of his life. It was a feature of his preaching on almost all occasions to speak extempore and to explain his message in a clear and simple manner. Charlotte's school-friend Ellen Nussey, who visited Haworth in 1833, later wrote down her impressions of Patrick's preaching:

Mr Brontë always addressed his hearers in extempore style, very often he selected a parable 'from one of the Gospels' which he explained in the simplest manner, sometimes going over his own words and explaining them also, so as to be perfectly intelligible to the lowest comprehension. (Ellen Nussey's 'Reminiscences', quoted from Smith, *Letters*, vol. 1, p. 600)

Patrick also took very seriously his responsibility to assist his parishioners in all ways that he could. During the winter of 1825–6, when poverty was widespread in the West Riding of Yorkshire, he had the duty of appointing a new parish clerk. Two candidates applied for the position. After due consideration, Patrick reported that 'Owing to the hardness of the times, and very nearly the equality of merit', he had decided to appoint them both, to operate in alternate months and to share the dues. When one of his churchwardens, Enoch Thomas, the landlord of the King's Arms, was suffering from acute depression, Patrick wrote to George Taylor, the other churchwarden, with a novel suggestion for assisting him: 'I wish you, to have a tea party, soon, and to invite him among, the number of the guests; His mind, which is, in a very disordered state should be diverted, as much as possible, from his present way of thinking' (Green, *Letters*, pp. 168–9). Mindful of how he himself had been assisted in fulfilling his youthful ambitions, he was always anxious to help young people to make something of their lives. When a young Haworth man applied to train as a teacher, Patrick wrote a sympathetic letter to the National Society in his support: 'Knowing him, as I well do, I think, he would be an acquisition, to the Society. I am only afraid, that as he will very probably be abashed, the Examiner may not discover his intrinsic worth, whilst many of far less merit, might shew off, to greater advantage' (Green, *Letters*, pp. 173–4). His concern to assist those in need is seen in a letter which he wrote to Eliza Brown, the younger sister of Martha, the parsonage servant. It seems that she was an unmarried mother and had left her little baby girl with her family in Haworth. In 1859, the eighty-two-year-old Patrick Brontë had the sad task of telling her that the little girl had died from scarlet fever. His letter reveals his skill in responding to the needs of a sad and troubled individual. Very gently and sensitively he broke the news of her baby's death:

After some time, it was hoped she was recovering, and |that| the danger was past, However, She rather suddenly got worse; and worse, till at last she seem'd to sleep away, till she closed her eyes, on time, and open'd them in eternity, I doubt not in an Eternity of glory and bliss. Thus she has made an exchange infinitely for the better. (Green, *Letters*, pp. 279–80)

Patrick also devoted himself assiduously to the wider role required of a clergyman in the nineteenth century, and he showed himself to be an able and effective campaigner on a variety of issues. He led the township's efforts to obtain improvements in the water supply and the system of sanitation. Also, from his earliest days in Ireland he had a consuming interest in education, and when he came to Haworth in 1820 he found that, in addition to there being no Church of England day school, there was not even a Sunday school. This state of affairs was probably due to the general poverty of the inhabitants and also to the large number of Dissenters in the parish. Patrick determined to remedy this situation, and in 1831 he persuaded the church trustees to release land for the building of a Sunday school.

Twelve years later, he began a remarkable campaign to establish a church day school in Haworth. Between August 1843 and April 1845, he wrote twenty-six letters to the National Society in his efforts to obtain grants to establish and maintain a school. His passionate concern is well revealed in his letter of 8 December 1843:

Owing to the people being generally poor ... it really seems to me, that as well might You require us to raise £1500 – as £15 – Had I, any money to spare, I would, myself, subscribe liberally, but My humble means, are already exhausted ... Surely ... there can be only a few applications, stronger or more just than mine. (Green, *Letters*, p. 159)

In a postscript, he added: 'Be so kind, as to excuse mistakes, as I am now advanced in Years, and my sight has become dim.' This heartfelt letter obviously made an impression on the officials of the society, and they agreed to send a master. The school opened in January 1844 and was an immediate success. Patrick was delighted and told the secretary: 'We have, now, between one and two hundred children. . . . The little creatures find that the way to ⟨knowledge⟩ |wisdom,| is the road to pleasure, and go on in their work for the acquisition of knowledge, with alacrity and delight' (Green, *Letters*, p. 163).

Patrick also wrote frequently to the local papers on various subjects of contemporary interest. Although his early upbringing in Ireland had implanted in him a deep distrust of Roman Catholicism, his sense of realism led him in 1829 to support a limited form of Catholic emancipation. In a similar manner, although the opposition of local nonconformists to the payment of church rates had a serious effect on the church in Haworth and privately he felt bitter on the subject, in public he advocated a conciliatory attitude, and he opened a voluntary subscription in order to raise the money necessary for church expenses.

Patrick was firmly opposed to the widespread use of capital punishment, which as late as 1830 was the stated penalty for 220 offences. He wrote several letters on this subject, arguing that 'fine, imprisonment, and hard labour, duly moderated as to durance and degree, would . . . answer the ends of justice infinitely better' and that many criminals, given time 'for repentance and amendment', might ultimately 'become useful members of society'. He also expressed strong opposition to the Poor Law Amendment Act of 1834, which established workhouses with deliberately harsh conditions as a deterrent to 'going on the parish'. He wrote a trenchant letter to the *Leeds Intelligencer* under the uncompromising heading 'Liberty or Bondage: To the Labourers, Mechanics, and Paupers or Slaves of England', in which he argued that the bill must be repealed and that if his readers would 'petition, remonstrate, and resist powerfully but *legally*', 'God, the father and friend of the poor' would crown their efforts with success.

Patrick Brontë's long ministry at Haworth shows him to have been a conscientious and devoted clergyman anxious to exercise a beneficial influence in his local community. He was, however, well aware of the criticisms made of him after the publication of Mrs Gaskell's biography of Charlotte. Writing to her on 30 July 1857, he said: 'I do not deny that I am, somewhat e⟨x⟩ccentric [*sic*]. Had I been numbered amongst the calm, sedate, <u>concentric</u> men of the world, I should not have been as I now am, and I should, in all probability, never have had such children as mine have been' (Green, *Letters*, p. 258). The letter's conclusion aptly epitomizes the simple, practical nature of his Christian faith: 'I am not in the least offended, at your telling |me| that I have faults I have many – and being a Daughter of Eve, I doubt not, that you also have some. Let us both try to be wiser and better, as Time recedes, and Eternity advances' (Green, *Letters*, pp. 258–9).

NOTES

1 Dudley Green, *Patrick Brontë: Father of Genius* (Stroud: Nonsuch, 2008), p. 353.
2 *Ibid.*, p. 127.
3 *Ibid.*, p. 128.
4 Dudley Green (ed.), *The Letters of the Reverend Patrick Brontë* (Stroud: Nonsuch, 2005), p. 37. Subsequent references are included in the text.

CHAPTER 5

A mother and her substitutes: Maria Brontë (née Branwell), Elizabeth Branwell and Margaret Wooler

Bob Duckett

One of the appeals of the Brontë story is the sympathy we have for the motherless children, three of whom survived to become world-famous authors. Significantly, many of the central characters in the Brontë novels are themselves orphans: William Crimsworth and Frances Henri (*The Professor*), Shirley Keeldar (*Shirley*), Lucy Snowe (*Villette*), Heathcliff (*Wuthering Heights*) and, of course, Jane Eyre. Then there is the appeal of how these heroes and heroines survived their motherlessness to become strong, independent people. Another interest is in how the Brontë sisters treated mothers and parenting in their novels and how these views were influenced by their own mother and mother-substitutes. This chapter focuses on the Brontës' mother, Maria Brontë (*née* Branwell), and on two of these mother-substitutes, Aunt Branwell and Margaret Wooler.

MARIA BRONTË (NÉE BRANWELL) (1783–1821)

Maria Branwell, the Brontës' mother, was born on 15 April 1783 in Penzance to Thomas and Anne Branwell. Maria was the eleventh of twelve children, although by the time of her birth six had already died.

Maria's father, Thomas (1746–1808), was a prominent Methodist tradesman in the grocery business; he imported luxury goods such as tea, which he sold wholesale or through his grocery shop in Penzance Market Square. He owned a profitable amount of property in the town and nearby, including a five-bedroom Georgian house, stables, a malthouse, an inn and quite a few acres of farming land. His brother Richard was also a successful businessman, and their sisters made good marriages. In 1789, Thomas was elected to be one of the '12 Assistants to the Corporation'. The value of his estate on his death in 1808 was £3,500, suggesting that his mercantile business had prospered. Maria's mother, Anne Carne (1743–1809), was the daughter of a Penzance silversmith and watchmaker and a cousin of William Carne, the town's first banker.

7 A copy of a portrait of Maria Brontë, *née* Branwell, made by her daughter
Charlotte in October 1830

Seven of the children of Thomas and Anne Branwell survived into
adulthood.[1] Maria's only surviving brother was Benjamin Carne Branwell
(1775–1818), who followed in his father's footsteps as a merchant and a
member of the corporation, being elected mayor of Penzance in 1809.
Maria's elder sister Jane (1773–1855) married John Kingston, a Wesleyan
minister and missionary who saw service in North America. The couple
separated, Jane returning to Penzance in 1809 with her daughter Eliza.

Maria's youngest sister was Charlotte Branwell (1789–1848), who married her first cousin, Joseph Branwell (Richard's son), a successful clerk, schoolmaster, accountant and banker. A third sister, Elizabeth (1776–1842), features later in this account.

After the deaths of both parents, the three unmarried sisters continued to live together until Maria, early in 1812, travelled to Yorkshire to stay with her aunt Jane Fennell, her father's sister, who had married the Methodist schoolmaster John Fennell. John had just been appointed the first headmaster of the Wesleyan school Woodhouse Grove at Apperley Bridge near Bradford.

It was here that Maria met Patrick Brontë, who had been appointed examiner in classics. The immediate attraction between Patrick Brontë and Maria Branwell was strong and the courtship brief. She was twenty-nine and he was thirty-five. From Maria's surviving letters we get a picture of a gentle, lively and intelligent young woman. On reading these letters in February 1850, her daughter Charlotte wrote to Ellen Nussey: 'There is a rectitude, a refinement, a constancy, a modesty, a sense, a gentleness about them indescribable. I wish [s]he had lived and that I had known her' (Smith, *Letters*, vol. II, p. 347).

Yet Maria was someone who knew her own mind. To Patrick she wrote: 'For some years I have been perfectly my own mistress, subject to no control whatever – so far from it, that my sisters who are many years older than myself, and even my dear mother, used to consult me in every case of importance, and scarcely ever doubted the propriety of my opinions and actions.' There was clearly love here: 'I do not, cannot, doubt your love, & here, I freely declare, I love you above all the world besides!'[2] It was a passionate relationship, as the births of six children in less than nine years testify.

Patrick and Maria married in nearby Guiseley on 29 December 1812. Most of their married life was spent at Thornton where, despite the constant pregnancies, childbirths and child-minding, Maria made friends and was socially active. Miss Elizabeth Firth, who lived with her widowed father nearby, kept a journal, and in the five years it covered, the two families were in each other's company on average once a week.[3]

The Brontës' first child, Maria, was baptized in 1814. There followed in rapid succession Elizabeth (1815), Charlotte (1816), Branwell (1817), Emily (1818) and Anne (1820). Just three months after Anne's birth the family moved to Haworth.

Mrs Brontë fell critically ill in January 1821, probably with uterine cancer, and died on 15 September that year, aged thirty-eight. Writing to his former employer, John Buckworth, in November 1821, Patrick spoke of her 'seven months of more agonizing pain than I ever saw anyone endure'.[4] At the time of their mother's death, Charlotte was five, Branwell four, Emily three and Anne just twenty months old. Charlotte recalled just one hazy memory of her mother playing with Branwell.

ELIZABETH 'AUNT' BRANWELL (1776–1842)

Mrs Brontë's sister, Elizabeth Branwell, was born on 2 December 1776, three months before Patrick Brontë. In 1808, after the death of her father, the mother and sisters shared a house; but in December 1812, Maria and Charlotte Branwell both married. Their sister Elizabeth stayed in Cornwall but visited Maria in Thornton in May 1815 for the baptism of her niece, Elizabeth, and to help look after the two babies. She stayed for a year and witnessed the baptism of Charlotte. In May 1815, Elizabeth Firth recorded in her journal that Mrs Brontë and Miss Branwell had called, and 'On Sunday, August 16th, Mr. Brontë's second daughter was christened Elizabeth by Mr. Fennell. My Papa was godfather. Miss Branwell and I were godmothers.' On 28 July 1816, 'I took leave of Miss Branwell. She kissed me and was much affected. She left Thornton that evening.'[5]

The death of Maria found Elizabeth back in Yorkshire to help her brother-in-law look after his motherless children. In his letter to Buckworth (27 November 1821), Patrick wrote: '[A]fterwards ... Miss Branwell ... arrived, and afforded great comfort to my mind, which has been the case ever since, by sharing my labours and sorrows, and behaving as an affectionate mother to my children' (Green, *Letters*, p. 43). Elizabeth stayed on to look after her sister's children. It was no small sacrifice: she was forty-four years of age, at a stage in life when she could have been living quietly and comfortably among the society of her numerous friends and relatives in Penzance.

Ellen Nussey recalled in her 'Reminiscences' that

She [Elizabeth] always dressed in silk. She talked a great deal of her younger days; the [gaieties] of her native town, Penzance in Cornwall, the soft warm climate &c. She very probably had been a belle 'among her acquaintance', the social life of her younger days she appeared to recall with regret ... she would be very lively and intelligent 'in her talk', and tilted argument without fear against Mr. Brontë. (Smith, *Letters*, vol. 1, p. 597)

The maids called her a 'bit of a tyke', though since Elizabeth was the authority and taskmaster in the household, neither servants nor strong-minded and independent children would be unbiased. Mrs Gaskell sums her up as '[a] kindly and conscientious woman with a good deal of character' (Gaskell, *Life*, p. 49).

Mr Brontë's income was small, and he had incurred huge debts in paying for his wife's treatment. Even with Aunt Elizabeth generously paying for her own board, she would, as housekeeper, have had to exercise great economy. Possibly she contributed to the costs of sending four of the children to the Clergy Daughters' School in Cowan Bridge, but after the tragic consequences there, she turned her bedchamber into a schoolroom during the day and taught her nieces and nephew what she could. The influence Elizabeth had on the children would have been considerable. She it was who established the regime by which the household ran smoothly, and she it was who educated the children in sewing and the household arts. The girls made their own clothes and some of their father's. In addition there was sewing for charity, and there were daily lessons. Not what high-spirited children – who must have been a handful – wanted when they could be out playing!

One witness said that 'Charlotte and her aunt once paid a visit to one Mrs. G. Charlotte suddenly burst out jeering at her aunt's old-fashioned clothes. The hostess rebuked her rudeness severely, adding that unless she apologized she was never to come there again.' Yet in her description of Miss Branwell, Ellen Nussey was complimentary: 'She always wore a shoulder shawl, the caps were always dainty, the dresses always good and becoming, she wore black silk for afternoon wear. She took snuff out of a very pretty gold snuff box.'[6] But throughout her twenty-year guardianship, Elizabeth Branwell had to make her clothes and those of the family last as long as possible.

Like any mother, Aunt Branwell had to curb the enthusiasm of her charges for playing outdoors and visiting. In late 1832, Charlotte wished her friend Ellen Nussey to stay, but Aunt objected to visitors in winter, and the visit did not take place until the summer of 1833. In 1838 Charlotte and Ellen Nussey were anxious to go to the east coast, but Aunt demurred and instead suggested that they all go on holiday to Liverpool. The holiday did not happen. 'Aunt – like many other elderly people – likes to talk of such things but when it comes to putting them into [practice], she rather falls off', wrote Charlotte to Ellen (Smith, *Letters*, vol. I, p. 197). Poor Aunt Branwell! She was sixty-two, and these were violent times, with troops being sent to Leeds and Hull to counter Chartist violence. It is worth noting that Patrick did consult Elizabeth and upheld her governance.

As is well known, Elizabeth Branwell supported the girls financially. In 1841 she agreed to lend them £100 towards establishing a school of their own. This was transmuted into a loan to enable Charlotte and Emily to go to Brussels to enhance their qualifications. Aunt's money also enabled the nieces to publish their *Poems* and to advance money for the publication of *Wuthering Heights* and *Agnes Grey*.

It was while the two sisters were in Brussels in the autumn of 1842 that Elizabeth Branwell died, just two months short of her sixty-sixth birthday. Branwell was with his aunt during her last weeks and wrote to his friend, Francis Grundy, that she had been 'for twenty years as my mother', lamenting, 'I have now lost the guide and director of all the happy days connected with my childhood' (Barker, p. 404).

It is hard to overcome the notion that the life of Elizabeth Branwell was a sad and unfulfilled one, and clearly she did sacrifice what was a congenial life in Penzance society for a harsh one in Yorkshire. But it was from Elizabeth Branwell, as much as from their father, that the three nieces learned the virtues of honesty and a sense of duty.

MARGARET WOOLER (1792–1883)

On 17 January 1831, Charlotte Brontë became a pupil at Roe Head School in Mirfield, some twenty miles south-east of Haworth. Patrick Brontë had held two curacies in the area and had a number of friends there. The school had opened the previous year and was run by Miss Margaret Wooler and three of her sisters. It quickly acquired a good reputation, with most of the pupils coming from local professional and mill-owning families. It was here that Charlotte met her lifelong friends Ellen Nussey and Mary Taylor.

Margaret Wooler was the eldest of eleven children. Her father, Robert Wooler (1770–1838), was a maltster, corn-miller, farmer and owner of several properties in the Batley–Dewsbury area of Yorkshire. He was evidently prosperous, for his children were well educated: his six daughters were all teachers or governesses; two of his sons became doctors, and one was a clergyman.

The school appears to have been well run, and Charlotte thrived. She left in June 1832 but returned there with Emily in July 1835, Charlotte as a teacher and Emily as a pupil. Emily, though, was not happy there and left after three months, her place being taken by her sister Anne. Early in 1838 the school was relocated to Heald's House in Dewsbury Moor, but Charlotte resigned her position in December of that year, Margaret

Wooler already having announced her retirement. In 1841 Margaret offered the headship to Charlotte, but Charlotte declined the offer and went to Brussels the following year.

As headmistress, Margaret Wooler can be credited with recognizing Charlotte's potential and she played a large part in developing her talent, so much so that Charlotte won many prizes for attainment. Margaret's influence on Emily and Anne is less clear, though Anne seems to have been reasonably successful as a governess. Chapter 6 of Elizabeth Gaskell's *Life of Charlotte Brontë* contains a glowing account of Margaret Wooler's teaching, and there is much in this account to indicate that the Brontë sisters were fortunate to have Margaret Wooler as a teacher.

Initially, Charlotte seems not to have appreciated Margaret Wooler's qualities and actually quarrelled with her, notably over Anne's illness in 1838, though Charlotte admitted in a letter to Ellen Nussey that 'with all her faults I should be sorry indeed to part with her' (Smith, *Letters*, vol. 1, p. 180). Margaret Wooler, her elder by twenty-four years, was able to give Charlotte the respect she needed from an older woman. They kept in touch, and as the years went by they became close friends. Thus Charlotte asked Ellen Nussey in 1846: 'Give my sincere love to Miss Wooler when you see her – Give her my address too and tell her to write to me here[,] indeed I shall enclose a scrap of paper which you must deliver to her' (Smith, *Letters*, vol. 1, p. 496).

Thirty-five letters from Charlotte to Margaret Wooler survive, plus other letters to members of the extended Wooler family. Among the many down-to-earth topics covered in these letters is life assurance, Charlotte (and Emily) thanking Margaret Wooler for her advice on the matter. Charlotte also writes about her shares in the railways and health matters, and she comments on books read and on their respective families. She seeks Margaret's advice on investing the money she received from *Jane Eyre* and also information on lodgings in Scarborough. Wider matters discussed are the doctrine of universal salvation and Charlotte's changing sentiments concerning war. Charlotte writes a heartfelt letter about Emily's death, and she understands the suffering Margaret's brother Thomas has experienced under the 'tyranny of Hypochondria'. In another letter she tells Margaret Wooler of her joy on seeing her father recover his sight.

Margaret Wooler stayed at Haworth for ten days in 1851, and Charlotte stayed with her in Filey in 1852 and later in Hornsea. In 1853, there was a rift between Charlotte and Ellen which lasted for six months. This rift was healed by Miss Wooler, to whom Charlotte expressed her gratitude in a letter dated 12 April 1854: 'Ellen and I are – I think – quite friends again – thanks, in a great measure to the kind mediating word which "turned away wrath." "Blessed are the peace-makers!"' (Smith, *Letters*, vol. III, p. 242; Charlotte's underlining).

Margaret Wooler's motherly concern shows in her cautioning Charlotte about her London visits and about her friendship with Harriet Martineau. Her counsel was also in evidence over advice given with regard to Charlotte's relationship with Mr Nicholls, and possibly over James Taylor's earlier marriage proposal. Miss Wooler was one of the few guests invited to Charlotte's wedding; on Patrick's last-minute absence, she gave the bride away.

Patrick described Margaret Wooler to Elizabeth Gaskell as 'a clever, decent and motherly woman' (Green, *Letters*, p. 234); and Margaret's nephew, Sir Thomas Clifford Allbutt, characterized her as 'a woman of unusual brains and accomplishments, especially a fine Italian scholar ... a keen-witted, ironical, and very independent Yorkshire woman'.[7]

The more Charlotte looked to her own future as an unmarried spinster, the more important Margaret Wooler became as a role model. Charlotte thus wrote in a letter to Margaret, dated 30 January 1846: 'I speculate much on the existence of unmarried and never-to-be married women nowadays and I have already got to the point of considering there is no more respectable character on this earth than an u[n]married woman who makes her own way through life quietly pers[e]veringly, without support of husband or brother' (Smith, *Letters*, vol. I, p. 448).

If Mrs Brontë was the mother the Brontë children barely knew and Elizabeth Branwell the surrogate mother they never loved, then Margaret Wooler was, at least for Charlotte, the wise counsellor and kindly confidante that the young woman needed.

NOTES

1 Most previous accounts of the Branwells say that just five of the family survived into adulthood (namely Jane, Benjamin, Elizabeth, Maria and Charlotte), but the recent genealogical study by Richard G. Grylls, *Branwell & Bramble: A Brief History of a West Cornwall Clan* (Tring, Herts.: Richard G. Grylls, 2006), points out that the first-born, Ann, was twenty-three when she died and that the second-born, Margaret, married when she was twenty-one, though the date of her death is unknown.

2 Dudley Green (ed.), *The Letters of the Reverend Patrick Brontë* (Stroud: Nonsuch, 2005), pp. 325 and 331. Subsequent references are included in the text.

3 According to Annette Hopkins, quoted in Margaret Lane, 'Maria Branwell',
   BST, 18.93 (1983), 215.
4 Dudley Green, *Patrick Brontë: Father of Genius* (Stroud: Nonsuch, 2008),
   p. 93.
5 C. Mabel Edgerley, 'Elizabeth Branwell: The "small, antiquated lady"', *BST*,
   9.47 (1937), 106.
6 Both quotations in this paragraph are from Edgerley, 'Elizabeth Branwell',
   p. 111.
7 From a memoir of Allbutt quoted by Smith in *Letters*, vol. 1, p. 99.

CHAPTER 6

Patrick Branwell Brontë

Victor A. Neufeldt

Branwell (as he was known) was born on 26 June 1817 at Thornton, west Yorkshire, the fourth of six children of the Revd Patrick Brontë (1776–1861) and Maria Brontë, *née* Branwell (1783–1821). Educated at home by his father, he soon developed a fondness for classical history and languages, translating passages from the New Testament and the works of Homer, Virgil, Horace, Ovid, Seneca and Lucian. Since Patrick placed few restrictions on what his children read, Branwell, blessed with a lively imagination and intellectual curiosity, read a wide range of material from an early age, including literature, history and current affairs. He was particularly fond of *Blackwood's Edinburgh Magazine*, especially its coverage of the French Revolution and the Napoleonic campaigns, the American War of Independence and West African exploration. With his sisters he was receiving art and music lessons by the time he was twelve, learning to play the flute, piano and organ. Though 'a little below middle height' according to his friend Francis Leyland, Branwell was 'slim and agile', and at the age of twenty-two 'good looking, with a shock of red hair brushed forward over his high forehead, long side-burns and a straight prominent nose. Vivacious and witty, he excelled at conversation and was impressively erudite.' His voice, Leyland recalled, 'had a ringing sweetness, and the utterance and use of his English were perfect'.[1]

After the deaths of their mother and the two eldest sisters, Maria and Elizabeth (1825), Branwell and his remaining sisters – stimulated by their reading, and using such toys as wooden soldiers and musicians – began to make up and act out plays. Under the leadership of Charlotte and Branwell these 'Young Men' plays evolved into the complex saga of the imaginary Glass Town Federation, situated in the Ashantee country of West Africa, which Charlotte and Branwell in turn developed into the story of the kingdom of Angria and finally abandoned in 1839.

With the creation of 'Branwell's Blackwood's Magazine' in June 1829, eleven-year-old Branwell revealed his ambition to become the poet and

8 A caricature self-portrait of Branwell Brontë, *c.* 1840

man of letters he saw exemplified by Christopher North and James Hogg in
Blackwood's. In this, his first full year of writing, Branwell assumed the roles
of editor and publisher of a magazine; author and publisher of two volumes
of poetry; writer of critical commentary on the poems; playwright; travel
writer; writer on natural history; reporter; Sergeant Bud as author of both
a prose tale and a letter to the editor; reviewer of Bud's edition of the poems
of Ossian; and author of 'Nights', modelled on the 'Noctes Ambrosianae' in
Blackwood's. Until 1836, when he submitted his first poem for publication
to *Blackwood's,* his work continued to be written and edited by a variety of
personae, all with distinctive personalities, who frequently comment on
aspects of literary composition, especially poetry, and offer critical and
satirical commentary on both Branwell's own work and that of his sisters.
He continued to use such personae to the very end, and all but one of his
published works appeared under the name of 'Northangerland', the chief
protagonist of his Angrian saga.

From 1829 to 1837 Branwell maintained a prodigious output of poems,
verse drama and prose. Eleven poems appeared in two volumes of poems

'published' (i.e. in Glass Town) by 'Young Soult the Rhymer' (spelled 'Ryhmer' by Branwell); the verse drama was also a separately 'published' volume. Branwell, more venturesome than Charlotte in experimenting with verse form, rhyme patterns and metrics at this time, was consciously propagating an image of himself as a poet and man of letters, an image with some contradictory features. On the one hand, the sober and scholarly Sergeant Bud publishes an edition of Macpherson's *Ossian* with 'notes and commentarys & c'; the same scholarly persona reappears in the guise of Moses Chateaubriand, who not only provides elaborate learned commentaries on Young Soult's poems, but also censures the poet's excesses and irregularities. On the other hand, the romantic posturing of the rebellious and undisciplined Young Soult the Rhymer becomes the subject of a number of satirical comments and sketches by Charlotte,[2] and by Branwell himself.[3]

Until the end of 1831 Branwell mainly thought of himself as Young Soult, the poet of Glass Town, published in Glass Town. After 1831, however, Young Soult rapidly disappears and a new dual conception emerges. Branwell continues as the chronicler of the Glass Town and Angrian saga, but he also becomes 'P. B. Brontë', producing poems in his own right. Ten of these poems are fair copies, and seven of the ten are written in ordinary cursive script rather than the usual print writing; three others, while in the print writing, are part of a manuscript volume of very legible fair copies. All are dated and either signed by Branwell or have his initials at the beginning. While the separation from Glass Town and Angria is obviously not complete, many of the poems are of a classical and philosophical bent, discussing the nature of human existence and the transitoriness of human happiness. As early as the age of fourteen, Branwell was thinking of publication in the real world.

Branwell's division of interests worried Charlotte. In her famous 1834 caricature of him as 'Patrick Benjamin Wiggins', she foresees the potential dangers of his inability to act with undivided purpose, for Branwell's divided conception of himself as a writer also had to compete with his interests in music, painting and civic activity. His poetic ambitions notwithstanding, he decided as early as 1833 to become a professional portrait painter and in 1834 began to take lessons from William Robinson, a society portrait painter in Leeds. The two family portraits – the 'Pillar Portrait' (or *The Brontë Sisters*) and the 'Gun Group' – date from this period.[4] In the same year he began plans to enrol in the Royal Academy of Arts in 1835, plans that were never realized (Barker, pp. 227–31). In addition, he taught in the Haworth Sunday School, established by his father in 1832, was a secretary of the Haworth Temperance Society established in 1834, joined the Freemasons in 1836, serving as secretary, and became interested in and involved with local politics, assisting in January 1837 with the establishment of the Haworth Operative Conservative Society, which he served first as secretary, then as chairman.

Failure to enrol in the Royal Academy prompted not only Branwell's immediate return to writing, but also his feverish attempt to gain literary employment and to get himself published. In December 1835, he sent a letter to *Blackwood's* offering himself as a replacement for James Hogg, and he followed this in April 1836 with his poem 'Misery'; in January 1837 he again wrote to the magazine's editor, requesting an interview to present a sample of his prose. His bombastic tone ensured that his letters went unanswered.[5] This last appeal was contemporaneous with Charlotte's letter to Robert Southey asking his advice on whether she could earn a living from her writing. Not to be outdone, Branwell sent Wordsworth the manuscript of a poem called 'The Struggles of Flesh with Spirit/Scene I – *Infancy*', asking him to pass judgement on it because at the age of nineteen he wished to 'push [himself] out into the open world' with his writing.[6] Unfortunately, neither *Blackwood's* nor Wordsworth replied to his letters, so he continued to compose and revise poems for publication, unchecked and unguided, while also continuing with his Angrian chronicles, though it became increasingly clear during 1837 that the imaginative impetus for the latter was failing. At the same time he continued to prepare himself to become a portrait painter.

During 1837 and early 1838 – until he left for Bradford – he added five poems to the notebook he had begun in late 1835 with the first draft of 'Misery', all fair copies signed or initialled, although some are incomplete. More significantly, he began a new notebook into which he entered between March 1837 and May 1838 revisions of twenty-six earlier poems, eight new poems, and translations of six odes of Horace. In it 'P. B. Brontë' reaffirms his dedication to poetry in 'The Spirit of Poetry', one of the two poems in the notebook not originally composed by an Angrian persona. Also, at the very end of 1837 he began work on a prose narrative, which, although still featuring Alexander Percy, is not set in Africa but in Yorkshire, and in which he rebukes Charlotte as a 'writer who loved more to dwell upon Indian Palm Groves or Genii palaces than on the wooded manors and cloudy skies of England'.[7] In short, Branwell essentially abandoned Angria at the end of 1837 and turned more and more to writing long poems not based on an Angrian source and complete in themselves: public pieces meant for publication.

Yet early in 1838 he decided to set up as a professional portrait painter in Bradford. Although he received some commissions, the venture was not a success,[8] and he returned to Haworth in February 1839. Except for the first draft of 'Sir Henry Tunstall', he seems not to have composed any new poems while he was at Bradford, nor immediately after his return, when he began a regulated programme of study with his father to prepare to take up teaching.

However, while at Bradford Branwell had become actively involved with an artistic and literary circle which included Joseph Bentley Leyland and his brother Francis. Stimulated by the friendship he developed with Joseph, he began the practice of passing manuscripts on to Leyland for criticism. While employed as tutor for the Postlethwaite family at Broughton-in-Furness, from January to June 1840, he attempted once more to establish a literary career, this time as a poet and translator. On 15 April 1840 he sent Thomas De Quincey a revised draft of 'Sir Henry Tunstall' and translations of five odes of Horace. Five days later he sent Hartley Coleridge a revised draft of the poem 'At Dead of Midnight-Drearily' and translations of two odes of Horace. He wrote to Coleridge that he was 'about to enter active life' and needed to ascertain whether he could earn a living by 'periodical or other writing' and by translations of classical authors.[9] While De Quincey did not reply, Coleridge obviously responded positively, for Branwell spent 1 May with him at Nab Cottage, near Rydal Water. Encouraged by the visit, he continued work on the translations, sending Coleridge book 1 of the odes on 27 June, just after he had been dismissed from his post as tutor (the reasons for his dismissal are unclear). Although Coleridge began to draft a very positive and encouraging reply, he unfortunately never completed and sent the letter.[10]

Meanwhile Branwell's literary activity was once more curtailed, this time by his appointment as assistant clerk at the Sowerby Bridge railway station on the newly opened Leeds and Manchester railway on 31 August 1840. Not until he became clerk in charge of the station at Luddenden Foot, on 1 April 1841, did he again find time and energy for literary composition. Contrary to the traditional view that Branwell's days at Luddenden Foot consisted of little more than lack of attention to duty, idleness and drunken debauchery, the move provided a new impetus to his literary aspirations. Five years before his sisters appeared in print and just over a month after the move, on 5 June 1841, he achieved his lifelong ambition when his poem 'Heaven and Earth' appeared in the *Halifax Guardian* under the pseudonym 'Northangerland', the first of eighteen poems to appear in various Yorkshire newspapers, all but one under the same pseudonym. In August he not only published a second poem in the *Guardian*, this time a political satire over his own initials, but he also began to enter drafts of poems into a new small notebook. Though some of the poems were autobiographical, indicating an awareness that he was not making the most of his talents because of his over-absorption in the pleasures of the moment, most are full of ambition, energy and optimism. Some of the credit for all this activity must be given to his circle of artistic friends in Halifax, who met at various hotels and inns to read their manuscripts aloud to one another for criticism.

Branwell's dismissal from his post in March 1842 because of a discrepancy in the accounts (he was never suspected of theft or fraud) spurred him on again to try to establish himself as a poet. Between April 1842 and January 1843, he published nine poems – three of which were new; six were revisions of the new poems in the 1837–8 notebook – and one prose article on the engraver Thomas Bewick in Yorkshire newspapers (the *Halifax Guardian, Bradford Herald* and *Leeds Intelligencer*). In the article on Bewick, which reflects a strong Wordsworthian influence, Branwell attempts to define and articulate beliefs and principles concerning poetry which he had been develop-ing since he described, in 1835, what 'real' poetry is all about, as opposed to what his sisters were writing.[11] Those principles are perhaps best demonstrated in his sonnets, his most disciplined com-positions, which he revised repeatedly, with up to four versions extant. They are certainly among his best poems. Additionally, he wrote one other new poem and revised six more during this period, all of them intended for publication. He also made an effort to draw attention to his poems, sending samples of his work to James Montgomery, *Blackwood's*, Caroline Bowles, James and Harriet Martineau and Leigh Hunt.[12]

However, Branwell still had to earn a living, and so from January 1843 to July 1845 he was employed as a tutor by the Robinsons at Thorp Green, where Anne was already a governess. During this time he produced six new poems, two of which – and two others, written earlier – he published in the *Yorkshire Gazette* within ten weeks of his dismissal from Thorp Green because of 'proceedings ... bad beyond expression', possibly an affair with Mrs Lydia Robinson. What the actual details of the alleged affair were is not clear, but Branwell apparently believed that Mrs Robinson's affection for him was sincere and that she would marry him when her invalid husband died.[13] However, Branwell's claim that Mr Robinson prevented the marriage by changing his will so as to disinherit Mrs Robinson should she do so is false. The reasons for the claim are unclear. It may have been a face-saving story, or it may have been a story created by Mrs Robinson to forestall any advances by Branwell.[14]

Despite his distraught state, Branwell embarked on several ambitious projects during 1845–6. Immediately after his dismissal he began revisions of three earlier poems, the second of which was to be the first canto of a long poem. However, the first two remained unfinished; the third became part of his unfinished novel 'And the Weary Are at Rest', begun in the summer of 1845. He set out to write the novel, he wrote to Joseph Leyland, because 'in the present state of the publishing and reading world a Novel is the most saleable article' (letter reprinted in Smith, *Letters*, vol. I, pp. 423–4). Before the end of 1845 he completed four new poems, two of which were published in the *Halifax Guardian*. He began 1846 with another poem in the *Guardian*, composed seven others, including a topical poem on the heroism of Sir Robert Sale and Sir Henry Hardinge, intended for publication, and began an epic in several cantos about Morley Hall, which was connected with the Leyland family. Although the death of Mr Robinson on 26 May and Mrs Robinson's rejection of him greatly upset and distracted Branwell, by October he was back at work on 'Morley Hall' and two other poems concerned with historical figures facing defeat and despair, begun in late 1846 or early 1847.[15] In all, he produced ten poems in 1846.

In 1847, however, it became apparent that whatever his intentions might be, Branwell's will and ability to write were fading rapidly. After Lydia Robinson's rejection he lapsed into alcoholism, dependence on opiates and debt, causing the family much distress, embarrassment and, on the part of Charlotte, bitterness over talent wasted. He seems to have been unaware of his sisters' 1846 volume of poetry and of their novels published in 1847, and there is no evidence that any of his family were aware of his publications. Yet he published one poem in the *Guardian*, fittingly entitled 'The End of All', just four months before the publication of *Jane Eyre*, and sent another to Leyland asking if 'it would be worth sending to some respectable periodical like *Blackwood's Magazine*'.[16] However, his health had deteriorated severely and he died at the parsonage on 24 September 1848, aged thirty-one. The cause of death was probably tuberculosis aggravated by delirium tremens, although the death certificate states it as 'chronic bronchitis – Marasmus' ('marasmus' meaning a wasting away of the body). He was buried in the family vault in his father's church on 28 September.

NOTES

1 Barker, p. 334, and Francis A. Leyland, *The Brontë Family with Special Reference to Patrick Branwell Brontë*, 2 vols. (London: Hurst and Blackett, 1886), vol. I, p. 266.

2 Christine Alexander, *The Early Writings of Charlotte Brontë* (Oxford: Blackwell, 1983), pp. 64–6; Christine Alexander (ed.), *An Edition of the Early Writings of Charlotte Brontë*, vol. I (Oxford: Blackwell, for the Shakespeare Head Press, 1987), pp. 127, 180–3, 309–11.

3 Victor A. Neufeldt (ed.), *The Works of Patrick Branwell Brontë*, 3 vols. (New York: Garland, 1997–9), vol. I, p. 175.

4 Christine Alexander and Jane Sellars, *The Art of the Brontës* (Cambridge University Press, 1995), pp. 73–6, 307–12.

5 In all, he wrote to *Blackwood's* six times. See Christine Alexander, 'Readers and Writers: *Blackwood's* and the Brontës', *Gaskell Society Journal*, 8 (1994), 54–69.

6 See Neufeldt, *The Works of Patrick Branwell Brontë*, vol. II, p. 588. Margaret Smith reprints Branwell's letter in *Letters*, vol. I, pp. 160–2.

7 Neufeldt, *The Works of Patrick Branwell Brontë*, vol. III, p. 186.

8 See Alexander and Sellars, *The Art of the Brontës*, pp. 82–5, 323 and 327–33.

9 Victor A. Neufeldt (ed.), *The Poems of Patrick Branwell Brontë* (New York: Garland, 1990), pp. 442–3.

10 *Ibid.*, pp. 522–4.

11 See Victor Neufeldt, 'The Child is Parent to the Author: Branwell Brontë', in Christine Alexander and Juliet McMaster (eds.), *The Child Writer from Austen to Woolf* (Cambridge University Press, 2005), pp. 173–87. Branwell's criticism, in 1837, of Charlotte's preference for the exotic over the homely (see above) is germane to the ideas expressed in the Bewick article.

12 See Neufeldt, *The Works of Patrick Branwell Brontë*, vol. III, p. xxvi.

13 The matter is discussed at some length in Barker, pp. 458–69, and Neufeldt, *The Works of Patrick Branwell Brontë*, vol. III, pp. 403, 470, 473 and 481–2.

14 See Barker, pp. 493–6; Smith reprints two pertinent letters from Branwell to Leyland in *Letters*, vol. I, pp. 414–15 and 475–7.

15 See Neufeldt, *The Works of Patrick Branwell Brontë*, vol. III, pp. 492 and 494.

16 J. Alexander Symington and C. W. Hatfield (eds.), *Patrick Branwell Brontë: A Complete Transcript of the Leyland Manuscripts Showing the Unpublished Portions from the Original Manuscripts* (privately printed, 1925), p. 42.

CHAPTER 7

Charlotte Brontë

Dinah Birch

Charlotte Brontë can seem a more substantial figure than her siblings. Born in 1816 as the third daughter of Patrick and Maria Brontë, she was the eldest of the four Brontë children who survived childhood, and she took a dominant role in their activities. She lived longer and wrote more than Branwell, Emily and Anne, and left a larger body of documentary material after her death. Nevertheless, her place in the extraordinary family that worked and wrote together in the parsonage at Haworth remains the necessary starting-point for an understanding of her work. She was a daughter, niece and sister before she became a poet and novelist, and throughout her life those identities remained intertwined.

The shared world of the Brontë children allowed their creativity to flourish, but its intimacy did not exclude competitive alliances. During her childhood, Charlotte's closest relations were with the restlessly ambitious and talented Branwell. Branwell's decline as a young man strained the family's emotional and practical resources to their limits, changing the dynamics that had motivated the children's prolific early writing. Like her sisters, Charlotte had a keen eye for the limitations and imbalances inherent in the conventional structures of the middle-class family in the early nineteenth century. She is unremittingly sharp, and sometimes bitter, about the constraints placed on the lives of women. Yet her underlying loyalties did not falter. Even after Branwell's death, and the subsequent deaths of Emily and Anne, Charlotte's devotion to her father meant that she continued to see herself in the context of the family. When she married Arthur Bell Nicholls, her father's curate, she chose not to leave the parsonage and spent the final months of her life as both daughter and wife, still living in her childhood home.

Charlotte faced the loss of Branwell, Emily and Anne with a courage that remains moving: 'Still I have some strength to fight the battle of life', she wrote to Ellen Nussey on 14 July 1849 (Smith, *Letters*, vol. II, p. 230). But her resilience had been developed long before, for her early experience of the family was defined by bereavement. She was five when her mother died in 1821. The stalwart Aunt Branwell then took charge of the household, and two older girls, Maria and Elizabeth, helped to look after the younger children. Maria seems to have grown up especially quickly in the absence of her mother, developing into a clever and energetic child who directed family pastimes. During the years in which Charlotte's sense of herself and her place in the world was formed, she was free of the need to take responsibility for her brother and sisters. She was a middle child, with motherly elder sisters and smaller siblings who would look up to her. It was a secure and cheerful position.

The pain of losing both Maria and Elizabeth to tuberculosis, a disaster perhaps hastened by the rigours of the Clergy Daughters' School, transformed Charlotte's role within the family. At the age of nine, she was propelled into the situation of the eldest girl in a motherless group of children. The intensity of her grief is recalled in *Jane Eyre*, where the decline and death of the patient Helen Burns at Lowood School is in part a memory of Maria's final illness. Writing to her publisher's reader W. S. Williams on 28 October 1847, she told her correspondent that he had been right in believing in the reality of Helen Burns' character – 'I have exaggerated nothing there: I abstained from recording much that I remembered respecting her, lest the narrative should sound incredible' (Smith, *Letters*, vol. 1, p. 553). Literary historians have suggested that Charlotte's description of Lowood's harsh regime, with its burnt porridge, plain uniforms and unjust discipline, may have been unfair to the school founded by the Evangelical minister William Carus Wilson;[1] but it evidently reflects a trauma that Charlotte did not forget as an adult. Throughout both her early writings and her published fiction, she reflects on exile, imprisonment, oppression and isolation. These were central concerns of the Romantic literature from which she drew many of her models, but her individual perspectives were shaped by the events of her childhood.

Charlotte's lifelong attachment to Haworth was not a matter of timidity, for among the values that she took from her family, and particularly from her father, was that of resolute self-determination. Patrick represented a firm centre of authority in the home, but his rule allowed a remarkable freedom of thought in his children. Their reading was wide and uncensored. School text-books were supplemented by newspapers and periodicals like *Blackwood's Magazine*, the lively and opinionated Tory journal that became such a central presence in the imaginative life of the children, and later the vigorous and equally Tory *Fraser's Magazine*. The young Brontës also read a diversity of religious, scientific, philosophical and literary books drawn from the collections of Patrick Brontë and Elizabeth Branwell, or borrowed from Keighley's circulating library and Mechanics' Institute. The notion that the children led a dreary life in the 'remote Yorkshire parsonage' (Gaskell, *Life*, p. 70) has long since been overturned. However deeply Charlotte felt the loss of her mother, and of Maria and Elizabeth, she was an active and sociable child, and her lessons and domestic duties left ample time for walks, toys, games and independent reading.

In 1826, Patrick gave his son twelve toy soldiers; the children called them 'The Young Men', and each claimed one as a special possession. Charlotte named her 'noble' soldier the 'Duke of Wellington', and he became her 'chief man' through much of her writing as a child.[2] Branwell named his soldier 'Bonaparte', Wellington's great rival. Emily's solemn soldier was called 'Gravey'; Anne called hers 'Waiting Boy'. A complex series of dramas and stories gradually evolved around these figures and their companions, later recorded in minuscule handwriting in a series of miniature hand-made books. The children projected their own personalities and interests into these increasingly sophisticated fantasies and adventures, their structures primarily derived from the diverse range of material they had encountered in their reading. Charlotte and Branwell created an imaginary country called Angria; Emily and Anne invented Gondal. Little survives from the Gondal saga, but a great deal of narrative material from the Angria of Charlotte and Branwell remains. The companionable rivalry that drove the relations between the two elder children formed their stories and poems. Branwell's exuberant writings describe politics, military conflicts and aggressive adventures, while Charlotte was more interested in evoking exotic settings and complex romantic lives for her characters. Traditional divisions within gendered identities were reflected in these differences. Charlotte's heroines are beautiful and melancholy; as they helplessly await the attentions of their powerful but unreliable lovers, their glamour is bound up with their sorrow. But her customary narrator, 'Charles Townshend', adopted an unmistakably masculine perspective, and Charlotte distanced herself from female inwardness. She wrote about women's suffering, but she claimed the privileges of male insight into their captivating distress. This doubleness, established very early in Charlotte's habits as a writer, persisted long after she had abandoned the luxuriant landscapes of Angria.

Deeply and almost obsessively involved in her Angrian writings, Charlotte had to negotiate a difficult transition between the intensities of her adolescent imagination and the demands of life as an independent adult. She was helped by the need to leave Haworth to prepare for life as a teacher, the most practicable professional option for a girl in her position. In 1831, when she was almost fifteen, she was sent to Roe Head School, not far from Huddersfield. Small and relaxed, the school was run by the kindly Margaret Wooler and her three sisters, and it offered an old-fashioned but serious education. Charlotte throve during her eighteen months as a pupil at Roe Head, making real connections outside her family circle for the first time. Her closest friend, Ellen Nussey, was pious and sensible; but Ellen's calm influence was balanced by the presence of the independent-minded Mary Taylor, who constantly challenged Charlotte's inclinations to self-abnegation. Both of these school-friends remained close to Charlotte in adult life.

Roe Head was crucial to Charlotte's development as a writer. She acquired a reputation as a storyteller among her fellow pupils and discovered that her literary accomplishments could command respect. On returning to Roe Head as a teacher in 1835, she earned money for the first time – in scanty amounts, as her acerbic friend Mary pointed out, but enough for her to be self-sufficient, and also to pay for Emily's education at Roe Head. She had become an adult. The transformation was not welcome in every respect, for it meant distancing herself from the imaginative life of her childhood. In her second year as a teacher, Charlotte records her frustration. She has been thinking of Angria:

Then came on me rushing impetuously. all the mighty phantasm that this had conjured from nothing from nothing [*sic*] to a system strong as some religious creed. I felt as if I could ⟨have⟩ have written gloriously – I longed to write. The Spirit of all Verdopolis of all the mountainous North of all the ⟨woodland the⟩ woodland West of all the river-watered East came crowding into my mind. if I had ⟨it⟩ had time to indulge it I felt that the vague sensations of that moment would have settled down into a narrative better at least than any thing I ever produced before. But just then a Dolt came up with a lesson. I thought I should have vomited[.] (Quoted in Barker, p. 255)

Charlotte relished the independence that life outside the parsonage had brought, but she frequently found the daily realities of teaching in a school exasperating. Her experiences as a domestic governess, after leaving her post at Roe Head, were equally wearisome. And yet she did not give up her ambition to found and run a school with the help of Emily and Anne. It was a prospect that would allow them a larger measure of autonomy than salaried employment could offer, a freedom that she had witnessed in the lives of Margaret Wooler and her sisters. Charlotte formed the plan of enrolling, with Emily, at a Belgian school, to improve their languages and increase their chances of success. Her months as a pupil and then teacher at the Pensionnat Heger turned out to be both traumatic and transformative. The prosperous Catholic bourgeoisie she encountered in Brussels represented a disturbing challenge to the values she had absorbed from the vigorously self-improving commercial society of provincial Yorkshire. Still more painfully, she fell in love for the first time – with Constantin Heger, who was married to the school's *directrice*. It was an attachment that caused Charlotte real misery, but it initiated a profitable change in her writing. The discipline that Heger's severe tuition imposed on her habits of composition, which had tended to be ornate, was of real value. Charlotte's aching desire for Heger prompted her to find a new balance between her persistent engagement with women's passive modes of distress and the need to claim a reasoned control over her life's direction.

The projected school found no pupils, and the scheme was abandoned. Charlotte began to hope that writing might provide a better career. Impressed by a chance discovery of Emily's poems, she hit on the scheme of publishing a collection of poetry to which each of the sisters would contribute. The volume, funded by money inherited from Aunt Branwell, appeared in 1846. It sold only two copies, but the reviews were encouraging, and Charlotte was exhilarated by seeing her work in print. The three sisters had a significant body of fiction to hand, and Charlotte quickly followed the appearance of the poems by offering their novels to a series of publishers – *The Professor, Wuthering Heights* and *Agnes Grey*. The initial response was lukewarm, but eventually Thomas Newby agreed to publish *Wuthering Heights* and *Agnes Grey*. Publishers showed no interest in Charlotte's *The Professor*, which was not published until 1857. But George Smith (of Smith, Elder & Co.) suggested that his firm might consider a three-volume work by Charlotte. She jumped at the chance, and within weeks she had sent him *Jane Eyre*, the intense and partly autobiographical novel she had begun in 1846. It appeared in October 1847, and *Agnes Grey* and *Wuthering Heights* followed in December.

Jane Eyre was the book that changed Charlotte's life. It was dramatically successful, selling 2,500 copies within three months at a time when the average print run for a new novel was 700 copies, and being reprinted repeatedly.[3] Not only did it relieve her from immediate financial anxieties (she earned £100 for the copyright, and eventually received £500 for the book), but it provided a triumphant entrance into the literary world. Charlotte was thrilled to hear of Thackeray's approval, and gratified by the sense of communication with a wide readership. She was initially sheltered by a pseudonym, 'Currer Bell', concealing her identity from family and friends. 'What author would be without the advantage of being able to walk invisible? One is thereby enabled to keep such a quiet mind', she wrote to W. S. Williams, literary adviser to Smith, Elder & Co. and Charlotte's loyal friend and supporter (Smith, *Letters*, vol. II, p. 4). Even Patrick did not know of his daughters' authorship until the following year, and 'Currer Bell' remained largely anonymous until 1849. Privacy gave Charlotte confidence, but it also made her vulnerable. In July 1848, she felt compelled to visit George Smith's London office in person, to identify the novels' authors. It was the first of several encounters with the literary life of London (or 'Babylon', as Charlotte sardonically called it; see Gaskell, *Life*, p. 325), and despite being acutely conscious that she and Anne would be seen as 'queer, quizzical looking beings – especially me with my spectacles' (letter to Mary Taylor of 4 September 1848, in Smith, *Letters*, vol. II, p. 113), she was excited and pleased by the deferential interest that came her way as a successful author.

She immediately began to write a third novel, begun in 1848 as 'Hollow's Mill' but published in 1849 under the title *Shirley*, the name of its firm-minded heroine. Before she could finish it, the slow disaster of the consecutive deaths of Branwell, Emily and Anne, all victims of pulmonary tuberculosis, unfolded. In her life as in her fiction, Charlotte saw work as the remedy for grief: 'Labour must be the cure, not sympathy – Labour is the only radical cure for rooted Sorrow', she wrote to Williams on 25 June 1849, four weeks after Anne's death (Smith, *Letters*, vol. II, p. 224). Memories of Emily and Anne are reflected in the characters of Shirley Keeldar and Caroline Helstone. Neither should be seen as a portrait of one of Charlotte's lost sisters; but the complexities of *Shirley*, which is as angry and sad as it is spirited, are to some extent a response to the short and shadowed lives of her siblings. Like *Jane Eyre*, the novel defies oppression – not just the domestic oppression that men could exercise over women, but the political oppression Charlotte saw in relations between masters and workmen. *Shirley* is, understandably, not a light-hearted book. But it ends hopefully, as Shirley and Caroline survive and marry, and the mill-owner Robert Moore acquires a more enlightened understanding of his responsibilities as an industrialist.

Charlotte's determination and optimism persisted, in the face of every setback. The response to *Shirley* was broadly positive, with some hostile exceptions – including a condemnatory review by the previously sympathetic G. H. Lewes, which evoked Charlotte's fierce indignation; a letter of hers to Lewes, probably written in January 1850, consists of a single sentence: 'I can be on my guard against my enemies, but God deliver me from my friends!' (Smith, *Letters*, vol. II, p. 330). Her fourth and final novel, *Villette*, which she began in 1851 and published in 1853, proved hard to complete. Charlotte was lonely. Despite visits to London, and new and rewarding friendships with writers (including Harriet Martineau and Elizabeth Gaskell), she missed the supportive companionship that her siblings had provided. She may have developed an affection for George Smith, her ebullient publisher; if so, her hopes for romance came to nothing. Whether or not she had wanted to marry Smith, her relations with him certainly became more distant after he announced his engagement to another woman in 1853.

Charlotte's quiet life as a clergyman's daughter in Haworth continued alongside her new literary celebrity. It was in Haworth that she worked and wrote, though the small community could not provide a range of social distractions that might have helped her cope with her increasing sense of isolation. Finally, however, Haworth provided her with a husband, and a new kind of family life. Overcoming the resistance of Patrick, and her own earlier reluctance, Charlotte accepted a proposal of marriage from Arthur Bell Nicholls, her father's curate. His courtship had been patient and passionate, and though it is not clear that Charlotte loved him with the fervour that she had once felt for the temperamental Monsieur Heger, his dogged loyalty finally won a response. They were married in 1854, when Charlotte was thirty-eight years old. The union was happy, and Charlotte began to write another novel. But her domestic contentment was short-lived. Pregnancy was followed by complications, and on 31 March 1855 she died, her father and husband beside her. She was no longer the 'poor, obscure, plain, and little' (*Jane Eyre*, II.viii.253) woman who had caught the world's attention with *Jane Eyre*, and the passing of a major writer was widely recognized and mourned. Two years later, Elizabeth Gaskell published her brilliant if misleading account of her friend in *The Life of Charlotte Brontë*, and the complex, shifting story of her literary legacy began to develop.

NOTES

1 Barker gives a balanced account of the school on pp. 118–41.
2 See Christine Alexander (ed.), *An Edition of the Early Writings of Charlotte Brontë*, 2 vols. (Oxford: Blackwell, 1987–91), vol. 1 (Oxford: Blackwell, for the Shakespeare Head Press), pp. 123–4.
3 The figure is supplied by Alexis Weedon in *Victorian Publishing: The Economics of Book Production for a Mass Market, 1836–1916* (Aldershot: Ashgate, 2003), p. 97.

CHAPTER 8

Emily Brontë

Lyn Pykett

Emily Brontë, by general agreement an extremely reserved woman, has often seemed remote and 'biographer-proof'.[1] Apart from *Wuthering Heights* and her poems, she left few written traces: three unrevealing letters; four diary papers, modelled on Byron's mode of detailing his activities at particular times of the day; and a dozen or so French essays from her Brussels period. Her prose contributions to the Gondal writings about an imaginary island in the North Pacific, on which she worked with Anne from about 1833, might have thrown valuable light on her cast of mind and creative process; but they have disappeared.

Another problem for biographers is that Emily's life and character have been refracted through the impressions of commentators who were more interested in Charlotte or Branwell, and through a mist of myth and legend. In particular, Charlotte Brontë, in seeking to act as the 'interpreter' who 'ought always to have stood between [Emily] and the world', constructed an influential myth of a solitary, untutored, romantic genius writing from 'the impulse of nature', and possessing a creative gift of which she was not (or possibly not *yet*) master. Charlotte's Emily is a series of paradoxes: a woman of strong feeling but '[undemonstrative] character'; possessing a 'magnanimous' but 'warm and sudden' temper and 'unbending' spirit;[2] interested in other people, but rarely exchanging a word with them.[3] According to Charlotte, Emily was both less and more than a woman as commonly understood by the Victorians: 'Stronger than a man, simpler than a child, her nature stood alone.'[4] Charlotte is also the main source for the view that there was 'a certain harshness in her powerful [and] peculiar character'.[5]

In 1820, aged just under two, Emily moved to the parsonage at Haworth which was to be her home until her death, at the age of thirty, in December 1848. She was soon acquainted with death: her mother died two months after her own third birthday, and her two eldest sisters died in quick succession when she was six. Despite these losses – about whose psychological consequences we can only speculate – Emily seems to have enjoyed a stable, happy and boisterous childhood in a lively, close-knit family and a comfortable home cared for by her mother's sister Elizabeth Branwell. She was particularly close to her younger sister Anne: they were 'like twins', Charlotte's friend Ellen Nussey observed, 'inseparable companions, and in the very closest sympathy'.[6] Emily always remained deeply attached to the domestic space of her home, as she did to the wild beauty of the moors which surrounded it, and spent only four brief (often unhappy) periods away from Haworth.

Emily's first absence from home was in November 1824, when she joined her elder sisters at the new Clergy Daughters' School at Cowan Bridge. She left in June 1825, following a typhoid outbreak and the deaths (from tuberculosis) of Maria and Elizabeth. Rather surprisingly, given her later reputation for strangeness and awkwardness with strangers, the six-year-old Emily, one of the youngest pupils, seems to have been made a school favourite: 'little petted Em' was 'quite the pet nursling of the school', who 'Reads very prettily & Works a little'.[7] After Cowan Bridge, Emily stayed at home for ten years, helping with domestic chores and being educated by her father, aunt and, latterly, Charlotte. As well as receiving formal lessons on the usual subjects, she shared in rambles with their father on the moors, an important part of the Brontës' education. They also attended exhibitions in Leeds and concerts in Haworth and had drawing and music lessons. Emily became a proficient pianist, according to Ellen Nussey's reminiscences (Smith, *Letters*, vol. 1, p. 599), developing a particular taste for Beethoven. She also read widely, without restriction, the books in her father's library and books borrowed from local subscription libraries; she was particularly well versed in the novels of Scott and the poems of Byron and Shelley. Emily also had ready access to newspapers and periodicals. During this period she grew into the girl whom Ellen Nussey recalled as graceful, attractive, with 'kind⟨ly⟩, kindling, liquid eyes' that rarely looked directly at other people, and very 'reserved', except when displaying her delight in the beauties of the moors (Smith, *Letters*, vol. 1, p. 598).

Something of the bustling, apparently carefree nature of Emily's life during her childhood and adolescence can be seen in her diary paper for 24 November 1834:

I fed Rainbow, Diamond, Snowflake Jasper phesant . . . Branwell went down to Mr Drivers and brought news that Sir Robert peel was going to be invited to stand for Leeds Anne and I have been peeling Apples\ for/ Charlotte to make an apple pudding ... papa opened the parlour Door and ... gave Branwell a Letter saying ... read this and show it to your Aunt and Charlotte – The Gondals are ⟨disc⟩ discovering the interior of Gaaldine

Sally mosley is washing in the back Kitchin ...

... Anne and I have not tid[i]ied ourselves, done our bed work \or/ done our lessons ... [or] our music excercise which consists of b majer Taby said on my putting a pen in her face Ya pitter pottering there instead of pilling a potate ... (finished pilling the potatos papa going to walk Mr Sunderland [their piano teacher] expected[.] (Barker, pp. 220–1)

In portraying the warm, lively chaos of the morning Emily segues contentedly and seamlessly between the kitchen, the world of politics, letters, visits, music lessons and her imaginary world of Gondal. She also reveals a sense of humour.

Eight months later, Emily exchanged this happy domestic scene for Roe Head School, accompanying Charlotte on her return to her former school as a teacher. At seventeen, Emily felt awkward as one of the oldest pupils; she also disliked rote learning and the lack of privacy and time for Gondal creation. Suffering an acute form of homesickness, she became ill and returned home in November. Charlotte later attributed Emily's situation to her need for the 'Liberty' without which she would perish, and to her inability to endure the 'change from ... her own very noiseless, very secluded, but unrestricted and inartificial mode of life, to one of disciplined routine'.[8] Emily's happiness with her re-immersion in her two favourite places, the domestic world of the parsonage and her own imagination, is evident in the diary she wrote with Anne on 26 June 1837:

Charolotte working in Aunts room Branwell reading Eugene Aram to her Anne and I writing in the drawing room – Anne a poem ... I Agustus Almedas life 1st vol ... papa gone out. Tabby in the Kitchin – the Emperors and Empresses of Gondal and Gaaldine preparing to depart from Gaaldine to Gondal to prepare for the coranation which will be on the 12th of July Queen Victoria ascended the throne this month. Northangerland in Moncey's Isle – Zamorna at Eversham. [A]ll tight and right in which condition it is to be hoped we shall all be on this day 4 years[.] (Barker, p. 271)

As in her other diary papers, Emily records the ages that she and her siblings will have attained a year hence and speculates on where and in what state they will be, indicating an insecurity about the future created by the deaths of her mother and elder sisters and by the relatively precarious financial position of the remaining Brontë children.

A year later Emily was seeking to earn a living as a teacher at Law Hill, a school with about forty pupils, half of them boarders. Although she was not a particularly unpopular teacher, a former pupil recalled that Emily found it difficult to associate with others and that her 'work was hard because she had not the faculty of doing it quickly' (Barker, p. 294). In a letter to Ellen Nussey, written on 2 October 1838, Charlotte reported that Emily's work was 'hard labour from six in the morning until near eleven at night, with only one half-hour of exercise between. This is slavery. I fear she will never stand it' (Smith, *Letters*, vol. 1, p. 182). In fact Emily withstood the rigours of her slavery quite well at first, writing many poems, including such well-known works as 'Loud without the Wind was Roaring' and 'A Little While, a Little While'. However, her poems became increasingly gloomy as autumn deepened into winter, and they ceased altogether when she returned to Law Hill after Christmas. Again her health broke down, and she returned home – this time to a fairly solitary existence. Her birthday paper for 30 July 1841 places her alone in the dining room and records the places where her siblings were employed. She notes the sisters' plans for establishing a school and wonders whether, a year hence, 'we shall still be dragging on in our present condition or established to our hearts' content'. Emily tries to imagine the circumstances in which the diary might be opened at the specified time, 'when Anne is 25 years old or my next birthday after – if – all be well':

I guess that . . . we (ie) Charlotte, Anne and I . . . shall be all merrily seated in our own sitting-room in some pleasant . . . and flourishing seminary having just gathered in for the midsummer holydays our debts . . . paid off . . . papa Aunt and Branwell will either have been or be coming to visit us – it will be a fine warm . . . evening very different from this bleak look-out . . . Anne and I will perchance slip out into the garden . . . to peruse our papers. I hope either this [or] something better will be the case –

The Gondalians ⟨are⟩ are at present in a threatening state but there is no open rupture as yet . . . I have a good many books on hand – but I am sorry to say that as usual I make small progress with any – however I have just made a new regularity paper! (Barker, p. 358)

Preparation for establishing their school was the ostensible reason for Emily's and Charlotte's nine-month stay in a Brussels boarding school in 1842. En route for Brussels (accompanied by their father), the sisters spent three packed days in London, visiting art galleries. Charlotte seems to have been the chief instigator of these visits, but Mary Taylor (who accompanied them to London) reported that Emily was also well informed on the paintings and statues and always had an opinion of her own to offer (Gaskell, *Life*, p. 172). In Brussels, Emily again experienced school as a place where she did not fit in. However, as Charlotte later recalled, Emily overcame her initial 'sinking' and 'rallied through the mere force of resolution'.[9] Emily survived by immersing herself in her Gondal writings, piano lessons and work. Working hard to improve her French, she also studied German and developed the interest in German Romanticism which clearly informs her novel and poems.[10] She made no new friends: with the exception of Louise de Bassompierre, who found her more sympathetic and approachable than Charlotte, the pupils did not much like her, and invitations to spend Sundays with an English family ended when they tired of her tendency to talk – if at all – in monosyllables.

Emily was more loquacious in objecting to a proposal from their tutor M. Heger that she and Charlotte should write essays modelled on classic French authors on a topic set by him. However, he prevailed, and she threw herself into the task. Heger was impressed and puzzled by the results and by his pupil, who had 'a head for logic, and a capability of argument, unusual in a man, and rare indeed in a woman', but whose powers, he suggested, were weakened by a 'stubborn tenacity of will, which rendered her obtuse to all reasoning where her own wishes, or . . . sense of right, was concerned' (Gaskell, *Life*, p. 177). Like other observers of Emily, Heger was unable to fit her qualities into his conception of femininity: 'She should have been a man', he confided to Mrs Gaskell. Despite this problem, Heger's assessment of Emily was quite shrewd. His sense that she should have been 'a great navigator' (Gaskell, *Life*, p. 177) seems to accord with the self-conception (or aspiration) of the woman who, in the Brontës' childhood games, named her soldier after Sir William Parry, the Arctic explorer. Moreover, Heger's view of Emily's unyielding will in the face of opposition and difficulty accords with the oft-repeated recollection of John Greenwood (the Haworth stationer) of the silent, practical resolve with which 'this fragile creature' separated two large fighting dogs while several grown men looked on, afraid to intervene:

She never spoke a word, nor appeared in the least at a loss what to do, but rushed . . . into the kitchen, took the pepper box, and . . . [sprang] upon the beasts – seizing Keeper around the neck with one arm, while with the other, she dredges well their noses with the pepper, and separating them by force of her great will.[11]

The final chapter of Emily's life began with her return home from Brussels on her aunt's death. She took over responsibility for running the household and managing the sisters' legacies from their aunt (leaving the money where it was, invested in railway shares). Emily's final diary paper (for 30 July 1845) suggests that this was – apart from Branwell's further deterioration – a happy and productive period for her:

> [W]e have cash enough for our present wants with a prospect of accumolation – we are all in decent health – only that papa has a complaint in his eyes and with the exception of B[ranwell] who I hope will be better and do better, hereafter. I am quite contented for myself – not as idle as formerly, altogether as hearty and having learnt to make the most of the present and hope for the future with less fidgetiness that I cannot do all I wish ... and merely desiring that every body could be as comfortable as myself and as undesponding and then we should have a very tolerable world of it – (Barker, pp. 455–6)

Emily also details a short holiday in York with Anne, where her main pleasure was imagining various Gondal characters 'escaping from the Palaces of Instruction to join the Royalists who are hard driven at present by the victorious Republicans' (Barker, p. 451). She seems not to have noticed that – as Anne's diary paper reveals – her sister was depressed and losing interest in Gondal.

Emily's equanimity was disturbed in the autumn of 1845, when Charlotte happened to find the poems which Emily had begun copying into two notebooks in 1844 and urged publication (see Chapter 16). Despite her outrage at Charlotte's violation of her privacy, Emily agreed on condition that they were published pseudonymously; she also removed the Gondal references. She played no part in efforts to obtain a publisher for the volume of poems by Currer, Ellis and Acton Bell. From about October 1845 Emily had also been writing *Wuthering Heights*, which was sent to publishers with her sisters' novels by July 1846. At first Emily accepted Charlotte's attempts to take control of their literary careers; but in 1847, after silences and rejections, she and Anne accepted Thomas Newby's offer of publication at their own expense. She later resisted Charlotte's efforts to move her younger sisters on more generous terms to her own publisher, Smith, Elder & Co. Reviewed with varying combinations of grudging admiration and outrage as an extraordinary book, *Wuthering Heights* was to remain a unique work. There is some circumstantial evidence that Emily began a second novel, but no manuscript survives. Emily would certainly have had good reason to immerse herself in her imaginary worlds in her final year, which was dominated by Branwell's problems, persistent drunkenness, ill-health and, finally, death. Shortly after his funeral in September Emily herself became ill, refusing all medical help until 19 December, the day of her death. A few days later

Charlotte sent a fitting epitaph to Ellen Nussey: 'She has died in a time of promise – we saw her taken from life in its prime' (Smith, *Letters*, vol. II, p. 157).

NOTES

1 John Hewish, *Emily Brontë: A Critical and Biographical Study* (London: Macmillan, 1969), p. 9.
2 All preceding quotations in this paragraph are from Charlotte Brontë's 'Biographical Notice of Ellis and Acton Bell', quoted from Smith, *Letters*, vol. II, where the relevant passages are found on pp. 746, 747, 742 and 746, in that order.
3 This picture of Emily is conveyed in Charlotte Brontë's 'Editor's Preface' to Charlotte's 1850 edition of *Wuthering Heights*, quoted from Smith, *Letters*, vol. II, pp. 748–51; see esp. p. 749.
4 From the 'Biographical Notice', in Smith, *Letters*, vol. II, p. 746.
5 See her letter to W. S. Williams of 2 Nov. 1848; Smith, *Letters*, vol. II, p. 133.
6 This often-quoted remark on the two sisters occurs in Ellen's reminiscences of the Brontës in the 1830s, written many years later; the account is reprinted in Smith, *Letters*, vol. I, where the quoted observation is found on p. 598.
7 From the school's superintendent and its admissions register, quoted in Barker, p. 134.
8 From Charlotte Brontë's 'Prefatory Note' to 'Selections from Poems by Ellis Bell', quoted from Smith, *Letters*, vol. II, p. 753.
9 *Ibid.*
10 On Emily's interest in German Romanticism, see Stevie Davies, *Emily Brontë: Heretic* (London: Women's Press, 1994), pp. 49–51.
11 Winifred Gérin, *Emily Brontë: A Biography* (Oxford University Press, 1972), pp. 146–7.

CHAPTER 9

Anne Brontë

Maria Frawley

A tension essential to understanding Anne Brontë permeates the poetry of 'Acton Bell' – one between home, figured as 'that little spot, / with gray walls compassed round' in the poem called 'Home', and the eternal beyond, represented in the poem 'Views of Life' as 'that blessed shore / Where none shall suffer, none shall weep'.[1] Indeed, home and heaven may be thought of as the twin compass points used by Anne Brontë to navigate and understand her life experiences, whether away from, or back in, Haworth Parsonage or contemplating her destiny, irrespective of where she happened to be at the time.

The youngest and still least well-known and appreciated of the Brontë sisters, Anne was born on 17 January 1820, a few months before the family moved from Thornton to Haworth. She lost her mother, Maria Branwell Brontë, little more than a year and a half later. Anne's aunt Elizabeth Branwell – who had moved in with the family to help when Maria became ill – consequently played a key role in raising Anne during the early childhood years, but so did her father, the Revd Patrick Brontë, and her siblings, especially her sisters Charlotte and Emily. Anne would have been just four years of age when her four sisters (Maria, Elizabeth, Charlotte and Emily) were sent off to the Clergy Daughters' School (made infamous by Charlotte's later depiction of it as Lowood in *Jane Eyre*). By virtue of her age, she was spared some of the trauma when her elder sisters Maria and Elizabeth fell ill while at the Clergy Daughters' School and died shortly after returning home.

However young she was when she encountered these early losses, Anne's childhood and the intensely close relations formed with her remaining siblings were surely affected by the mark that death had left on those who raised her. Biographers of the Brontës make much of the pairings between siblings suggested by the juvenilia – Charlotte and Branwell working together to create the imaginary worlds of Glass Town and Angria, Emily and Anne together creating the Gondal saga. Letters to

9 Portrait of Anne Brontë by her sister Charlotte, *c.* 1833

and from Charlotte Brontë paint a more kaleidoscopic picture, however, with Charlotte as likely to refer to 'Anne and I both' or 'Anne and I ditto' as to 'Emily and Anne', 'Emily and I' or 'Emily, Anne & myself'. The relationships forged during the early years when the three sisters worked together in the kitchen alongside the beloved family servant Tabitha Aykroyd, read the books and magazines to be found in their father's library or through the circulating libraries in nearby Keighley, sketched and painted, explored the moors surrounding their home and began to channel their imaginative energies towards writing projects are characterized by a powerful sense of shared experience. This closeness lent emotional urgency to the many leave-takings and reunions that punctuated their young adult lives as they individually left home, either for schooling or for work.

Anne first left Haworth Parsonage at fifteen, when she took Emily's place at Roe Head School after her sister had become ill from homesickness. Although Anne, like Emily, struggled with her separation from home and family – at one point experiencing a religious crisis, eased by spiritual comfort administered by the Moravian minister James La Trobe – she remained for two years, earning an award for good conduct in December 1836.

The pattern of struggle – unhappiness and dissatisfaction competing with acceptance and stoic endurance – repeats itself in Anne's professional experiences. A few years after her stint at Roe Head, in 1839, she left home again, this time to begin employment as a governess for the Ingham family, who resided at Blake Hall in Mirfield. Charlotte's often-quoted description of the children Anne cared for as 'desperate little dunces' undoubtedly reflects the combination of frustration and resentment that her youngest sister conveyed in correspondence home. Nevertheless, her experience as a governess was crucial to her first foray into fiction-writing. Published in 1847 by Thomas Cautley Newby (in a volume with *Wuthering Heights*), Anne's first novel *Agnes Grey* memorably articulates the hardships endured by its young heroine in her role as governess to the Bloomfield family. Repeatedly treated with incivility, the narrator bemoans the incorrigible behaviour of her young charges and the unreasonable expectations of their parents. Despite her 'unremitting patience and perseverance' and her nightly pleas for 'Divine assistance', Agnes Grey is eventually discharged and returns home, to 'that dear, familiar place' associated throughout the narrative with 'rest and liberty', key concepts for all the Brontë sisters (iv.33).

Anne Brontë was likewise dismissed from her first governess position, allegedly because the Ingham children had not learned enough. As Juliet Barker summarizes, '[d]espite [Anne's] having done her best to instil some order and learning into her charges, the Inghams had found no visible improvement in them and held Anne responsible' (Barker, p. 318). Although Anne was able to return home in time to spend Christmas with her family, she left home again in the spring of 1840, fuelled by a desire to be self-sufficient.

That desire was strong enough to outweigh the attractions of staying in Haworth in close proximity to William Weightman, the new curate who had come to Haworth in 1839 to work with Patrick Brontë. Some biographers and critics have seen Weightman as an object of Anne's affection, and the subject of some of her poems (among them 'To —', 'Yes, thou art gone' and 'Dreams'); others – most notably Juliet Barker – contend that Charlotte, despite mocking him in some of her letters, was more infatuated with the young man than was her youngest sister. In any case, the poems of Anne's that are sometimes believed to have been inspired by Weightman undoubtedly depict strong desires, as when, in 'Dreams', she writes of a wish 'To know myself beloved at last / To think my heart has found a rest' (*Poems*, p. 113). 'Yes, thou art gone', also known as 'A Reminiscence', bemoans the fact that 'never more / Thy sunny smile shall gladden me' but ends wistfully: 'To think a soul so near divine / Within a form so angel fair / United to a heart like thine / Has gladdened once our humble sphere' (*Poems*, pp. 100–1). 'To —', a poem written in December 1842 which may have been prompted by news of Weightman's death, laments, 'And yet I cannot check my sighs / Thou wert so young and fair' (*Poems*, p. 87). Whatever the exact nature of Anne's feelings about William Weightman, his personality, beliefs and early death clearly fuelled the fires that were already animating her writing and would continue to stimulate her throughout her authorial career. As Marianne Thormählen observes, Anne Brontë viewed love itself 'as an actuator of and driving force in human development and spiritual pilgrimage'.[2]

When Anne left home in the spring of 1840 her destination was Thorp Green Hall, ten miles from York, where she would work as governess to the children of the Revd Edmund Robinson and his wife Lydia. Her poetry documents the intensity of her feelings of loneliness and homesickness experienced while at Thorp Green, as well as her occasional dissatisfaction and desire to leave. Even so, her work there not only was more long-lasting, but also ultimately proved more satisfying, than any other teaching job undertaken by one of the young Brontës – not least because Anne earned the respect and, eventually, the affection of her charges, who turned to her for advice. She was also able to travel a little with the Robinsons, who took summer holidays in the seaside town of Scarborough. A diary paper written in 1841 records a small degree of pride in having, since her last such recording, 'seen the sea and York Minster' (quoted in Barker, p. 359).

Anne Brontë's diary papers expose what appears to have been a lifelong tendency to take stock of her self, engaging in a kind of self-scrutiny, and to feel compelled to look ahead even while being deeply pessimistic about her prospects. As Edward Chitham comments with regard to Anne, '[t]o rethink one's life was almost a duty, and certainly an easing of pain'.[3] Just as notes pencilled on the flyleaves of her Bible – notably 'what where and how shall I be when I have got through?' – reveal a woman uncertain about but deeply desirous of change,[4] so the few diary extracts of Anne's that remain suggest a disconcerting combination of anticipation, pessimism and regret. The diary paper of 30 July 1841 is illustrative of this tone, for example as it looks backward through the years and then shifts forward, as Anne reflects: 'What will the next four years bring forth? Providence only knows. But we ourselves have sustained very little alteration since [1837]. I have the same faults that I had then, only I have more wisdom and experience, and a little more self-possession than I then enjoyed' (Barker, p. 359). Four years later, having left Thorp Green behind, she writes:

I wonder how we shall all be and where and how situated ⟨when we open this pap [er]⟩ on the thirtyeth of July 1848 ... [W]hat changes shall we have seen and known and shall we be much changed ourselves? I hope not – for the worse at least – I for my part cannot well be <u>flatter</u> or older in mind than I am now – (Barker, p. 455)

This particular disposition of Anne's, and the concern with how conditions influence one's character, manifest themselves in her second and more critically successful novel, *The Tenant of Wildfell Hall*, which appeared in 1848 and which the critic Elizabeth Berry has usefully described as exhibiting a 'contentious disquietude' in contrast to the 'contemplative equanimity' of *Agnes Grey*.[5] Portions of *The Tenant of Wildfell Hall* have long been believed to have been prompted by Anne's response to her brother Branwell's reckless behaviour, capitulation to alcoholism and early death; but the novel's sophisticated narrative technique and its confrontational approach to thorny social issues (involving gender ideology, marriage and property laws and class hierarchies) reveal a much more complex agenda on the author's part.

The novel's heroine, Helen Huntingdon, idealistically imagines herself capable of functioning as a moral beacon for the man she marries, but she gradually discovers herself powerless in the face of his irresponsible behaviour and dissolute propensities. Portions of the novel dedicated to Helen's diaries depict her, not unlike Anne Brontë herself, periodically taking stock of her life, reflecting on the past and anticipating the future. 'What have I done? And what will be the end of it?' begins one chapter (xix.139). Another records the heroine's early premonitions of her marital disaster; her 'bliss is sobered', her 'hopes diminished' and her 'fears increased' (xxviii.202). In a highly charged and poignant moment, she faces herself in a mirror and reflects on the loss of her idealism and how it has changed her. Like Anne Brontë herself, she feels she could not be 'flatter or older in mind', and her recognition of the debilitating nature of her condition inspires her to the courageous (and illegal) action of leaving her husband and taking their son to live in hiding. One critic has aptly described *The Tenant of Wildfell Hall* as 'a realist's response to the romanticization of violence and conflict that had occurred in her sisters' writings' (a judgement that perhaps goes some way towards explaining the famously caustic remark of Charlotte's, in her 'Biographical Notice of Ellis and Acton Bell', according to which *The Tenant of Wildfell Hall* was 'an entire mistake').[6]

In *The Brontë Myth*, Lucasta Miller observes that '[w]hen it was first published in 1848, Anne's *Tenant of Wildfell Hall* ... offended the shockable sections of society more than the other Brontë novels and ... intensified the critical outrage that had gathered around the Bells'.[7] Anne's own response to this reaction to her novel is seen in her 'Preface to the Second Edition', written in July 1848. The preface emphasizes the realist impulses that drove Anne's work. 'In the present work', she writes,

I find myself censured for depicting con amore, with 'a morbid love of the coarse, if not of the brutal,' those scenes which, I will venture to say, have not been more painful for the most fastidious of my critics to read, than they were for me to describe. I may have gone too far, in which case I shall be careful not to trouble myself or my readers in the same way again; but when we have to do with vice and vicious characters, I maintain it is better to depict them as they really are than as they would wish to appear. To represent a bad thing in its least offensive light, is doubtless, the most agreeable course for the writer of fiction to pursue; but is it the most honest, or the safest? (Preface, pp. 3–4)

Anne Brontë did not have long to contemplate the reception of her second novel. Just a few short months after she wrote her preface, her brother Branwell was dead and her sister Emily betrayed symptoms of the tuberculosis that would take her life before the year's end. At the beginning of 1849, Anne, too, was ill – too tired to do much and with the tell-tale cough that prophesied consumption. However 'patient in her illness' (Charlotte's description of Anne), the experience forced her lifelong concerns with death, the afterlife and the fragility of faith in the face of such pressures to resurface. Although professing 'no horror of death', she nevertheless wrote of desiring 'to do some good in the world before I leave it'.[8] Recognizing the likelihood that such hopes were vain, she urged Charlotte and their friend Ellen Nussey to accompany her to Scarborough so that she could enjoy, and possibly benefit from, the seaside climate. She died on 28 May, only a few days after arriving in Scarborough, and was buried there at a church overlooking the sea. Describing what had unfolded in a letter to her publisher's reader – by that time a friend – W. S. Williams, Charlotte wrote, 'I wanted her to die where she would be happiest – She loved Scarboro'' (Smith, *Letters*, vol. II, p. 216).

There is symbolic resonance in Anne Brontë's final resting-place. The literal distance from Haworth in some ways captures her distinctive position within her family, and her grave's very position in a small church-yard overlooking the sea suggests both the inevitability of confinement and the promise of unbounded expanse that marked Anne Brontë's inner world. Her gravestone identifies her as 'Anne Brontë, daughter of the Revd. P. Brontë'; but Anne Brontë, author and individual, remains something of an unknown entity, an extraordinary talent – like her siblings – who was painfully aware of thoughts, feelings, abilities and desires kept hidden from the world, including those closest to her. Some of the themes that dominate Anne's writing – secrecy, solitude and silence – paradoxically speak volumes about her sense of self. Indeed, Anne's poem 'A Fragment' (also known as 'Self-Congratulation'), which ends with the lines 'They little knew my hidden thoughts / And they will never know / The anguish of my drooping heart, / The bitter aching woe!' (*Poems*, p. 157), implies that she experienced a modicum of triumph in self-awareness of the control she exerted over her inner world. If, as Juliette Wells and Sandra Hagan contend, 'the shadow of her siblings' achievements' has obscured full appreciation of all that Anne Brontë accomplished,[9] some consolation is surely to be had in the knowledge that she transformed obscurity itself into subject matter for her writing, the matter of her art.

NOTES

1 Edward Chitham (ed.), *The Poems of Anne Brontë: A New Text and Commentary* (London: Macmillan, 1979; repr. 1987), pp. 100 and 119. Subsequent references are included in the text.

2 See Marianne Thormählen, 'Aspects of Love in *The Tenant of Wildfell Hall*', in Julie Nash and Barbara A. Suess (eds.), *New Approaches to the Literary Art of Anne Brontë* (Aldershot: Ashgate, 2001), p. 154. Although Thormählen's analysis is focused on Anne Brontë's second novel, the comment is applicable to almost all of Anne Brontë's writing.

3 Edward Chitham, *A Life of Anne Brontë* (Oxford: Blackwell, 1991), p. 155.

4 See my essay 'Contextualizing Anne Brontë's Bible', in Nash and Suess, *New Approaches*, pp. 1–13 for a fuller elaboration on this remark and others appearing in Anne's Bible.

5 Elizabeth Hollis Berry, *Anne Brontë's Radical Vision: Structures of Consciousness*, ELS Monograph Series, 62 (University of Victoria, Canada, 1994), p. 108.

6 Charlotte's 'Biographical Notice' is quoted from Smith, *Letters*, vol. II, p. 745. The critic referred to is Mary Mark Ockerbloom; see the entry on 'Anne Brontë' on the website 'A Celebration of Women Writers': http://digital. library.upenn.edu/women/bronte/bronte-anne.html (accessed 17 Apr. 2012).

7 Lucasta Miller, *The Brontë Myth* (London: Jonathan Cape, 2001), p. 156.

8 These expressions occur in a letter of Anne's to Ellen Nussey, written on 5 Apr. 1849 and repr. in Smith, *Letters*, vol. II, p. 195.

9 Juliette Wells and Sandra Hagan, in the introduction to their *The Brontës in the World of the Arts* (Aldershot: Ashgate, 2008), p. 5.

CHAPTER 10

Friends, servants and a husband

Stephen Whitehead

'Resident in a remote district where education has made little progress, and where, consequently, there was no inducement to seek social intercourse beyond our own domestic circle, we were wholly dependent on ourselves and each other.'[1] Charlotte's 'Biographical Notice' has influenced the popular image of the Brontë sisters' huddled isolation perhaps more than any other text. Aspects of the 'Notice' have been challenged by Brontë biographers and historians of Haworth; but even for those who accept the text, ideas of isolation diminish when we consider the breadth of the Brontës' 'domestic circle'.

The children's relationships with their father and their aunt are dealt with elsewhere in this volume, but there were others within the domestic circle, namely the family servants, whom the Brontë sisters were ever ready to acknowledge. To Charlotte, Tabby Aykroyd was 'like one of our own family', as she wrote to Ellen Nussey in December 1836 (Smith, *Letters*, vol. 1, p. 159). Emily's and Anne's diary papers describe the doings of Tabby and Martha Brown seamlessly along with the rest of the family, and when Charlotte was from home, she wrote to Martha, concluding her letters, 'I am dear Martha, your sincere friend, C. Brontë.'

Haworth Parsonage is a small, cold house, and the warmest room was the kitchen; 'Tabby's kingdom [where] the copper pans shone like gold. It was a snug, warm, crooning place.'[2] The Brontë children gravitated towards 'Tabby's kingdom', and sharing the housework with the servants established strong bonds of loyalty. When Tabby broke her leg in a fall in December 1836, the Brontë sisters nursed her themselves, in defiance of their aunt; and when, three years later, Tabby left the parsonage for a spell of rest with her sister, Charlotte wrote to Ellen: 'I manage the ironing and keep the rooms clean – Emily does the baking and attends to the Kitchen [–] We . . . prefer this mode of contrivance to having a new face among us' (Smith, *Letters*, vol. 1, p. 206).

It was, by 1839, fifteen years since Tabby had been 'a new face'. In 1824 she had replaced the Garrs sisters, who had come with the Brontës from

83

Thornton.[3] Tabby was born in 1771, she never married, and little is known of her life before she came to the parsonage. According to Mrs Gaskell, Tabby 'abounded in strong practical sense and shrewdness' (Gaskell, *Life*, p. 63). She took the children for walks, she was a great storyteller and she knew all the complex relationships of blood and property that linked the old families of Haworth. A professed Calvinist, she nonetheless maintained the ancient anthropomorphic traditions of the countryside.

With her leg still troublesome, Tabby left the parsonage in 1839 for a three-year spell of recuperation with her sister. Fresh domestic help was needed, and Mr Brontë found it in the person of his sexton's second daughter, eleven-year-old Martha Brown, who would remain with him at the parsonage until his death in 1861.

The Brontës were cautious in accepting people into their domestic circle; but as they had accepted Tabby, so they accepted Martha, and after the deaths of Branwell, Emily and Anne, Martha was indispensable to Charlotte. Charlotte's letters are laced with references to Tabby's and Martha's involvement in family affairs and, as the years passed, with concern for their health. After Tabby returned to the parsonage from her sister's, early in 1843, she was retained on only the lightest of duties. For the last twelve years of her life she shared the little servants' bedroom with Martha, fifty-seven years her junior, until she died six weeks before Charlotte, on 17 February 1855.

The photograph of Martha Brown shows a neat, spirited woman with large, dark eyes. The Brown family lived at Sexton's House, a hundred yards from the parsonage. They were the Brontës' closest neighbours, and they became more intimately involved with them than any other family in Haworth. As sexton, John Brown worked closely with Mr Brontë; his wife, Mary, and at least three of Martha's sisters, Eliza, Tabitha and Hannah, all worked, at different times, at the parsonage. The Browns' taking-in of Arthur Bell Nicholls as a lodger, between 1845 and 1853, added a further dimension to the relationship, as did John Brown's friendship with Branwell.

Branwell, as a boy, had more liberty to venture beyond the domestic circle than had his sisters. His personality inclined him to it, and he developed a fairly comprehensive set of friends and companions. However, dazzled as these acquaintances were by Branwell's brilliance, they mostly deserted him when his brightness dimmed, and only Francis Grundy and John Brown stood by him to the end. John Brown was thirteen years older than Branwell, and biographers are equivocal on the benignancy or otherwise of his influence. Brown initiated Branwell into

Freemasonry and the associated life of the local inns; but it was to John Brown that Mr Brontë turned in July 1845, when Branwell returned home from Thorp Green in disgrace, asking him to accompany Branwell on what he hoped might be a restorative week in Liverpool and North Wales. The hope turned out to be a forlorn one.

None of the Brontë sisters enjoyed being away from home. Charlotte's and Emily's first experience of it, at the Clergy Daughters' School, had ended in tragedy, and so it would have been with trepidation that Charlotte set off alone, in January 1831, to board at the Misses Wooler's school at Roe Head near Dewsbury. Charlotte was lonely and homesick, but she was soon adopted by another new girl, Ellen Nussey, who had the twin advantages of living in the neighbourhood and having local friends, the sisters Mary and Martha Taylor, enrolling with her.

Charlotte was a pupil at Roe Head for eighteen months, and in that time Ellen and Mary Taylor became her surrogate sisters and friends for life. Charlotte was regarded as a dreamer, Ellen as sentimental and Mary as a passionate extrovert. The three friends were thus very different; but they were all clever and always together at the top of the class. Charlotte and Ellen began corresponding even while they were at school, and in her edition of Charlotte's letters Margaret Smith traces the development of her 'ardent adolescent fondness' for Ellen (Smith, *Letters*, vol. 1, p. 3). Charlotte, Ellen and Mary all left Roe Head in June 1832, after which, although back home with her sisters, Charlotte's fondness for Ellen continued undiminished. Charlotte's attraction to Mary Taylor was less visceral. Mary was self-confident and combative, and for some time Charlotte was wary of her. Their opposing political views were drawn into open conflict over the progress of the 1832 Reform Bill, and it was in neither of their natures to conceal their principles. Mary's candour could be brutal. On the Brontë children's isolation she told Gaskell, 'I told her sometimes they were like growing potatoes in a cellar. She said sadly, "Yes! I know we are!"' (Gaskell, *Life*, p. 84). Mary, who, like Ellen, was pretty, also told Charlotte she was ugly, a remark that Charlotte never forgot.

Mary Taylor was a fiercely independent radical thinker who would, through her journalism and her novel *Miss Miles*, contribute to the nineteenth-century debate on 'the woman question'. By 1840, she had slipped the family leash and gone to live on the Continent, earning her living as a music and English-language teacher. Mary, who never married, was ever chivvying Charlotte and Ellen to assert their independence, and it was her influence that took Charlotte and Emily to Brussels. When, in 1844, Mary Taylor announced her intention to emigrate, Charlotte told

Ellen that she felt as if 'a great planet fell out of the sky' (Smith, *Letters*, vol. I, p. 372); but Mary made enough money in New Zealand, from retail distribution and land dealing, to return home after fourteen years, and she never needed to work again.

The young Mary and Charlotte shared literary aspirations, and Mary's later, surviving correspondence is characterized by a keen critical ear, dry humour and lively debates on politics and literature. Ellen sometimes felt left out of her friends' intellectual correspondence. More often, however, it was Charlotte and Ellen who were, as Joan Bellamy puts it, 'huddling together to fend off the cold winds of Mary's energetic challenges'.[4]

The fact is that Ellen and Mary represented two conflicting sides to Charlotte's own personality: Ellen – passivity, piety and self-effacement; Mary – ambition, frankness and self-fulfilment. They represented Charlotte's heart and her head, and Charlotte responded to the one with love and to the other with admiration. 'God bless her – I never hope to see in this world a character more truly noble', Charlotte wrote of Mary in 1840, in a letter to Ellen (Smith, *Letters*, vol. I, p. 234); of Ellen herself, she wrote, ten years later, to W. S. Williams: 'When I first saw Ellen [–] we were contrasts ... now – no new friend, however lofty or profound in intellect, ⟨could be to me what Ellen is⟩' (Smith, *Letters*, vol. II, p. 323).

Literary aspiration was an aspect of Charlotte's life that she did not share with Ellen. Even when she was correcting the proofs of *Jane Eyre* while staying at Brookroyd, in September 1847, Charlotte did not tell Ellen what she was doing, and it was only after Emily's death that Ellen was shown the novels. The bonds of sisterhood had been uncommonly strong in the Brontës; but even beyond that, these three great artists had been one another's literary mentors, collaborators and critics. Ellen was never part of that world, and Mary was in New Zealand; it was a void in Charlotte's life that would be filled by her new-found professional literary friends.

Charlotte's first point of contact with her publishers, Smith, Elder & Co., was with their reader, William Smith Williams. Williams was an intelligent and a generous man, steeped in the world of literary publishing. He was a friend to such luminaries as Thackeray, G. H. Lewes and Harriet Martineau, and he made clear in his correspondence with Charlotte that he respected her as their equal. Desperately lonely at home, Charlotte soon wrote letters to Williams which went beyond literary matters to an outpouring of her aching grief and her anxieties for herself and her father.

Before long, Charlotte extended this personal correspondence to the principal of Smith, Elder & Co., George Smith. Smith was a bachelor, eight years Charlotte's junior; and during her many visits to London, Charlotte stayed with Smith's family, his mother and his sisters. The success of *Jane Eyre* and *Shirley* encouraged Smith to develop his friendship with his best-selling author, and Ellen and the servants sensed romance; but any such idea was crushed in November 1853, when Smith became engaged to a London sherry heiress. After that, Charlotte's relationship with Smith rapidly cooled, and five months later Charlotte was herself engaged to be married.

'True friendship', Charlotte once wrote to W. S. Williams, 'is no gourd springing in a night and withering in a day' (Smith, *Letters*, vol. II, p. 323). Charlotte's literary friends, who after 1850 included Elizabeth Gaskell, filled the intellectual void left by the deaths of Emily and Anne; but none of them became the 'true friends' of the parsonage domestic circle – those few with whom Charlotte had lived in Parsonage Lane or at Roe Head and who had succoured one another through illness and bereavement. One who fulfilled these criteria, but whom Charlotte only gradually acknowledged, was Arthur Bell Nicholls.

Nicholls had come to Haworth in May 1845, shortly before Branwell and Anne returned from Thorp Green. Nicholls lived with the Brown family, the Brontës' close neighbours, and as Mr Brontë's curate, he was in and out of the parsonage on a daily basis. Nicholls witnessed the decline and death of Branwell and the deaths of Emily and Anne; he conducted Branwell's memorial service and Emily's funeral, and for the next three and a half years he saw, at first hand, the emotional and physical effects of those deaths on Mr Brontë and his last surviving child. In those years when Charlotte so desperately needed a bosom companion in Haworth, there was, in fact, one available; and on 13 December 1852, he declared himself.

Letters home to her father in 1851 and 1852 indicate that Charlotte was warming to her father's curate – five out of six letters ask that her good wishes be passed on to him – and when Nicholls proposed marriage to her, she did not refuse him. The proposal was rejected by Mr Brontë, and with such vehemence that Charlotte deferred to her father's will. Mr Brontë traduced his formerly cherished curate up and down the chapelry; Nicholls felt forced to resign, and in May 1853 he left to take up a curacy near Pontefract. With no lead coming from Charlotte, John Brown and Martha fell in behind Mr Brontë. 'I am sorry for one other person whom nobody pities but me', Charlotte wrote to Ellen; 'Martha is bitter against him: John Brown says he should like to shoot him' (Smith, *Letters*, vol. III, p. 101; the underlining is Charlotte's). Ellen was equally affronted by Nicholls' proposal and wrote to Mary Taylor in New Zealand to tell her so, but Mary was having none of it: 'You talk wonderful nonsense abt C. Brontë', Mary wrote in reply, '[i]t is an outrageous exaction to expect her to give up her choice in a matter so important' (Smith, *Letters*, vol. III, p. 228). Charlotte and Nicholls corresponded in his exile and met secretly when Nicholls visited his friend the Revd Joseph Grant at Oxenhope. By the spring of 1854, Charlotte had managed to persuade her father to relent. The couple were married on 29 June, and Nicholls was reinstated as Mr Brontë's curate.

Ellen's opposition to Charlotte's engagement chilled the relationship between the old friends. Once the matter was decided, however, Ellen made a show of accepting the new order, and warmth returned to Charlotte's letters to her. But when, in November, Nicholls exacted a promise from Ellen to destroy Charlotte's letters, on the grounds that they might one day become public, it was an intrusion too far. Ellen abandoned all show of accommodation to Nicholls, and she resented him for the rest of her life.

There is no doubt that Mr and Mrs Nicholls' brief marriage was a happy one. When she knew that she was dying, Charlotte could reassure Ellen, 'I find in my husband . . . the best earthly comfort that ever woman had' (Smith, *Letters*, vol. III, p. 326). Nicholls stayed on in Haworth after Charlotte's death to look after his father-in-law for the last six years of his life, and during that time Martha Brown warmed to Charlotte's widower. After Mr Brontë's death, Nicholls and Martha were the last of the parsonage household. It was a bond that they both acknowledged, and when Nicholls returned to his native Ireland he asked Martha to go with him. Martha declined that invitation, but between 1862 and 1878 she paid at least five visits to Banagher, some of several months' duration, and the two of them maintained an affectionate correspondence until Martha's death in 1880.

Trust based on long familiarity was the sole passport to the Brontë domestic circle. There were one or two more who entered it, but then died too young. One such was Martha Taylor, Mary's younger sister. Martha was between Anne and Emily in age, and she helped extend the Nussey–Taylor–Charlotte friendship to Anne and Branwell and even Emily. Martha was 'Miss Boisterous', outspoken and original like her sister. If she lacked Mary's good looks and high intellect, she made up for it with her infectious *joie de vivre*, and her death from cholera, in Brussels in October 1842, was deeply felt at the parsonage.

Another Brontë insider was the Revd William Weightman, who died of cholera just four weeks before Martha Taylor. He was then twenty-eight and had been Mr Brontë's curate since 1839. Christine Alexander and Margaret Smith have summarized Weightman's character as 'charming to all, kind and generous to the poor, and diligent in his clerical duties'. A fellow classicist, Weightman was to Branwell 'one of my dearest friends'. All three sisters were a little in love with him, and at Weightman's funeral Mr Brontë described his relationship with his curate as 'like father and son'.[5]

If few entered the Brontë circle, there were many who touched it. Ellen Nussey was the youngest of twelve children and Mary Taylor the fourth of six, and Charlotte took a lively interest in all of their siblings. One of Ellen's brothers, Henry Nussey, proposed marriage to Charlotte. After another brother, George, was admitted into long-term care in a York mental hospital, his fiancée, Amelia Ringrose, went on to marry one of Mary Taylor's brothers, Joseph. Charlotte remained friends with Joe and Amelia Taylor until the end of her life.

There are families in Haworth who claim familiarity with the Brontës: the Heatons of Ponden, the Taylors of Stanbury and three branches of the Greenwood family are the most significant.[6] But none has a claim to intimacy any stronger than the odd formal tea-party invitation and oral tradition. The heads of these families were either church land trustees or churchwardens, and their Brontë connections derive from Mr Brontë's professional position. There is no primary evidence of intimacy with his daughters.

When a member of a small community achieves celebrity, as the Brontës did in Haworth, neighbours take pride in their vicarious association. The paucity of evidence for 'social intercourse beyond our own domestic circle' seems to support Charlotte's claim, but the scope of that domestic circle should prevent exaggerated ideas of their isolation.

NOTES

1 'Biographical Notice of Ellis and Acton Bell', repr. in Smith, *Letters*, vol. II, p. 742.
2 James M. Hoppin, 'An American Visitor for Mr Brontë', *BST*, 15.4 (1969), 327.
3 On the Garrs and the Brontës, see Marion Harland, *Charlotte Brontë at Home* (New York: Knickerbocker Press, 1899), p. 16.
4 Joan Bellamy, *'More Precious than Rubies': Mary Taylor, Friend of Charlotte Brontë, Strong-Minded Woman* (Beverley: Highgate Publications, 2002), p. 9.

5 Christine Alexander and Margaret Smith (eds.), *The Oxford Companion to the Brontës* (Oxford University Press, 2003), p. 531.
6 An extremely useful source of information on these and other local families is provided by Robin Greenwood, 'Who was Who in Haworth during the Brontë Era 1820–61', unpublished typescript, 4th edn (2005); copy in the library of the Brontë Parsonage Museum, Haworth.

The Brontës' sibling bonds

Drew Lamonica Arms

The Brontës' sibling relationships were, in a word, intense. In an 1841 letter to Henry Nussey, the brother of her confidante Ellen Nussey, Charlotte Brontë praised her Haworth home for the 'profound, and intense affection which brothers and sisters feel for each other' (Smith, *Letters*, vol. 1, p. 255). Thirty years later, Ellen herself insisted that 'intelligent companionship and intense family affection' were essential to her friend's literary success.[1] More than a century later, Juliet Barker concluded her comprehensive *The Brontës* reaffirming Nussey's view: 'Without this intense family relationship, some of the greatest novels in the English language would never have been written' (Barker, p. 830). Such intense emotional and intellectual understanding among three sisters (and a brother, for a time) is certainly not unique, but the Brontës uniquely formed and fostered their relationship by writing together. For this close-knit family, sibling bonds carried an intensity that was ultimately enabling, 'setting them in a free place' to exercise their genius (Gaskell, *Life*, p. 247). However their lives may have been limited by their gender, locale, economic status – even their health – the liberating and prolific writing of the sisters' partnership prevailed.

Recognizing the Brontës' sibling relationships as an important part of their art not only helps to illuminate their writing practices – *how* the Brontës wrote – but also reminds us that this family relationship was a necessary precondition for writing to happen at all. Biographers and critics have described the essential sibling context in various ways: family 'mediated' the sisters' relationship to writing; family was 'an institution for literary production'; family was a 'defining community' that also served as a 'locus of literary activity' and 'vehicle for publication'.[2] From the earliest juvenilia to their published novels, when the Brontës thought of themselves as writers, they thought of themselves as *sibling* writers. Even in taking the masculine-sounding pseudonyms Currer, Ellis and Acton to mask their identities as female authors, they presented themselves to the public as a family, the brothers Bell. The interdependence of family relationship and writing was fundamental to their experiences as authors.

The collaborative writing endeavour began in the Brontës' childhood, arising out of the early loss of their mother and two elder siblings, Maria and Elizabeth. Playing and writing together filled a void and forged bonds. But the early writings were not enacted in sorrow; writing together brought matchless joy in the lives of the Brontë children: 'the highest stimulus, as well as the liveliest pleasure we had known from childhood upwards', Charlotte wrote in 1850, 'lay in attempts at literary composition'.[3] If the deaths of Charlotte's two eldest sisters launched a ferment of literary activity in the Brontë household, the deaths of her two younger sisters threatened to silence the lone survivor.

The Brontës' practice of writing in sibling partnerships, begun in the juvenilia, underscores the dual nature of their creative process: the siblings used writing to identify themselves as a family but also to assert individuality within their strong family likeness. In his correspondence with Elizabeth Gaskell, Patrick Brontë recalled how his children formed a little society among themselves, united by their common efforts in acting and composing 'their little plays'.[4] The Brontë children eventually split into two separate and intense pairings: Charlotte and Branwell battling over the course of events in Angria, and Emily and Anne adopting the distinctly different imaginative landscape of Gondal. Despite this division, the sibling groups shared information about their stories: Emily's 26 June 1837 diary paper, for example, reveals that she and Anne were aware of Angrian events, and Gondal's plot development closely parallels Angria's. Charlotte and Branwell's writing partnership began to dissolve in 1839, as Charlotte sought to distance herself from Branwell's increasingly dissipated lifestyle. While Emily's and Anne's collaboration on Gondal lasted well into their adult lives, it became a process through which they could also reveal disagreement and divergence. Nevertheless, when the three sisters decided to publish a joint collection of poems, they made their public appearance as a family unit, though they left out Branwell, who was the first to have poems printed in local periodicals. The decision to publish resumed the 'habit of communication and consultation' that the sisters had enjoyed in childhood and encouraged them to embark on the more profitable course of writing novels.[5]

Gaskell's *The Life of Charlotte Brontë* provides the lasting image of the sisters' ritual: they

retained the old habit, which was begun in their aunt's life-time, of putting away their [needlework] at nine o'clock, and beginning their steady pacing up and down the sitting room. At this time, they talked over the stories they were engaged upon, and discussed their plots. Once or twice a week, each read to the others what she had written, and heard what they had to say about it ... It was on one of these occasions, that Charlotte determined to make her heroine plain, small, and unattractive, in defiance of the accepted canon. (Gaskell, *Life*, p. 247)

In her obituary of Charlotte Brontë, Harriet Martineau claimed that Charlotte's desire to prove to her sisters 'that they were wrong – even morally wrong – in making their heroines beautiful as a matter of course' was the impetus behind *Jane Eyre*.[6] Even though Charlotte professed that she seldom made changes based on her sisters' comments, it seems clear that the writings and opinions they shared in these nightly conversations prompted Charlotte to write her heroine different.

Excluded from their writing practices and confidence, Branwell nevertheless exerted a certain influence on the appearance and character of Jane Eyre. In much modern criticism, the Brontës' only brother serves their genius solely as an example of self-destructive, drunken indulgence that the sisters shaped into art, most obviously in Emily's Hindley Earnshaw and Anne's Arthur Huntingdon and Lord Lowborough. But Branwell was a formative influence on the family writing dynamic, particularly Charlotte's literary development. Charlotte's reliance on male narrators throughout her early writings and for her first novel *The Professor*, for example, can be directly linked to her artistic partnership with Branwell: she set herself against his commanding position in the early plays not by creating strong female characters, as Emily and Anne did in Gondal, but by appropriating maleness. Her fascination with Byronic romance was prompted by Branwell's own great admiration for the poet, and her juvenile stories are filled with beautiful women swept up by her Byronic hero Zamorna – with one exception.

Elizabeth Hastings is a plain and undersized governess, independent, strong-minded, self-respecting and regarded by most readers as a prototype for Jane Eyre. Charlotte wrote her story (titled 'Henry Hastings', 24 February – 25 March 1839) pondering Branwell's decline and her deteriorating relationship with him. In it, she casts Branwell's creation Henry Hastings as a brother and introduces a sister-heroine far different from her usual Angrian beauties (but not so different from herself). Composed in the month following Branwell's return home from his failed stint as a portrait painter in Bradford, 'Henry Hastings' is the only one of Charlotte's early writings to centre on a brother–sister relationship. Throughout the story, Elizabeth struggles to reconcile her deep familial loyalty with her moral repugnance for a once-beloved brother who is now a fugitive soldier wanted for desertion, drunken conduct, murder, even attempted regicide. In the end, Charlotte has it both ways: the sister-character saves her brother from execution through the force of her supplication, and the sister-author escorts him out of the story, alive but disgraced. The sibling-rescue plot allows Elizabeth Hastings a measure of self-worth wholly lacking in other female characters of Charlotte's juvenilia. Charlotte was clearly inspired by her heroine's growing self-esteem as she then has Elizabeth reject Sir William Percy's offer that she become his mistress, even though Elizabeth acknowledges the strength of her love for him. This scene is replayed in Jane Eyre's rejection of a similar proposal by Rochester.

The iconic character of Jane Eyre, then, has origins in sisterly debate and the changing dynamics of a brother–sister relationship. With Gaskell's description of the sisters' nightly exchanges in mind, critics have proceeded to read their novels as reciprocal commentaries on one another – an intertextual dialogue through which they expressed differences of opinion and outlook within the family group. The uncontrollable passion of *Wuthering Heights* has been read as responding to the chilly realism of *The Professor*; Anne's *The Tenant of Wildfell Hall* as a corrective to the excesses of *Wuthering Heights*; and the description of Arthur Huntingdon as a more sobering look at the lifestyle that we quickly forgive Rochester.[7] Much can be gained by this kind of exploration in revealing both similarities and departures, helping to discredit the myth of Brontë 'oneness', a myth launched by the earliest reviewers who took *Wuthering Heights*, *Agnes Grey* and *Jane Eyre* to be written by the same hand. By insisting on publishing with the same surname, the sisters brought on the unforeseen but inevitable conflation of their individual identities, many readers insisting that the Bell brothers must be a single author. Both Charlotte and Anne defended their separate identities in prefaces to later editions of their works. While Emily never championed her individuality publicly, privately she insisted upon her authorial integrity as Ellis Bell, refusing to be identified by anything other than her *nom de plume* even after Charlotte and Anne informed Charlotte's London publishers that the Bells were three sisters. Charlotte's purpose in writing the 'Biographical Notice of Ellis and Acton Bell' in 1850, following the deaths of Emily and Anne, was not primarily to reveal them as women, but to depict them as individuals.

Long before publishing together, Emily and Anne had consciously used writing to establish artistic and ideological differences of opinion, a habit carried out in their juvenilia and poems through companion pieces. Emily's poem 'AS to GS' (19 December 1841), for example, responds to the attitude towards a mother's death expressed in Anne's 'An Orphan's Lament' (1 January 1841).[8] Though Emily's poem was written almost a year after Anne's, both were composed during the Christmas holidays when Anne was home from Thorp Green and the sisters could review their Gondal writings together. With the mother's death, the orphan in Anne's poem sees the loss of all earthly affection and laments the long years ahead without companionship: 'Where shall I find a heart like thine / While life remains to me, / And where shall I bestow the love / I ever bore for thee?' (lines 44–7). Emily's poem begins with a retort to these sentiments. Appropriately, her poem is constructed as one sibling's address to another. The character AS (probably Alfred Sidonia) immediately distinguishes himself from GS (Gerald Sidonia) with a rebuke: 'I do not weep, I would not weep; / Our mother needs no tears: / Dry thine eyes too, 'tis vain to keep / This causeless greif [*sic*] for years' (lines 1–4). AS rejects the idea of perpetual mourning and the selfish desire for restored companionship with the mother on earth. When Charlotte prepared Emily's poem for publication in 1850, she titled it 'Encouragement', and either she or Emily changed its internal Gondalian reference: 'Gerald' became 'Sister', thus making the poem literally an address to a sister. 'AS to GS' is one of the early glimpses into Emily's shifting views of the afterlife, and Anne's poem provides the outlet for her sister's response. It is generally thought that Anne lost her enthusiasm for Gondal: her poem 'Self-Communion' is often cited as evidence of her wanting to free herself from Emily's immersion in their imaginary world. Still, even after writing *Agnes Grey* and *Wuthering Heights*, both sisters wrote Gondal poems on the same day (14 September 1846) about the same subject (the republican war in Gondal), which suggests that they were discussing, planning and collaborating on their literary creation almost to the end.

The end of her sisters' lives proved to be Charlotte Brontë's greatest trial. In a letter to W. S. Williams, she admitted to being a writer dependent upon the 'gentle spur of family discussion' (Smith, *Letters*, vol. II, p. 513); but *Villette*, as Heather Glen points out, 'was conceived and written in unprecedented isolation'.[9] *Villette* marks Charlotte's creative attempt to deal with loss and memory amid the realities of a solitary existence – the last sounding Bell. It is a journey also ventured by her most compelling and autobiographical heroine Lucy Snowe. With the decline and deaths of her siblings, Charlotte suffered a crisis of identity as an author. Struggling to finish the last third of *Shirley* in the aftermath of Emily's death and as Anne's health was failing, Charlotte wrote to

Williams, 'My literary character is effaced for the time ... Should Anne get better, I think I could rally and become Currer Bell once more' (Smith, *Letters*, vol. II, p. 168). Time and again, Charlotte stressed that her authorship was subject to a healthy sibling relationship; without it, Currer Bell's abilities seemed to fail her. She told Williams about her loss of confidence: 'Worse than useless did it seem to attempt to write what there no longer lived an "Ellis Bell" to read' (Smith, *Letters*, vol. II, p. 203).

Even after submitting part of the manuscript of *Villette* to her publishers in 1852, Charlotte admitted to George Smith, 'I have sometimes desponded and almost despaired because there was no one to whom to read a line – or of whom to ask a counsel' (Smith, *Letters*, vol.III, p. 74). Despite the critical success of *Villette*, Charlotte expressed uncertainty over how to begin her next novel without her sisters to consult. She returned to a recurrent theme of both the juvenilia and her early writing experiences: sibling rivalry. Charlotte repeatedly framed rivalries within male sibling partnerships throughout her early writings; indeed, the Angrian plot was driven by the rivalry between Charlotte's Zamorna and Branwell's Northangerland. Her juvenilia contain numerous prototypes of *The Professor*'s industrial tyrant Edward Crimsworth and his younger brother William, who reappear as Edward and William Ellin in fragments written between April and July 1853, before Charlotte's own death in March 1855.

Charlotte Brontë's interest in the dynamics of sibling rivalry lasted her entire writing life. It was a subject she knew well: the pursuit of self-expression within familial bonds had inspired her greatest work and shaped her authorial identity. In her letter to Henry Nussey, she remarked:

[M]y home is humble and unattractive to strangers but to me it contains what I shall find nowhere else in the world – profound, and intense affection which brothers and sisters feel for each other when their minds are cast in the same mould, their ideas drawn from the same source – when they have clung to each other from childhood and when family disputes have never sprung up to divide them. (Smith, *Letters*, vol. I, p. 255)

Despite Charlotte's claim, the creative and emotional intimacy among the Brontë siblings was not always the harmonious union of like minds: throughout their lives, the sisters both supported and challenged one another, allowing each to find a distinct literary voice. For the Brontë sisters, home – and no place like home – offered the liberty to be together and to be themselves, and this meant the freedom to write. Writing in collaboration reinforced the Brontës' sense of family solidarity. It was also the means by which they established, asserted and explored individual differences among siblings cast in the same mould, raised in like circumstances and spaces, placed in similar life experiences as daughters, sisters, governesses and authors, whose devotion to one another was both profound and intense. For many readers, balancing the inevitable influences they had on each other's writings with the uncommon distinctiveness of each is the greatest challenge and highest stimulus in studying the lives and works of the Brontës.

NOTES

1 In her 'Reminiscences', quoted from Smith, *Letters*, vol. i, p. 601.
2 Andrew Elfenbein, *Byron and the Victorians* (Cambridge University Press, 1995), p. 127; Drew Lamonica, *'We are Three Sisters': Self and Family in the Writing of the Brontës* (Columbia: University of Missouri Press, 2003), p. 62. See Elfenbein's chapter 'Byron at the Margins: Emily Brontë and the Fate of Milo', pp. 126–68, and Lamonica's chapter 'The Family Context: Writing as Sibling Relationship', pp. 36–66.
3 'Biographical Notice of Ellis and Acton Bell', repr. in Smith, *Letters*, vol. ii, p. 742.
4 Dudley Green (ed.), *The Letters of the Reverend Patrick Brontë* (Stroud: Nonsuch, 2005), p. 239.
5 The quotation is from Charlotte's 'Biographical Notice'; see Smith, *Letters*, vol. ii, p. 742.
6 *Daily News*, 1 Apr. 1855, quoted in Gaskell, *Life*, p. 247.
7 See Elfenbein, *Byron and the Victorians*, p. 145; Edward Chitham, 'Diverging Twins: Some Clues to *Wildfell Hall*', in Edward Chitham and Tom Winnifrith, *Brontë Facts and Brontë Problems* (Basingstoke: Macmillan, 1983), pp. 91–103; and Elizabeth Langland, *Anne Brontë: The Other One* (Basingstoke: Macmillan, 1989), chapter 2.
8 Derek Roper (ed.), *The Poems of Emily Brontë* (Oxford: Clarendon Press, 1995), pp. 128–9; Edward Chitham (ed.), *The Poems of Anne Brontë: A New Text and Commentary* (London: Macmillan, 1979; repr. 1987), pp. 78–9.
9 In Heather Glen (ed.), *The Cambridge Companion to the Brontës* (Cambridge University Press, 2002), p. 138.

CHAPTER 12

Juvenilia

Christine Alexander

The Brontë juvenilia are famous in English literature for their unique record of the early creative life and writing experience of four talented authors. *Jane Eyre* and *Wuthering Heights* owe much in content and style to the imaginary worlds of Angria and Gondal and to Charlotte's and Emily's apprenticeship in writing during their teenage years of collaboration and constructive rivalry with their siblings. The sisters' growth as writers was visibly fostered by their experimentation with a variety of different genres. The secret world of this early writing, hidden at first from adult eyes by its minuscule script and later locked in private portable writing desks, also reveals uncensored personal and public concerns appropriated and transformed from adult nineteenth-century society.

As children of the parsonage, the young Brontës had little contact with other Haworth village children. The Revd Patrick Brontë explained to Elizabeth Gaskell that '[a]s they had few opportunities of being in learned and polished society, in their retired country situation, they formed a little society amongst themselves' and developed their own childhood games.[1] They acted out little plays of their own based on tales of local legend or fairy stories told by their servant Tabby, on early history and geography books, magazines and newspapers and on Mr Brontë's own enthusiasm for military and literary heroes and for the politics of the time. As soon as they could read, they had free access to their father's bookshelves: crude scribbled sketches of faces and animals adorn the margins of such works as *The Gardens and Menagerie of the Zoological Society Delineated* (1830) and Dryden's translation *The Works of Virgil* (1824). They read *Blackwood's Edinburgh Magazine* and *Fraser's Magazine*, both of which promoted the contemporary fashion for 'hero-worship'. Mr Brontë's passion for literature – for Milton and Bunyan, Wordsworth, Scott and Byron in particular – and his own habit of writing and publishing encouraged his children to emulate his example.

Mr Brontë's gift to Branwell of a box of twelve toy soldiers, on 5 June 1826, was instrumental in initiating the most famous of the children's games: the Young Men's Play that eventually grew into the sagas of Glass Town, Angria and Gondal. Both Charlotte and Branwell recorded the event and the enthusiasm with which they named 'the Twelves', gave them characters and homelands and began to weave the narrative of Glass Town around them.[2] Branwell had had other sets of toy soldiers that had formed the basis of his war games, but with the collaboration of his sisters the soldiers were given both a political and a social context in which they became explorers, conquerors, colonizers and rulers of a federation of lands in West Africa, centred on the magnificent Great Glass Town that had risen magically at the delta of the Niger. The children invented not only public but also private lives for their 'chief men' – the Duke of Wellington (Charlotte), Napoleon, later Sneaky (Branwell), Parry (Emily) and Ross (Anne), the two greatest antagonists of recent history in Europe and two famous Arctic explorers. Influenced by *The Arabian Nights*, the Brontës themselves assumed the roles of 'Chief Genii' (Tallii, Branii, Emmii and Annii) guarding their respective heroes, directing mortal affairs and intervening in the plot for fun, as if they were Greek gods. Branwell invented a language called the 'Young Men tongue' and had a particular penchant for killing off characters, whom his long-suffering sisters had to 'make alive' again in order to preserve the narrative.

Two other related plays were invented in the next two years: 'Our Fellows' Play' (1827), influenced by *Aesop's Fables* and basically a continuation of Branwell's earlier war games, and the Islanders' Play (1827–8), which caught the imaginations of Charlotte and Emily in particular.[3] For the Islanders, the Brontës each had three heroes (Charlotte again chose the Duke of Wellington, together with his two sons Arthur and Charles). British islands were soon replaced by fictitious ones, one with a palace school to educate the nobility and dungeons where Branwell and Emily delighted in punishing miscreant children. The stories jointly composed and acted by the Brontës were allegories of political events, a mixture of the real and the purely fictional. Wellington is the subject of an attempted assassination in one story, and he bravely rescues his kidnapped sons in another. In yet another he becomes the saviour of Ireland, oppressed under the bigotry of the Roman Catholic Church. In Charlotte's 'Tales of the Islanders' we learn how the Brontë family excitedly received the news of the passing of the Catholic Emancipation Bill, and we see Charlotte's comic version of Wellington (now Prime Minister of Britain) in conference with his cabinet at 10 Downing Street, London.

This intermixing of actual events, people and places with the fictitious world of the Islanders became habitual in the children's play and was continued in their writing. The islands, rebellions of rival aristocratic pupils, dungeons and even the moorland scenery in the Islanders' Play all became part of the Gondal saga, which Emily and Anne established in about 1831.

By 1829 Charlotte and Branwell, rival leaders of the early plays, had begun to chronicle their histories on scraps of paper and in tiny hand-made booklets; and by 1830 events and characters from the Young Men's Play and the Islanders' Play had merged into what we now refer to as the Glass Town and Angrian saga. The central story, like that of Gondal, is the struggle for power by rival aristocratic characters whose tangled love affairs and political intrigues affect many 'High Life' and 'low life' inhabitants of their respective countries. The four kings of the Glass Town Federation form alliances that reflect the Brontës' own relationships: Wellington and Sneaky (Charlotte and Branwell) together with their sons represent one faction and Parry and Ross (Emily and Anne) with their family and entourage form another. The situation is quickly complicated by Branwell's introduction of a new hero, Alexander Percy ('Rogue', later Lord Ellrington and Duke of Northangerland), and by Charlotte's narrative preference for Wellington's two sons as more flexible characters to explore: her favourite hero Arthur Wellesley, Marquis of Douro and later Duke of Zamorna and King of Angria, and Charles Wellesley (later Charles Townshend), her chief narrator and pseudonym. The love-hate relationship between Percy and Zamorna (again reflecting the creative relationship between brother and sister) provides the motivation for most of the political, social and cultural life of the saga.

Throughout the saga, wars and political upheavals are chronicled in obsessive detail by Branwell and form the background to many of Charlotte's stories which focus on the entangled love affairs of Zamorna and Percy and their many wives and mistresses. The cynical Lord Charles records Zamorna's marriages (to Helen Gordon, Marian Hume and Mary Percy), his mistresses (chiefly Mina Laury, Sofala, Rosamond Wellesley and Caroline Vernon), his children (who are destined to repeat their father's disastrous relationships) and his friends, artists, writers and political associates. Percy has an equally colourful coterie, ranging from former pirates, cattle thieves and revolutionaries (for example Naughty, Caversham, Simpson and O'Connor) to French noblemen (like Montmorency) and the Ashantee leader Quashia. He develops from the early pirate and republican revolutionary 'Rogue' into a cynical aristocrat on his marriage to Zenobia Ellrington; and as Northangerland, he evolves into the sinister Gothic villain-hero of Romantic literature, Branwell's alter ego. His unnatural hatred for his sons Edward and William Percy begins a theme of antagonism between two brothers that was later to appear in Charlotte's *The Professor*.[4]

Events centre first on the Glass Town Federation and its principal city Verdopolis (formerly the Great Glass Town) and then move to Angria, a new kingdom in the east, created in 1834 to reward Zamorna for protecting the Federation from encroaching Ashantee tribes and their French and Arab allies. Zamorna, as King of Angria, appoints Northangerland (now his father-in-law) as Prime Minister, but Northangerland remains in league with his old republican associates and leads a rebellion against Zamorna. Mary Henrietta, Northangerland's beloved daughter and Zamorna's wife, becomes a pawn in their complex and unresolved power struggle.

The gradually evolving plot is documented in numerous poems, articles, histories, dramas, speeches, short stories and novelettes, ostensibly by a variety of Glass Town writers for a fictitious audience. Charlotte and Branwell adopted several pseudonyms, depending on the genre. With characteristic undisciplined exuberance, Branwell wrote prodigiously first as 'Young Soult the Rhymer' or the historians Captain Sir John Flower (Viscount Richton) and Captain John Bud; then as the wayward Angrian writers Henry Hastings and Charles Wentworth; and later as Northangerland, whose career he traced relentlessly first in novelettes like 'The Pirate' and 'The Politics of Verdopolis' and then in a series of unstructured chronicles. Charlotte at first moved her ideal hero (the early Arthur Wellesley, Marquis of Douro) closer to Northangerland's ruthlessness, indulging in the new Byronic personality she created for him as Zamorna (the change in name reflecting his modified persona) in long romances like 'High Life in Verdopolis' and 'The Spell', which are nevertheless undercut by her scandal-loving ironic narrator Lord Charles Wellesley. Passion for her hero and his Angrian world sustained her during her lonely years as a teacher, but it also became an obsession at this time; the 'Roe Head Journal' records her feelings of guilt about her 'infernal world', and the novelette 'Mina Laury' explores the all-consuming self-abnegating love in which the later Jane Eyre refuses to indulge. Elizabeth Hastings, 'the little dignified governess', 'dependent on nobody' yet 'burning for warmer, closer attachment',[5] proudly denies William Percy's seductive overtures, heralding her author's efforts to retreat from Angrian romance. Although in Charlotte's last novelette, 'Caroline Vernon', the heroine is again a victim of romance, the emphasis is on Caroline's vulnerability, her limited situation and frustrated personality; and the cynical narrator Charles Townshend reduces the would-be Gothic seducer Zamorna to an absurd and ageing 'tom-cat'.

From the beginning, the Glass Town and Angrian saga was dominated by Charlotte's and Branwell's heroes; the imaginary kingdoms of the younger siblings are portrayed by Charlotte and Branwell as old-fashioned, parochial (Yorkshire in character rather than Oriental or African) and mundane. Emily and Anne, who contributed to the plays but may not have written about them at this stage, gradually lost interest. When Charlotte left for school at Roe Head in 1831, they broke from Branwell's dominance and began inventing the play that would nourish their relationship as 'twins' and provide Emily with an imaginative world that would sustain her creativity for the rest of her life.

There are no surviving prose manuscripts by Emily or Anne relating to any of the sagas. Information about Gondal remains confused and uncertain, although a number of critics have attempted to reconstruct the plot, chiefly to show that Gondal represents *Wuthering Heights* in the making.[6] But all that survive of the Gondal juvenilia are Emily and Anne's poems, narrated by imaginary characters to express moments of crisis or deep feeling. They function like Wordsworth's 'spots of time', recording particular lyrical episodes rather than providing insights into the events of the Gondal saga. There are a few fragmentary lists of characters and places in old geography books, and Emily and Anne's diary papers provide tantalizing references that indicate the extent to which the imaginative world of Gondal formed an integral part of the sisters' everyday existence. They also show that the early Glass Town methods of acting out events and of writing episodes in random order are particular features of Gondal.

The poems focus on the violent passions of the strong-willed heroine Augusta Geraldine Almeda (A. G. A.) and on the power struggles of Julius Brenzaida, who at one time was either her husband or her lover. As in the Glass Town and Angrian saga, these two central characters are surrounded by friends, lovers and enemies, but their relationships are uncertain. The action moves between the North Pacific island of Gondal, divided into four kingdoms ruled by rival families, and Gaaldine, a newly dis-covered island in the south. Savage passion, imprisonment, murder and internecine warfare characterize the saga. A. G. A., the subject and speaker of many of Emily's poems, becomes Queen of Gondal, but is murdered during a bloody civil war between royalists and republicans. Julius Bren-zaida, equally ambitious and ruthless, is made emperor, but soon assassinated. Recurring themes and images of isolation, exile, confinement and death prefigure those of *Wuthering Heights*.

The juvenilia testify to the extraordinary literary ambitions of the Brontës. From the time they were able to read and write, they modelled themselves on the male writers they found in the pages of *Blackwood's Edinburgh Magazine* and imitated the format and style of its pages. They played at print culture, writing their own monthly magazine in 1829–30. The transformation of its title from 'Branwell's Blackwood's Magazine' to 'Blackwood's Young Men's Magazine' and then simply 'The Young Men's Magazine' indicates not only the passing of the role of editor from Branwell to Charlotte but also the gradual take-over of the real adult model into the imaginary reality of Glass Town with its fictitious contributors and audience (see Figure 10). The little hand-made magazines and newspapers with their tiny script that imitated print were originally intended to correspond to the size of the twelve-inch toy soldiers, but they soon increased in size (although the minuscule print

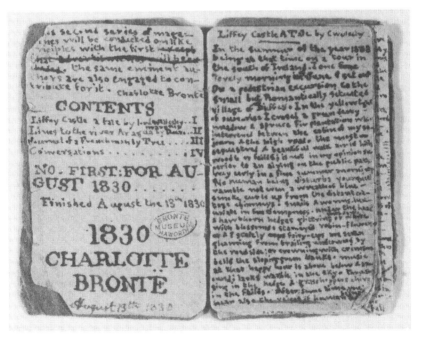

10 'The Young Men's Magazine', August 1830, by Charlotte Brontë, one of the early 'little books' made by the Brontës as children

remained a distinguishing feature, allowing the authors to squeeze hundreds of words onto a single page) and took on a life of their own.

The ability to adopt different roles in their plays and to write from the viewpoints of a variety of characters gave the teenage Brontës a surprisingly sophisticated notion of the power of fiction. As fictitious authors, they could create and recreate the same events; as editors, they had the power to censor or deny versions of 'truth'; as the omniscient 'Chief Genii' (or 'Little King and Queens' in the Islanders), they could comically invent a further dimension of control over editors and authors; and as inventors of the whole saga, they relished the ironic possibilities that their multiple layers of reality created. Charlotte (as Lord Charles) satirized Branwell's pomposity as the poet Young Soult and ridiculed his often excessive enthusiasm for music or boxing through her depiction of his character Patrick Benjamin Wiggins, while at the same time mocking herself and her sisters from her brother's supposedly superior point of view.[7] Through the eavesdropping Lord Charles, Charlotte could gratify her penchant for scandal and the romance of 'High Life' while laughing at her own indulgence; her detached narrator punctures her romantic bubbles and provides her with the ironic distance needed to explore the motivations of her characters. Yet she was not unaware of the limits of her identity as author: she was after all a child writer whose voice is confined, like that of Lord Charles, to an imaginative world. Although she occasionally glimpsed the powerlessness of her situation,[8] she continued to relish her ambivalent relationship with her narrator and to practise the sophisticated cat-and-mouse games she would later play with her readers in *Villette*. Branwell, however, became lost in the labyrinth of Glass Town and Angria; he increasingly identified with the dissolute but powerful Northangerland, refusing or unable to confront reality. The early image he cultivated as a man of letters (as the historians Flower and Bud) gave way to an undiscriminating narrator (Hastings or Wentworth) of formless narratives and long poems that trace Branwell's own decline through the deteriorating fortunes of his alter ego. For both brother and sister, the sheer sense of fun and excitement evident in their earlier manuscripts is replaced in their later juvenilia by an absorbed exploration of personal concerns and the search for a mature authorial identity.

Charlotte referred to the vast literary enterprise that was Glass Town, Angria and Gondal as 'scribblemania'. When she was twenty-four, her own manuscripts alone exceeded in volume all her later published novels. Although, in March 1837, she found herself unable to heed Robert Southey's warning against indulging in daydreams (Smith, *Letters*, vol. I, p. 166), she was growing increasingly dissatisfied with what she now saw as Angria's lurid exoticism. In late 1839 she wrote a fragmentary manuscript that can be read as her 'Farewell to Angria': 'I long to quit for a while that burning clime where we have sojourned too long . . . & turn now to a cooler region.' Her subsequent manuscripts show an increased effort to adapt her creative visions to reality: her goal was now the 'grey and sober' scene of *The Professor*. But as *Jane Eyre* attests, Charlotte's Angrian world provided a rich apprenticeship for the writing of her greatest novel.

Both Emily and Anne continued to exploit their Gondal world into adulthood, although Anne was never as committed as Emily to their intensely emotional and violent creation. Her Gondal compositions were written almost entirely at home, while under Emily's influence. As Emily gradually withdrew into her private sphere, Anne's own interests asserted themselves, shifting away from the shared fiction with Emily. For Emily, Gondal provided a creative frame within which she could explore her personal concerns; it could never be abandoned. Gondal was an essential part of the 'intentional dreaming' that encompassed both her Gondal and her personal poetry, and provided a creative context for *Wuthering Heights*.[9] As late as May 1848, seven months before her death, Emily was working on a Gondal civil-war poem: even after the publication of *Wuthering Heights*, her creative life continued to be nourished by her early fantasy world and by the habit of making literature.

NOTES

1 C. W. Hatfield and Mrs C. M. Edgerley (eds.), 'The Reverend Patrick Brontë and Mrs. E. C. Gaskell', *BST*, 8.43 (1933), 92.

2 In Charlotte's 'The History of the Year' (1829) and 'The Twelve Adventurers', later retold by Branwell in 'The History of the Young Men'.

3 Detailed descriptions can be found in Christine Alexander, *The Early Writings of Charlotte Brontë* (Oxford: Blackwell, 1983), pp. 27–52.

4 See 'Two Rival Brothers', *ibid.*, pp. 219–33.

5 'Henry Hastings', in Heather Glen (ed.), *Charlotte Brontë: Tales of Angria* (London: Penguin, 2006), pp. 287–8.

6 For a summary of Gondal reconstructions see Christine Alexander and Margaret Smith (eds.), *The Oxford Companion to the Brontës* (Oxford University Press, 2003), pp. 218–19. See also Janet Gezari (ed.), *Emily Jane Brontë: The Complete Poems* (Harmondsworth: Penguin, 1992), pp. xxix–xxxii.

7 'My Angria and the Angrians', in Christine Alexander (ed.), *An Edition of the Early Writings of Charlotte Brontë*, vol. II (Oxford: Blackwell, for the Shakespeare Head Press, 1991), part 2, p. 250.

8 See, for example, 'Strange Events' in the 'Young Men's Magazine' and the 'Roe Head Journal'. Heather Glen expertly explores this issue in 'Configuring a World: Some Childhood Writings of Charlotte Brontë', in Mary Hilton, Morag Styles and Victor Watson (eds.), *Opening the Nursery Door: Reading, Writing and Childhood 1600–1900* (London and New York: Routledge, 1997), pp. 229–31.

9 Janet Gezari, *Last Things: Emily Brontë's Poems* (Oxford University Press, 2007), p. 7.

CHAPTER 13

The Brussels experience

Sue Lonoff

The Brontë sisters are so closely associated with Haworth and the moors that a wider European connection seems implausible for many readers. But in fact, Charlotte and Emily both crossed the Channel in 1842 to study at a boarding school or *pensionnat* in Brussels, and Charlotte returned there in 1843 to become a teacher and a pupil. While this experience seems not to have influenced Emily's future writing, it would prove crucial to two of Charlotte's novels and significant to all four. The *pensionnat* would also be the setting for the great emotional drama of her life.

Charlotte's fascination with French language and culture incited this adventure. At fourteen, she had translated part of an epic poem by Voltaire; at fifteen, she won the French prize at the Misses Wooler's school; and at sixteen, she wrote a letter in often faulty French to Ellen Nussey. French scenes and characters pervade her early fiction, and Paris was for her the epitome of glamour, with a knowledge of its language in itself a sign of the speaker's sophistication. More practically, French was the first foreign language that young English ladies were expected to learn. If she and her sisters were to open a school – as all three hoped to do in the early 1840s – they would need to increase their proficiency.

This was the rationale behind the appeal that Charlotte made to her Aunt Branwell when, on 29 September 1841, she wrote to ask for a loan that would enable her and Emily to study abroad for half a year. She did not dare to try for Paris, which would have been expensive and too sinful for her father. Instead, she proposed going 'to Brussels, in Belgium', where she could perfect her French and 'even get a dash of German'. Friends then resident in Brussels could help her find 'a cheap and decent' school with 'respectable protection'; once there, she could make 'connections far more improving, polished, and cultivated, than any [she] had yet known' (Smith, *Letters*, vol. 1, p. 268). These were the motives calculated to convince her aunt; but to Ellen, she wrote of 'such a strong wish for wings ... such an urgent thirst to see – to know – to learn' and to escape from the routines that were stifling her (Smith, *Letters*, vol. 1, p. 266). Happily, Aunt Branwell consented, so Charlotte started looking for a school. In late January 1842, one Mrs Jenkins, the wife of the British chaplain in Brussels, put her in touch with the directress of the Pensionnat Heger. Terms were soon settled, and so on 8 February, Charlotte set out with Emily and her father. They spent three days in London, which the sisters saw for the first time. Then they took a packet boat to Ostend and made their way to Brussels, arriving at 32 rue d'Isabelle on the morning of 15 February (see Figure 11).

The school in which they would remain for nearly nine months was run by an exceptional couple. Claire Zoë Parent had founded it in 1830, in a building with a garden that Charlotte would celebrate in both *The Professor* and *Villette*. Four years later, Mlle Parent met Constantin Georges Romain Heger, a teacher at Brussels' leading school for boys. His ability was so apparent that she soon asked him to teach for her too. They married in 1836. By the time the Brontës arrived, they had three daughters; their first son would be born six weeks later.

11 A view of the rue d'Isabelle, Brussels, showing the Pensionnat Heger on the left

The fact that a growing family lived on the premises added one more contrast to the schools that the Brontës had attended in Yorkshire. With eighty to one hundred boarding and day students, it was certainly larger. The 'faculty' consisted of three full-time teachers and seven 'Masters' who taught subjects like music and drawing. An additional staff of full- and part-time workers tended to the school, the household and the garden. Madame Heger ran this considerable enterprise, and she was the one in charge of discipline. Her husband was its professor of literature and rhetoric, as well as her ally and consultant, especially in matters pertaining to teaching. At thirty-two, he was five years younger than his wife and only seven years older than Charlotte. A charismatic teacher with a fiery temper and a fervour for his *métier*, he was to become the dominant force in the sisters' education abroad.

As Elizabeth Gaskell explains, Heger first observed these new English pupils closely. At nearly twenty-six and twenty-three, Charlotte and Emily were not only much older than the other pupils but worlds apart in background and outlook. They were staunch Protestants in a Catholic school whose curriculum was, as the school prospectus announced, 'basé sur la Religion'.[1] Preternaturally shy, they clung to each other and avoided the others. But they were also exceptionally gifted and determined to learn. Heger therefore proposed to teach them by a method he sometimes used with advanced French and Belgian pupils. Instead of drilling them in grammar and vocabulary, he would read them extracts from works by major French writers and then analyse those excerpts, pointing out their strengths and weaknesses. After that, the sisters were to compose an essay (*devoir*) that would imitate the extract, but choosing their own subjects and expressing their own thoughts. Imitation was anathema to Emily, who told him that they would 'lose all originality of thought and expression' if they consented. Charlotte too objected at the outset, but because he was her teacher, she obeyed (Gaskell, *Life*, p. 178).

Whatever their opinion of Heger's assignments, both sisters submitted essays to him, Emily probably gritting her teeth and Charlotte with increasing dedication. Twenty of hers and nine of Emily's have survived, and although it is not always possible to identify the assignments that prompted them, most were composed as exercises that respond to a teacher's instructions. Only a few of those essays, however, explicitly imitate his models. Several others appear to be reflections based on passages and poems that he dictated. Sometimes he would give them the outline for an essay and ask them to flesh it out. At other times he would ask them to compose a letter or, in one case, an invitation. Gaskell says that as the sisters progressed, he asked them to synthesize contrasting versions of the same subject or event. As Charlotte's command of French increased, she would write longer, more elaborate essays on classical, historical and biblical subjects. But these date from her second year at the *pensionnat*, after Emily had returned to Haworth.

Emily's months on the Continent cruelly tested her powers of endurance. Never happy away from the moors and the parsonage, she underwent an ordeal that could only have been aggravated by her scanty knowledge of French. For while Charlotte had arrived with a grounding in the language, as well as a passion for proficiency in it, Emily's only French had been self-taught. And yet, a little more than three months after her arrival, she wrote 'The Cat' ('Le Chat'), an indisputably original essay with only minor errors in grammar:

'But,' says some delicate lady, who has murdered a half-dozen lapdogs through pure affection, 'the cat is such a cruel beast, he is not content to kill his prey, he torments it before its death; you cannot make that accusation against us.' More or less, Madame ... You yourself avoid a bloody spectacle because it wounds your weak nerves. But I have seen you embrace your child in transports, when he came to show you a beautiful butterfly crushed between his cruel little fingers; and at that moment, I really wanted to have a cat, with the tail of a half-devoured rat hanging from its mouth, to present as the image, the true copy, of your angel.[2]

'The Butterfly' ('Le Papillon'), another of Emily's Belgian essays, has also been widely discussed and reproduced as an example of her unique vision. Emily may not have liked Heger, whose methods were directive and, for her, overbearing. But he recognized her exceptional gifts – her 'powerful reason', 'strong, imperious will' and 'faculty of imagination' (Gaskell, *Life*, p. 177) – and his assignments compelled her to display them. During those months, she studied German, the piano and drawing as well as French. At home, she had been the family's most accomplished pianist; here too her talent was recognized, so that by late summer she was giving lessons to the daughters of a recently arrived English family. Charlotte was also recruited as a teacher – in her case of English. Although the sisters were not paid for this work, it offset the costs of the additional lessons that they themselves were taking.

Madame Heger ran her school with a careful attention to economy, but she did not stint on measures that would keep the 'young ladies' healthy and well fed. If the descriptions of pastries and coffee in *Villette* may be taken as reminiscences of the fare offered by Madame, Charlotte rated the *pensionnat* highly where food was concerned. The students were each assigned to one of three classes, depending on age and level of achievement, and sat at their desks for three hours in the morning and two in the afternoon. Ample time was allocated for meals, recreation, sewing and study. When the weather permitted, they exercised in the large garden; Charlotte must often have walked beneath the trees that Lucy Snowe describes in *Villette*. They were also taken on walks in the country, sometimes bearing sketch-pads so that they could draw from nature. Emily and Charlotte both returned to Haworth with sketches from this period. All the boarders slept in a dormitory; but because the Brontë sisters were so much older than the others, they were given beds and washstands curtained off at the end of the long room. They resisted the breaks built into the schedule, preferring to spend their spare time studying. Nonetheless, these living conditions kept them well and facilitated progress.

Charlotte's progress in French was further stimulated by her growing admiration for Heger. The man whom she initially described to Ellen Nussey as 'a little, black, ugly being' (Smith, *Letters*, vol. 1, p. 284) would become the professor whose approval she craved and then the nucleus of her emotional life – in Brussels and, for painful years, in Haworth. By all estimates but Emily's, Heger was a teacher so intellectually magnetic that he could make his pupils share his literary passions as well as his insights. In the classroom, he could fly into a tantrum and, after bringing many pupils to tears, not only console but enrapture them with his readings and interpretations. The texts that he selected ranged from the classics to the latest works of the French Romantics (so long as they were not too racy for young feminine ears). Charlotte had never before encountered a professor with his breadth of learning or a teacher so committed to literature. She saw him in the few private lessons that he gave the sisters, heard him in the classroom and occasional evening lectures, read his often copious comments on her essays and, unsurprisingly, crossed the boundary from esteem to one-sided love.

Her approval was not unqualified. As Gaskell says, both Charlotte and Emily 'were Protestant to the backbone' (*Life*, p. 185). Never having been in a Catholic country before, much less in a school suffused with that religion, Charlotte expressed her disdain in letters home, and her resistance in several of her essays. For example, when Heger asked her to imitate a passage about a martyr named Eudorus, she responded with an essay about Anne Askew, a Protestant tortured to death in Tudor England for refusing to convert to Catholicism. In this respect, both Hegers were more tolerant than she was. Madame Heger exempted the sisters from the mandatory daily Mass, and Heger never criticized attacks in her essays that were patently against his own faith. His critiques focused on word choice, the effects she was creating and especially method. Charlotte had grown up with the Romantic belief that masterpieces were born of genius under the sway of inspiration. Heger insisted that even the greatest raw talent required training and study. Charlotte laboured to please him and follow his precepts, borrowing his books to study further. And yet, perhaps ironically, none of her Belgian essays are as gripping as Emily's. Still, Heger's lessons about craftsmanship and style would influence the work of her maturity.

The school term ended on 15 August 1842 and was followed by the long vacation. The Brontës could not afford to go back to Haworth, but they spent this period productively. Charlotte's friend Mary Taylor had preceded her to Brussels and remained nearby, with members of her family. While continuing to study, the sisters had more time to investigate the city. It was probably during this period that Charlotte saw the art exhibition that figures in the famous 'Cleopatra' chapter of *Villette*.

By the time classes resumed, the Brontë sisters had received permission to complete a year abroad. But the sudden death of Aunt Branwell on 29 October forced them to cancel their plans. On 6 November they departed from Antwerp, arriving in Haworth two days later. Emily would never leave home again. But Charlotte yearned to return to the *pensionnat*, and in this desire she was aided by the man who had unwittingly inspired her yearning. Heger had given her a letter for her father, in which he lavishly praised the sisters' progress and suggested that another year of study would make them even better qualified to teach. He added an offer of employment that Charlotte happily accepted. And so at the end of January 1843, she again set off for the school, where she would become Mademoiselle Charlotte and teach English to the first class.

For the first few months, all seemed to go well despite Emily's absence. Charlotte wrote to Ellen Nussey that Madame Heger had welcomed her 'with great kindness' (Smith, *Letters*, vol. 1, p. 308); she was taking German lessons; and in addition to her regular teaching, she was giving a weekly lesson in English to Heger and his brother-in-law. But by March she was starting to complain of loneliness, and by late June she reported to Ellen that reserve had replaced Madame's kindness. While this transformation baffled her, the reason is not hard to reconstruct: Charlotte's devotion to the man she would later call 'the only master that I have ever had' was becoming all too apparent.[3] Zoë Parent-Heger did not worry about her husband straying; indeed, he had failed to notice the nature of this adult pupil's attachment. But if other eyes saw what hers had perceived, gossip could create a scandal that would threaten her school and their livelihood. Confrontation had never been her method, and a scene would only have intensified the trouble, so instead she quietly kept watch over Charlotte and managed her husband's agenda so that he and Charlotte had limited contact. The English lessons stopped. Heger continued to lend Charlotte books, but they rarely conversed. She was left with the loneliness that her disdain for the other teachers and pupils had fostered.

As the summer approached, her letters grew increasingly bitter. Heger, she wrote to Branwell on 1 May 1843, was the only 'black Swan' in a household where everyone else was dense and false. Although her hatred of his wife was still nascent, she accused Madame of being 'always cool & always reasoning' (Smith, *Letters*, vol. 1, p. 317). Correspondingly, in her essay 'The Death of Napoleon' ('La Mort de Napoléon'), she attacked 'Mediocrity' ('La Médiocrité') for being too cold and limited to comprehend Genius.[4] By now, the essays she submitted to Heger had become her main means of gaining his attention and approval. He would give a copy of this one to Gaskell after Charlotte's death, but he eliminated this passage and made other massive revisions.

By late June, Charlotte was depressed and ailing. Her claim that Madame paid her no attention may well have been accurate: confronted with a teacher so potentially disruptive, the directress may have hoped that isolation would persuade her to leave. Charlotte thought about returning to Haworth; she wrote to Ellen that she dreaded the coming long vacation, when she would be left in the deserted building. Nevertheless, she remained. On 1 September, on the brink of a breakdown, this daughter of an Anglican clergyman entered the Cathedral of Ste Gudule and confessed to a Catholic priest. She would draw on that episode ten years later with Lucy Snowe's confession to Père Silas.

Classes resumed, and as the autumn wore on Charlotte's disillusion deepened. In October, she tried to resign. Madame Heger promptly accepted, but when Heger told her to remain, she stayed on. Finally, in mid December, Charlotte brought herself to leave. On Christmas Day, she dined with the couple who had recommended the *pensionnat* to her. On New Year's Day, Madame Heger accompanied her to Ostend. Before she departed, Heger gave her a poetry anthology and a diploma attesting to her qualifications in French. The sisters would never open the school that had provided the rationale for her Brussels experience, but Charlotte would strive to keep up her French and included it in all four of her adult novels whenever she could.

After returning to Haworth, she wrote Heger four letters. Apparently he answered the first, but the unrestrained expression of her feelings in the others dissuaded him from writing again. Madame Heger nonetheless preserved those letters, probably as a potential defence against claims that her husband had incited this response. Charlotte underwent two years of torment before her one-sided passion receded. But its residues, and all of her Brussels experiences, became reconstructed in her fiction. Readers of *Villette* who had met Heger recognized him instantly as Paul Emanuel, the professor who loves Lucy Snowe. However, they disclaimed any resemblance between Madame Heger and Charlotte's two schemers, Zoraïde Reuter of *The Professor* and Simone Beck of *Villette*.

NOTES

1 The prospectus is reprinted in Smith, *Letters*, vol. 1, p. 287; Smith translates the French expression as 'founded on religious principles' (p. 288).

2 Sue Lonoff (ed. and trans.), *Charlotte Brontë and Emily Brontë, the Belgian Essays: A Critical Edition* (New Haven: Yale University Press, 1996), pp. 56–8. The French original reads: '"Mais", dit quelque dame délicate, qui a meurtri une demi-douzaine de bichons par pure affection, "le chat est une bête si cruelle; il ne se contente pas de tuer sa proie, il la tourmente avant sa mort; vous ne pouvez faire cette accusation contre nous." A peu près Madame ... Vous évitez vous-même un spectacle sanglant, parce qu'il blesse vos faibles nerfs; mais j'ai vous vue embrasser avec transport votre enfant, quand il venait vous montrer un beau papillon écrasé entre ses cruels petit doigts; et, à ce moment, j'ai voulu bien avoir un chat, avec la queue d'un rat demi-englouti, pendant de sa bouche, à présenter comme l'image, la vraie copie, de votre ange' (pp. 57–9).

3 In a letter to Heger himself, written on 24 July 1844, she referred to him as '[le] seul maître que j'ai jamais eu'; see Smith, *Letters*, vol. 1, p. 356; Smith's translation is found on p. 358.

4 Lonoff, *The Belgian Essays*, pp. 284–5.

CHAPTER 14

The Brontë correspondence

Margaret Smith

The postal system for letters in England before 1840 was fairly efficient, but it was complicated by the hierarchy of main roads, cross-posts, and 'bye-posts'. After 1784 letters could be conveyed by mail-coach along a network of main post-roads, and delivered to post offices in large towns. From these, local 'penny posts' might be operated, in addition to the cost per mile on the main roads. Thus, Mr Brontë's letter to Mrs Franks of Huddersfield went by a cheap local penny post on 29 April 1831, as did Charlotte's letter to Ellen Nussey on 13 January 1832. Timing was unreliable, and the cost was complicated by the existence of bye-posts, short roads connecting places to a main post road. In a letter from Mr Brontë to Mrs Franks of Huddersfield, dated 13 June 1836, he expressed his fear that the letter he had written to his daughters Charlotte and Anne, who were at Roe Head School (about twenty miles from Haworth), might not reach them in due time 'owing to a bye-post'. Fortunately, it did reach them.

Another difference from the reformed system introduced in 1840 was that the postage fee had to be paid by the receiver of the letter. Charlotte began her letter to Ellen Nussey of 4 July 1834 with an apology: 'You will be tired of paying the postage of my letters but necessity must plead my excuse for their frequent recurrence' (Smith, *Letters*, vol. I, p. 129). The lowest postal rate for a single-sheet letter was fourpence for up to fifteen miles, rising to one shilling for a distance of up to 300 miles. Two sheets cost twice as much as a single sheet, the resulting 'heavy letter' being charged by the quarter ounce. In order to reduce the recipient's expense, the first page of a letter could be written normally, then turned through 90 degrees so that the rest of the message could be written across the same page. Charlotte could manage this technique quite skilfully, taking care as far as possible that the original horizontal lines remained legible. But she was aware of the difficulties. Her long, lively, crossed letter to Ellen of 4 July 1834, with its affectionate teasing and its long list of books recommended for Ellen to read, ends, 'If you can read this scrawl it will be to the credit of your patience' (Smith, *Letters*, vol. I, p. 131).

In 1837, Rowland Hill (1795–1879) initiated a major change in the postal system when his pamphlet *Post Office Reform* was published. He proposed that there should be a uniform rate of postage regardless of distance throughout England, and his schemes were put into effect in 1840. The cost of posting a letter was to be paid by the sender, who would affix a prepaid postage stamp either to the address panel on the folded letter, which was sealed with a wafer, or to an envelope. Most of Charlotte Brontë's letters written before and in 1840, and some written after that year, were sent folded and sealed, with the recipient's address on the outer fold. Printed or adhesive penny stamps were available from 6 May 1840, and after this date letters could be enclosed in envelopes. The new system was very efficient: Charlotte's corrected proofs were usually received by her publishers in London on the day after she had posted them. Letters to and from the European Continent, carried by packet boats, were costly;

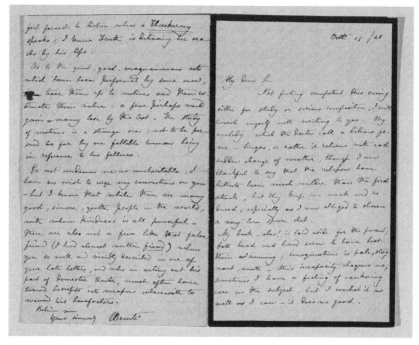

12 A letter by Charlotte Brontë to W. S. Williams, her publisher's reader,
dated 18 October 1848

and when Charlotte and Emily were in Brussels in 1842–3 they sent home packets of letters by travelling friends for distribution in England.

But Charlotte received and replied to letters from even further afield. In early November 1851 she sent to Ellen Nussey a letter she had received from James Taylor (?1817–1874), a Scotsman employed by the publishers Smith, Elder & Co., who had sent Taylor to India to foster their trading interests there. On 15 November she wrote to him, assuring him that both his letters had reached her safely, 'the note of the 17th. Septbr. and the letter of the 2nd. Octbr' (Smith, *Letters*, vol. II, p.716). She sympathized with his complaints about the lack of intellectual attraction in Bombay society, and (perhaps not very tactfully) gave him a list of her own experiences in summer: she had been to London, heard Thackeray's lectures, seen 'Rachel' acting, heard D'Aubigné's, Melville's and Maurice's preaching, and visited the Crystal Palace. By 1851 the postal service to India was efficiently run. For many years the route had been via a six-month voyage round the Cape of Good Hope, but now steamships could take the mail to Alexandria, from where it would be carried overland to Suez and transferred to a steamship to complete the journey to Bombay.

One of Charlotte's best friends, Mary Taylor, had emigrated to New Zealand, arriving in Wellington on 24 July 1845 and finally returning to Yorkshire in 1860. A letter from Mary to Charlotte, dated June–July 1848, described her difficulties in despatching her letters to Britain:

I looked for a ship to carry a letter to you. There was a little thing with one mast, & also HMS <u>Fly</u> & nothing else. If a cattle vessel came from Sydney she would probably return in a few days & would take a mail, but we have had east wind for a month & nothing can come in ... 'July 1' The Harlequin has just come from Otago & is to sail for Singapore <u>when the wind changes</u> & by that route ... I send you this. (Smith, *Letters*, vol. II, p. 87; underlining in the letter)

Unfortunately Mary destroyed all except one of Charlotte's letters to her; but that one, written on 4 September 1848, is a graphic account of Charlotte's impetuous visit to London with her sister Anne to prove their separate identities to their publishers (Smith, *Letters*, vol. II, pp. 111–15).

All the members of the Brontë family of Haworth were highly literate. Mr Brontë valued literacy all the more because he had worked hard to gain it: over 200 letters by him survive. His earliest known letter was written on 4 July 1806, the year when he graduated from St John's College, Cambridge, offering himself as a candidate for holy orders. His formal correspondence with clerics on church matters and with newspaper editors on topics of public concern is courteous, earnest and

practical. Such formal letters outnumber those on more personal and
intimate family matters; but he writes movingly about his family trage-
dies. There is a touching mixture of pride and sorrow in his words when
he writes to inform Mrs Gaskell of his daughters' achievements, and in
his simply stated relief in a letter of February 1855 to Sir James Kay-
Shuttleworth that his own poor sight 'has been gradually improving', so
that 'under Providence . . . it may suffice for my wants.'[1]

In a letter to Ellen Nussey of February 1850, Charlotte Brontë described
the moving experience of reading her mother's letters:

Papa put into my hands a little packet of letters and papers – telling me that they
were Mamma's and that I might read them – . . . it was strange to peruse now for
the first time the records of a mind whence my own sprang – and most strange –
and at once sad and sweet to find that mind of a truly fine, pure and elevated
order. They were written to papa before they were married – there is a rectitude,
a refinement, a constancy, a modesty, a sense – a gentleness about them indescribable. (Smith, *Letters*, vol. II, p. 347)

When Clement Shorter won Mr Nicholls' trust in 1895, he was given this
'little packet', and he hoped there would be 'no breach of confidence' in
publishing such private letters – one of them addressed to 'My dear saucy
Pat' – in his *Charlotte Brontë and her Circle* of 1896.

The most prolific letter-writer in the family was Charlotte. About 950
of her letters have been found, most of them in the original manuscripts,
some in transcripts made by Ellen Nussey, and others in faded photo-
copies of manuscripts in the collection made by William Law of
Honresfeld in the late nineteenth century. Very few letters from Anne
and Emily Brontë survive. Our understanding of both sisters has to be
derived more from Charlotte's references to them and from their novels
than from their own letters. Forty-two letters from Branwell Brontë are
known. They make sad reading, including as they do his ambitious early
letters to the editor of the prestigious *Blackwood's Magazine*. They provide
the evidence for his later pitiable trajectory through his work as a railway
clerk, his dismissal for negligence and finally his craving for drink after
his dismissal from his tutorship at Thorp Green.

Ellen Nussey's long friendship with Charlotte Brontë, and her indignant
reaction to a misleading article published in *Sharpe's London Magazine*
for June 1855, made her wish to have a true account of Charlotte's life.
The magazine had emphasized the 'improper' elements in *Jane Eyre*, such
as Rochester's 'real wicked oaths', and had recalled the influential
Quarterly Magazine's decision that the novel was written by a man who

had masculine ideas about women's clothes. Ellen considered that a biography by Mrs Gaskell would provide a 'just and honourable defence' of Charlotte. At first Mr Brontë had merely laughed at the *Sharpe's* article, but he soon changed his mind. Mrs Gaskell had written to him, expressing warm sympathy, after Charlotte's death, and he asked her to write a biography. She realized that for a just and accurate account she would need to see as many as possible of Charlotte's letters. Arthur Nicholls, Charlotte's husband, found and sent about a dozen letters chiefly addressed to Emily, with the occasional letter to her father and brother and one to Aunt Branwell.[2] Few more letters from Charlotte to family members have survived. We have altogether fifteen letters to her father and three empty envelopes addressed to him, eight letters to Emily, and a single brief note to Anne, included in one of two letters addressed to Branwell. Three letters from Emily and five from Anne have been found.

The dearth of letters from Emily is not surprising: her brief note to Ellen of May 1843 concludes: '[Anne] will be here in a week or two and then if she be willing I will get her to write you a proper letter – a feat that I have never performed' (Smith, *Letters*, vol. i, p. 319). Charlotte's letters to Emily are more revealing, for she knew that she could confide absolutely in her discretion. Emily had been with Charlotte in Mme Heger's school in 1842, and in May 1843, when Emily was back in Haworth, Charlotte reported that two of the teachers at the school hated each other like two cats and quarrelled venomously. Mlle Sophie said Mlle Blanche was 'heartless, insincere, and vindictive ... she is the regular spy of Mme Heger ... M. and Mde Heger rarely speak to me' (Smith, *Letters*, vol. i, pp. 319–20). One can see in such a letter the genesis of *The Professor* and *Villette*.

Mrs Gaskell had to select her excerpts from the letters judiciously. She assured George Smith that she would exclude all that ought to be considered private and personal in Charlotte's letters to him; but she had a sense of humour and, happily for us, she retained some of Charlotte's bold, lively and unladylike expressions in letters to other correspondents. In a letter of September 1840, Charlotte told Ellen Nussey that a high wind had made her 'strongly inclined to dance a jig ... I think I must partake of the nature of a pig or an ass' (Smith, *Letters*, vol. i, p. 228). Mrs Gaskell's biography is also the primary source for a few letters – including Charlotte's letter to Emily of July 1839, beginning 'Mine Bonnie Love' – a phrase recalling Charlotte's love for Burns' poems. But she had to be selective and to conceal identities. She also occasionally misread words or paraphrased sentences. In a letter from Charlotte to Ellen Nussey of 7 April 1840, a 'most stormy meeting' became 'a stirring meeting' (Smith, *Letters*, vol. 1, p. 213).

Mrs Gaskell's *Life* created a renewed interest in the Brontës' lives and work, and contributed to the dispersal of precious Brontë manuscripts – already regarded as treasures. She included an autograph letter from Charlotte in a collection she sent to Abigail B. Adams (1808–89) 'to be sold for the benefit of the Sanitary Commission' during the American Civil War. Mr Brontë was asked by various people for Charlotte's letters as mementoes, and, one hopes reluctantly, cut up into small sections a letter from Charlotte in which she had described the 'black desolate reef of rocks' in Filey, where she and Ellen had stayed after Anne's death in Scarborough. Arthur Nicholls refused to provide entire letters for Mrs Gaskell's use in the *Life*, but he responded to autograph-hunters with tiny fragments of Charlotte's letters.

In 1863 Ellen Nussey decided that an edition of letters, approved by herself, should be published to set the record straight about Charlotte's character. She wrote to M. Heger to ask for his help in producing an edition – an embarrassing request which he refused on the ground that confidential letters revealing 'les battements de ce pauvre cœur malade' ('the beating of this poor sick heart') should not be published. Ellen must have been surprised by this reference to a 'sick heart'. She would certainly have been horrified had she read Charlotte's four extant letters to M. Heger – especially that of 8 January 1845, telling him that she could find 'ni repos ni paix' ('neither rest nor peace') because she had waited so long in vain for a letter from him (Smith, *Letters*, vol. 1, p. 378). Charlotte begged him to write, declaring that she had suffered torments for eight months. In her last surviving letter to him, written on 18 November 1845, she begs desperately for his compassion. She has kept her promise not to write for six months, but now she is suffering because she is the slave of a 'dominant fixed idea'. When he does not write, 'j'ai la fièvre – je perds l'appétit et le sommeil – je dépéris' (Smith, *Letters*, vol. 1, p. 435; 'I am in a fever – I lose my appetite and my sleep – I pine away'). Mrs Gaskell had actually seen these letters in May 1856, but she had concealed the intensity of Charlotte's attraction to M. Heger. On 6 June 1913, Heger's son Paul gave the four surviving letters to the British Museum. They were published for the first time, with translations, in *The Times* for 29 July 1913.

From 1869 until 1892 Ellen persisted in her wish to have more of Charlotte's letters published. In 1870 the American firm Scribner's paid her £100 for a selection in its magazine *Hours at Home*, in which the texts were heavily edited and unreliable. From October 1870 *Hours at Home* was replaced by *Scribner's Monthly*, and for this Ellen provided valuable reminiscences of her early friendship with Charlotte in the number for May 1871.[3] In 1876 she sent to Thomas Wemyss Reid, the editor of the *Leeds Mercury*, a memoir including quotations from Charlotte's letters. Though it included valuable accounts of her friendship with Charlotte, it was inaccurate in details, for Ellen's memory was failing; and Arthur Nicholls wrote to Reid, expressing his dismay: Ellen had been unmindful of what was due to the memory of the dead and the feelings of the living.

In 1882 a Brontë enthusiast, Sidney Biddell, suggested that Ellen might prepare a volume of the letters with a short preface and notes; and in 1887 she sent most of her letters to the local antiquarian J. Horsfall Turner to be printed. Printing continued until spring 1889, when she decided that it should be halted and that the original manuscripts should be returned to her. When they were, Ellen claimed that fifty to sixty manuscripts were missing. In 1891 she asked the journalist Clement King Shorter to produce an edition of the letters, and, fearing intervention by Nicholls over the copyright, she arranged for the burning of all but about twelve copies of the collection. Shorter advised her in 1892 that a friend would give her £100 for the manuscripts, while he would write a biography of the Brontës from which Ellen would receive two-thirds of the profits. The friend was Thomas James Wise, then highly esteemed but revealed in 1934 as a forger of fake early editions. On 23 November 1895 Shorter paid Arthur Nicholls £150 for the copyright in Charlotte's letters. This enabled him to publish much new material: Charlotte's letters to William Smith Williams, James Taylor and the Wheelwright sisters were lent to him, and were safely returned. Shorter's *Charlotte Brontë and her Circle* (1896) was therefore the most comprehensive collection of letters up to that date. Unfortunately it was marred by misreadings, and sometimes by the insertion of passages from one letter into another. Shorter's *The Brontës' Life and Letters* of 1908 had similar drawbacks. Meanwhile Wise continued to buy, through Shorter, letters and manuscripts from Mr Nicholls and other owners. Although Wise gave fourteen letters to the Brontë Society when he was its vice-president, he continued to sell Brontë manuscripts to English and American libraries, so that when he and the untrustworthy Alexander Symington produced the Shakespeare Head edition of the Brontës' letters in 1932, mistakes were inevitable since they had no direct access to many of the manuscripts.

The Brontë Society aims to add genuine letters to its already fine collection. In 1974 Mrs Elizabeth Seton-Gordon, the granddaughter of George Smith, generously gave her rich collection of Brontë letters to the society. Letters advertised for sale by auction are carefully assessed by examining their provenance, handwriting, paper, ink and any watermarks to make sure that they are not forgeries.

NOTES

1 Dudley Green (ed.), *The Letters of the Reverend Patrick Brontë* (Stroud: Nonsuch, 2005), p. 225.
2 On the history of the Brontë letters, see Smith, *Letters*, vol. 1, pp. 27–71.
3 Repr. *ibid.*, pp. 589–95.

CHAPTER 15

Portraits of the Brontës

Jane Sellars

Branwell Brontë's portrait of his sisters Charlotte, Emily and Anne (see Figure 13) is one of the most famous literary portraits in the world. This image, and his portrait of Emily (see Figure 14), attract large numbers of visitors to the National Portrait Gallery in London. Yet Branwell was not a great painter, and these are not great portraits. The fascination is with the sitters. The visual images that the teenage artist created of his sisters have endured into the twenty-first century as a significant influence on our perception of the Brontës, their writing and their lives.

History has handed down to us altogether three portraits of the Brontës made in their own lifetimes.[1] The first is Branwell's 'Pillar Portrait' of about 1834, mentioned above, so called because of the pillar in the centre of the group where Branwell painted himself out of the picture.[2] Then there is the fragment portrait of Emily Brontë, hacked from the portrait called 'the Gun Group' of about the same date.[3] The third is George Richmond's 1850 drawing of Charlotte Brontë, famous author of *Jane Eyre* (see Figure 15). Richmond's portrait established a kind of pictorial symbol for the face of Charlotte Brontë that persists to this day. But the story of the Brontë portraits begins with the seventeen-year-old Branwell picking up his paintbrush and oil palette and ordering his sisters into position, telling them to leave a very important space in the middle for the portrait of the artist as a young man.

From an early age, Branwell had a natural talent for drawing. Often, like his sisters, he copied from engravings. Unlike his sisters, however, he employed colour in a robust and imaginative way and added quirky touches of his own to the subject. As a boy, along with the girls, he had lessons from the Keighley artist John Bradley (1787–1844), and he had expensive lessons from the Leeds painter William Robinson (1799–1838). Robinson was a pupil of Sir Thomas Lawrence (1769–1830), the leading British portrait painter of the early nineteenth century, who portrayed most of the important personalities of the day in his polished and

13 *The Brontë Sisters*, the so-called 'Pillar Portrait', by the sitters' brother
Branwell Brontë, *c.* 1834

flattering style. The purpose of Branwell's art lessons was of course to support his ambition to become a professional artist. He drafted a letter to the Royal Academy of Arts, asking how to go about applying for a place at the schools there, and for many years it was assumed that he went to London with an interview in his sights but got waylaid by the city's public houses and came home again. Now we do not think that he ever went

14 A fragment portrait of Emily Jane Brontë by her brother Branwell, torn from the so-called 'Gun Group' portrait, *c.* 1834, now lost

15 George Richmond's portrait of Charlotte Brontë. Coloured chalk drawing, 1850

to London at all. One thing is certain: when he painted the group portraits of himself and his sisters, it was with a career as an artist in view.

When we go to the National Portrait Gallery to look at Branwell's paintings of his three sisters, we find them, unsurprisingly, in the room dedicated to great Victorian writers and other artists. Most of the other paintings in the room were painted when the subject was at the height of his or her fame. Despite the date given for the painting, many people who gaze at the portrait in the National Portrait Gallery will look at the teenage Brontë sisters as if they were painted when they were famous writers. Contemplating these three pale girls in their dark dresses, set against a dark impenetrable background with the ghostly shadow of their degenerate brother's figure in between them, they are reading the Brontës' life story – a story that in 1834 had barely begun. Why is it that when we look at this portrait we sense intimations of what was to come? The painting has become imbued with our knowledge of the Brontës' biographies, of their struggle to become writers, the early deaths that took away their chance of becoming prolific and celebrated literary figures, the cold, dark atmosphere of their Haworth home and the burden of their brother's wasted life upon them all. To a great degree, this is because this is our only known image of the three Brontë sisters together in their lifetimes, and it illustrates every book ever written about the Brontës. But there is also something else there, and that is to do with the way that Branwell chose to represent his family.

What, then, were Branwell's intentions when he created this picture? What were the influences on him as an artist? Why, in fact, did he paint it at all?

The three Brontë sisters are placed against a very dark background, three-quarter length, standing, with Anne on the left, Emily in the middle and Charlotte on the right, each with a hand placed on a small desk or table in the foreground. Anne and Emily are seen three-quarter face, with Anne looking up to the right, displaying a very slight squint. It is worth noting here that Anne is in fact the most depicted Brontë sister. As the youngest in the family, she must have been the most easily coerced by her elder siblings to pose for her portrait, for there are three portrait drawings of Anne by Charlotte in the Brontë Society's collection.[4] Emily looks straight at the viewer, and Charlotte gazes off to the left. The controversial yellow-brown pillar, painted over Branwell's self-portrait, separates the group.[5] One of the physical aspects of the three faces is the different colours of the girls' eyes: Anne's are blue, Emily's a greenish blue and Charlotte's brown. Much later in life, Charlotte's eyes were remarked upon by George Smith, her publisher, as her only beautiful feature: 'Her head seemed too large for her body. She had fine eyes, but her face was marred by the shape of the mouth and by the complexion.'[6] The Brontë girls are dressed alike in plain gowns with white muslin collars, the dress colour of each reflecting the colour of her eyes. All three have reddish-brown hair parted in the centre with ringlets covering their ears.

Charlotte's hair is piled in a topknot, as befits her age, whereas the other two appear to have short, loose hair. Their faces are pale, with touches of pink in the cheeks. In front of them there is a simple table with a book lying on it.

Branwell has composed his group portrait according to particular principles of painting. There is a well-known portrait of the three Waldegrave sisters painted by Sir Joshua Reynolds in 1780 in the National Gallery of Scotland, Edinburgh.[7] At first sight one would not associate the frilled femininity of the Waldegrave women with the image of the Brontës, but there are elements in common. Reynolds was the great elevator of British portraiture. It was he who established the Grand Manner that was to dominate British art for centuries. His stranglehold on the Royal Academy ensured that this tradition was carried down the generations, all the way to the teenager Branwell Brontë painting his sisters in 1834, learned in diluted form from his teacher William Robinson. Reynolds arranged his three female sitters in a close group in distinctly different poses. Branwell attempts the same, with each Brontë girl looking in a different direction. Reynolds' drapery creates a dark foil for the girls' pale faces, something imitated by Branwell in his use of a dark, featureless background. Whereas the Waldegrave sisters have their embroidery to denote feminine accomplishments, the Brontës have a book laid on a plain desk. Unlike Reynolds, Branwell has made no attempt to suggest any kind of interior, nor has he inserted a tantalizing glimpse of landscape in the top right corner. His figures emerge from the darkness. The dark shadows encourage the viewer to concentrate attention on the figures and faces of the girls, a method that he employs in most of his portraits.

In 1838 to 1839, Branwell survived for a year in Bradford as a provincial portrait painter. His subjects were not aristocratic families, great statesmen or famous writers; instead he painted local mill-owners and tradesmen and their families. Quite a number of his subjects were from Haworth: for example, his friend John Brown, the musician Thomas Parker and Maria Ingham, daughter of the Taylor family of Stanbury.[8] Although John Brown is allowed a flourish of stormy sky, and Parker has a violin in the background, all of Branwell's subjects emerge from the same darkness that enfolds his teenage sisters.[9]

When considering what Branwell's intentions were when he painted the portrait of his sisters, one fact that one must keep in mind is that the experience of looking at paintings first hand was not something to which any of the Brontës had easy access. There was the famous family visit to the 1834 exhibition of the Royal Northern Society for the Encouragement of the Fine Arts in Leeds, where not only did they first encounter the work of Branwell's teacher, William Robinson, but also the sixteen-year-old Charlotte had two drawings on show.[10] But that visit was a rare opportunity to look at the real thing. Ordinarily the Brontës were restricted to looking at engravings of famous paintings in books and magazines or, given the limitations of illustration at that period, to reading detailed reviews of works on display at the Royal Academy and elsewhere. Branwell would certainly have been able to read about the theory of the Grand Manner in painting, and to follow the fortunes of the most famous painters of the day and their forerunners.

For example, the name of George Romney (1734–1802) was one that Branwell must have known. Although he predates Branwell by several decades, Romney's work marks a high point of achievement in British portraiture, and his influence lingered on. Romney could, in fact, have been a role model for Branwell: he spurned the Royal Academy and never became a member, and he dedicated the greater part of his life to his art, leaving his wife alone in Cumbria for forty years in order to pursue his career. He specialized in portraits of society women and was obsessed by Emma Lady Hamilton. In 1768 Romney painted a huge portrait of the Leigh family, now in the National Gallery of Victoria, Melbourne, Australia. It is considered to be his supreme achievement, incorporating eight intensely observed figures in an elaborately patterned composition. Jared Leigh was a solicitor, and he wanted to show off his family as prosperous, educated and elegant, set against a background of classical architecture in an Arcadian landscape.

Leigh thus had pretensions for himself and his family, which Romney has willingly accommodated in his painting. Branwell Brontë must surely have had a similar purpose in the way that he portrayed his sisters. He was of course training to be an artist at the time, and it was natural that his sisters would be his models. However, with his choice of poses, the dramatic dark background, the matching costumes, the book on the table and the serious expressions, Branwell clearly aimed to convey the impression of a distinguished and learned family. This speaks of his ambition not only for himself but for his siblings as well.

In 1834 Branwell also painted the family portrait known as 'the Gun Group'.[11] All that survives of this painting is the fragment with the image of Emily. The painting has a convoluted history. It is believed that Arthur Bell Nicholls, Charlotte's widower, took the complete canvas back to Ireland with him after Patrick Brontë's death in 1861 and subsequently destroyed the greater part of the picture out of dislike, preserving only the image of Emily because he considered it a good likeness. Tracings of the individual figures of the sisters made by John Greenwood, the Haworth stationer, are in the Brontë Parsonage Museum collection at Haworth. There is an engraving of 1879 in Horsfall Turner's book *Haworth Past and Present*, and in 1989 a photograph of the painting was found in Dr Mildred Christian's papers at the Brontë Parsonage Museum. This photograph was apparently copied from a daguerrotype or ambrotype and is known to have belonged to Martha Brown, the Brontës' servant, and to have been used by Horsfall Turner as the basis for his book illustration. The photograph is indistinct, but it gives us enough information to decipher Branwell's portrait group.[12]

Here Branwell takes centre stage, with Anne and Charlotte on his left and Emily on his right. A dead game bird and a pile of books and papers are spread untidily across the table around which they sit, and in the crook of his arm the artist holds a shotgun, hence the title. In the presentation of himself as the sportsman holding the gun, with his booty displayed on the table in front of him, Branwell puts a specific emphasis on his own masculinity, which contrasts with the perceived femininity of his sisters' literary pursuits, also symbolized by objects on the table. His figure towers above the girls, and he alone meets the viewer's eye, while the women look inwards towards one another. The perception of the family intended here is that they should be identified with the aristocracy, or at the very least the gentry, whose lives are devoted to the leisure pursuits of sport and literature.

There is another painting in the National Portrait Gallery that was purchased by the gallery in 1906, when it was described as a portrait of Charlotte Brontë.[13] There is, however, no reliable provenance to prove that this picture of a young woman reading a book is a portrait of her. During my seven years as Director of the Brontë Parsonage Museum in the 1990s, I was presented with numerous paintings and drawings of Victorian women whose owners were convinced that the sitter was Charlotte. Occasionally, photographs appeared as well.

Photography was in its infancy in the Brontës' lifetimes, but immediately after Charlotte's death in 1855 the carte-de-visite emerged, enabling the celebrity photograph to become commonplace. Writers, painters, actors, scientists, the aristocracy and royalty – all turned towards the camera, and their images were peddled to the general public. It seemed extraordinary that there was no famous photograph of Charlotte Brontë to illustrate the biographies and the endlessly reprinted novels. Then, in 1984, the staff of the National Portrait Gallery discovered in their archives a glass negative from the photographer Emery Walker's studio that was labelled 'from a carte-de-visite of Charlotte Brontë, taken within a year of her death' (see Figure 16).[14] It was accompanied by a copy of a letter that Walker had written to George Smith, Charlotte's publisher when he returned the carte-de-visite, confirming that he had taken a negative from it and noting that 'So far as I can ascertain the photograph has never been published.' The carte-de-visite itself was left to the Brontë Society by Smith's granddaughter in 1986, bringing the story full circle. It is only in the last twenty-five years, therefore, that this photographic portrait has begun to appear in books about the Brontës. Charlotte was known to have been unhappy about her own appearance, and it seems logical to assume that she vetoed the publication of the photograph in her own lifetime. In 1991 Audrey Hall produced a privately published

16 A carte-de-visite photograph believed to be of Charlotte Brontë, *c.* 1854. Part of the collection of Emery Walker

booklet to argue the case for a photograph of a woman she believed to be Charlotte Brontë, found in the papers of a descendant of Charlotte's lifelong friend Ellen Nussey; but this image lacks the convincing provenance of the Walker photograph.[15]

In a letter written in September 1853, after her first visit to Haworth, Elizabeth Gaskell described how Charlotte showed her 'a rough, common-looking oil-painting, done by her brother, of herself, – a little, rather prim-looking girl of eighteen, – and the two other sisters, girls of 16 and 14, with cropped hair, and sad, dreamy-looking eyes.'[16] With her description of 'sad, dreamy-looking eyes', Mrs Gaskell set the tone for our perception of the Brontës: they are dreamy, otherworldly, already infected with the grief of their lives to come. Or perhaps the lives that Mrs Gaskell is going to write for them. It is this great weight of Brontë biography that we cannot help but bring to bear on our idea of the painting, and hence on the Brontës' lives. But I also think that the physical appearance of the three sisters' portrait, and of the sad little fragment of Emily, affects our idea of the Brontës.

The three sisters' portrait bears the scars of years spent hidden on top of an Irish cupboard. The paint has flaked off in broad lines across the surface of the picture where it was roughly folded and stuffed out of sight. There are holes where it was ripped off the nails that fixed it to the wooden stretcher. Mrs Gaskell gives her readers the impression that when Charlotte showed her the painting she was ashamed of it because Branwell had painted it, and he was responsible for a large part of his sisters' misery. Arthur Nicholls clearly did not like it, given his lack of care for the object. Indeed, it is extraordinary under the circumstances that he saved it at all. Had this history not been known or not been considered important to the Brontë story, the National Portrait Gallery picture restorers would have filled in the holes, painted out the scars and cleaned up the picture, thus depriving it of some of its most telling details. I cannot think of any other painting in a national collection that has been allowed to keep the marks of its bad treatment. The Brontë family portraits thus cease to be mere paintings. They are no longer just the work of the artist's hand and eye. Instead, through the interpretations of legions of biographers from Mrs Gaskell onwards, they have become complex symbols of the sitters' lives and achievements.

NOTES

1 They are now all in the National Portrait Gallery, London. In the Brontë Parsonage Museum at Haworth, there is also a well-known oil portrait of Charlotte by John Hunter Thompson, a local artist who was a friend of Branwell's. Although Thompson had met Charlotte, his portrait was painted after her death.

2 See Christine Alexander and Jane Sellars, *The Art of the Brontës* (Cambridge University Press, 1995), pp. 310–11.

3 *Ibid.*, pp. 307–10.

4 *Ibid.*, pp. 210–11 and 230.

5 The pillar has caused controversy in the past, with suggestions that it was Charlotte who painted out the figure of Branwell after his death. For information about the discovery of the under-painted figure, see Ingeborg Nixon, 'The Brontë Portraits: Some Old Problems and a New Discovery', *BST*, 13.68 (1958), 233.

6 George M. Smith, 'Charlotte Brontë', *Cornhill Magazine*, Dec. 1900, p. 784.

7 To see an image of *The Ladies Waldegrave*, NG 2171, go to www.nationalgalleries. org (accessed 17 Apr. 2012).

8 See Alexander and Sellars, *The Art of the Brontës*, pp. 323, 327–8 and 330–1, respectively.

9 Branwell's portraits of his Haworth subjects are normally on show in the room at the Brontë Parsonage Museum that was formerly his studio.

10 See Alexander and Sellars, *The Art of the Brontës*, pp. 228–30.

11 *Ibid.*, pp. 307–10.

12 See Juliet Barker, 'The Brontë Portraits: A Mystery Solved', *BST*, 20.1 (1990), 3–11.

13 NPG 1444, unknown woman, formerly thought to be Charlotte Brontë, no date, artist unknown. For an image, see www.npg.org.uk/collections (accessed 17 Apr. 2012).

14 Juliet Barker, 'Charlotte Brontë's Photograph', *BST*, 19.1–2 (1986), 27–8.

15 Audrey W. Hall, *A Suspected New Photograph of Charlotte Brontë* (Keighley: J. L. Crabtree, 1991).

16 J. A. V. Chapple and Arthur Pollard (eds.), *The Letters of Mrs Gaskell* (Manchester University Press, 1966), p. 249.

CHAPTER 16

The poetry of the Brontës

Janet Gezari

In the spring of 1846, the poems of Anne, Charlotte and Emily Brontë 'stole into life' (Gaskell, *Life*, p. 237). This birth had an unusually long history, and Charlotte was its midwife. From childhood, the three sisters and their brother Branwell had been writing and self-publishing prose tales, verse, plays and journalism. Charlotte tells the story of how she and her sisters came to publish *Poems* in her 'Biographical Notice of Ellis and Acton Bell', written to accompany the 1850 edition of *Wuthering Heights* and *Agnes Grey*:

One day, in the autumn of 1845, I accidentally lighted on a MS. volume of verse in my sister Emily's handwriting. Of course, I was not surprised, knowing that she could and did write verse: I looked it over, and something more than surprise seized me, – a deep conviction that these were not common effusions, nor at all like the poetry women generally write. I thought them condensed and terse, vigorous and genuine. To my ear they had also a peculiar music – wild, melancholy, and elevating. (Smith, *Letters*, vol. II, p. 742)

While Charlotte was persuading Emily that her poems merited publication, Anne took the opportunity to show her poems to Charlotte, who attributed to them 'a sweet sincere pathos of their own' (Smith, *Letters*, vol. II, p. 743). Juliet Barker imagines that Emily was enraged by Charlotte's having trespassed in the Gondal world she shared with Anne; but Emily's poems had, from the beginning, laid claim to a life of their own apart from her Gondal prose (Barker, p. 479). In proof of this, she had begun transcribing some of them into two notebooks about a year earlier. Emily was indignant at her elder sister's unlicensed reading of her poems, but it took only hours for Charlotte to win forgiveness and only days for Emily to agree that the three sisters should seek a wider audience for their poems.

They did not invite their brother Branwell to participate in their project. Because Charlotte was so capable a correspondent, we know most about how she felt and least about Emily's feelings, but Branwell's

134

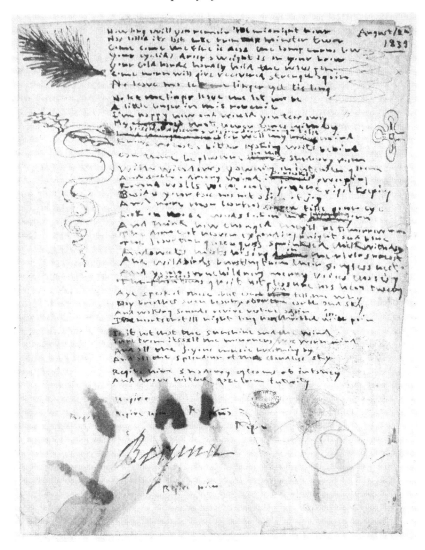

17 Manuscript of Emily Brontë's poem 'How long will you remain?', dated 12 August 1839

behaviour would have distanced all three sisters from him. Dismissed in disgrace from his post as tutor at Thorp Green in late July, Branwell was living at home in the autumn of 1845. He sought but failed to find employment and at the same time sought and found oblivion in alcohol. But Branwell's literary career was already different from those of his sisters

in important respects. He had succeeded in publishing a poem in the
Halifax Guardian in 1841 and would publish fourteen more poems in
three Yorkshire newspapers before his death in 1848.[1] Of the four siblings,
only Branwell and Charlotte had long dreamed of making their way in
the world as writers, but Branwell's ambitions and expectations were
different from Charlotte's. The difference is marked not only by the
publication of his poems in local newspapers but also by his repeated
efforts to interest *Blackwood's Magazine* and various literary luminaries
in them. Unlike his sisters, he also had a circle of artistic young men
outside Haworth with whom to share his poems. There is no evidence
that in 1845 he would have connected his literary future to that of his
sisters, anticipated careers for any of them as women of letters or eagerly
joined them in a joint publication.

Poems (1846) comprises nineteen poems by Charlotte and twenty-one
poems each by Emily and Anne. The usual arrangement is for a poem by
one sister to be followed by one poem each by the other two. In some
cases, contiguous poems have a common subject; in others, poems seem
to respond to each other by taking up a common theme. For example,
three consecutive poems – Anne's 'If this be all', Charlotte's 'Life' and
Emily's 'Hope' – address the abstractions signalled by Charlotte's and
Emily's titles. The moods of these poems differ in characteristic ways:
Anne's is gloomy about love's absence, friendship's loss, sin's triumph and
her own inability to make a difference in the world; Charlotte's is cheery
and full of good counsel meant to hold despair at bay; Emily's poem
registers a wider range of feelings than either Anne's or Charlotte's, and
her transactions with hope or life are more various, deceptive and unresolved. The number of encouraging reviews that *Poems* received (three)
exceeded by one the number of copies actually sold within the first year.
Discouraged but not humbled, the sisters sent copies of the remaindered
book as presents to writers they admired, including Tennyson,
Wordsworth, De Quincey and Hartley Coleridge. Charlotte's accompanying note strikes the proper tone of wry self-deprecation. The book
is offered 'in acknowledgement of the pleasure and profit' that the
recipients have 'often and long' provided to its authors, not in pursuit
of their assistance or approval (Smith, *Letters*, vol. 1, pp. 529–30).

Despite its small sales, the importance of *Poems* for our understanding of
the Brontë sisters as poets is considerable. All of them had grown up reading
and writing poetry. In addition to the Bible, Shakespeare and Milton,
their particular models – and Branwell's – included the eighteenth-
century poetry of James Thomson, William Cowper and Robert Burns;

the nineteenth-century poetry of Scott, Wordsworth, Byron, both Samuel Taylor and Hartley Coleridge, Shelley and Tennyson; songs, devotional verse and hymns, especially those of Isaac Watts; as well as the poetry and verse published in newspapers, magazines and the annuals in vogue in the second quarter of the nineteenth century. Anne wrote a poem titled 'To Cowper' that salutes him as a kindred soul, and Branwell's poem titled 'Robert Burns' suggests his identification with Burns' ambitions and his unhappy end.

Unlike Emily and Anne, Charlotte almost entirely gave up writing poetry after 1845, and also unlike them, she had only three recent poems to contribute to their joint venture. Later, when her fame renewed interest in her poems, she referred to them as 'juvenile productions; the restless effervescence of a mind that would not be still' (in a letter of 1850 to Elizabeth Gaskell; Smith, *Letters*, vol. II, p. 475). One reviewer, Sydney Dobell, confirmed Charlotte's critical judgement by noting that the Bell brothers shared 'the instinct of song' but shared it unevenly. Only in Emily's poems, Dobell wrote, did this instinct manifest itself as 'an inspiration which may yet find an audience in the outer world'.[2] Emily's poem 'A Death Scene' appeared in the *Halifax Guardian*; that paper had presumably received a review copy of *Poems* that it declined to review. This was the same journal in which Branwell had published his poem 'Heaven and Earth' five years earlier.

The Brontës punctuated the poems they chose to publish according to current practice, and references to Angria or Gondal, the empires the Brontës had invented as adolescents, were removed from them. Although Charlotte and Anne had lost interest in Angria and Gondal by this time, Emily's last poem – the only poem she is known to have written after *Wuthering Heights*, 'Why ask to know what date what clime' – is a Gondal poem and so bears witness to the continuing role that Gondal played in her imaginative life. Nevertheless, only six of the poems she selected for publication in 1846 came from her 'Gondal Poems' notebook, probably the notebook Charlotte found and the one into which Emily transcribed poems inspired by Gondal characters and situations. Fifteen more poems were taken from the notebook known as the Honresfeld manuscript.

Charlotte contributed fewer poems to *Poems* than her sisters, but hers are usually longer than theirs. She and Branwell each wrote fewer poems than either Emily or Anne but more lines of verse than Emily and Anne combined. *Poems* begins with Charlotte's poem 'Pilate's Wife's Dream', which sets a tone for the volume as a whole and shares important features with Charlotte's other contributions. Because the subject of Pilate's wife had a long history in the visual arts, it would not have signalled that this was a book of poems by women, a signal the sisters hoped to prevent by adopting their masculine-sounding pseudonyms. But 'Pilate's Wife's Dream' does mark the importance to these poems of female perspectives, dreams and visions. Charlotte's immediate source is Matthew 27:19, in which a dream motivates Pilate's wife to warn her husband not to condemn Jesus, 'that innocent man'; but two aspects of Charlotte's representation of Pilate's wife are her own. First, her heroine is unhappily married to a husband whose 'cold and crushing sway' she abhors and whose efforts at intimacy with her she resists. Second, she does not actually warn him not to condemn Jesus. When she imagines doing so, she is first constrained by doubts about the dream she has had and then distracted from any practical course of action by her vision of Christ's eventual triumph. Achieving a 'firmer trust' and 'higher hope', she decides to await further instructions rather than speak to Pilate.

In 'Mementos', objects that have survived their owner inspire a narrative about passionate, abandoned women (mothers, daughters) and powerful but vicious men (husbands, fathers). *Shirley* shows what Charlotte could make of this material in the medium of the novel. In the poem, 'keepsakes' that have become 'relics' inspire the story of a woman's oppressive marriage to a dissolute husband, her 'blest' youth before marriage, and the birth of a daughter she does not live long enough to know. The poem then proceeds to tell the story of this daughter, who grows up without her mother and alienated from her father:

> She crossed the sea – now lone she wanders
> By Seine's, or Rhine's, or Arno's flow;

Either the speaker does not know where the daughter is, or her exact location does not matter to the poet, so that one European river will do as well as another. The poem then imagines the daughter's death and narrates the father's suicide. His soul now 'groans, / In hell's eternity'. Having begun with particular abandoned objects in a remembered room, the poem ends with an abandoned soul – or nearly; in the last stanza, there is a turn characteristic of many of Charlotte's poems when the speaker seeks 'to rally mirth' in 'some more cheerful room'.

'Mementos' shows Charlotte experimenting with some of the poetic forms available to her. It begins with iambic tetrameter lines and alternating rhymes but soon shifts into couplets and thereafter toggles between quatrains and longer strophes, mixing couplets and alternating rhymes.

Trimeter lines begin to appear about halfway through the poem, producing a succession of traditional ballad stanzas. The poem's imagery is conventional and predictable. Sometimes – especially when the rhythm of the lines is working well – an image can be fresh and compelling, but Charlotte's poetry does not achieve the original expressive force that characterizes her novels. There it transforms even dense and syntactically awkward writing into luminous prose.

Emily is the only one of the Brontës whose experience and its record in the poems were, from the beginning, nourished by both mysticism and Stoic philosophy. 'No Coward Soul Is Mine' is one poem in which we can mark her enduring claim to an authority of her own. Even her mysticism feels both authentic and original: what she seeks and writes about in several poems is not union with a transcendent deity, but release into a state of undifferentiated being where subject and object are one, and the imagination has sovereign authority. Her own creative experience is often the subject of her poems, as it is of Charlotte's; but regardless of whether Emily is writing in her own voice (as in 'No Coward Soul Is Mine') or in another's (as in the lines below from 'The Prisoner [A Fragment]'), the physical qualities of her verse are essential to the feeling it conveys:

> 'He comes with western winds, with evening's wandering airs,
> With that clear dusk of heaven that brings the thickest stars.
> Winds take a pensive tone, and stars a tender fire,
> And visions rise, and change, that kill me with desire.'

Form – the leisurely hexameter couplets, the balanced phrases and clauses, the steady placement of the caesura in the middle of the line, assonance and consonance – is indissolubly connected to content, the feeling of openness and gradually intensifying anticipation that the lines express.

Although Emily's poetry shares some of its vocabulary with the poetry of her siblings, the language and rhythms of her best poems show that she possesses something far exceeding the 'faculty of verse' that all the Brontës shared.[3] Her ear is more musical than the ears of her siblings, and her poems register more fully than theirs the urgencies of her distinctive voice. Charlotte's best poems, 'The Visionary' and 'Often rebuked, yet always back returning', were written after Emily's death but under her tutelage. Charlotte attributed both poems to Emily when she published them in 1850.[4]

Anne's poems resemble Emily's more closely than Charlotte's, and not always because the sisters often composed verse in response to the same Gondal occasions. 'Lines Composed in a Wood on a Windy Day', for example, reminds us of 'High waving heather 'neath stormy blasts bending', with which it shares a powerful sense of the mutability of natural forms, an insight into what Wordsworth called 'the one life within us and abroad', and an expressive use of feminine endings:

> My soul is awakened, my spirit is soaring
> And carried aloft on the wings of the breeze;
> For above and around me the wild wind is roaring,
> Arousing to rapture the earth and the seas.

But Anne's poems are more didactic than Emily's and more doctrinal than Charlotte's. One of the poems she contributed to the 1846 volume, 'A Word to the "Elect"', expresses her commitment to universalism, a doctrine that asserts that none of God's creatures is consigned to eternal doom. Anne was especially influenced by hymns, many of which she transcribed into her own music manuscript book. A few of her own hymns have been included in modern editions of *The Methodist Hymn Book* and other hymnals.[5] Anne's best-known hymn encourages the believer to hold fast to faith and cling to God's love, whatever the difficulties:

> Believe not those who say
> The upward path is smooth,
> Lest thou should stumble in the way
> And faint before the truth.

These lines are smooth and predictable. Their lack of rhythmic interest is an advantage for words designed to be set to music. Like all of Anne's poems, this one expresses her considered view of life as well as her conviction that poetry can soothe a troubled soul and sustain faith.

The assertion that Branwell is the second-best poet in the family after Emily is more often made than supported by any evidence. He shared with Charlotte, his writing partner from 1829 to 1837, what she called (in the letter to Mrs Gaskell quoted above) the 'restless effervescence' of a mind unable to be still. Educated in classical literature, as his sisters were not, Branwell not only composed poems of his own but also translated thirty-seven of Horace's odes. He sent some of these translations to De Quincey and Hartley Coleridge, along with poems of his own composition. De Quincey did not acknowledge his receipt of them, but Coleridge did, apparently positively, although he was ultimately either alienated or simply insufficiently energetic to promote

Branwell's career. Branwell's translations of Horace provide interesting evidence of his poetic ambition and his competence as a reader of Latin, but he could hardly have chosen a writer less suited to his own sensibility and experience. Familiarity with poetry, enthusiasm, and even perseverance and hard work – these last being virtues Branwell is often thought to have lacked – characterize Branwell's translation project, but what he produced were versified cribs.

Although Branwell wrote competent poems like 'Heaven and Earth' on conventional religious themes, his best poems are about 'miserable me' and explore a 'communion of vague unity' with something inanimate.[6] 'Me' in the poem titled 'The End of All' may be Angria's Northangerland grieving over his wife's death, although Northangerland's mood in this poem chimes with Branwell's in the two unpublished autobiographical poems titled 'Lydia Gisborne' (Gisborne was Lydia Robinson's maiden name). In 'Real Rest' the speaker addresses an anonymous corpse, and in 'Penmaenmawr' he contrasts his own unsteadiness and torment with the insensibility of an ancient mountain. In 'Letter from a Father on Earth to his Child in the Grave', a father finds comfort in his dead infant's unchanging aspect, so superior to his own 'restlessness and worrying care'. The lines which describe the suffering that conjoins and dooms the poem's lovers in 'Penmaenmawr' are full of facile gloom and tired diction:

> I knew a flower whose leaves were meant to bloom
> Till Death should snatch it to adorn the tomb,
> Now, blanching 'neath the blight of hopeless grief
> With never blooming and yet living leaf;
> A flower on which my mind would wish to shine,
> If but one beam could break from mind like mine . . .

The Byron of *Don Juan* anticipates this speaker's staleness, and the Coleridge of 'Dejection: An Ode' may have spawned his image of a beamless soul. These comparisons suggest, among other things, the extent to which Branwell's development as a poet was limited by his susceptibility to the influence of established poets as well as by his inability to compellingly oppose anything to his longing for oblivion. Branwell may have been the most competent versifier in the Brontë family; but his verse lacks the originality found in the poems of his sisters – especially those of Emily. Her remarkable achievement as a poet has long been recognized by readers and will continue to receive critical and scholarly attention.

NOTES

1 See Victor A. Neufeldt (ed.), *The Poems of Patrick Branwell Brontë* (New York: Garland, 1990), p. xxv.
2 From 'Poetry of the Million', quoted in Miriam Allott (ed.), *The Brontës: The Critical Heritage* (London: Routledge & Kegan Paul, 1974), p. 61.
3 The phrase is Wordsworth's, quoted by Robert Southey in his letter to Charlotte, who had sent him some of her poetry in 1836. Smith, *Letters*, vol. I, p. 166.
4 In *Last Things: Emily Brontë's Poems* (Oxford University Press, 2007), pp. 138–47, I discuss both 'The Visionary' and 'Often rebuked, yet always back returning' and make the case for Charlotte's authorship of the latter.
5 Edward Chitham (ed.), *The Poems of Anne Brontë: A New Text and Commentary* (London: Macmillan, 1979; repr. 1987), p. 34.
6 These phrases appear in 'The End of All', line 29, and 'Penmaenmawr', line 68.

CHAPTER 17

Literary influences on the Brontës

Sara J. Lodge

It was once commonplace to declare that the Brontës' works were defined by their singularity. A romantic myth, fostered by Charlotte's biographical notice of her sisters and Elizabeth Gaskell's *Life of Charlotte Brontë*, emphasized the isolation of Haworth Parsonage and the untutored genius that flourished there. *Wuthering Heights* in particular, with its narrative of troubled inheritance, was pronounced by May Sinclair in 1912 to be 'absolutely self-begotten and self-born. It belongs to no school; it follows no tendency',[1] while Virginia Woolf, in 1925, could still claim that 'Charlotte Brontë ... owed nothing to the reading of many books'.[2] Modern criticism, on the contrary, has emphasized the Brontës' immersion from childhood in a rich print culture which made them aspire to write and model their writing, imagery and conception of authorship on a variety of literary sources.

It is important to recognize that the question of influence is never neutral. Whether it is F. R. Leavis asserting, in *The Great Tradition*, that Charlotte can claim 'no part in the great line of English fiction',[3] Sandra Gilbert and Susan Gubar identifying *Wuthering Heights* as a radical feminist rewriting of Milton's *Paradise Lost*[4] or Harold Bloom countering that Emily's argument with Milton is wholly prefigured in Byron's *Manfred*,[5] appraising the effects of earlier literature on the Brontës' work inevitably involves critical investments in the relative value of tradition and originality. In addition, such appraisals engage conceptions of influence itself, whether as a benign inheritance or a site of discursive struggle.

We know a good deal about what the Brontës read.[6] Each child owned a personal copy of the Bible and Prayer Book, which they knew inside out. The parsonage also possessed copies of Hannah More's *Moral Sketches*, John Bunyan's *Pilgrim's Progress*, Isaac Watts' *Doctrine of the Passions* and Milton's *Paradise Lost*. The last three were seminal influences and constant sources of quotation. Among the store of classical texts in Patrick Brontë's library were Homer, Horace, Virgil and Dryden's translation of the *Aeneid*; Branwell used these to study Latin and Greek, and there is evidence that Emily translated parts of the *Aeneid* and the *Ars poetica*. All the children were familiar with Shakespeare's plays from a young age: references to them appear in their earliest creative experiments and recur in the later work, for example in Charlotte's *Shirley* where Caroline Helstone persuades her future husband to read *Coriolanus*, which offers sly insights into his own temperament.[7]

When Charlotte was twelve, the parsonage acquired Thomas Bewick's *History of British Birds*, whose detailed engravings of different species and vignettes of rural scenes offered a portal into imaginary landscapes. Emily copied the whinchat and ring ouzel; Charlotte copied the tree sparrow, the cormorant and a vignette of a lonely man fishing in the rain. Bewick's descriptions of birds' habitats were often intense and dramatic; he followed his water birds into the polar tundra:

There a barrier is put to further enquiry, beyond which the prying eye of man must not look, and there his imagination only must take the view, to supply the place of reality. In these forlorn regions of *unknowable* dreary space, this reservoir of frost and snow, where firm fields of ice, the accumulation of centuries of winters, glazed in Alpine heights above heights, surround the pole, and concentre the multiplied rigours of extreme cold; even here ... there appears to subsist an abundance of animals, in the air, and in the waters.[8]

This sublime idea of territory at the extremity of human conception was deeply attractive to children who also revelled in the exotic fantasy landscapes of *The Arabian Nights Entertainment*, James Ridley's *Tales of the Genii* and *Aesop's Fables*. Bewick's 'forlorn regions of *unknowable* dreary space' become an objective correlative for Jane Eyre's lonely inner self at the beginning of Charlotte's novel and a source of her artistic inspiration. Among natural-history writers, the Brontës also admired John James Audubon and Gilbert White.

The young Brontës read various periodicals: the *Leeds Mercury* and *Leeds Intelligencer* newspapers, *Fraser's Magazine* and the *Methodist Magazine* (to which Aunt Branwell provided access) and literary annuals such as the *Forget Me Not*, illustrated gift-books featuring work by celebrity authors with particular emphasis on images of female beauty and on female writers – among them Felicia Hemans, whose *Songs of the Affections* Charlotte later gifted to Ellen Nussey. Undoubtedly the most powerful periodical in their lives, however, was *Blackwood's Edinburgh Magazine*, an innovative monthly miscellany of poetry, tales and articles on subjects ranging from literature to history, geography and politics. In *Blackwood's*, they encountered Gothic stories by James Hogg ('the Ettrick Shepherd') and accounts of German novellas such as E. T. A. Hoffmann's *Das Majorat* ('The Entail'), which would influence *Wuthering Heights*. *Blackwood's* poets included David Moir ('Delta'), whose elegiac stanzas, spare style, and ballads of Scottish history are echoed in 'complete lines, even whole poems' of Emily and Anne's Gondal writing (Barker, p. 274).

Eighteenth-century prose writers and poets formed a staple of the Brontës' literary diet. Charlotte read *Gulliver's Travels* early in life, and by the age of twenty-four she knew Samuel Richardson's novels, including the seven-volume *Sir Charles Grandison*; histories by Charles Rollin and David Hume; and biographies such as Samuel Johnson's *Lives of the Poets* and Boswell's *Life of Johnson*. Among the eighteenth-century poets, the Brontës read Alexander Pope (whom Charlotte disliked), James Thomson, James Macpherson, Edward Young, Oliver Goldsmith and particularly William Cowper, whose poem 'The Castaway' was a family favourite. Anne later wrote a poem 'To Cowper', in which she addressed the central irony and pathos of his life: the fact that, as a Calvinist, he did not believe in the certainty of his own redemption.

> Sweet are thy strains, Celestial Bard,
> And oft in childhood's years
> I've read them o'er and o'er again
> With floods of silent tears.[9]

Anne Brontë's delicate address negotiates the difficult boundary between pity and respect. Anne's often deliberately plain religious lyrics and the concern her novels display with depression, particularly religious melancholy, as well as the promise of universal salvation, reflect her continued interest in the questions posed by Cowper's life and art. In addition, her poetry reveals an affection for meditative and devotional verse, including that of Thomas Gray and Charles Wesley.

It was, however, Romantic writing that fired the Brontës' passion for passion. In 1834, Charlotte breathlessly recommended Ellen Nussey to 'read Scott alone all novels after his are worthless' (Smith, *Letters*, vol. 1, p. 130). Her enthusiasm was still undimmed in 1847, when she had St John Rivers present Jane Eyre with a copy of *Marmion*: 'one of those genuine productions so often vouchsafed to the fortunate public of those days – the golden age of modern literature. Alas! the readers of our era are less favoured' (*Jane Eyre*, III.vi.370). All the Brontës read Scott avidly, but Emily's particular sense of ownership is reflected in the fact that in the Islanders' Play, begun when she was nine, Scott was her chosen figure and the Isle of Arran her island. From Scott, Emily and her sisters absorbed aspects of narrative technique and characterization, including the use of dialect voices and the depiction of northern landscape as a site embodying historical conflict. Critics have noted that Lockwood in *Wuthering Heights* has many of the features of a narrator in a Scott novel such as *Waverley*: he is a young urban outsider, southern, inhibited, an 'emotional tourist' in the wilder northern realms he visits. However, Emily wrongfoots any reader who expects a transformation akin to Waverley's. In U. C. Knoepflmacher's view, this upset is 'quite calculated. Readers who had been led to expect Lockwood to turn into the hero of his own tale were obviously disappointed to find him displaced by his more anarchic anti-type'.[10] Scott's *Life of Napoleon* (1827) was a source for Branwell and Charlotte's Angrian fantasies, which revive the Duke of Wellington and the backdrop of the Napoleonic Wars.

Of the Romantic poets, Byron's figure looms largest in the Brontës' literary pantheon. While many young minds were shielded from his more scandalous works, the young Brontës read him fearlessly. Both his poetry and drama and Thomas Moore's *Letters and Journals of Lord Byron, with Notices of his Life* (1830) had potent effects. Charlotte copied engravings illustrating Byron's poetry and life, and these sketches closely resemble her descriptions of Angrian characters. As Heather Glen remarks: 'The developing figure of Zamorna is a markedly Byronic one: heroic, accomplished, magnetically sexually attractive, aristocratically careless of the world's opinion, and ... with a dark and sinful past.'[11] In Branwell and Charlotte's Angrian tales, Caroline Vernon falls in love with Zamorna, her guardian, who nurtures their incestuous union but annihilates her with his mystical power. In *The Professor*, Frances is excited by reading Byron, whose work was synonymous with ungovernable sexual power for a whole generation. Traces of the sinful, accomplished, upper-class renegade who falls dangerously in love with his charge remain in *Jane Eyre*'s Rochester. *Wuthering Heights* is, meanwhile, indebted to the incestuous passion in *The Bride of Abydos* and *Manfred*; as several critics have noticed, Heathcliff's appeal to Cathy in Lockwood's dream: 'Cathy, do come. Oh do – *once* more! Oh! my heart's darling, hear me *this* time – Catherine, at last!' (1.iii.24) closely resembles Manfred's invocation of Astarte: 'Speak to me! though it be in wrath; – but say – / I reck not what – but let me hear thee once – / This once – once more!'[12]

The poetry of Shelley, Coleridge and Wordsworth was also essential reading in the Haworth household, alongside Robert Burns, Thomas Campbell, Thomas Moore and Robert Southey. Shelley's *Epipsychidion* has been identified as another important source for *Wuthering Heights*, while, as Lyn Pykett argues, Emily 'seems constantly to have been rewriting Shelley's "Ode to the West Wind", most notably in "Aye, there it is! It wakes tonight!", which ends with a Shelleyan Platonic vision of the soul escaping from the imprisoning body'.[13] Emily was also deeply engaged by the poetical philosophy of Coleridge and Wordsworth. As Janet Gezari suggests, Emily's poem 'A Day Dream' responds both to Coleridge's *Rime of the Ancient Mariner* and Wordsworth's 'Resolution and Independence'. At the start of 'A Day Dream', the speaker is a joyless guest at the wedding of May and June; she sadly sinks into a reverie, a 'fit of peevish woe' which dwells on the inevitability of winter and of death. Like Coleridge's Mariner and Wordsworth's dejected poet, she is, however, reawakened to the benign force of nature through a vision of 'a thousand thousand gleaming fires . . . kindling in the air'. That vision restores her to a sense of 'universal joy' which can comprehend mortality as a boon, on which immortality depends.[14]

Anne, too, responded to Wordsworth, producing in 'Dreams' a conscious echo of his 'Daffodils':

> While on my lonely couch I lie
> I seldom feel myself alone,
> For fancy fills my dreaming eye
> With scenes and pleasures of its own.[15]

Notably, however, Anne's poem borrows Wordsworth's couch but changes the sitter: her poem speaks of a young woman's longing for a child. Branwell produced a poem, 'The Struggles of Flesh with Spirit/ Scene I – *Infancy*', self-consciously indebted to 'Ode: Intimations of Immortality', and made the mistake of sending it to Wordsworth – 'a divinity of the mind' who, extremely irritated, failed to reply.[16] Charlotte similarly wrote to Southey of her poetic ambitions and received a now-famous rebuff, recommending that she concentrate on domestic duties. The Romantic poets lived in the imaginations of the budding writers as models of authorship whom they conceived stooping, as Charlotte told Southey, 'from a throne of light & glory' (Smith, *Letters*, vol. i, p. 166).

Emily and Charlotte's sojourn in 1842–3 in Brussels, where they studied with M. Heger, introduced them to French Romantic writers such as Chateaubriand, Hugo, Lamartine, Millevoye, Alfred de Musset, Nodier and Bernardin Saint Pierre, whom they read in the original French. Emily learned German, an enthusiasm that probably stemmed from and reinforced her interest in the German works (Schiller, Hoffmann, Goethe) reviewed in translation in *Blackwood's*.[17] The context created by the Brussels experience and French writing is vital to Charlotte's work, especially *The Professor* and *Villette*. The latter seems particularly indebted to the novels of George Sand, which Charlotte borrowed from her friends the Taylors. According to a letter of hers to G. H. Lewes, written on 12 January 1848, she especially valued *Consuelo* (1842–3), Sand's novel in which an outwardly nun-like heroine conceals a passionate inner life (Smith, *Letters*, vol. II, p. 10). Mary Ward, an astute late Victorian critic, stressed the influence of Hugo, de Musset and Sand on Charlotte's intellectual development, remarking that *Jane Eyre* was 'linked in various significant ways with the French romantic movement'.[18]

We know more about Charlotte's reading as an adult than about that of her siblings. An 1840 letter to Hartley Coleridge demonstrates her familiarity with the works of Jean-Jacques Rousseau and with novelists such as Charles Dickens, James Fenimore Cooper and Edward Bulwer Lytton (Smith, *Letters*, vol. I, p. 241). She read, and eventually met, Harriet Martineau and William Thackeray, having praised the latter's work as that of 'the first social regenerator of the day' in her preface to *Jane Eyre*. Her publisher forwarded unfamiliar novels, including those of Jane Austen, whose greatness she questioned in the 1848 letter to Lewes mentioned above (Smith, *Letters*, vol. II, p. 14). It is clear that *Shirley*, though set in the historical context of the Luddite riots, is influenced by the mid-nineteenth-century trend towards social novels (by Dickens, Benjamin Disraeli, Charles Kingsley and others) which explored conflicts between capital and labour. Charlotte, however, did not want to write a tear-jerking account of working-class suffering. She read Frances Trollope's *The Life and Adventures of Michael Armstrong, the Factory Boy* (1840) and strove *not* to emulate its melodramatic depiction of starved and beaten child characters. Interestingly, she encountered Elizabeth Gaskell's industrial novel *Mary Barton* (1848) mid-way through writing *Shirley* and felt the need to differentiate her own social novel from it. As Margaret Smith observes, *Shirley* deliberately avoids the working-class hero and many of the dramatic manoeuvres in *Mary Barton*: a pursuit of the industrialist's attempted assassin, a last-minute rescue from the law and a 'death-throes' reconciliation scene.[19] As Sally Shuttleworth has noticed,[20] Charles Kingsley's verse drama *The Saint's Tragedy; or, The True Story of Elizabeth of Hungary* (1848), which caused Charlotte's eyes to 'rain', is a significant influence on *Villette*. An anti-Catholic propaganda-piece typical of its period, Kingsley's drama describes a queen who was found, on her wedding night, covered in self-inflicted lacerations, unable to reconcile her sexual desires with her religious feelings. She falls into the hands of a venal priest, who sadistically exploits her self-torturing piety. In *Villette*, Lucy Snowe barely escapes falling into the hands of a Roman Catholic priest while in a state of morbid self-doubt.

Arguably, however, the most important literary influences on the Brontës were the Brontës themselves. Patrick Brontë was a published author of didactic poems and stories, including *The Cottage in the Wood*, the tale of a rake's reform. *Jane Eyre* responds to Anne's earlier governess novel *Agnes Grey*, whose quiet and plain first-person narrator describes a process of eroding self-confidence under the thoughtless tyranny of employers before fate eventually reunites her with the good-but-plain clergyman she loves. Equally, *The Tenant of Wildfell Hall* responds critically to *Jane Eyre* and *Wuthering Heights*. Anne's novels have a strong anti-Romantic strain: rejecting the rakish figure of Arthur Huntingdon, who abuses his wife and child, her female artist heroine makes a sober and fulfilling Victorian second marriage, gladly leaving the excesses of the Regency and its self-absorbed cultivation of extreme states of feeling behind her. In *Shirley*, Mrs Pryor's maiden name is Grey, and she has been an ill-used governess. Even after Anne's death, Charlotte could not, it seems, wholly abandon the habit of competitive and collaborative writing that characterizes the Brontës' oeuvre.

NOTES

1 May Sinclair, *The Three Brontës* (London: Hutchinson, 1912), p. 223.

2 Virginia Woolf, *The Common Reader* (London: Hogarth, 1925), p. 200.

3 F. R. Leavis, *The Great Tradition* (London: Chatto & Windus, 1948), p. 27.

4 Sandra M. Gilbert and Susan Gubar, *The Madwoman in the Attic: The Woman Writer and the Nineteenth-Century Literary Imagination* (New Haven: Yale University Press, 1979; repr. 2000), pp. 248–308.

5 Harold Bloom (ed.), *Emily Brontë's* Wuthering Heights (New York: Chelsea, 1987), p. 5.

6 See Christine Alexander and Margaret Smith (eds.), *The Oxford Companion to the Brontës* (Oxford University Press, 2003), pp. 54–6; Barker, esp. pp. 145–50; and Marianne Thormählen, *The Brontës and Education* (Cambridge University Press, 2007), pp. 136–49.

7 See Paul Edmondson, 'Shakespeare and the Brontës', *Brontë Studies*, 29.3 (Nov. 2004), 189–91, and Margaret J. Arnold, 'Coriolanus Transformed: Charlotte Brontë's Use of Shakespeare in *Shirley*', in Marianne Novy (ed.), *Women's Re-Visions of Shakespeare* (Chicago: University of Illinois Press, 1990), pp. 76–88. On Emily's knowledge of Latin, see Edward Chitham, *The Birth of* Wuthering Heights: *Emily Brontë at Work* (Basingstoke: Macmillan, 1998), chapter 2.

8 Thomas Bewick, *A History of British Birds*, vol. II: *Water Birds* (Newcastle: Longman, 1832), pp. xiv–xv.

9 Edward Chitham (ed.), *The Poems of Anne Brontë: A New Text and Commentary* (London: Macmillan, 1979; repr. 1987), p. 84.

10 U. C. Knoepflmacher, *Emily Brontë:* Wuthering Heights (Cambridge University Press, 1989), p. 28.

11 Heather Glen (ed.), *Charlotte Brontë: Tales of Angria* (London: Penguin, 2006), p. 485.

12 See Andrew Elfenbein, *Byron and the Victorians* (Cambridge University Press, 1995), pp. 152–3.

13 Lyn Pykett, *Emily Brontë* (Basingstoke: Macmillan, 1989), p. 29.

14 Janet Gezari, *Last Things: Emily Brontë's Poems* (Oxford University Press, 2007), p. 37.

15 Chitham, *The Poems of Anne Brontë*, p. 113.

16 Apparently Wordsworth communicated his lively disgust with the letter to friends, who gossiped about it. See Smith, *Letters*, vol. I, pp. 160–2.

17 On the Brontës' knowledge of German, see Thormählen, *The Brontës and Education*, pp. 115–17.

18 Mary ('Mrs Humphry') Ward (ed.), *Jane Eyre* (Smith, Elder & Co., 1899), p. xxxviii.

19 See Rosengarten and Smith's 1981 edn of *Shirley* for Oxford World's Classics, p. xii.

20 Sally Shuttleworth, *Charlotte Brontë and Victorian Psychology* (Cambridge University Press, 1996), p. 227.

CHAPTER 18

The Brontës' way into print

Linda H. Peterson

The Brontë sisters have often been mythologized as native geniuses, tucked away in a remote parish of Yorkshire, who rose to literary fame despite their lack of professional training or knowledge of the publishing world. While the sisters suffered, at least initially, from their remoteness from literary London, this myth of naïveté is at odds with known facts of the sisters' production and dissemination of their work. Even as children, Charlotte, Emily and Anne Brontë, along with their brother Branwell, studied the literary periodicals that came their way and imitated the style, content and material form in little magazines of their own. As young adults the sisters pored over literary annuals, such as the *Forget Me Not* and *Literary Souvenir*, reading the poems and stories and copying the elaborate engravings that accompanied them. When, as adults, the sisters decided to venture into print, Charlotte took it upon herself to purchase a professional handbook for authors to learn techniques of manuscript preparation.[1] Throughout their brief careers the sisters were keen observers of the cultural milieu in which their work circulated, with Charlotte carrying on a detailed correspondence with her publisher, Smith, Elder & Co., about the business practices of the literary marketplace.

The Brontës' education in print culture began with the study of *Blackwood's Edinburgh Magazine* and *Fraser's Magazine*. The first they read during the 1820s, by courtesy of a neighbour; the second they received from 1831 onwards, when their Aunt Branwell took out a regular subscription. According to their biographer Juliet Barker, *Blackwood's* 'truly [changed] their lives': the children 'absorbed its Tory politics, made its heroes, from the Duke of Wellington to Lord Byron, into their own heroes and copied its serio-comic style' (Barker, p. 149). That serio-comic style, exhibited particularly in the column 'Noctes Ambrosianae', in which imaginary drinking companions sit round a table at a tavern and converse about literature and politics, may not have served Branwell well. He not only tried to imitate the literary drinking parties but also imbibed the jocular, masculine style of the column, using it inappropriately when he wrote to the editor of *Blackwood's* to offer his services. Nonetheless, for all the Brontë children, *Blackwood's* was both educational and inspirational. Charlotte and Branwell produced a homemade version, 'Blackwood's Young Men's Magazine', written in a minuscule handwriting to mimic printed text and filled both with contemporary figures whom they had encountered in the magazine and with fictional characters to populate their invented political kingdoms and romantic counterplots. As the Brontës developed as writers, *Blackwood's* provided models for popular fiction, gave access to the work of such prominent poets as James Hogg and Felicia Hemans and shed light, via its reviews, on contemporary literary taste.

Arguably, though, it was *Fraser's Magazine* that taught the Brontë sisters their most practical lessons in authorship. In 1830 the magazine initiated a series of engraved portraits and verbal sketches of prominent British authors. This 'Literary Gallery' began with depictions of the editors of leading London magazines; it included the 'Fraserians' sitting round a table toasting their publisher and continued with portraits of eight literary women, 'Regina's Maids of Honour', as *Fraser's* called them.[2] Carol A. Bock has shown how, through its portraits, columns and reviews, *Fraser's* 'set itself up as literary advisor to "the ingenious Pupil of the Muse"'; it 'repeatedly addressed itself to prospective contributors and literary hopefuls whom it characterized as youthful, inexperienced, and sorely in need of ... advice'.[3] The Brontës were just such literary hopefuls when they began reading *Fraser's* as teenagers.

What lessons in authorship would they have absorbed? The magazine offered general advice: 'that coming forward [as an author] is a tricky process, one fraught with danger and personal risk for men and women alike'.[4] To negotiate the dangers, *Fraser's* taught literary aspirants how to be modest yet determined, successful without seeming egotistical or self-absorbed. Beyond general principles, the Brontë sisters would have learned specific lessons about women's authorship, as depicted in 'Regina's Maids' and individual portraits that *Fraser's* published of Mary Russell Mitford, Caroline Norton, Laetitia Landon, Harriet Martineau and their female contemporaries. They would have learned that literary women must be properly domestic – as in Mitford's appearance within her village home, surrounded by flowers and attended by a faithful dog, or in Caroline Norton's portrait as a dutiful wife pouring tea for her husband. They would have learned that love poetry and romantic fiction were appropriate genres for women – as in *Fraser's* praise of Landon for choosing 'the tender passion as the theme for woman' – whereas politics and 'economical philosophy' were deemed unacceptable, as evidenced in the caricature of Martineau for writing her *Illustrations of Political Economy*. And they would have learned that excessive preening or self-display was inappropriate – as in the satire on Lady Morgan adjusting her hat in 'a cheval glass'.[5]

Such lessons in gender and genre were reinforced by the Brontës' reading of literary annuals. These lavishly illustrated books, typically produced for gift-giving during the holiday season, contained fiction and verse that reflected a presumed feminine interest in love and courtship, whether thwarted or fulfilled. All three sisters studied *Friendship's Offering* (1829), *The Literary Souvenir* (1830) and *Forget Me Not* (1831), taking from them lessons in art and authorship. Charlotte painstakingly reproduced engravings of Bolton Abbey, a Gothic ruin, and an 'Italian Scene' with a dreamlike landscape. Anne copied picturesque scenes like Robert Batty's 'Ober Wessel on the Rhine'. Both Charlotte and Emily copied 'The Disconsolate', a print depicting a young woman grieving, a sympathizing dog at her feet.[6]

From the landscapes, the Brontës imbibed the pictorial aesthetic that permeated so much poetry of the 1830s and 1840s. From the poem by Landon (L. E. L.) written to accompany 'The Disconsolate' (and others like it), they learned the conventions of the lyric lament. They absorbed, too, the features of sentimental domestic verse, with its enshrinement of the home. Selections in the sisters' first volume, *Poems of Currer, Ellis, and Acton Bell* (1846), show all these influences. Charlotte's 'The Lonely Lady' depicts a poetess straight out of Landon – with pale but perfect features, wearied of 'trying all her harp's symphonious powers', and in her grief virtually transforming herself into a 'sculpture effigy' within a 'Gothic pile'. One of Anne's lyrics depicts the anguish of a young maiden who silently suffers the loss of her lover: 'He came not nigh – he went away / And then my joy was past'. In another, 'Home', Anne describes 'a lovely scene' under 'softly smiling skies', yet expresses a stronger longing for the 'little spot, / With gray walls compassed round' that is her home. Such maidenly anguish or devotion to domesticity may not have led to great poetry, but it sold well in literary annuals and ladies' magazines. Emily wrote passionate lyric laments in her private journals, and she published a powerful example, 'Remembrance', in the 1846 *Poems*. If Emily was also influenced by a Wordsworthian tradition of nature poetry and a Byronic tradition of philosophical rebellion, thus making her verse seem more masculine than her sisters', it is nonetheless the case that she absorbed the influence of the periodicals and annuals before she launched into print.

Of course, popular feminine genres were not the only ones the Brontës encountered in early nineteenth-century print; they also read ballads, elegies, sonnets, dramatic monologues and devotional verse. Anne made use of this wider range by submitting two devotional pieces to *Fraser's Magazine* in 1848: 'The Three Guides' and 'The Narrow Way', published in August and December respectively.[7] Recognizing that *Fraser's* constructed itself as a masculine periodical, Anne shrewdly read its gender politics and offered a poetic genre suitable for its pages.

When it came to transforming their manuscripts into a book, however, Charlotte took the lead. In her description of the sisters' entry into public authorship, she emphasizes both Romantic masculine power and Victorian feminine decorum:

One day, in the autumn of 1845, I accidentally lighted on a MS. volume of verse in my sister Emily's handwriting. ... [S]omething more than surprise seized me, – a deep conviction that these were not common effusions, nor at all like the poetry women generally write. I thought them condensed and terse, vigorous and genuine. To my ear they had also a peculiar music – wild, melancholy, and elevating. ... Meantime, my younger sister quietly produced some of her own compositions ... I could not but be a partial judge, yet I thought that these verses too had a sweet sincere pathos of their own.[8]

Charlotte maintains the Romantic myth of genius in describing Emily's poetry while associating Anne's with sincere feminine feeling. In this account, she presents herself as the most professional – insisting that they arrange a small selection of their poems, consulting an Edinburgh publisher for advice and buying *The Author's Printing and Publishing Assistant* to learn details of book production.[9] In this guidebook, Charlotte would have read about the printing process; about paper, type and fonts; about preparing a clean manuscript and reading proofs; about choosing bindings and decorative devices; and about advertising.

Charlotte took these practical matters seriously when she negotiated the details of book production with Aylott and Jones, publishers of the *Poems of Currer, Ellis, and Acton Bell* (1846). She requested that their work 'be printed in 1 octavo volume of the same quality paper and size of type as Moxon's last edition of Wordsworth'. Though she misjudged the relation of manuscript to printed pages, and so had to adjust down from 'royal octavo' to 'duodecimo', she nonetheless insisted on '*clear* type', having learned its importance from her guidebook. She asked for 'long primer', the recommended type for poetry and duodecimo volumes.[10] Once such details had been settled, Charlotte paid the printer's bill and began discussing advertisements and review copies.[11] She acted as the agent of Currer, Ellis and Acton Bell – pseudonyms chosen because they were not exactly masculine, but sufficiently ambiguous to avoid 'what is called "feminine"'. As Charlotte explained: 'we had the impression that authoresses are liable to be looked upon with prejudice'.[12]

The stillbirth of the *Poems* probably had little to do with the gender of the authors or with their names: it sold only two copies and received few reviews. This result was predictable since, from the 1830s when the market for poetry began to decline, the publishing watchword was 'Poetry don't sell'.[13] Despite their disappointment, the sisters determined to make their way as authors and try the market for fiction, composing short novels even before their verse appeared in print. Charlotte's increasing knowledge of the publishing business informed her enquiries to Aylott and Jones about selling their fiction, even as moments of naïveté surfaced in her letters. For example, when Charlotte informed them that 'C. E. & A. Bell are now preparing for the Press a work of fiction', she added, 'it is not their intention to publish these tales on their own account' – thus signalling that she understood the difference between the poetry and fiction markets, whereby poets must bear the cost of publication whereas novelists received up-front payments for copyright of their manuscripts. When Aylott and Jones (presumably) advised her that they did not publish fiction on this basis, she asked more questions: whether it might be better to submit a work of three volumes or offer 'contributions to a periodical'; which publishers would be likely to look favourably on submissions of fiction; and whether she must ask for a personal interview or simply 'write to a publisher' (Smith, *Letters*, vol. 1, p. 462).

We do not know what counterparts in the fiction business Aylott and Jones recommended. We might surmise that Charlotte tried Saunders and Otley, given her knowledge of their *Author's Printing and Publishing Assistant.* We know that she sent an unsuccessful enquiry to Henry Colburn about 'three tales' comprising 'a work of fiction in 3 vols.' (Smith, *Letters*, vol. 1, p. 481); in this strategy, the sisters were aiming at the market for the 'triple-decker', a staple of circulating libraries. But we can be sure that she tried multiple publishers, for the publisher George Smith told Elizabeth Gaskell, Charlotte's first biographer, that when he received the manuscript of *The Professor*, the brown paper parcel it came in bore the crossed-out addresses of other publishers to whom the manuscript had been sent before – thus revealing prior 'houses in the trade to which the unlucky parcel had gone, without success' (Gaskell, *Life*, p. 255). Eventually, when Thomas Newby of Cavendish Square,

London, accepted *Wuthering Heights* and *Agnes Grey* but not *The Professor*, Charlotte found a home with Smith, Elder & Co. at 65 Cornhill – not placing her first novel, but successfully submitting *Jane Eyre* to this reputable firm.

Newby's publishing practices are now considered 'shifty'.[14] At the time, however, his proposal to Emily and Anne reflected a common practice adopted with unknown authors: he agreed to print 350 copies, asking for £50 to cover costs and contracting to return the money once 250 copies were sold. If Newby had fulfilled this contract, he would not today be execrated in biographies of the Brontës. But Newby under-printed, failed to show the authors proofs, left errors uncorrected and never returned their £50 or sent profits when the novels became best-sellers. As Charlotte put it in a letter to George Smith after receiving a £100 payment for *Jane Eyre*, 'Your conduct to me has been such that you cannot doubt my relatives would have been most happy, had it been in their power, to avail themselves of your proposal respecting the publication of their future works' (Smith, *Letters*, vol. II, p. 29). Nonetheless, Anne felt she could not leave Newby, and she published her second novel, *The Tenant of Wildfell Hall*, with his firm – this time receiving a £25 payment on publication and another £25 when sales reached 250 copies.[15]

After her sisters' deaths, Charlotte took their novels to Smith, Elder & Co. for a new edition, published in 1850 with a 'Biographical Notice' describing her sisters' brief lives and literary careers. Newby was reluctant to let go, claiming (falsely) that he held copyright and threatening legal action. Despite the obstacles he created, Smith negotiated the transfer of Emily's and Anne's novels to his firm and even induced Newby to send Charlotte £30 in additional payment for Anne's second book. Charlotte remained loyal to Smith, Elder & Co. – 'my kind friends at Cornhill'.[16]

That loyalty was less about financial profits than about fair dealing and steady encouragement. (Charlotte received, in the end, £500 for each novel – a solid remuneration in an era when £50 and £100 were common payments, but nothing like the £800 and £1000 figures of the 1870s.)[17] In her 'Biographical Notice' Charlotte tells not only of her sisters' literary ambitions, but of her own. She describes 'the chill of despair' that invaded her heart when her first novel failed to find acceptance anywhere, and then her grateful surprise when, despite an official rejection, a letter from Smith, Elder & Co. 'discussed its merits and demerits so courteously, so considerately, in a spirit so rational, with a discrimination so enlightened, that this very refusal cheered the author better than a vulgarly-expressed acceptance would have done' (Smith, *Letters*, vol. II, p. 744). With that first letter, Charlotte knew she had found a publishing firm interested in literature – committed to financial profits, of course, but also committed to books of intellectual and artistic merit, familiar with trends in print culture and supportive of literary aspirants whose work showed promise. Throughout her career she stayed with Smith, Elder & Co., publishing *Shirley* in 1849 and *Villette* in 1853, with *The Professor* appearing posthumously in 1857.

NOTES

1 *The Author's Printing and Publishing Assistant* (London: Saunders and Otley, [1839]).

2 See 'The Fraserians', *Fraser's Magazine*, 11 (Jan. 1835), 27, and 'Regina's Maids of Honour', *Fraser's Magazine*, 13 (Jan. 1836), 80.

3 Carol A. Bock, 'Authorship, the Brontës, and *Fraser's Magazine*: "Coming Forward" as an Author in Early Victorian England', *Victorian Literature and Culture*, 29 (2001), 243.

4 *Ibid.*, p. 247.

5 See 'Mary Russell Mitford', *Fraser's Magazine*, 3 (May 1831), 410; 'Caroline Norton', *Fraser's Magazine*, 3 (Mar. 1831), 222; 'Laetitia Landon (L. E. L.)', *Fraser's Magazine*, 8 (Oct. 1833), 433; 'Harriet Martineau', *Fraser's Magazine*, 8 (Nov. 1833), 576; and 'Lady Morgan', *Fraser's Magazine*, 11 (May 1835), 529.

6 See Christine Alexander, 'Educating "The Artist's Eye": Charlotte Brontë and the Pictorial Image', in Sandra Hagan and Juliette Wells (eds.), *The Brontës in the World of the Arts* (Aldershot: Ashgate, 2008), pp. 18–21, as well as Christine Alexander and Jane Sellars, *The Art of the Brontës* (Cambridge University Press, 1995).

7 Acton Bell, 'The Three Guides', *Fraser's Magazine*, 38 (Aug. 1848), 193–5, and 'The Narrow Way', *Fraser's Magazine*, 38 (Dec. 1848), 712.

8 See Charlotte's 'Biographical Notice of Ellis and Acton Bell', repr. in Smith, *Letters*, vol. II, pp. 742–7.

9 For the detail that Charlotte 'bought a small volume, from which to learn all she could on the subject of preparation for the press', see Gaskell, *Life*, pp. 231 and 526n.

10 *Author's Printing and Publishing Assistant*, p. 50.

11 See the letters to Messrs Aylott and Jones of Jan.–May 1846, in Smith, *Letters*, vol. I, pp. 449, 453, 454 and 470.

12 From the 'Biographical Notice', Smith, *Letters*, vol. II, p. 743. On the sisters' choice of pseudonyms, see Marianne Thormählen, 'The Brontë Pseudonyms', *English Studies*, 75.3 (May 1994), 246–55.

13 See Lee Erickson, 'The Market', in Richard Cronin, Alison Chapman and Antony H. Harrison (eds.), *A Companion to Victorian Poetry* (Oxford: Blackwell, 2002), pp. 345–60.

14 See Elisabeth Sanders Arbuckle, 'Newby, Thomas Cautley (1797–1882)', *Oxford Dictionary of National Biography*, online edn, Sept. 2010, http://www.oxforddnb.com/view/article/47457 [accessed 15 May 2012].

15 According to Charlotte Brontë writing to George Smith on 18 Sept. 1850, Newby thus made the two £25 payments, but he failed to send a promised £50 on the sale of 400 copies; Smith, *Letters*, vol. II, p. 473.

16 Letter to W. S. Williams, 16 Apr. 1849, in Smith, *Letters*, vol. II, p. 203; Charlotte uses variants of this phrase throughout her correspondence.

17 For Charlotte's profits, see Smith, *Letters*, vol. II, p. 29, n. 2.

CHAPTER 19

Reading the Brontës: their first audiences

Stephen Colclough

The novelist William Thackeray was one of the earliest readers of *Jane Eyre*, and his reaction to the novel reveals the excitement felt by many Victorian readers: 'I wish you had not sent me *Jane Eyre*. It interested me so much that I have lost (or won if you like) a whole day reading it at the busiest period.' Both Charlotte's publisher George Smith and the anonymous reviewer for *Fraser's Magazine* also recalled being unable to put it down; the latter, having begun the novel on a winter's evening, 'finally married Mr Rochester about four in the morning'. All three were, of course, privileged readers: Smith was reading Charlotte's manuscript, and Thackeray and the reviewer had been sent copies by the publisher.[1] They were excited by the text, but they also read for professional reasons: to judge the quality of a manuscript, to assess a literary competitor and to produce a review. This chapter sets out to explore how other, less privileged readers accessed the Brontës' work when it was first published.

How does the work of the Brontës fit into the context of early to mid-Victorian publishing? All the first editions of the novels – with the exception of *The Professor* (1857) – appeared in the format most commonly associated with Victorian fiction, the three-volume novel. *The Professor* was famously too short for this format, and T. C. Newby published *Wuthering Heights* and *Agnes Grey* together in a three-volume edition, with Anne's shorter novel occupying the final volume. The typical print run of a three-decker was 1,000 copies, up to half of which might be sold directly to the commercial libraries before publication. However, the three-volume novel was not the only, or even the major, form in which fiction was published at this time. From the 1830s onwards it was common to find novels published in parts. For example, Dickens' *Dombey and Son* (1846–8) first appeared in twenty parts at 1s each, a format perfected by the author in the previous decade. Part-issue was a unique form, packaging fiction together with illustrations and surrounding the whole in a wrapper covered in advertisements. As with Thackeray's *Vanity Fair* (1847–8), a bound version of the whole run was usually made available for 21s when it concluded, and a traditional three-decker was issued at around the same time, so that the novel was available to several different audiences at once. Serialization in newspapers and magazines was also common. *Oliver Twist* (1837–9) appeared in *Bentley's Miscellany*, and Dickens' own magazine *Household Words* (1850–9) published some of his own and other novelists' work.

By appearing only in the traditional three-volume format, the work of the Brontës looked significantly different from that which appeared in part-issue or serialized form. For its first audience, a serialized novel gradually revealed its contents over several months and illustrations were an integral part of the text, whereas the first readers of *Jane Eyre* could press on until they married Rochester in the early hours of the morning. However, as the three-decker was more expensive to buy than these other formats, it is likely that many first readers would have borrowed rather than bought the Brontës' work. The price of a new three-volume novel was set at 31s 6d (£1 11s 6d) in the 1820s and remained the same until the 1890s.[2] As Simon Eliot has argued, even for a middle-class family with an income of £400 per year, 31s 6d was 'a huge sum', representing about 'twenty percent of gross weekly income' or 'close to the total disposable income available to such a middle-class family'. Even for a lawyer earning £1,000 per year, 31s 6d was 8 per cent of his weekly income.[3]

Borrowing a book in the 1840s and 1850s entailed its own strategies of acquisition and reading, but before moving on to discuss what kinds of library stocked the sisters' work, we need to know how these first readers would have become aware of its existence. Both buyers and borrowers relied on printed sources for information about new books. In order to be successful, a book needed to be advertised and reviewed both in the metropolitan newspapers and in general intellectual weekly magazines, such as *The Athenaeum*. Charlotte Brontë was aware of this need for publicity, requesting that the publishers of *Poems* (1846) send out review copies and place advertisements in eight periodicals and two newspapers (letter to Aylott and Jones of 7 May 1846; Smith, *Letters*, vol. I, p. 470). Smith, Elder & Co. ran an effective campaign for *Jane Eyre*, which was advertised in *The Literary Gazette* on 16 October 1847 as one of three 'new novels' about to be published and was included among a longer list of 'new books' in *The Athenaeum* on the same day. From 13 October 1847 onwards, regular advertisements also appeared in a range of newspapers. That Smith, Elder & Co. anticipated that many readers would borrow rather than buy is suggested by the fact that most of these advertisements advised that it was 'now ready at all the Libraries'. The efficacy of sending out review copies is suggested by the fact that extracts from favourable assessments in *The Atlas* and *The Weekly Chronicle* appeared in these adverts within two weeks of the book's being first announced.[4] By the time the novel had gone into a second three-volume edition in January 1848, the advertising campaign (which was now for the book alone) included extracts from up to ten reviews.[5] From December 1847, Newby's advertising campaign for *Wuthering Heights* and *Agnes Grey* deliberately associated the work of Ellis and Acton Bell with Charlotte's already successful novel. Newby's use of the phrases 'Mr Bell's Successful New Novel' and 'The Popular New Novelist' echoed Smith, Elder & Co.'s description of *Jane Eyre* as the 'New Work of a New Novelist', and his use of extracts from reviews declaring the affinity between *Wuthering Heights* and Charlotte's novel was designed to encourage readers of the latter to acquire the new text.[6] The absence of any author's name from some of Newby's advertisements was perhaps even designed to encourage readers to assume that all three novels were the work of the same author.[7] Whether they bought or borrowed, the experience of many of the Brontës' first readers was framed by these advertising campaigns, which frequently quoted from reviews and encouraged the novels to be compared in terms of style and subject matter.

If many first readers borrowed rather than bought the novels, how were they acquired? By the 1840s many towns included a commercial circulating library from which books could be rented, usually after the payment of a yearly, quarterly or monthly subscription. The most famous Victorian circulating library, Charles Mudie's Select Library, was founded in Bloomsbury in 1842. In the 1840s, Mudie's offered a wide selection of periodicals and books – not just fiction – to 'Town' (i.e. London) subscribers at an annual fee of one guinea, a fee which would enable them to have a single volume out at a time. 'Country' subscribers, who wanted books delivered, and those who wanted more volumes paid higher subscription rates. In February 1848, for example, a three-guinea subscription gained a town reader one year's access to 'Twelve Volumes (exchangeable at pleasure)' from Mudie's own list, or from the latest lists of a number of publishers including Smith, Elder & Co. For those who could afford to join, both *Jane Eyre* and *Wuthering Heights* were available to be ordered from Mudie's 'List of New and Choice Books' in February 1848.[8] Although cheaper than buying individual novels at 31s 6d, Mudie's fees were still a substantial outlay for a middle-class family of the sort described above. As an alternative, some commercial libraries offered shorter subscription periods, such as weekly or daily rates, and some even charged by the volume borrowed.

Surviving catalogues and advertisements for other commercial libraries suggest that the Brontë novels were widely available from circulating libraries both large and small. In October 1847, the circulating library run by Mrs Deighton from her bookseller's shop in Worcester included *Jane Eyre*, and it was still being listed as a 'new addition', along with *Wuthering Heights* and *The Tenant of Wildfell Hall*, in November 1848. Deighton's mimicked Mudie's one-guinea annual subscription; but the minimum fee was 3s 6d for one month, and this entitled the reader to 'one set of books' (i.e. all three volumes of a novel) rather than the single volume available from Mudie.[9] In the same year, the annual subscription to Thomas Griffiths's Circulating Library in Ludlow charged an expensive-sounding two guineas for access to just 555 titles, but non-subscribers could borrow *Jane Eyre* – a new addition to the catalogue that year – for as little as 3d per volume. In the mid 1850s another small circulating library, F. T. Vibert's in Penzance, stocked all of the novels apart from *Wuthering Heights* for an even cheaper 2d per volume; but they needed to be returned within four days. Similarly, in 1856, Thurnam's Circulating Library in Carlisle charged its non-members 1d per volume 'per evening' or 2d per week, thus allowing swift readers to complete *Wuthering Heights* for just one or two pence, depending on the edition.[10]

Who had access to these libraries? Margaret Beetham has argued that the mid-Victorian circulating library gave women who had 'some domestic comfort' access to a greater range of texts than ever before, especially if they could afford to have their books delivered. There is substantial evidence that the Brontë sisters themselves borrowed books from commercial libraries in nearby Keighley.[11] However, the clientèle of circulating libraries was not restricted to women. Mudie's selection of 'new and choice' books was designed to appeal to all the members of a family who might choose to visit his premises at the same time. Advertisements drawing attention to the fact that commercial libraries stocked novels by the Bell brothers also had the effect of underlining that these were fashionable texts. Mudie's adverts were prominently placed to catch the eager reader's eye. That on the front page of *The Literary Gazette* for 29 January 1853, for example, announced that the Select Library had acquired 150 copies of *Villette*, first advertised as a forthcoming publication just two weeks previously.[12] The novel's popularity is signalled by the increase in the number of copies to 200 just a few days later.[13] One side-effect of such popularity was that once the rush to read was over, 'surplus copies' were made available to subscribers at a reduced price. *Villette* was offered for sale from Mudie's surplus stock at 19s, for example, just over three months after it first appeared on the library's shelves.[14] This does not mean that borrowing had stopped, however, and *Villette* continued to be advertised for rent into the following year. By January 1854 its surplus price had been reduced to 9s, bringing the novel to a new audience of purchasers, including other library owners who might buy to rent it out again.[15] Commercial circulating libraries needed to sell books in order to maintain their profits, and as the advertisement for *Villette* at 13s from Cawthorn and Hutt's Library suggests, copies of the novel that had already been circulated were quite widely available within a few months of publication.[16] However, it is worth remembering that 9s is still a hefty price in comparison to the 2s 6d that would buy a middle-class reader a reprint novel at a railway station.

Not all nineteenth-century libraries were commercial, though many charged an entry fee or had rules regarding access. For example, Patrick Brontë's 5s admission fee and weekly contribution of twopence gave him access to the reading room and library of the Keighley Mechanics' Institute. There were more than 700 institutes in Britain by 1851, usually attended by professionals and clergymen (as was Keighley's) rather than the working-class mechanics that they were intended for.[17] Most had libraries; and despite a reputation for the serious study of 'useful knowledge', many of these included fiction. My own survey of catalogues failed to find any Brontë novels, but was too small to be conclusive, and it is likely that some among the 700 would have stocked the sisters' work. Subscription libraries served a similarly middle-class readership. These libraries emerged in significant numbers in the latter half of the eighteenth century, and they are related to the book-clubs and reading societies that flourished in the same period. Like the commercial libraries, they relied upon money generated by subscriptions; but they usually catered for only a small membership, both new members and books being elected by committee. For example, in 1850 members of the Northampton General Library paid an annual fee of one guinea and became full 'proprietary' members only after five years. Full members nominated books to be ordered by a committee that met each month. Both *Jane Eyre* and *Shirley* were included in the 1850 catalogue, *Villette* and *Wuthering Heights* being added in 1854.[18] In the mid 1850s, similar libraries in Manchester and Lichfield contained all of Charlotte's novels but nothing by her sisters, while Kingston-upon-Hull had everything except *The Tenant*.[19] If the circulating library is sometimes imagined as a female space, subscription libraries are usually associated with a predominantly male readership and a preponderance of serious works. However, this is perhaps a more accurate description of the Georgian rather than the Victorian subscription library. In 1854, thirty-three of the ninety 'shareholder' members at the Lichfield Library were women (eighteen of whom were not married). As one may expect of a cathedral city, many members were clergymen or professionals; but it is important to remember that members did not necessarily borrow only for themselves, and it was common practice for texts to be shared through reading aloud.

Circulating libraries, Mechanics' Institutes and subscription libraries all charged their members a fee. Throughout the 1840s, there was a concerted campaign to establish free libraries open to all which resulted in the Public Libraries Act of 1850. The Act was 'severely restricted' because it was 'confined to boroughs of populations exceeding 10,000; required a poll of ratepayers; and included a rate cap'. With considerable opposition to 'culture on the rates', only twenty-seven library authorities had been founded by the mid 1860s.[20] The real growth in public libraries began in the 1870s; but wherever they were established in the 1850s, these libraries gave new opportunities for working-class readers to acquire books. Most included fiction. The surviving catalogues of the Manchester Free Library reveal that these new library spaces included work by the Brontës. In 1854 the Manchester lending department included both *Jane Eyre* and *Wuthering Heights*, and by 1857 the Hulme branch was offering multiple copies of all of Charlotte's novels and a single copy of the 1852 edition of the sisters' poetry. In the same year, the Ancoats and Ardwick branch included an original copy of the *Poems* (1846) and new single-volume reprints of *Jane Eyre*, *Shirley* and *Villette*.[21] Manchester was perhaps unusually well stocked with novels, but even the smaller collection of the Liverpool Free Public Library included *Shirley*.[22] We do not know whether *Shirley* lay neglected on the shelves or was read and returned until its pages began to decay, as no borrowing records survive from this time, but the ordering of multiple copies at Manchester suggests that the Brontë novels were being borrowed from such venues during the 1850s.

This chapter suggests that the Brontë novels were available from a range of libraries that charged for access, the multiple copies of *Villette* ordered by Mudie allowing a significant number of middle-class subscribers to read the text simultaneously soon after it was published. Smaller, cheaper libraries, the selling-on of surplus copies and the free public libraries (where available, when they arrived) also meant that contact with these texts in the first years after publication was not restricted to those who could afford 31s 6d or Mudie's one-guinea fee.

NOTES

1 Miriam Allott (ed.), *The Brontës: The Critical Heritage* (London: Routledge & Kegan Paul, 1974), pp. 70 and 152. Smith's remarks are quoted by Barker, p. 527.
2 The abbreviations refer to the old British currency, in which there were 12 pence ('d') in a shilling ('s'). 20 shillings made up a pound and 21 a guinea.
3 Simon Eliot, '"Never Mind the Value, What about the Price?"', *Nineteenth-Century Literature*, 56.2 (2001), 166–7.
4 *The Literary Gazette*, 30 Oct. 1847, p. 776; *The Athenaeum*, 30 Oct. 1847, p. 1115.
5 *The Examiner*, 22 Jan. 1848, p. 63; *The Athenaeum*, 22 Jan. 1848, p. 74.
6 *The Examiner*, 19 Feb. 1848, p. 128; *The Examiner*, 29 Jan. 1848, p. 80.
7 On Newby's deliberate confusion over the authorship of the Bell texts, see Allott, *Critical Heritage*, p. 11 and Chapter 18 in this volume.
8 *The Athenaeum*, 26 Feb. 1848, p. 1.
9 *Berrow's Worcester Journal*, 28 Oct. 1847 and 23 Nov. 1848.
10 *Catalogue of the Circulating Library of T. Griffiths Jun., Bull-Ring Ludlow* (Ludlow, [1850]); *A Catalogue of F. T. Vibert's Circulating Library Market-Place, Penzance* (Penzance, [185?]); *Catalogue of Thurnam's Circulating Library Carlisle* (Carlisle, 1856).
11 Margaret Beetham, 'Women and the Consumption of Print', in Joanne Shattock (ed.), *Women and Literature in Britain 1800–1900* (Cambridge University Press, 2001), pp. 59–60; Bob Duckett, 'Where Did the Brontës Get Their Books?', *Brontë Studies*, 32.3 (Nov. 2007), 193–206.
12 *The Literary Gazette*, 29 Jan. 1853, p. 1.
13 *The Examiner*, 5 Feb. 1853, p. 95.
14 *The Athenaeum*, 14 May 1853, p. 578.
15 See the advertisement in *The Manchester Times*, 4 Jan. 1854, headed 'To Librarians and Others'.
16 *The Athenaeum*, 18 June 1853, p. 724.
17 Duckett, 'Where Did the Brontës', p. 195; Marianne Thormählen, *The Brontës and Education* (Cambridge University Press, 2007), pp. 19–20.
18 *A Catalogue of the General Library, Northampton* (Northampton, 1854).
19 *A Catalogue of the Books Belonging to the Permanent Library, Lichfield 1854* (Lichfield, 1854); *Catalogue of the Library of the Portico Library, Manchester* (Manchester, 1856); *A Catalogue of the Subscription Library at Kingston-upon-Hull* (Hull, 1855).

20 Alistair Black, *A New History of the English Public Library: Social and Intellectual Contexts, 1850–1914* (London: Leicester University Press, 1996), pp. 19–20.

21 *Manchester Free Library: Catalogue of the Lending Library* (Manchester, 1854); *Catalogue of the Hulme Branch Lending Department, November 1857* (Manchester, 1857); *Catalogue of the Ancoats and Ardwick Branch Lending Department, December 1857* (Manchester, 1857).

22 *Catalogue of the Liverpool Free Public Library* (Liverpool, 1855).

PART II

Scholarship, criticism, adaptations and translations

CHAPTER 20

Brontë biography: a survey of a genre

Tom Winnifrith

George Smith published *Jane Eyre* in 1847, earning fame and fortune for himself at the beginning of a long and distinguished career. He also won undying gratitude from the reading public. Fifty years later he published the Haworth edition of the works of the Brontës, and this too has been very useful to generations of students. The text of the novels is reliable, there are pleasant black and white photographs, and Mary ('Mrs Humphry') Ward provided good introductions. She was herself a famous novelist at the time and, like her uncle Matthew Arnold, a discerning critic and admirer of Emily Brontë. In other respects Emily and Anne fare less well in the Haworth edition. Smith included Charlotte's 'Biographical Notice' to the 1850 edition, which damns Anne with faint praise and praises *Wuthering Heights* with faint damns. He also produced selections from the poetry of the three sisters which Charlotte had edited in a very cavalier fashion. Finally, he added Elizabeth Gaskell's *Life of Charlotte Brontë*.

The inclusion of Gaskell's biography not only makes Charlotte the principal Brontë, but has led to the belief that the lives of the Brontës were, like their novels, dramatic, exciting, wild and sad like the landscape near Haworth and the atmosphere of *Wuthering Heights*. Gaskell (whose novels are not all as cosy as *Cranford*) exaggerated the savagery of life at Haworth, ignoring the proximity of large industrial towns; but she was fairly restrained in drawing parallels between fact and fiction. Attempts to equate Lowood and Cowan Bridge had caused trouble. Later biographies were less careful. Smith's decision to publish Gaskell's *Life* probably encouraged readers to see the novels as autobiographical, a vision damaging to biography and criticism.

As editor of Gaskell's biography in the Haworth series, Smith chose Clement Shorter. The decision was again unfortunate, although perhaps inevitable. Shorter owned or had access to material which could supplement Gaskell's account. In addition, he had – or claimed he had – the right to publish this material. In 1895 he had purchased both manuscripts and copyright for himself and T. J. Wise from Mr Nicholls in Ireland. In *Charlotte Brontë and her Circle* (1896), Shorter included new and unpublished letters; he produced more in the Haworth edition of 1900; and in 1908 he added still further letters in the two-volume *Life and Letters*, for many years the standard reference work for aspiring biographers.

Shorter was by profession a journalist. He was genial but unscrupulous, not worried about letting the truth get in the way of a good story. His dealings with Arthur Nicholls and Ellen Nussey were not honestly conducted, although the more dishonest Wise has taken most of the blame. The two published a great deal of material which they copied very badly and scattered widely. It took at least two generations before the flaws of Shorter and Wise as editors and as men were generally recognized.[1] As a literary editor Shorter is equally at fault. He begins by extolling Gaskell's biography as one of the most famous of its genre: Gaskell on Charlotte Brontë is compared to Lockhart on Scott and Boswell on Johnson as the author of a definitive biography. More recent Brontë biographers have shown that this was an exaggerated claim.

Shorter's preface supplies a useful list of seventeen works on various members of the Brontë family published between 1857 and the end of the century.[2] To this number in the period before the First World War we must add Shorter's *Life and Letters* and May Sinclair's *The Three Brontës*. Both writers take some of the emphasis away from Charlotte, who was now beginning to lose some of her stature as a novelist. Sinclair's book is worth reading, as it captures better than Gaskell the painful conflict all three sisters faced between the calls of duty and feminine freedom. Unfortunately for both biographers, a nasty surprise was waiting in the shape of four letters from Charlotte to Monsieur Heger published in 1913. Shorter had maintained that there was nothing improper about Charlotte's feelings for her teacher. Gaskell had known about this doomed love affair, had judged that it would be thought improper and had explained Charlotte's sadness on her return from Belgium by her anticipating Branwell's decline. Sinclair was shocked by the discovery that her feminist icon had been tainted by love for a married man. Most students of the Brontës seized upon the letters as proof that Charlotte's novels were indeed autobiographical, Heger, a married masterful Belgian schoolmaster, being the obvious model for a series of heroes who are married or masterful or Belgian or teachers or a combination of these attributes. Shorter printed the letters to Heger without comment in a revised edition of *Life and Letters* in 1914.

The Heger letters were a godsend to those who thought that there was some mysterious key to the Brontës which would open up the real secrets of their lives.[3] English literature was now a respectable subject in British and American universities, but a reaction against Charlotte as a writer and hostility to biography as an aid to literary criticism left the way open to amateurs rather than scholars. Both F. R. Leavis and his Oxford contemporary, the biographer and literary historian Lord David Cecil, thought little of Charlotte; and Winifred Gérin's *Charlotte Brontë: The Evolution of Genius*, published in 1967, was in a way a reaction against the groves of academe.

Gérin's biography was, as its title indicates, complimentary to Charlotte. It was published by the Oxford University Press and has a skeleton apparatus of footnotes and references. As evidence for Charlotte's letters, she quotes the 1908 edition of Shorter and the enlarged Shakespeare Head version edited by Wise and J. A. Symington. Wise's incompetence and dishonesty have already been mentioned. Symington was not much better. Only in recent years, thanks to the labours of Christine Alexander, Victor Neufeldt and Margaret Smith, have there been satisfactory editions of the juvenilia, poetry and letters of the Brontës, and of modern biographers only Juliet Barker seems fully cognizant of the inadequacy of the Shakespeare Head. Smith's edition of the letters is of course now a fully satisfactory substitute.

While painting a sympathetic and lively picture of Charlotte, and indeed of her three siblings, deftly managing not to tell the same story in the four separate books, Gérin is weak on texts and dates owing to the imperfections of Shorter, Symington and Wise. She is also too ready to fill her biographies with incidents derived from the novels. Thus Charlotte's life in Brussels, dull and lonely, is filled with incidents from the life of Lucy Snowe, lonely but far from dull. Anne Brontë is assumed to have been in love with the Revd William Weightman because Agnes Grey loves a clergyman whose name begins with a W. Emily Brontë, an enigma even to her family, by all accounts painfully shy and withdrawn, becomes more like Shirley Keeldar, bold and outspoken although hardly handsome and rich. In view of the pitiful lack of evidence about Emily and Anne, Gérin occasionally falls back on their poetry, where the Gondal element must act as a deterrent against autobiographical interpretations.

In writing about Branwell, and to a lesser extent Anne, Gérin had to face the problem that had it not been for their more famous siblings, neither would have been a figure of note. The scandal at Thorp Green provided sensational material which Gaskell had to suppress. Gaskell had seen the younger members of the family through Charlotte's eyes, and Charlotte had – with the best of intentions – done Branwell and Anne and even Emily no service in her 1850 'Biographical Notice'. Previous biographers of the family, like May Sinclair, the Hansons, Phyllis Bentley and Margaret Lane, had given too much weight to Charlotte. By concentrating on one Brontë at a time, Gérin was able to give a more rounded account, although the book on Charlotte is much the longest. Almost simultaneously with the publication of Gérin's book on Branwell, Daphne du Maurier, yet another novelist to try her hand at Brontë biography, had produced a more sensational account of the Robinson affair. Gérin gains by the contrast, although nobody can be certain exactly what happened to cause Branwell's dismissal and subsequent collapse.

Emily, as a more noteworthy literary figure, had attracted biographies before Gérin, but not very good ones. She had been at Cowan Bridge with Charlotte and in Brussels for nearly a year, two important periods of Charlotte's life which had caused Mrs Gaskell much difficulty. She left a few short and uninteresting letters and diary entries and some powerful poems, reasonably edited for the first time in 1941 by C. W. Hatfield. They were difficult to interpret autobiographically, although two other writers on Emily, John Hewish and Edward Chitham, have tried to do this. Some poems by both Emily and Anne are personal rather than connected with Gondal, but even these do not shed a great deal of light on the life of either author. The lines 'so hopeless is the world without, the world within I doubly prize' make it clear that the rich world of Emily's imagination had little to do with the dreary life of a lonely spinster in Haworth Parsonage. The prose narratives of Gondal and a possible second novel by Emily, if by some miracle they should turn up, would not add a great deal to our knowledge of Emily, and Fannie Ratchford's too imaginative reconstruction of the Gondal story in *Gondal's Queen* is of little help for biographers. The Angrian narratives of Charlotte and Branwell, now properly edited, make it clear that all the Brontës used fiction as an escape from, rather than a reflection of, reality.

The books by Hewish, Gérin and Chitham on Emily are a great deal better than the justly derided work of Virginia Moore, which sought to prove that Emily fell in love with a Belgian called Louis Parensell. This turns out to be a misreading of a poem entitled 'Love's Farewell'. The gradual production of proper texts eliminated such misreadings, although real-life Heathcliffs to match M. Heger occasionally crop up. Other factors contributed to the arrival of a spate of biographies in the last quarter of the twentieth century. Charlotte's reputation has recovered from the strictures of Cecil and Leavis, and three large-scale biographies of her by Margot Peters, Rebecca Fraser and Lyndall Gordon attest to this fact. Peters' book, *Unquiet Soul*, and Gordon's *A Passionate Life* show the influence of the feminist movement, which became very important in Brontë studies at this time. In 1976 Helene Moglen combined criticism with biography in *The Self Conceived*, and in 1979 Gilbert and Gubar published their revolutionary study *The Madwoman in the Attic*. Even Fraser, whose title is neutral, mentions Charlotte's tempestuous spirit on her first page.

Fraser is comparatively kind to Mr Nicholls and Mr Brontë, who tend to be regarded as figures thwarting Charlotte's genius in other biographies. Juliet Barker's comprehensive work on all the Brontës restores the balance, although in the process Charlotte becomes a rather less attractive figure. Recently there have been sympathetic studies of Mr Brontë by Dudley Green and of Mr Nicholls by the Cochranes. Apart from his brief moment of glory as Charlotte's husband Arthur Nicholls had no particular claim to distinction, although the initial rejection of his suit, his devoted attention to Mr Brontë and the long twilight of his retirement in Ireland, faithfully preserving Brontë relics, make a good story. Green tries to make a case for Patrick Brontë as a noteworthy figure in his own right, attempting to co-operate with Dissenters and more liberal in his politics than often represented. Mr Brontë had been the subject of previous biographies, one partly written by Gérin's husband, and he does gain a place in *The Oxford Dictionary of National Biography*; but it seems foolish to pretend that Patrick Brontë would have been particularly famous if he had not been his daughters' father. Of course, his progress from Irish poverty to respectability as a clergyman in the Church of England and then the tragic poignancy of his life as a widower outliving all his six children is almost worthy to be the subject of a Brontë novel. There have also been full-length studies of Ellen Nussey, an uninteresting figure who fortunately preserved Charlotte's correspondence to her, and of Charlotte's older friend Mary Taylor, a more enterprising character whose letters from Charlotte have not survived, with one exception.[4]

In *The Brontë Myth* Lucasta Miller casts a cold if fair eye on the eccentricities of Brontë biography, concluding that each generation of biographers writes the book it desires, and possibly deserves, to fit in with contemporary prejudices. The above brief summary of Brontë biographies considers books only. In addition, there have been biographical articles, most notably in *Brontë Society Transactions*, later reborn as *Brontë Studies*. Not all of these have been scholarly, and many show a tendency to confuse fact and fiction, and to equate biography with hagiography. In this they follow Gérin, who also follows them. More recently this valuable periodical has favoured criticism at the expense of biography, though there is still a considerable proportion of the latter, minor figures like the Cornish Branwell cousins and Robinson descendants receiving undue attention. Nevertheless, the Brontë Society has done yeoman service in keeping the Brontë record straight in spite of the efforts of Shorter, Wise and Symington, whose misdemeanours have still to be fully exposed.

NOTES

1 Wise's exposure as a forger of first editions took place in 1934. I drew attention to his role in the Brontë saga in *The Brontës and their Background: Romance and Reality* (London: Macmillan, 1973), pp. 6–8, 10–19 and 195–201. Shorter, whose widow claimed nominal copyright of Brontë material until the 1980s, has not been blamed to a similar extent.

2 The list includes Leyland's work on Branwell, Robinson's book on Emily and Yates' study of Patrick. For bibliographical information on these books, and on works by authors mentioned both in the running text and in subsequent notes, see the 'Further reading' section for this chapter at the back of this volume.

3 Other works in the mysterious-key category include William Wright (Ireland), Alice Law (Branwell as author of *Wuthering Heights*), Romer Wilson (a mystic Emily), Virginia Moore (a Lesbian Emily as well as Louis Parensell), G. Elsie Harrison (Methodism) and Kathleen Franks (anorexia).

4 Joan Bellamy and Barbara Whitehead provide some new information. Mary Taylor, rather surprisingly, gets a mention in *The Oxford Dictionary of National Biography*.

CHAPTER 21

Mid-nineteenth-century critical responses to the Brontës

Miriam Elizabeth Burstein

Charlotte Brontë's death in 1855, shortly followed by the appearance of Elizabeth Gaskell's biography in 1857, sparked critical retrospectives on both sides of the Atlantic. By this time, the earlier confusions about who wrote what had disappeared; no longer did critics compare Currer Bell's 'unformed writing of a giant's hand' in *Wuthering Heights* to her mature style in *Jane Eyre*.[1] The puzzle of authorship solved, critics found themselves contemplating the relative strengths of the three sisters and their individual legacies. This brief overview thus traces the Brontës' reception for the two decades after Charlotte's death, a period bookended by the reviews of *The Life of Charlotte Brontë* at one end and the joint appearance of Thomas Wemyss Reid's *Charlotte Brontë: A Monograph* (1877) and Algernon Charles Swinburne's *A Note on Charlotte Brontë* (1877) – both rejoinders to Gaskell – at the other.

The reception history of the Brontës during this period is unavoidably Charlotte-centric. Tom Winnifrith sums up the situation: during the nineteenth century, 'Charlotte was everywhere; Emily, apart from a few brave dissenting voices, was nowhere.'[2] (Even here, Anne is non-existent.) While the power of 'Ellis Bell's' novel was acknowledged from the first, before the identity of the author was known, Charlotte's 'Biographical Notice', along with her 'Preface' to *Wuthering Heights* published in the novel's 1850 edition, introduced a biographical focus that shaped all subsequent discussion of the text. Gaskell's *Life* thus consolidated, rather than originated, the Victorian interest in reading the Brontës through a biographical lens. Soon popular biography would overwrite all of the novels – and not just for the Brontës' Anglo-American readers.[3] However, by the late 1850s *Wuthering Heights* enjoyed little of the recognition accorded to Charlotte's work. For example, Patsy Stoneman finds no cases of the novel being adapted for the stage, unlike *Jane Eyre*, and virtually no intertextual references until the last two decades of the nineteenth century.[4] Anne, meanwhile, quickly lapsed into obscurity. The sister most easily appropriated for conventional narratives of feminine domestic piety, she had, Margaret Oliphant claimed, 'no right to be considered at all as a writer but for her association with these imperative spirits'.[5] Mrs Oliphant's dismissal summed up four decades of tepid critical response which alternately praised Anne for her personal virtues and, in the case of *The Tenant of Wildfell Hall*, castigated her for impropriety. Emily's reputation began its recovery with the appearance of Mary F. Robinson's *Emily Brontë* (1883); Anne's would have to wait until twentieth-century feminism. Consequently, Charlotte occupies the starring role in any account of the Brontës' reception.

The template for assessing the Brontës' relative merits was established in the 1850s. Although those who praised Emily noted 'a genuine originating power' beyond anything that Charlotte's creations evinced, only Charlotte obtained a reputation as a fully fledged artist.[6] Emily was wildly imaginative, but lacked technical finesse; Anne understood proper novelistic technique, yet her work was 'less original and striking' than her sisters'.[7] But Charlotte, as Mrs Gaskell argued, was not only deeply attuned to the power of language; she was also intensely and minutely self-conscious about how it was employed (Gaskell, *Life*, pp. 246–7). For Victorian readers, although *Jane Eyre* was the most *popular* novel, Charlotte's strength was best displayed in *Villette*, with the 'irascible' yet 'strangely effective' M. Paul Emanuel especially praised.[8]

Moreover, critics found Charlotte's work refreshingly realistic. One reader, ranking Charlotte with Elizabeth Barrett Browning and Germaine de Staël, argued that while Emily was 'disgusted at her own picture' in *Wuthering Heights* and Anne 'weird [and] unnatural', Charlotte's representations were always 'within the rational and real'.[9] For some, however, Charlotte's realism derived from ignorance, not sophisticated observation. This was especially true when it came to men: 'She thought men habitually talked before women in the way she makes one of them talk', complained the High Church *Christian Remembrancer* of characters like Rochester; 'she thought men generally were like, in their principles, practice, and manners, the men she describes'.[10] Even worse was the 'unblushing and rampant' evil that permeated Emily's and Anne's novels, thanks to Branwell's dread influence (120). For all that, though, Charlotte had 'genius' (123).

Some critics commented on the painful aspects associated with Charlotte's acknowledged genius, and it was pointed out that the affective impact of her tales went beyond the characters to encompass the author herself. In an essay on George Eliot (to whom Charlotte was frequently compared), a contributor to the liberal Catholic magazine *The Rambler* wrote that Charlotte 'probes, with a pen dipped in vitriol, the festering sores of a corrupt humanity, triumphing almost, in proud but bitter superiority, over the foibles and hypocrisies of a world which she has tried and found wanting to her spirit's deepest needs'.[11] The novels seemed to reveal some deep and unresolved disappointment. Even worse, Charlotte's very genius could be a loose cannon. Some, like Margaret Oliphant, felt that Charlotte's brilliant depictions of rebellious women like Jane Eyre inspired later, lesser novelists to a new erotic brazenness.[12] Peter Bayne, who wrote on Charlotte several times, worried that *Jane Eyre* was particularly 'unhealthy', owing to the novel's clear fascination with the alluring Rochester; instead of sticking to its moral, *Jane Eyre* successfully (and wrongly) turns Rochester into a figure of desire.[13]

That being said, if Charlotte was undoubtedly the family's most brilliant novelist, readers of the Brontës' *poetry* insisted on Emily's superiority. At best, Charlotte was no more than '[c]orrect'.[14] By contrast, Emily was, one critic insisted, one of the few nineteenth-century women writers with a 'true poetical faculty', along with Christina Rossetti and Elizabeth Barrett Browning; this faculty manifested itself in the 'passion, energy of thought, and daring' which characterized her admittedly imperfect work.[15] Following Charlotte's lead as editor of the poems, critics praised Emily in particular for her evocations of nature, which 'have a pre-Raphael-like minuteness and fidelity; but they have far more; they have that atmospheric power which is the truest test of genius, and which puts us instantly *en rapport* with the spirit of the scene and the mind of the artist'.[16] In addition, critics pointed to the forcefulness of her work and its record of spiritual struggle. Many came away from her poetry with a sense of profound desolation. Linking Emily's poetic strengths to her problematic spirituality, E. S. Dallas argued that 'Ellis . . . is somewhat of a heathen, and writes in the utmost despair: she writes calmly, but with intensity; and from the intensity of her woe there issues a music of expression which Currer, with all her wonderful felicity of diction, never attained'.[17] Although another reader found Emily alone possessed of the 'real Divine afflatus',[18] that is not the same thing as saying that her poetry was *conventionally* pious or 'religious', as most found Anne's to be.[19]

This question of spirituality tapped into the nineteenth century's obsession with the Brontës not as authors, but as women. At least one distraught critic confessed that after reading Gaskell's biography, he or she 'became far more interested in the fate of the woman, than in the discipline and development of the authoress'.[20] For some sceptical readers, Mrs Gaskell's biography over-emphasized Charlotte's feminine normality. One reviewer from the USA complained that Mrs Gaskell reduced Charlotte to her own conventional womanhood, which explained 'her anxiety to show how dainty-nice were her habits, how simple yet careful her choice of dress, her "three offers of marriage," and some every-day talk about potatoes and cooking'.[21] Despite such grumblings, and despite the difficulties involved in shoehorning Emily into any idealized account of domesticity, the Brontës found their way into such Anglo-American biographical collections of exemplary women as *Daughters of Genius* (1886), *Some Eminent Women of our Time* (1883), *Women of Fashion and Representative Women of Society* (1878), *Women of Worth: A Book for Girls* (1863), *Working Women of this Century* (1869) and *World-Famous Women* (1891).

Granted, some naysayers persisted – *Godey's Lady's Book and Magazine* concluded that '[the Brontës] suffered like martyrs; but they did not try to make themselves amiable' – but the consensus of popular biographies was that the sisters were properly domestic, whatever their fiction suggested.[22] While critics crowned Charlotte as one of the period's great creative minds, they also sought to claim her as the protagonist of a great modern Christian epic. The word 'heroine' appears more than once, inflating Gaskell's far more modest claim that Charlotte was a 'heroine to her servant Martha, – and to those who knew her best' (*Life*, p. 347). 'It is not only coming to be believed', enthused one reviewer, 'that Brontë was a genius in some high sense; it is making itself felt that she was a heroine, not only great but good, and good as great'.[23] Such moral heroism trumped artistic achievement. Paradoxically enough, the lessons propagated by books of this kind meant that 'Charlotte Brontë ... was harnessed to an image of moral virtue within the home to such an extent that the fact that she had written books was almost forgotten'.[24]

Although the interest in Brontë biography temporarily eclipsed more literary-critical approaches, in 1877 Thomas Wemyss Reid and Algernon Swinburne jointly re-ignited the question of the Brontë literary legacy. Wemyss Reid's *Charlotte Brontë: A Monograph* was initially serialized in *Macmillan's Magazine* in 1876, then published in volume form in the following year.[25] In his memoirs, Wemyss Reid ruefully commented that his book was 'coldly received by the critics'; nevertheless, not only did it sell extremely well, but it also inspired Swinburne to write his own study.[26] Wemyss Reid combined new research into the primary sources (including Charlotte's correspondence with Ellen Nussey) with critical reassessment, seeking to explode what he felt was Gaskell's exaggeratedly melancholy vision of the Brontës and their upbringing – as well as charges that Charlotte's work was 'rude in language and coarse in thought'.[27]

Wemyss Reid's assessments of the Brontës are unoriginal in themselves. Emily is the outstanding poet, not Charlotte (p. 77), and there is little to be said about Anne. Similarly, Reid admits to being appalled by *Wuthering Heights*. Despite its undoubted power, the novel leaves any right-minded reader revolted: 'Nobody can pretend that such a story as this ever ought to have been written; nobody can read it without feeling that its author must herself have had a morbid if not a diseased mind' (p. 202). Despite offering some excuses for Emily's style (themselves descended from Charlotte Brontë's own reworking of her sister's life), Reid argues that the genius in her work is the genius of literary *promise*, as opposed to mature literary *accomplishment*; the one exception to this rule is Heathcliff, whom, like many earlier critics, Reid sees as a truly unique and masterful creation (p. 206). Alone among the sisters, Charlotte displays fully developed literary powers. Wemyss Reid finds that unlike her siblings, Charlotte's work charts a clearly defined emotional arc, from the 'hope' which emerges from the otherwise glum *The Professor* (p. 222) to the 'key of almost absolute hopelessness' (p. 224) which characterizes what he believes to be her masterpiece, *Villette* (p. 224). If *Villette* marks Brontë's psychological nadir, it also, however, turns out to represent the full flowering of her 'genius' (p. 223).

While Wemyss Reid sought to restore Charlotte to her proper place in the literary firmament, Swinburne's *A Note on Charlotte Brontë* (1877; reprinted in 1894) revised the canon of British novelists altogether, using the occasion of George Eliot's final novel, *Daniel Deronda* (1876), to do so. Many critics, including Wemyss Reid, had compared Brontë and Eliot. Swinburne, however, invokes the Brontë 'genius' to displace Eliot from the pinnacle of nineteenth-century female artistry. (This was not a principled attack: Swinburne had somehow arrived at the conclusion that Eliot was persecuting him.[28]) It is here that Swinburne notoriously describes Eliot as 'an Amazon thrown sprawling over the crupper of her spavined and spur-galled Pegasus' (p. 25).[29] If, Swinburne concedes, Charlotte lacks Eliot's intellectual development, she nevertheless possesses 'a type of genius directed and moulded by the touch of intelligence' (p. 20). Celebrating the force of a dominating imagination over civilized intellect, Swinburne (echoing Sydney Dobell) argues that Charlotte was one of the few authentic geniuses whose creations '[compel] us without question to positive acceptance and belief' (p. 9).[30] Charlotte's (and Emily's) ability to fully *master* the reader outstrips the skill of every other female or male English novelist, living or dead.

At times, Swinburne's argument becomes confused because he often celebrates one sister and then illustrates his claims by a quotation from the other. He concedes that Emily is by far the better poet. (Anne remains unmentioned.) Nevertheless, Charlotte reigns supreme. Unlike Wemyss Reid, who usually considers Charlotte's work in isolation, Swinburne matches Charlotte Brontë against the greats of English and Continental literature, whether Sir Walter Scott, George Sand or Miguel de Cervantes; even when her work fails, as he believes it does in *Shirley*, he finds glories in it equal to 'Pindar or to Shelley or to Hugo' (p. 56). As a novelist, Charlotte found the poetry that eluded her actual verse, equalling classical and nineteenth-century poets renowned for their passionate lyricism. By contrast, even when Swinburne appears to praise Eliot, as when he celebrates the skill obvious in her work from the beginning or admires her pitch-perfect children, he does so only to highlight Brontë's greater powers. Charlotte's very lack of 'baby-worship' (p. 54) – which would seem, by Victorian standards, to mark her out as fatally unfeminine – is merely the necessary flaw that highlights her strength. If anything, Eliot becomes too feminine, too grounded in novelistic convention, whereas Charlotte Brontë turns out to belong to the international canon of literary (not merely novelistic) greatness.

Needless to say, Swinburne failed to eject Eliot from the British literary pantheon. But, as Wemyss Reid said in his *Memoirs*, with the publication of his own and Swinburne's two works, he had not 'long to wait before [seeing] the Brontë cult a great and growing factor in our literary life'.[31]

NOTES

1 [Sydney Dobell], 'Currer Bell', *The Palladium*, 1 (Sept. 1850), 166.

2 Tom Winnifrith, 'Charlotte and Emily Brontë: A Study in the Rise and Fall of Literary Reputations', *The Yearbook of English Studies*, 26 (1996), 14.

3 See O. R. Demidova, 'The Reception of Charlotte Brontë's Work in Nineteenth-Century Russia', *The Modern Language Review*, 89.3 (July 1994), 692–3. As Demidova goes on to point out, the biographical information at hand could be bizarre (pp. 693–5). On biographical readings in the 1850s, see Carol A. Bock, 'Reading Brontë's Novels: The Confessional Tradition', in Elsie Browning Michie (ed.), *Charlotte Brontë's* Jane Eyre: *A Casebook* (New York: Oxford University Press, 2006), pp. 25–9. Elizabeth Langland argues that Brontë criticism did not escape this biographical obsession until the 1960s; see 'The Receptions of Charlotte Brontë, Charles Dickens, George Eliot, and Thomas Hardy', in Patrick Brantlinger and William B. Thesing (eds.), *A Companion to the Victorian Novel* (Oxford: Blackwell, 2002), p. 394.

4 Patsy Stoneman, *Brontë Transformations: The Cultural Dissemination of* Jane Eyre *and* Wuthering Heights (Hemel Hempstead: Harvester Wheatsheaf, 1996), pp. 57–8. Cf. Joanne Wilkes, *Women Reviewing Women in Nineteenth-Century*

Britain: *The Critical Reception of Jane Austen, Charlotte Brontë, and George Eliot* (Aldershot: Ashgate, 2010); Wilkes notes the difficulties Victorian critics had with Emily (pp. 19–20).

5 Mrs [Margaret] Oliphant, 'The Sisters Brontë', in *Women Novelists of Queen Victoria's Reign: A Book of Appreciations* (London: Hurst and Blackett, 1897), pp. 28–9.

6 'Reading Raids. No. VI – Currer, Ellis, and Acton Bell', *Tait's Edinburgh Magazine*, 22 (July 1855), 421.

7 [W. C. Roscoe], 'Miss Brontë', *The National Review*, 5.9 (July 1857), 140.

8 'Charlotte Brontë and the Brontë Novels', *North American Review*, 85 (Oct. 1857), 325.

9 'Charlotte Brontë', *The Presbyterian Quarterly Review*, 6.22 (Sept. 1857), 301–2.

10 'The Life of Charlotte Brontë', *The Christian Remembrancer*, 34 (July 1857), 90. Subsequent references are included in the text.

11 'George Eliot's Novels', *The Rambler*, n.s. 4.10 (Nov. 1860), 82.

12 [Margaret Oliphant], 'Novels', *Blackwood's Edinburgh Magazine*, 102 (Sept. 1867), 258–9. For Oliphant's unease, see Wilkes, *Women Reviewing Women*, pp. 120–3.

13 Peter Bayne, 'Novels and Novel-Reading', *The Christian World Magazine* (Jan. 1868), 9.

14 'The Brontës', *Every Saturday: A Journal of Choice Reading*, n.s. 4 (26 July 1873), 103.

15 'Poetesses', *Littell's Living Age*, 97 (June 1868), 819, 820.

16 'The Life and Writings of Emily Brontë (Ellis Bell)', *The Galaxy*, 15.2 (Feb. 1873), 228. On Charlotte's construction of Emily as nature poet, see Susan R. Bauman, 'Her Sisters' Keeper: Charlotte Brontë's Defence of Emily and Anne', *Women's Writing*, 14.1 (2007), 30.

17 [E. S. Dallas], 'Currer Bell', *Blackwood's Edinburgh Magazine*, 82 (July 1857), 89.

18 'Reading Raids. No. VI', 422.

19 E.g. 'Charlotte Brontë', *The Athenaeum*, 19 May 1877, 634.

20 'Charlotte Brontë', *The Eclectic Review*, n.s. 1 (June 1857), 630.

21 'Charlotte Brontë', *Emerson's Magazine and Putnam's Monthly*, 5.39 (Sept. 1857), 269.

22 'Charlotte Brontë', *Godey's Lady's Book and Magazine*, 55 (Sept. 1857), 275.

23 'Charlotte Brontë', *The Presbyterian Quarterly Review*, 6.22 (Sept. 1857), 286; Charlotte as Christian 'heroine' appears again in 'Biography', *The Christian Examiner*, 43 (July 1857), 147.

24 Lucasta Miller, *The Brontë Myth* (London: Jonathan Cape, 2001), p. 84.

25 T. Wemyss Reid, *Charlotte Brontë: A Monograph* (New York: Scribner, Armstrong, & Co., 1877).

26 T. Wemyss Reid, *Memoirs of Sir Thomas Wemyss Reid, 1842–1885*, ed. Stuart J. Reid (London: Cassell, 1905), pp. 234, 235.

27 Wemyss Reid, *Charlotte Brontë: A Monograph*, p. 229. Subsequent references are included in the text.

28 Or so he told Edmund Gosse in 1878; see Gosse's *Portraits and Sketches* (New York: Charles Scribner's Sons, 1914), p. 15.

29 Algernon Charles Swinburne, *A Note on Charlotte Brontë* (1877; repr. London: Chatto & Windus, 1894), p. 25. Subsequent references are included in the text.

30 [Dobell], 'Currer Bell', p. 162.

31 Wemyss Reid, *Memoirs*, p. 235.

CHAPTER 22

Brontë scholarship and criticism, 1920–1970

Herbert Rosengarten

Well into the twentieth century, writing about the Brontës was firmly anchored in biography and dominated by Elizabeth Gaskell's *Life of Charlotte Brontë* (1857), which shaped critical responses for decades by the emphasis it placed on notions of saint-like suffering and isolated genius. Added impetus was given to biographical approaches by the publication in 1913 of Charlotte's letters to her Belgian 'master', Constantin Heger. The letters threw a new light on Charlotte's yearnings and frustrations, renewing the debate about the extent to which she had drawn on her own experiences and feelings to create her fictional characters.

Discussion about the Brontë family was further fuelled by the newly developing field of psychoanalytic criticism, which sought to interpret literary works and their authors in the light of Freudian ideas about parent–child relationships, the role of the unconscious and the repression of sexual impulses. Lucile Dooley's 1920 'Psychoanalysis of Charlotte Brontë',[1] with its dubious identification of Charlotte's 'Father-complex' and the neurotic compulsions that found expression in her novels, opened the way for wide speculation about the workings of the unconscious in the Brontë children, whose family life was now discovered to have implanted seeds of frustration, repression, self-doubt and unconscious longings that burst forth in their novels and poetry. Rosamond Langbridge thought Charlotte Brontë's story 'the saddest life that one has ever heard of' and pinned the blame firmly upon Patrick Brontë, whom she depicted as callously selfish and ill-tempered, 'the ugly product of a hideous religion'. The experience of Cowan Bridge left its mark, too – 'What a feast of exploration for the modern psycho-analyst is here in these harrowing records of suppressed and crippled childhood!'[2]

As the century progressed, other academics – especially in North America – attempted to unravel a variety of psycho-sexual complexes. Freud was invoked to suggest the presence of unconscious sexual tension and its release in Jane Eyre's exchanges with St John Rivers.[3] The extraordinary relationship between

Heathcliff and Cathy was explained in terms of the incest taboo.[4] Wade Thompson traced the connection between infanticide and sadism in *Wuthering Heights*, which depicts a perverse world of adult cruelty and violence towards motherless children, 'a world in which the young and the weak live in constant peril'.[5] For Thomas Moser, the power of Emily's novel lay in Heathcliff as the embodiment of untrammelled sexual energy, the Freudian id unleashed; whether she knew it or not, says Moser, Emily Brontë, 'the intense, inhibited spinster of Haworth', was writing a paean to Eros, and conveyed a sense of Heathcliff's masculine power through sexually charged images.[6] Moser's gender stereotyping was rejected in 1971 by Carol Ohmann, who placed his essay in a long line of critiques by male readers conditioned, in her view, to read Brontë through the blurred lens of sexual prejudice.[7]

Freud offered one avenue to an understanding of the Brontës; Jung provided another, especially in his identification of a shadow self that the individual must learn to acknowledge in order to achieve maturity. Heathcliff offered himself readily as the type of the Dark Hero. Writing in 1928, Romer Wilson determined that the key to understanding Heathcliff lay in Emily's childhood. Jealous of all the attention received by Branwell, young Emily fostered 'a dark soul in herself, a dark thing that grew and grew upon her and ultimately possessed her, body and soul'.[8] Wilson's conclusions were echoed and extended by Virginia Moore, who argued that Heathcliff is the means by which Emily works out the grief and suffering she experienced after some unknown horror and betrayal by either a male or a female lover. Moore's hypotheses make little sense; but like others before and after her, she overcame the lack of hard information by the free use of her own powers of what she termed 'psychological divination' and 'responsible imagination', the result being an overheated account verging on the pseudo-mystical.[9]

The very dearth of information about Emily helped to fuel the growing curiosity about her life and the mystery of her unique and extraordinary novel. The twentieth century saw a growth in her critical reputation along with a concomitant decline in Charlotte's. One of the most important proponents of this revised estimate was Lord David Cecil, who in his 1934 study *Early Victorian Novelists* describes Charlotte as a naïve Victorian moralist, while Emily is seen as a mystic, able to apprehend a transcendent reality ungoverned by conventional ideas of right and wrong. Though Cecil was willing to praise Charlotte as 'our first subjective novelist, the ancestor of Proust and Mr. James Joyce and all the rest of the historians of private consciousness', he condemned her novels as '[f]ormless, improbable, humourless, exaggerated, uncertain in their handling of character'.[10]

Wuthering Heights, in contrast, he praised for its structural and thematic coherence; the plot follows a pattern created by the dynamic of storm and calm, the complementary cosmic forces that in Cecil's view underlie Emily's view of the workings of nature and are embodied in the contrasting settings of Wuthering Heights and Thrushcross Grange and their respective inhabitants.

Cecil's interpretation was felt by some to impose a scheme untrue to the workings of the narrative. Miriam Allott thus questioned whether the book's ending really figures the restoration of harmony that Cecil had claimed, since the new order at the end is one that excludes all that Heathcliff stands for, a kind of restless passion that cannot be absorbed by conventional society – 'for the purposes of ordinary life [Heathcliff] will not do'.[11] To Richard Chase the resolution of cosmic conflict in both *Wuthering Heights* and *Jane Eyre* comes at a cost, representing 'the triumph of the moderate, secular, naturalistic, liberal, sentimental point of view over the mythical, religious, tragic point of view'.[12] Regardless of such challenges, David Cecil's reading would retain its appeal for the next half-century because it offered an accessible and persuasive account of the novel's complex structure, and also because it provided a convincing rationale for Heathcliff's appeal: Cecil drew him not as the typical villain of melodrama, but as a figure of almost mythic proportions expressive of the deep forces uniting humankind and nature.

Not all interpreters of the Brontë novels looked to the play of cosmic forces to account for their power or saw the characters as embodiments of mythic archetypes. The growing availability in the 1920s and 1930s of hitherto unpublished materials, especially poems and juvenile writings, led to the realization that the sisters' published works were not *lusi naturae* or autobiographical outpourings, but the productions of skilful and practised writers. Though not the first to connect the Brontës' adult writings to their juvenilia, the American librarian and scholar Fannie Ratchford offered a plausible reconstruction of the fantasy worlds of Angria and Gondal in *The Brontës' Web of Childhood* (1941), showing how they anticipated many elements of theme and character in the Brontës' maturer compositions. Drawing on C. W. Hatfield's research for his excellent edition of Emily's poems, Ratchford attempted an outline of the Gondal epic, noting drily that the fact that many of Emily's poems are about Gondal 'turns into nonsense the hundreds of pages of Brontë biography based on the subjective interpretation of her poems'.[13] Her work would culminate in *Gondal's Queen: A Novel in Verse by Emily Jane Brontë* (1955), a recreation of Gondal made up of Emily's poems linked by Ratchford's own prose narrative. Subsequent scholarship has challenged some of her findings; but the real value of Ratchford's contribution lay in providing an important corrective to ideas about untutored genius or mystic revelation by showing that the Brontës had served long apprenticeships as writers.

The Victorians had acknowledged that the Brontë sisters' novels possessed power and drama, but saw them as the crude products of untaught sensibilities – a view tied to the idea of female authorship as somehow lacking in intellect and rigour. By the middle of the twentieth century, however, the lessons of New Criticism had taught academic readers to pay closer attention to the internal clues provided by the text, including the workings of symbol and metaphor, and this encouraged a new appreciation of the Brontës' handling of language and narrative. Mark Schorer's 1949 essay identifying patterns of nature imagery in *Wuthering Heights* and Dorothy Van Ghent's exploration in 1952 of Emily's suggestive use of window images moved Brontë criticism towards a more formalist hermeneutic.[14] A stream of such analyses followed, from examinations of the symbolic and structural functions of imagery in *Jane Eyre* and *Villette* to studies of Charlotte's transformation of first-person narrative as a means of revealing the irrational workings of human personality.[15] Formalist readings also gave more attention to issues of narrative structure, especially point of view; notions of the 'unreliable narrator' led to reassessments of the roles and responsibilities of Lockwood and Ellen Dean, no longer seen merely as neutral observers but rather as participants influencing the action in *Wuthering Heights* and our perceptions of the outcome.[16]

With formalism in the ascendant in the academy, the 1960s saw a surge of critical interest in all the Brontës. Charlotte, emerging from her sister's shadow and now admired as the forerunner of novelists like Lawrence and Woolf, was the focus of book-length studies by Robert Bernard Martin (1966) and Earl A. Knies (1969), both of whom explicitly rejected the biographical approach in favour of thematic and structural analyses.[17] For Martin, it was important to treat Charlotte's novels as seriously conceived works of art. W. A. Craik, publishing a study of all the Brontë novels in 1968, was equally insistent on the need to treat the sisters' work as serious art, extending this criterion to Anne's writing 'to assess her place as an independent novelist, not merely as an interesting minor appendage'.[18]

The 1960s also brought renewed interest in the lives of the Brontë family. Anne, so rarely in the critical spotlight, was the subject of two biographies in the same year (1959): one by Ada Harrison and Derek

Stanford, the other by Winifred Gérin.[19] On the strength of *The Tenant of Wildfell Hall*, Stanford made a strong claim for Anne to be regarded as 'our first realist woman author', eclipsing Mrs Gaskell in her ability to expose 'the motives of domestic drama'.[20] Between 1959 and 1971 Winifred Gérin published biographies of each of the Brontë children, the best undoubtedly her study of Charlotte (1967).[21] Her book *Branwell Brontë* appeared in 1961, a year after Daphne du Maurier's *The Infernal World of Branwell Brontë*. Both biographies went some way towards softening the unflattering portrait drawn by Mrs Gaskell and eliciting sympathy for their subject without attempting to excuse Branwell's excesses and self-indulgence. Mr Brontë too came in for some rehabilitation: the ill-tempered figure conjured up by the *Life* was replaced by a caring and tolerant husband and father, first in Annette B. Hopkins' study *The Father of the Brontës* (1958), then by John Lock and W. T. Dixon's more detailed (but frustratingly unannotated) biography *A Man of Sorrow* (1965).

An added dimension to biographical study was provided by critics who placed the Brontës' novels in the context of nineteenth-century English society, particularly the regional society to which the family belonged. Much of this kind of critical response was limited to identifying the real-life equivalents that were thought to have inspired the Brontës' characters and settings. Despite Charlotte's denial of allegations that she drew on her acquaintance for her fiction (in a letter to Ellen Nussey dated 16 November 1849; Smith, *Letters*, vol. II, p. 285), critics and biographers were not dissuaded from looking for the real-life equivalents to her places and characters – especially in *Shirley*, which chronicles well-documented historical events in the West Riding and draws on Charlotte's acquaintance for some of its characters. Throughout the century of its existence (1895–2001), the Brontë Society's *Transactions* made an extensive contribution to such scholarship. A more searching enquiry into the social, religious and political underpinnings of Victorian English society as depicted in Charlotte's novels would have to wait until the last quarter of the twentieth century.

Wuthering Heights, too, was searched for its correspondences to 'real life'. C. P. Sanger's unpretentious but telling 1926 essay, *The Structure of Wuthering Heights*, showed how carefully Emily Brontë had constructed her novel in relation to family pedigree, chronology, topography and the law of entail.[22] Sanger's practical approach won praise from Emily's biographer Charles Simpson, who observed that '*Wuthering Heights* has suffered more than most novels from a surfeit of theoretical criticism';[23] he limited his own discussion of the novel to a consideration of Emily's possible use of local stories about feuding families in Halifax. The novel's solid grounding in quotidian details led the English Marxist critic Arnold Kettle in mid-century to pronounce the subject of *Wuthering Heights* to be 'England in 1847 ... The story of *Wuthering Heights* is concerned not with love in the abstract but with the passions of living people, with property-ownership, the attraction of social comforts, the arrangement of marriages, the importance of education, the validity of religion, the relations of rich and poor'. Kettle sought to rescue the novel from those he called 'transcendentalists' and read it instead as the account of a rebellion by a member of the oppressed working class against corrupt and decadent nineteenth-century capitalism.[24]

Kettle did not apply this model to Charlotte's novels; but Inga-Stina Ewbank's *Their Proper Sphere: A Study of the Brontë Sisters as Early-Victorian Female Novelists* (1966) identified women's poverty, and their consequent dependence on men, as a recurring theme in Charlotte's books. Ewbank's sober analysis of the critical double standards applied to women writers in the nineteenth century reflected a growing shift in academic study from the aesthetic to the social. She insisted that her book was not about feminism; but she nonetheless demonstrated how the Brontës consciously fought the prevailing view that women writers should confine themselves to being womanly. Like Harrison and Stanford before her, Ewbank praised the moral realism of Anne's novels, recognizing that, though her work might seem less interesting than that of her sisters, her novels tackle serious social problems head-on, especially in *The Tenant*'s unflinching depiction of the impact on family life of drunkenness and infidelity. Ewbank showed that in addressing such unpleasant subjects, Anne, though herself no feminist, was willing to speak with moral passion on behalf of all women, regardless of the charges of coarseness that were levelled against her by her contemporaries.

Ewbank's focus was primarily on the inequities suffered by women writers. Later feminist critics broadened their perspective to take in the Brontës' treatment of the 'woman question', examining the impact of Victorian patriarchy on women forced to disguise their feelings through sublimation or displacement. The artist as dramatized subject made a strong return in the 1970s, and critical interest focused once again on the inner lives of the Brontë sisters, though this time as representatives of their gender in an oppressive society rather than simply as tortured individuals. Kate Millett, writing in 1970, echoed the conclusions of Rosamond Langbridge forty years earlier, observing that *Villette* was the product of a mind oppressed by domestic tyranny and condemned to a life of servitude. Through Lucy Snowe, Charlotte Brontë reveals the self-hatred induced in women by centuries of subordination; in Millett's view, the novel is essentially about the heroine's escape to freedom – '*Villette* reads like one long meditation on a prison break'.[25]

Millett's essay marked a turning-point in writing about the Brontës in the latter part of the twentieth century: the Brontës' lives and works offered a wealth of materials to the women's studies courses then springing up in North America, and feminist scholars began to apply new criteria developed in conjunction with the psychological, formalist and Marxist approaches developed by their predecessors and fortified by Derrida and Lacan. It is worth noting that from the early 1970s onwards, coterminous with feminism's second wave, a majority of the books and articles about the Brontë sisters' lives and writings have been by women. Charlotte's own view of the 'condition of women' question was ambivalent: she deplored the plight of women in her time, yet objected to what she called the 'cant' surrounding the topic (in a letter to W. S. Williams of 12 May 1848; Smith, *Letters*, vol. II, p. 66). She would, however, have been pleased that her work, and that of her siblings, would give women ample 'exercise for their faculties, and a field for their efforts' (*Jane Eyre*, I.xii.109).

NOTES

1 Lucile Dooley, 'Psychoanalysis of Charlotte Brontë, as a Type of the Woman of Genius', *American Journal of Psychology*, 31.3 (July 1920), 221–72.

2 Rosamond Langbridge, *Charlotte Brontë: A Psychological Study* (New York: Doubleday, Doran, [1929]), pp. 3, 7 and 27.

3 Wayne Burns, 'Critical Relevance of Freudianism', *Western Review*, 20 (1956), 301–14.

4 For instance by Eric Solomon, 'The Incest Theme in *Wuthering Heights*', *Nineteenth-Century Fiction*, 14.1 (June 1959), 80–3.

5 Wade Thompson, 'Infanticide and Sadism in *Wuthering Heights*', *PMLA*, 78.1 (Mar. 1963), 70.

6 Thomas Moser, 'What is the Matter with Emily Jane? Conflicting Impulses in *Wuthering Heights*', *Nineteenth-Century Fiction*, 17.1 (June 1962), 12.

7 Carol Ohmann, 'Emily Brontë in the Hands of Male Critics', *College English*, 32.8 (May 1971), 906–13.

8 Romer Wilson, *All Alone: The Life and Private History of Emily Jane Brontë* (London: Chatto & Windus, 1928).

9 Virginia Moore, *The Life and Eager Death of Emily Brontë: A Biography* (London: Rich & Cowan, 1936).

10 David Cecil, *Early Victorian Novelists: Essays in Revaluation* (London: Constable, 1934), pp. 111 and 125.

11 Miriam Allott, '*Wuthering Heights*: The Rejection of Heathcliff?', *Essays in Criticism*, 8.1 (Jan. 1958), 47.

12 Richard Chase, 'The Brontës: A Centennial Observance', *Kenyon Review*, 9.4 (Autumn 1947), 505.

13 Fannie Ratchford, 'The Gondal Story', in C. W. Hatfield (ed.), *The Complete Poems of Emily Jane Brontë* (New York: Columbia University Press, 1941), p. 16.

14 Mark Schorer, 'Fiction and the "Matrix of Analogy"', *Kenyon Review*, 11.4 (Autumn 1949), 539–60; Dorothy Van Ghent, 'The Window Figure and the Two-Children Figure in *Wuthering Heights*', *Nineteenth-Century Fiction*, 7.3 (Dec. 1952), 189–97.

15 See, for example, Mark Schorer, 'Introduction', *Jane Eyre* (Boston: Houghton Mifflin, 1959), pp. v–xviii; Robert Heilman, 'Charlotte Brontë, Reason, and the Moon', *Nineteenth-Century Fiction*, 14.4 (Mar. 1960), 283–302; Robert A. Colby, '*Villette* and the Life of the Mind', *PMLA*, 75 (Sept. 1960), 410–19; and David Lodge, 'Fire and Eyre: Charlotte Brontë's War of Earthly Elements', in *Language of Fiction: Essays in Criticism and Verbal Analysis of the English Novel* (London: Routledge & Kegan Paul, 1966), pp. 114–43.

16 See, for example, James Hafley, 'The Villain in *Wuthering Heights*', *Nineteenth-Century Fiction*, 13.3 (Dec. 1958), 199–215.

17 Robert Bernard Martin, *The Accents of Persuasion: Charlotte Brontë's Novels* (London: Faber and Faber, 1966); Earl A. Knies, *The Art of Charlotte Brontë* (Athens: Ohio University Press, 1969).

18 W. A. Craik, *The Brontë Novels* (London: Methuen, 1968), p. 3.

19 Winifred Gérin, *Anne Brontë* (London: Allen Lane, 1959; rev. edn 1976).

20 Ada M. Harrison and Derek Stanford, *Anne Brontë: Her Life and Work* (New York: John Day Company, 1959), p. 236.

21 Winifred Gérin, *Charlotte Brontë: The Evolution of Genius* (Oxford University Press, 1967).

22 C. P. S[anger], *The Structure of* Wuthering Heights, Hogarth Essays, 19 (London: Hogarth Press, 1926). Some of Sanger's findings were qualified by A. Stuart Daley, 'The Moons and Almanacs of *Wuthering Heights*', *Huntington Library Quarterly*, 37 (1974), 337–53.

23 Charles Simpson, *Emily Brontë* (London: Country Life, 1929), p. 156.

24 Arnold Kettle, 'Emily Brontë: *Wuthering Heights* (1847)', in *An Introduction to the English Novel* (London: Hutchinson, 1951), vol. 1, pp. 139 and 154.

25 Kate Millett, *Sexual Politics* (Garden City, NY: Doubleday, 1970), p. 146.

CHAPTER 23

Brontë scholarship and criticism, c. 1970–2000

Sara J. Lodge

Despite modernist enthusiasm for *Wuthering Heights*, academic acceptance of the Brontës as canonical authors of the highest calibre was slow. Tom Winnifrith, mounting a defence of *Jane Eyre* as a great novel in 1977, could still lament that the very popularity of the novels and the family story, which led amateur enthusiasts to make the pilgrimage to the Brontë Parsonage Museum at Haworth, had stood in the way of the works' academic reputation: 'Such a cult has not found favour with the high priests of our more austere literary tradition, and just as there are some students of the Brontës who know nothing of any other major literary figure, so there are students of literature who profess to know almost nothing about the Brontës.'[1] The 1970s and 1980s saw major changes in how universities approached literary study, as structuralist and poststructuralist criticism and Marxist, feminist and postcolonial theory claimed that 'texts' and 'authors' were socially constructed entities whose interpretation was inherently political. The Brontë novels became more visible, but also more controversial, in an academic environment that emphasized the text as a contested site, and reading as necessarily partial and ideologically fraught.

Frank Kermode, discussing *Wuthering Heights* in the early 1970s, drew attention to the 'hermeneutic code' constituted by the inscription above the eponymous house's doorway and the chain of names (Catherine Earnshaw, Catherine Heathcliff, Catherine Linton) inscribed on the ledge by Lockwood's bed. These inscriptions, Kermode suggests, are emblematic of the way in which the novel *invites* the active reader to de-code its text, leaving a riddling gap in which the reader's imagination must operate, but equally deliberately *frustrates* our attempts – like Lockwood's – to come to a unitary understanding of what is read. We are left recognizing 'the intrinsic plurality of the text', which no 'single' reading can satisfactorily explicate.[2] Kermode's analysis ushered in a new era, influenced by deconstruction, in which readings of the Brontë novels would relish their indeterminacy: the sense in which these texts resist and elude interpretation even as they coerce us into following their narrative leads. In 1982, J. Hillis Miller argued that each passage in *Wuthering Heights* seems to ask to be taken as an emblem of the whole novel in that it teases us with the possibility of a system of signification, lying beyond it, which will make sense of the structure of the whole. But each of these tempting critical corridors leads to a blank wall; the 'secret truth of *Wuthering Heights* . . . is that there is no secret truth which criticism might formulate in this way. No hidden identifiable ordering principle which will account for everything stands at the head of the chain or at the back of the back.' In these circumstances, 'the best readings will be the ones which best account for the heterogeneity of the text, its presentation of a definite group of possible meanings which are systematically interconnected, determined by the text, but logically incompatible'.[3]

Readings of *Jane Eyre* likewise move from an emphasis on the organic unity of the text, and on the heroine's achievement of coherent and fulfilled selfhood as its plot outcome, to a standpoint that is more suspicious of Jane's story and of her self-constructed identity. Mark M. Hennelly (1984) argues that '[t]he plot of *Jane Eyre* seems . . . to plot against the reader by its dogged and mysterious indeterminacy'.[4] Hennelly notes that the text of *Jane Eyre*, from its opening, foregrounds the process of reading: it is full of incidents in which we identify with the 'reader' and thereby become conscious of the ways in which the text anticipates being read and manipulates its readers' responses, whether by direct address ('Reader, I married him') or through the device of the 'twice-told tale', where certain incidents are described by multiple characters in subtly different terms. We 'learn to read between the narrative lines and be especially alert for lacunae or blanks which signal Jane's crucial moments of self-suppression', becoming aware of the impossibility of a wholly candid or consistent narrative.

After 1980, *Jane Eyre*'s intense first-person narration concerns many critics. Annette Tromly (1982) suggests that Jane is an unintentionally unreliable narrator, akin to the psychologically troubled first-person narrators of Brontë's other novels, while Joseph Litvak (1992) regards Jane as a precocious actress, whose power-hungry performances we should distrust precisely because she so often presents herself in the opposite role of spectator.[5] Karen Chase (1984) argues that all the characters and landscapes in *Jane Eyre* embody some aspect of Jane that she must reject: this means that, ironically, she is both everywhere and nowhere in the text; her 'substantial self' remains evanescent and illusory.[6] Heather Glen

(2002) develops this sense of *Jane Eyre*'s undecidability, arguing that the novel exists simultaneously as two different stories:

Jane Eyre tells not a single, fictionally undermined story, but two opposing and incommensurate ones. The self at the centre of each appears in a radically different way: in one, as magically omnipotent, triumphing absolutely; in the other, as insubstantial, the constantly jeopardized object of forces beyond its control ... Those opposing configurations of triumphant omnipotence and imminent annihilation which animate her narrative remain to the end unresolved.[7]

Feminist readings of the Brontës dominate the critical landscape after 1970. Adrienne Rich (1973) argues that *Jane Eyre* has a 'special force' for women, because it tells a tale that is an allegory of female survival and triumph under an oppressive patriarchy: 'Jane Eyre, motherless and economically powerless, undergoes certain traditional female temptations, and finds that each temptation presents itself along with an alternative – the image of a nurturing or principled or spirited woman on whom she can model herself, or to whom she can look for support.'[8] Subsequent feminist readings would debate how far the Brontës' works described, critiqued, transcended or internalized the limitations of nineteenth-century women's lives. Sandra Gilbert and Susan Gubar's pioneering work *The Madwoman in the Attic: The Woman Writer and the Nineteenth-Century Literary Imagination* (1979) offers analyses of all the novels by Emily and Charlotte. Their thesis is that, like other nineteenth-century woman writers, the Brontës express their rebellion against patriarchy through texts that contain an overt and a covert story – of enclosure and escape – and an acceptable protagonist and a monstrous alter ego (Heathcliff, Bertha), the latter of whom acts out the destructive and monstrous rage that is the unacceptable face of women's anger. *Wuthering Heights*, they maintain, is a radical re-vision of Milton's *Paradise Lost*, in which Catherine falls from the wild and liberating 'hell' of the Heights to the stifling genteel 'heaven' of the Grange, a movement emblematic of the general drive to confine woman's ungovernable nature within the oppressive culture of Victorian femininity.

Gilbert and Gubar use psychoanalytic vocabulary to describe the novels' covert narratives, which are often visible in symbol, dream and landscape. They observe, for example, the phallic imagery of pillars used to describe the Revd Brocklehurst and St John Rivers in *Jane Eyre*, who are both associated with the 'superego': that part of the self, in Freudian terminology, that polices and inhibits our desires. Psychoanalytic Brontë criticism continues to flourish after 1970. Margaret Homans (1986), drawing on Lacanian theory, argues that both Emily and Charlotte struggle with the symbolic order of patriarchal language, which women must enter from the 'presymbolic' space of mother–child communion and which denies their natural mode of speaking the world as the price of admission to the masculine domain of written culture. The narrator, Lockwood, allows Emily to write as a 'son', using the figurative discourse privileged by patriarchy, but within Lockwood's narrative we catch glimpses of the 'daughter's' natural style; Catherine's diary – a fragmentary text, which she abandons to run on the moors (identified with the mother) – is indicative of the impossibility for women of both remaining true to their literal voice and writing within the patriarchal language of figuration: the first Catherine is doomed to die and the second to be acculturated and diminished.[9]

Later feminist criticism is preoccupied with language. Patricia Yaeger (1988), whose writing reflects the legacy of Julia Kristeva and Mikhail Bakhtin, argues, more positively, that both *Jane Eyre* and *Wuthering Heights* challenge the boundaries of patriarchal symbolic order by incorporating multiple voices and vocabularies: Jane learns French and is liberated into construing the verb 'to be' (*être*) in a way that empowers herself (Eyre); *Wuthering Heights* overcomes the anxiety of patriarchal influence represented in Lockwood's violence towards Catherine's ghost and transfers narrative power to the rumbustious, comic female voice of Nelly Dean.[10] Lyn Pykett (1989) also argues for Nelly Dean as a positive 'image of female resilience, resourcefulness and power' in *Wuthering Heights*, which she sees as a novel that productively crosses genres, incorporating Gothic, folk tradition and aspects of Victorian domestic realism to create a dramatic, polyphonic text which subverts convention.[11]

Feminist readings of the Brontës are frequently in debate with Marxist criticism. Terry Eagleton's *Myths of Power: A Marxist Study of the Brontës* (1975) offers a provocative account of economic and class relations throughout the Brontë novels. The 'deep structure' of Charlotte's works, he claims, involves a 'struggle between two ambiguous, internally divided sets of values'. These are the rational, energetic, individualistic and rebellious values of the bourgeois entrepreneur and the habits of piety, submission, culture and conservatism typical of the landed gentry. Charlotte's plots, in which these values spar but converge (*Jane Eyre* becomes both an independent professional and the wife of a landowner), mimic the actual negotiation occurring in the early nineteenth century between industrial capitalists and landed gentry to consolidate a new ruling class. Where Charlotte explores upward mobility, Emily in *Wuthering Heights* explores the freedom Catherine achieves by moving down and out – consorting with Heathcliff, who both represents the dream of temporary escape from dominating class and familial power structures and illustrates the ultimate triumph of those structures:

Heathcliff is robbed of liberty in two antithetical ways: exploited as a servant on the one hand, allowed to run wild on the other … In this sense there is freedom for Heathcliff neither within society nor outside it … It is a contradiction which encapsulates a crucial truth about bourgeois society. If there is no genuine liberty on its 'inside' – Heathcliff is oppressed by work and the familial structure – neither is there more than a caricature of liberty on the 'outside', since the release of running wild is merely a function of cultural impoverishment. The friendship of Heathcliff and [Catherine] crystallises under the pressures of economic and cultural violence, so that the freedom it seems to signify … is always the other face of oppression[.][12]

Marxist criticism naturally draws attention to the historical circumstances of industrialization, social division and labour disputes in which the Brontës' works were produced. Critics debate the extent to which their fiction collaborates with or interrogates contemporary power structures and ideology. Similarly, postcolonial criticism investigates the place of race, nation and empire in the cultural 'work' that the Brontës' texts perform. Jean Rhys' novel *Wide Sargasso Sea* (1966), which sympathetically imagines a Caribbean prehistory for Bertha Mason, had already questioned the union between Jane and Rochester as a celebratory 'end' for *Jane Eyre*. Gayatri Spivak (1985) notes that Jane's triumph is made possible by the elimination of Bertha, a representative of the colonized, racially 'other', subject who is described in bestial terms. St John Rivers, meanwhile, in a parallel to Jane's mission, concludes the narrative in Calcutta 'labouring for his race'. Readers need, Spivak argues, to move beyond the 'minimal diagnosis' of racism to recognize the complicity of criticism which ignores the race question in obscuring the wider imperial project of nineteenth-century literature. Subsequent critics, including Susan Meyer (1996), discuss Charlotte's treatment of slavery (sometimes presented as an analogue for female oppression under patriarchy) and empire; Elsie Michie (1996) and Terry Eagleton (1995) explore the status of Heathcliff as a representative of Ireland and its abused, rebellious status under British colonial rule; and more recently, Anne Longmuir (2009) has considered Belgium in *The Professor* and *Villette* as a site for Charlotte's negotiation between British and French cultural and political values.[13]

Before the 1980s, little critical attention lighted on Anne, or on the Brontës' poetry, and Branwell and Patrick were biographical bogeys. Juliet McMaster (1982), Elizabeth Langland (1989), Laura Berry (1996) and Maria Frawley (1996), among others, helped to restore Anne's visibility and to demonstrate her active participation in debates about narrative form, style and social issues (women's rights; education; child custody), in ways – demonstrably critical of Charlotte's and Emily's work – that blew apart her one-time image as the quietest sister. Juliet Barker's meticulous, revisionist group biography *The Brontës* (1994) likewise drew positive attention to Patrick and Branwell as writers whose contribution to the family's competitive and collaborative literary world had been neglected. From the 1980s onwards, the New Historicism, influenced by the work of Michel Foucault, emphasized the 'historicity' of cultural products such as novels: their embeddedness in a specific historical moment and cultural setting and the power dynamics of the social reality in which they operate. This critical trend produced new archival research, much of it on materials (newspapers, advertisements, medical treatises, educational prospectuses) previously ignored. In Brontë studies, it stimulated a more forensic scholarly interest in the Brontës' reading, juvenilia and letters, and in contemporary ideas and issues – from divorce legislation to governesses' pay, and from the situation of the woman artist to the treatment of the insane – with which they engaged. Sally Shuttleworth's 1996 investigation of Charlotte's works in the context of Victorian psychology is a prominent example.

Studies by Heather Glen (2002) of hard-line Victorian Evangelical propaganda as a context for *Jane Eyre*'s critique of Lowood, and by Marianne Thormählen (1993) of Anne's interest in theological, phrenological and temperance literature as a background to understanding Arthur Huntingdon's degenerate tendencies and capacity for salvation in *The Tenant of Wildfell Hall*, typify the careful work of historically orientated scholarship beyond the New Historicist domain. Most recently, the historicist turn has produced evaluations, such as Patsy Stoneman's *Brontë Transformations* (1996), of versions, adaptations, prequels, sequels and re-visions of the Brontës' works, on page, stage and screen, as themselves critical 'readings' that communicate social and political dimensions of both the original and the 'new' text. Indeed, the Brontës' works have come to be seen as 'intertexts' which, like all literature, necessarily absorb and transform other texts and are, in turn, absorbed and transformed: one cannot respond to these works without acknowledging the multiple forms of transmission through which they have been and continue to be mediated.

NOTES

1 Tom Winnifrith, *The Brontës* (London: Macmillan, 1977), p. 3.

2 Frank Kermode, '*Wuthering Heights* as a Classic', in *The Classic* (London: Faber and Faber, 1975); repeatedly reprinted, e.g. in Tom Winnifrith (ed.), *Critical Essays on Emily Brontë* (New York: Simon & Schuster, 1997), where the relevant passage is on p. 222.

3 J. Hillis Miller, '*Wuthering Heights*', in *Fiction and Repetition in Seven English Novels* (Cambridge, MA: Harvard University Press, 1982), p. 51.

4 Mark M. Hennelly, '*Jane Eyre*'s Reading Lesson', *ELH*, 51.4 (Winter 1984), 709.

5 Annette Tromly, *The Cover of the Mask: The Autobiographers in Charlotte Brontë's Fiction*, English Library Studies (University of Victoria, Canada, 1982), and Joseph Litvak, *Caught in the Act: Theatricality in the Nineteenth-Century English Novel* (Berkeley: University of California Press, 1992).

6 Karen Chase, *Eros and Psyche: The Representation of Personality in Charlotte Brontë, Charles Dickens, and George Eliot* (London: Methuen, 1984), p. 76.

7 Heather Glen, *Charlotte Brontë: The Imagination in History* (Oxford University Press, 2002), p. 64.

8 Adrienne Rich, 'Jane Eyre: The Temptations of a Motherless Woman', *Ms.*, 2.4 (Oct. 1973), repr. in, among others, Rich's *On Lies, Secrets and Silence: Selected Prose 1966–1987* (London: Virago, 1980), where the quoted passage is on p. 91.

9 Margaret Homans, *Bearing the Word: Language and Female Experience in Nineteenth-Century Women's Writing* (University of Chicago Press, 1986).

10 Patricia Yaeger, *Honey-Mad Women: Emancipatory Strategies in Women's Writing* (New York: Columbia University Press, 1988).

11 Lyn Pykett, *Emily Brontë* (Basingstoke: Macmillan, 1989), p. 107.

12 Terry Eagleton, *Myths of Power: A Marxist Study of the Brontës* (London: Macmillan, 1975), pp. 103–4.

13 For full references to the works mentioned in this paragraph, as well as the ensuing ones, see the 'Further reading' recommendations for this chapter at the back of this volume.

CHAPTER 24

Current trends in Brontë criticism and scholarship

Alexandra Lewis

When Lockwood, suffering from insomnia, examines the library of Catherine Earnshaw in *Wuthering Heights*, he finds it sparse and dilapidated. Not so the offerings of Brontë scholarship from the past decade: pages worldwide have continued to '[swarm] with Catherines' (*Wuthering Heights*, I.iii.15). According to the MLA International Bibliography, 2008–9 alone saw 140 books, chapters and articles published, and at least a further twenty dissertations written, with one or more of the Brontës as a main subject. For the period 2000–10, the figure is close to 900. Twenty-first-century Brontë scholarship has built on its extensive critical heritage by moving beyond likeness, sometimes blending inherited concerns and methodologies in such a way as to offer vital comment upon – and even to form – new trends within nineteenth-century studies generally. This chapter discusses some of these trends, also considering how the relevant critical approaches illuminate current debates about the purposes of literary scholarship.

First, some broad parameters: A fundamental critical shift appears to be taking place, with increasing institutional emphasis on cultural studies on the one hand and on the other a thoroughgoing interdisciplinarity, bringing various positions on the theoretical–historical spectrum into new forms of conversation. If the 'late-twentieth-century phenomenon known as "Theory"' is 'passing into history'[1] – an 'evaporation' that is evident in some, but not all, trends in Brontë criticism – the question of which theoretical (with a small 't') and methodological approaches might jostle for space, or join together, in its wake remains. So does the question of what these approaches aim to achieve. There is a dual challenge here: the multiple social, cultural, political, ideological and stylistic concerns that affect authors and readers need to be explored in ways that neither impose a single dominant, and thus potentially distorting, screen across the surface of literary works or genres, nor fail to situate the fabric of individual texts within their wider contexts. The boundaries of cultural, historical and interdisciplinary analysis are being redefined in subtle and searching ways. For the historian Martin Hewitt, writing in 2001, the field of Victorian studies was 'hamstrung by an unwillingness to move too far beyond traditional disciplinary objects of study, and by the [resulting] confusion of competing concepts of culture'. We need, Hewitt suggested, 'to develop a practice which ... considers the play of contingencies' across both discourse (that is, linguistic, textual and symbolic practices) and material conditions.[2] However, while interdisciplinarity thrives on exchange, it does not imply similitude of purpose, audience or aesthetics across all objects of analysis – and here a range of possible futures for Brontë scholarship opens up. An important task for the literary scholar in the coming decade will be to ensure that the processes of historical, biographical, theoretical and multidisciplinary contextualization develop in such a way as to inform rather than diminish close reading and the art of textual awareness.

Concern about how and why we read and interpret is crystallized in a number of key works which recently emerged in Brontë studies. Full-length works on Charlotte Brontë and the Brontë 'myth' from Heather Glen and Lucasta Miller respectively, and a chapter on Anne Brontë's 'exchange economy' in Garrett Stewart's *Novel Violence*, are variously concerned with the intersection of historical imagination and narrative form. Glen argues that readers today should look beyond apparently universal themes of private experience (desire, loneliness, ambition) and resist an 'intensity of identification' with Charlotte Brontë's characters that 'threatens to overwhelm the critical faculties'. Appreciating the intelligent use of particular registers of language in Brontë's work allows much that has been regarded as awkward, random and disruptive to be differently perceived, as speaking of a multifarious early nineteenth-century world. In Glen's study, the socially constructed medium of language in the novels is the necessary starting-point, and it is a medium which communicates the difference of Charlotte Brontë's concerns from ours. Rather than proceeding by reconstructing a history that will elucidate the novels, it is, for Glen, the very strangeness and alterity of their language that provides the 'prism' for us to (re)read the history we think we know.[3]

Garrett Stewart's 'narratography' of Victorian fiction opens with the claim to be a radically historicist study: his, too, is a historicism situated within the words themselves. Rather than assessing prose fiction as evidence for a particular view of the past, Stewart wants to read Victorian fiction as the Victorians might have read it – not by testing for sociological resonances but by 'processing' the prose, sentence by sentence, for 'the novelty of its language *as incident*, including its shock effects'. Of course, 'taking the context for granted' requires intimate knowledge of its joists and furnishings.[4]

This is an objective that Elaine Freedgood has approached from quite a different direction in *The Ideas in Things*. Influenced by lines of critical thinking ranging across Marxist cultural studies, postcolonial responses to imperialism and studies of power and subjectivity from Frantz Fanon and Sigmund Freud to Michel Foucault and Judith Butler, Freedgood emerges with a literal reading of material culture. Characterizing the mahogany furniture in *Jane Eyre* as metonymic 'souvenirs of sadism', she argues that deforestation and slavery imbue such objects with greater 'radiance' within the narrative, activating 'as yet unseen connections between historical knowledge and fictional form'.[5]

Aligned with the calls for renewed attention to context and detail rather than ahistorical universality is Lucasta Miller's plea for a re-privileging of text over myth in the biographical domain: arguing that we must determine where the cultural value of these artists is located, she maintains that 'it is time to turn the tables and put the writings first'.[6] This should certainly be achievable, given the high quality of biographical studies and encyclopaedic works of reference produced in the twenty-first century. Recent publication of Brontë juvenilia, with expert commentary, and the appearance of the third volume of Margaret Smith's magnificent annotated *Letters of Charlotte Brontë* also merit mention in this regard.

Since 1999, the republication of three major works in the history of Brontë scholarship has heralded both an affirmation of critical interest in race, class and gender and a recasting of the specific directions taken by the members of this 'leftist Holy Trinity'.[7] In a new introduction to the thirtieth anniversary edition of *Myths of Power* (2005), Terry Eagleton recognized that class in his study had edged aside gender as well as race and ethnicity, making his a 'pre-feminist' analysis in what he posits is now 'a post-feminist world'.[8]

The possibility of a post-feminist criticism is also raised by Elaine Showalter in the expanded edition of *A Literature of their Own* (1999). Weighing in on the theoretical–historical–narratological debate to suggest that the most important theoretical questions are not always philosophical but can be historical and cultural, and that narrative realism as practised by the Brontës has its own theoretical underpinnings, Showalter says that distinctions of gender may soon become matters of literary history. If this occurs it will, in Showalter's view, be 'because feminist criticism has succeeded in its task'.[9]

For Sandra Gilbert and Susan Gubar, however, feminist criticism is far from losing its impetus; instead, it faces a new post-millennial hurdle: regulation by the 'downsizing of the humanities'. By the second edition of their seminal work in 2000, the Madwoman is now 'in the Academy', and 'our challenge today' is to reconcile the personal, political and professional.[10] For Marlene Tromp and other contributors to a reassessment of *The Madwoman in the Attic* after thirty years, a third wave of feminist literary criticism continues to learn from the authors' collaborative approach.[11]

Indeed, an overview of Brontë scholarship since 2000 reveals that issues of race, class and gender have not so much lost their sharpness as gained new dimensions through unexpected points of convergence as well as through continued contestation. From Deborah Denenholz Morse's work on animal metaphors for imperialist encounters in *Wuthering Heights* to Sue Thomas' claim that signs of race and empire in *Jane Eyre* have been 'massively under-read', and on insufficiently historical grounds,[12] it is clear that postcolonial perspectives continue to generate questions and frameworks for analysis. An interest in transatlantic exchanges is steadily building, being visible in comparative analyses of the poetry of Emily Brontë and Emily Dickinson; the prose of Charlotte Brontë and Louisa May Alcott; and the social activism – a revision of the conventional marriage plot through temperance fiction – of Anne Brontë and Elizabeth Stoddard.[13]

Two recent studies extend analysis of collective class interests in the direction of individual psychology. In monographs on public politics and technologies of power respectively, John Plotz and John Murray examine the representational possibilities and behavioural dynamics of the working-class crowd in Charlotte Brontë's *Shirley* so as to reveal what Plotz describes as the role of economic exigencies in the production of Victorian interiority.[14] Conversely, Jonathan Rose's examination of the private responses (in letters and diaries) of working-class readers to the writing of authors including Charlotte Brontë exemplifies the growing scrutiny of reception history and the literary marketplace.[15]

A recent resurgence of interest in gender studies in relation to the Brontës has resulted in work on Victorian masculinities as well as in reappraisals of the theme of female self-realization. Demonstrating that reinvigorated theoretical perspectives combined with detailed attention to historical context and archival materials can at once inform and be directed by close textual analysis, Lisa Surridge traces the role of fiction and the press in publicizing domestic abuse and concerns over the law of coverture.[16] For Surridge, the double time-frame of Anne Brontë's *The Tenant of Wildfell Hall* (set in the 1820s and 1840s) contrasts Regency and Victorian mores in a way that helps consolidate a new model of mid-century manliness. Discussions of Brontëan men as leaders and lovers attempt to answer difficult but inevitable questions about the nature of sexuality and eroticism and about their links to power and authority during the nineteenth century.[17] Psychoanalytic theory continues to provide a conceptual apparatus for analyses of female sexuality in the Brontës' novels, from the Lacanian gaze in *Jane Eyre* to mothering and desire focused through the ideas of Freud, Melanie Klein and Nancy Chodorow.[18]

For Dinah Birch, some of the most productive thinking of the Victorian period is evident in Charlotte Brontë's 'refusal to accept rigid categories of gender' within the sphere of education.[19] The complexities of the Brontës' representations of processes of learning and instruction are, together with philosophies of child-rearing and knowledge acquisition, analysed in works by Thormählen, Gargano and Berry.[20] Since 1999, when Marianne Thormählen set out to remedy the 'comparative neglect of religion in the Brontë fiction',[21] there have been several sustained investigations of the profusion of views and experiences of faith in early nineteenth-century Britain and their relation to the texture of the novels.[22]

A late twentieth-century focus on what Gillian Beer called the two-way intellectual traffic between nineteenth-century science and literature paved the way for the expansion of two closely aligned areas in twenty-first-century Brontë scholarship: literature and medicine and (following Sally Shuttleworth's 1996 study) literature and psychology.[23] In line with the currently flourishing interest in the medical humanities – an inter-disciplinary field linking medical practice and education with the humanities, arts and social sciences – studies by Susan Rubinow Gorsky, Jane Wood, Anna Krugovoy Silver and Beth Torgerson have explored the ways in which nineteenth-century doctors and authors, the Brontës included, envisioned the mind–body divide in relation to depression of spirits, nervous debility, self-starvation, alcoholism and addiction.[24] The works of Emily and Charlotte Brontë are central to Janis Caldwell's identification of the 'double vision' of 'Romantic materialism': a way of reading the world through the books of Nature and Scripture.[25]

As part of these developments in medicine and literature, a still-evolving set of debates about memory and affect are taking shape in relation to the Brontës' novels and poetry. With reference to Emily Brontë's homesickness,

Linda Austin charts the metamorphosis of nostalgia from a disease to a cultural aesthetic.[26] Nicholas Dames has made claims for what he sees as Charlotte Brontë's textual effacement of memory through her use of metaphors drawn from phrenology and physiognomy, in line with his wider argument that recollection for the Victorians was, until the 1870s, 'among the least compelling of mental processes'.[27] In contrast, by uncovering nineteenth-century medical and narrative interest in mnemonic disruption – particularly disruption which occurs as a response to overwhelming external events, rather than simply as an inherent pathology or weakness – I have historicized interpretations of psychic trauma. The Brontës' complex engagements with late eighteenth- and early nineteenth-century debates about memory and its malfunctions reveal the early Victorian origins too often overlooked in genealogies of mental shock, showing that works of literature can extend and even anticipate scientific insights into mind and consciousness.[28]

Evaluations of nineteenth-century 'moral taste', ethics and sympathy are gaining prominence in discussions of the Brontës' lives and works, from the exploration of formative familial bonds to Christopher Lane's provocative suggestion that hatred underwrites citizenship in Charlotte Brontë's fiction.[29] Referring to the often-remarked-on depictions of cruelty and narrative indeterminacy in *Wuthering Heights*, Rachel Ablow argues that Emily Brontë views sympathy as a threat to female empowerment: her novel 'systematically resists' readers' sympathy in order to call attention to disguised gendered injustices.[30]

Efforts to secure greater visibility for the Brontë poetry and for Anne Brontë's prose have continued in the last two decades, with Janet Gezari's acclaimed *Last Things* and a volume dedicated to *New Approaches to the Literary Art of Anne Brontë*.[31] Another collection which, in responding to late twentieth-century trends, has shaped those trends anew for twenty-first-century scholarship is *The Brontës in the World of the Arts*. Taken together, the first eight contributions to that volume expand the critical focus from the Brontës' personal and thematic engagements with the visual arts (painting, engraving and drawing) to include music, acting and fashion. The final three essays address subsequent adaptation and intertextuality on page, stage and screen.[32] An interest in tracing the historical resonances of 'bizarre and outrageous' variations on the original *Jane Eyre*, developed in eight plays performed between 1848 and 1898 (republished in full by Patsy Stoneman),[33] points to another trend, or genre – that of modern rewritings and imaginative engagements with the Brontëan heritage. Novels such as *The Secret Diaries of Charlotte*

Brontë and *The Taste of Sorrow*,[34] as well as sequels and broader neo-Victorian responses to the Brontës' fictional worlds, have generated a concomitant body of scholarship.[35] These creative revisionings illuminate the problems and pleasures of all historical fictions: while they offer opportunities for insightful recuperation, they are attended by the risk of perpetuating inaccurate impressions which might in turn delimit the range of readings of the Brontës' own works. Will a blurring of the line between archive and imagination in twenty-first-century popular fiction contribute to new Brontëan myth-making of disturbing proportions? Or do the more compelling among these works register a wider turn away from modernist scepticism regarding the redemptive power of fiction towards a new vision (born of twenty-first-century optimism, desperation and uncertainty) which encompasses enduring Victorian cultural and literary models of empathy and transformation?

As glimpses of future trends emerge, including ecocritical analyses of the Brontë fiction and work conditioned by new forms of digital dissemination, it is clear that if Lockwood were to peruse a library composed of tomorrow's academic work on the Brontës, he would find plenty to keep himself occupied – and precious little to send him to sleep.

NOTES

1 An assertion made by Marianne Thormählen in the editor's preface to *English Now: Selected Papers from the 20th IAUPE Conference in Lund 2007*, Lund Studies in English, 112 (Lund, 2008), p. xvi.
2 Martin Hewitt, 'Victorian Studies: Problems and Prospects?', *Journal of Victorian Culture*, 6.1 (2001), 150, 153.
3 Heather Glen, *Charlotte Brontë: The Imagination in History* (Oxford University Press, 2002), pp. 1–2.
4 Garrett Stewart, *Novel Violence: A Narratography of Victorian Fiction* (University of Chicago Press, 2009), pp. 1–3.
5 Elaine Freedgood, *The Ideas in Things: Fugitive Meaning in the Victorian Novel* (University of Chicago Press, 2006), pp. 30, 6 and 29.
6 Lucasta Miller, *The Brontë Myth* (London: Jonathan Cape, 2001), p. 255.
7 Terry Eagleton's designation for race, class and gender in the introduction to the thirtieth anniversary edition of his *Myths of Power: A Marxist Study of the Brontës* (Basingstoke: Palgrave Macmillan, 2005), p. xiv.
8 *Ibid.*
9 Elaine Showalter, *A Literature of their Own: British Women Novelists from Brontë to Lessing* (1977), expanded edn (Princeton University Press, 1999), pp. xix and xxxiii. (Showalter feels that distinctions of nationality have already lost some of their sharpness.)

10 Sandra M. Gilbert and Susan Gubar, *The Madwoman in the Attic: The Woman Writer and the Nineteenth-Century Literary Imagination* (New Haven: Yale University Press, 1979; repr. 2000), pp. xlii–xliii.

11 Marlene Tromp, 'Modeling the *Madwoman*: Feminist Movements and the Academy', in Annette R. Federico (ed.), *Gilbert & Gubar's* The Madwoman in the Attic *after Thirty Years* (Columbia: University of Missouri Press, 2009), pp. 34–59.

12 Deborah Denenholz Morse, '"The Mark of the Beast": Animals as Sites of Imperial Encounter from *Wuthering Heights* to *Green Mansions*', in Morse and Martin A. Danahay (eds.), *Victorian Animal Dreams: Representations of Animals in Victorian Literature and Culture* (Aldershot: Ashgate, 2007), pp. 181–200; Sue Thomas, *Imperialism, Reform, and the Making of Englishness in* Jane Eyre (Basingstoke: Palgrave Macmillan, 2008), p. 4.

13 Michael Moon, '"No Coward Souls": Poetic Engagements between Emily Brontë and Emily Dickinson', in Meredith L. McGill (ed.), *The Traffic in Poems: Nineteenth-Century Poetry and Transatlantic Exchange* (New Brunswick, NJ: Rutgers University Press, 2008); Christine Doyle, *Louisa May Alcott and Charlotte Brontë: Transatlantic Translations* (Knoxville: University of Tennessee Press, 2000); Amanda Claybaugh, *The Novel of Purpose: Literature and Social Reform in the Anglo-American World* (Ithaca: Cornell University Press, 2007).

14 John Plotz, *The Crowd: British Literature and Public Politics* (Berkeley: University of California Press, 2000), p. 155; John C. Murray, *Technologies of Power in the Victorian Period* (Amherst, NY: Cambria Press, 2010).

15 Jonathan Rose, *The Intellectual Life of the British Working Classes* (New Haven: Yale University Press, 2001).

16 Lisa Surridge, *Bleak Houses: Marital Violence in Victorian Fiction* (Athens: Ohio University Press, 2005), p. 73.

17 Patricia Menon, *Austen, Eliot, Charlotte Brontë and the Mentor-Lover* (Basingstoke: Palgrave Macmillan, 2003), p. 1; Daniela Garofalo, *Manly Leaders in Nineteenth-Century British Literature* (Albany: State University of New York Press, 2008).

18 Beth Newman, *Subjects on Display: Psychoanalysis, Social Expectation, and Victorian Femininity* (Athens: Ohio University Press, 2004), p. 32; Jin-Ok Kim, *Charlotte Brontë and Female Desire* (New York: Peter Lang, 2003).

19 Dinah Birch, *Our Victorian Education* (Malden, MA: Blackwell, 2008), p. 90.

20 Marianne Thormählen, *The Brontës and Education* (Cambridge University Press, 2007); Elizabeth Gargano, *Reading Victorian Schoolrooms: Childhood and Education in Nineteenth-Century Fiction* (New York: Routledge, 2008); and Laura C. Berry, *The Child, the State, and the Victorian Novel* (Charlottesville: University Press of Virginia, 1999).

21 Marianne Thormählen, *The Brontës and Religion* (Cambridge University Press, 1999), p. 2.

22 See, for instance, J. Russell Perkin, 'Charlotte Brontë's *Shirley* as a Novel of Religious Controversy', *Studies in the Novel*, 40.4 (2008), 389–406, and

Diana Peschier, *Nineteenth-Century Anti-Catholic Discourses: The Case of Charlotte Brontë* (Basingstoke: Palgrave Macmillan, 2005).

23 Gillian Beer, *Darwin's Plots: Evolutionary Narrative in Darwin, George Eliot and Nineteenth-Century Fiction* (1983), 2nd edn (Cambridge University Press, 2000), p. 5; Sally Shuttleworth, *Charlotte Brontë and Victorian Psychology* (Cambridge University Press, 1996).

24 Susan Rubinow Gorsky, "'I'll Cry Myself Sick": Illness in *Wuthering Heights'*, *Literature and Medicine*, 18.2 (1999), 173–91; Jane Wood, *Passion and Pathology in Victorian Fiction* (Oxford University Press, 2001); Anna Krugovoy Silver, *Victorian Literature and the Anorexic Body* (Cambridge University Press, 2002); Beth Torgerson, *Reading the Brontë Body: Disease, Desire and the Constraints of Culture* (Basingstoke and New York: Palgrave Macmillan, 2005).

25 Janis McLarren Caldwell, *Literature and Medicine in Nineteenth-Century Britain: From Mary Shelley to George Eliot* (Cambridge University Press, 2004), p. 1.

26 Linda M. Austin, *Nostalgia in Transition, 1780–1917* (Charlottesville: University of Virginia Press, 2007).

27 Nicholas Dames, *Amnesiac Selves: Nostalgia, Forgetting, and British Fiction, 1810–1870* (Oxford University Press, 2001), p. 9.

28 Alexandra Lewis, 'Memory Possessed: Trauma and Pathologies of Remembrance in Emily Brontë's *Wuthering Heights'*, in Ryan Barnett and Serena Trowbridge (eds.), *Acts of Memory: The Victorians and Beyond* (Cambridge Scholars Publishing, 2010), pp. 35–53.

29 Drew Lamonica, *'We Are Three Sisters': Self and Family in the Writing of the Brontës* (Columbia: University of Missouri Press, 2003); Christopher Lane, *Hatred & Civility: The Antisocial Life in Victorian England* (New York: Columbia University Press, 2004), p. 85; see also Marjorie Garson, *Moral Taste: Aesthetics, Subjectivity, and Social Power in the Nineteenth-Century Novel* (University of Toronto Press, 2007).

30 Rachel Ablow, *The Marriage of Minds: Reading Sympathy in the Victorian Marriage Plot* (Stanford University Press, 2007), p. 45.

31 Janet Gezari, *Last Things: Emily Brontë's Poems* (Oxford University Press, 2007); Julie Nash and Barbara A. Suess (eds.), *New Approaches to the Literary Art of Anne Brontë* (Aldershot: Ashgate, 2001).

32 Sandra Hagan and Juliette Wells (eds.), *The Brontës in the World of the Arts* (Aldershot: Ashgate, 2008).

33 Patsy Stoneman (ed.), *Jane Eyre on Stage, 1848–1898: An Illustrated Edition of Eight Plays with Contextual Notes* (Aldershot: Ashgate, 2007).

34 Syrie James, *The Secret Diaries of Charlotte Brontë* (New York: HarperCollins, 2009), and Jude Morgan, *The Taste of Sorrow* (London: Headline, 2009).

35 See, for instance, Margarete Rubik and Elke Mettinger-Schartmann (eds.), *A Breath of Fresh Eyre: Intertextual and Intermedial Reworkings of* Jane Eyre (Amsterdam: Rodopi, 2007).

CHAPTER 25

Adaptations, prequels, sequels, translations

Patsy Stoneman

It was Charlotte Brontë's *Jane Eyre*, the first of the seven Brontë novels to be published (in October 1847), which first seized the public imagination. By January 1848, it was adapted for the London stage, and by the end of the century there were at least eight strikingly different stage versions. The earliest, written by John Courtney for London's working-class Victoria Theatre, invents a cast of vocal servants and relegates Rochester's friends to off-stage references. Charlotte Birch-Pfeiffer's *Die Waise von Lowood* ('The Orphan of Lowood'), performed throughout Europe and America for the rest of the century, presents Rochester as an impeccable lover since Bertha is the wife of his dead brother, while James Willing's 1879 play highlights Rochester's attempted bigamy through a parallel plot in which John Reed seduces Blanche Ingram with a mock marriage.[1]

The revolutionary impact of *Jane Eyre* itself depends on its spirited heroine, whose craving for love is matched by her dauntless integrity. Jane Eyre's courageous acknowledgement of love seemed to liberate women writers such as Dinah Craik, Julia Kavanagh, Rhoda Broughton and Mary Elizabeth Braddon,[2] so that Margaret Oliphant, writing disapprovingly in 1867, finds that heroines now 'live in a voluptuous dream, either waiting for or brooding over the inevitable lover'.[3] Film-makers of the twentieth century, however, mostly found Jane's love more appealing than her courage.[4] Christy Cabanne's blonde, ringleted Jane (1934) shows a good deal of spirit, but by mid century the novel was recuperated as a feel-good model of traditional courtship and marriage. Robert Stevenson's 1944 film with Orson Welles as Rochester and Joan Fontaine as Jane omits plot features which stress Jane's independence and instead focuses on her self-effacing love for the strong hero. Jane's wry and fearless replies to Rochester's first interrogation, for instance, are replaced in this film by her bending, at the snap of his fingers, to renew the water in which he is bathing his feet.

One reason why the novel continues to be reproduced, in fact, is its ambiguity of stance, so that an adaptor's emphasis can present the story as either radical or conservative. In the 1930s, *Jane Eyre* provided the template for novels as different as Winifred Holtby's *South Riding* (1936) (where the heroine leaves behind her the moody squire and his mansion to educate tomorrow's young womanhood) and Daphne du Maurier's *Rebecca* (1938) (where the heroine remains her husband's handmaid, nostalgic for his lost manor). It is now the archetype for Mills and Boon and Harlequin romances, in which a young heroine encounters an older, richer man whose rude or capricious behaviour eventually fails to disguise his need of her. Although his emotional vulnerability thus offsets his material dominance, 1970s feminists complained that this pattern showed women 'cherishing the chains of their bondage'.[5] The pattern has proved flexible with time – romances which once ended with a kiss and a promise of marriage now include satisfying sex and a fulfilling career for the heroine – but wary feminists point out that these 'more assertive, less virginal heroines are still seeking Mr Right'.[6]

Film, stage and television versions of *Jane Eyre*, from the 1970s onwards, have tried to present Jane as a heroine for a feminist age by stressing her stubborn negotiation of companionate marriage. Susannah York as Jane in Delbert Mann's 1970 version debates Bertha's rights with Rochester. Zelah Clarke in the television serial made by the British Broadcasting Company (BBC) in 1983 has the space of eleven episodes to develop her sparring conversations with Rochester (Timothy Dalton). Samantha Morton holds her own against a blustering Ciaran Hinds in Robert Young's version for London Weekend Television (1997). In the 2006 BBC version, Ruth Wilson as Jane delivers her 'equal, – as we are!' speech with fiery passion. Franco Zeffirelli's lavish 1996 film, however, shows that versions of *Jane Eyre* can still tip towards convention. While his young Jane stands up to her elders, and shares the Lowood head-shearing which marks her as a rebel, the later scenes, with Charlotte Gainsbourg as Jane, show her sinking into a protected femininity.

Cary Fukunaga's 2011 film is a beautifully balanced version, creating dramatic tension by beginning with Jane's escape to Moor House and enacting her previous life as intermittent flashback. The Gothic elements are played down – Bertha is a minor character, and there is no tearing of the veil – but accurate use of the novel's dialogue helps Mia Wasikowska and Michael Fassbender recreate Jane and Rochester's sparkling exchange of wit and their electric physical attraction.

Feminism had its impact on our view of the first Mrs Rochester. In Victorian *dramatis personae* she is simply 'The Maniac', theatrically valuable for her blood-curdling shrieks. A modern understanding of how madness can derive from women's lot has, however, prompted more sympathy. The landmark in this changed perspective is Jean Rhys' prequel story, *Wide Sargasso Sea* (1966), in which Bertha, under her original name of Antoinette Mason, tells the story of her childhood, education and marriage to the man we recognize as Mr Rochester, and of his revulsion from the sexual abandon he has himself encouraged in his wife. A hauntingly beautiful novel, *Wide Sargasso Sea* has achieved literary status quite apart from its function as increment to *Jane Eyre*. Remarkably, its narrative dovetails impeccably with its Victorian counterpart, adding resonance to our understanding of Rochester as well as of Bertha.

Wide Sargasso Sea has had its own impact on representations of *Jane Eyre*. While older stage versions of *Jane Eyre* are still performed, such as Helen Jerome's (1936) with its shrill and violent Bertha, newer dramas are more likely to show Bertha as beautiful and sad; and writers and dramatists now highlight parallels, rather than contrasts, between Jane and Bertha. This change of perception was reinforced by Sandra Gilbert and Susan Gubar's groundbreaking work *The Madwoman in the Attic* (1979), which argues that the 'madwoman' in many Victorian novels gives voice to the rage and desire which the decorous heroine must suppress.[7] Accordingly, Fay Weldon's stage version of *Jane Eyre* (1988) uses grey, life-sized dolls to emphasize the dreary conformity of Victorian women's lives. Polly Teale's 1997 version has the mad Bertha on stage throughout, doubling Jane's emotions in choreographed movements. Michael Berkeley's operatic version of 2000, with David Malouf's libretto, also has Bertha on stage as a constant implied commentary on the foreground action, and at different points in the opera Jane and Bertha sing and dance to the same suggestive theme from Donizetti's *Lucia di Lammermoor*, in which the reluctant bride goes mad after killing her bridegroom. All these versions follow *Wide Sargasso Sea* in making vivid use of Bertha's red dress.[8]

Jane Eyre was explicitly linked with Jean Rhys' novel in plays by Valerie Lucas and David Cottis (*Shadow in the Glass*, 1988) and by Debbie Shewell (*More than one Antoinette*, 1990), while Polly Teale's *After Mrs Rochester* (2003) includes the troubled Jean Rhys herself in the complex of parallels. Teale was also influenced by Paula Rego's challenging illustrations for *Jane Eyre*, exhibited in 2002. Rego, who says she came to *Jane Eyre* from *Wide Sargasso Sea*, uses the same model for Jane and Bertha and gives us a ruthless-looking, jack-booted Rochester. In *Come to Me*, where Jane hears Rochester's call, she appears in the grip of a fierce but indecisive desire: 'I put her doubting', Rego comments.[9]

Recent sequels to *Jane Eyre*, taken together, also suggest doubt about its outcome. Hilary Bailey's *Mrs Rochester* (1997) and Kimberley A. Bennet's coyly sexual *Jane Rochester* (2000) re-establish marital harmony after factitious alarms; but D. M. Thomas' *Charlotte: The Final Journey of Jane Eyre* (2000) shows Jane, in a postmodern tangle of Oedipal stories, escaping to the Caribbean from an unconsummated marriage. Textual instability is delightfully exploited in Jasper Fforde's *The Eyre Affair* (2001), where a time-travelling literary detective enters the world of *Jane Eyre* and changes its ending for ever.

Emily Brontë's *Wuthering Heights* now shares, or even exceeds, the status of *Jane Eyre*, but it was slow to achieve popular esteem. Though some early readers recognized its eery power, most were repelled by its harsh and amoral characters. It was not until the late nineteenth century that the aesthetic movement allowed writers such as Algernon Swinburne to see the novel as 'a poem' with 'the roll of a gathered wave',[10] and twentieth-century modernism allowed critics interested in structures of plot and imagery to see the characters as emanations of their wild setting. The earliest film version, made in 1920, was filmed on location in Haworth; and the link between characters and place was reinforced by Lord David Cecil's 1934 essay which reads Heathcliff and Catherine as 'children of the storm',[11] rather than as the morally responsible characters who people realist novels.

Certainly *Wuthering Heights* has attracted poets, musicians and dancers rather than novelists. Both Sylvia Plath (1961) and Ted Hughes (1998) have written poems called 'Wuthering Heights'. Three major ballet versions, at least five musicals and five operatic versions have been written, including an opera by Carlisle Floyd (1958). Film, stage and television versions have also gloried in the novel's tempestuous context. William Wyler's 1939 film, with Laurence Olivier as Heathcliff, begins with Lockwood fighting through a blizzard to banshee music by Alfred Newman. Bernard Herrmann, who wrote eery wind music for the Orson Welles *Jane Eyre* (1944), based his *Wuthering Heights* opera (1966; first performed in 1982) on Wyler's film, making a motif of the falling snow-flakes. Kate Bush's unearthly popular song 'Wuthering Heights' (1978) uses a high-pitched register for the ghostly Catherine's lament outside the window. Following the 1939 film, almost every visual adaptation shows us a ghostly reunion. Bernard Taylor's 1991 musical ends with a rejoicing song, 'Up Here with You', and Ralph Fiennes' fading through the walls of Peter Kosminsky's turreted Heights to find a transfigured Catherine (1991) is echoed by Robert Cavanah in David Skynner's London Weekend Television film (1998), and by Tom Hardy in Peter Bowker's 2009 version for Independent Television.

By contrast, Andrea Arnold's 2011 film offers a brutal earthiness. A hand-held camera and rapid intercutting of landscape shots with small natural creatures present characters immersed in a relentless physical environment where wind and rain replace dialogue. Shot in the Yorkshire Dales using local inexperienced actors, the film has no narrative frame and no second generation, but centres on a suffering black Heathcliff, whose response to Catherine's death is to flee into the landscape.

Unlike *Jane Eyre, Wuthering Heights* has seldom inspired other novelists by providing a template in which readers can see their lives reflected. Its narrative structure is complex, its location inhospitable, its ethical stance elusive, and the outcome for its major characters is so bleak that few can wish to emulate their lives. Its tragic pattern of love, moreover, is quite different from that of *Jane Eyre*. While *Jane Eyre* offers a still recognizable matrix for love and marriage, the lovers in *Wuthering Heights* are nostalgic for childhood and never consummate their love. Readers' uneasy fascination with and resistance to its world-view are indicated by the number of its parodies, from Stella Gibbons' *Cold Comfort Farm* (1932) to Michèle Roberts' 'Blathering Frights' (2001) by way of Bette Howells' *Wuthering Depths*, Lip Service's *Withering Looks* and the semaphore version of Monty Python's Flying Circus (all 1989).

Wuthering Heights has gained popular acceptance, in fact, not by virtue of its own world-view but by being merged with an existing archetype, which Denis de Rougemont calls 'the great European myth of adultery'.[12] The French artist Balthus, for instance, harshly emphasizes Catherine's provocative stance between Heathcliff and Edgar (1932–5). Adaptors feel at home with the eternal triangle, and they can make their mark on the material by shifting sympathies between the characters. Heathcliff in particular is susceptible to interpretation. While Victorian readers found him a kind of demon, Wyler's 1939 film presents him as a bewildered victim of Catherine's social climbing. Wyler omits all sign of his cruelty, including the persecuted second generation, while Catherine's relentless ambition is emphasized by the ludicrous luxury of the film's Thrushcross Grange. Sympathy for Heathcliff finds its acme in Cliff Richard's musical *Heathcliff* (1996), whose lead song plaintively asks whether he is 'a devil incarnate' or a 'misunderstood man'. Resentfully misunderstood, this

Heathcliff enjoins Catherine to 'learn what your sin has done', since 'nothing justifies / Reckless inhuman lies'. By contrast, Alice Hoffman's 1997 novel *Here on Earth* presents its Heathcliff figure, in present-day rural America, as inevitably cruel and possessive. Like Peter Bowker's 2009 Independent Television film, this novel assumes the template of adultery in explicitly sexual scenes.

Literary criticism has offered alternatives to the 'myth of adultery'. Terry Eagleton's *Myths of Power: A Marxist Study of the Brontës* (1975) presents a class analysis of the novel, focusing on Heathcliff's social placelessness, while Gilbert and Gubar's *The Madwoman in the Attic* (1979) shows Catherine not as a heartless social climber but as a disinherited female. Each of these insights could explain why the lovers look for escape (into nature, childhood or death) rather than social integration, but they have not shaped any striking adaptation of the novel. Luis Buñuel's Mexican film *Abismos de pasión* (1953) and Dino Millela's Italian opera *Una storia d'altri tempi* (1972) both place the events in a Catholic and fiercely patriarchal society, where Heathcliff is an outsider and Catherine an object of exchange between her brother and her husband; but while Buñuel's absurdly heightened tale of vendetta is parodic in effect, Millela presents the social constraints uncritically as tragic machinery.

Wuthering Heights is still a staple of provincial theatre, and new versions appear every year, although some producers are content with well-worn scripts such as John Davison's (1937), in which Catherine's scamper on the moors ends with Heathcliff carrying her home because she is tired! And whereas *Jane Eyre* has inspired writers to create new stories on the same plan, *Wuthering Heights* has mostly prompted sequels in the strict sense – what happens next – or stories which fill the gaps in Emily Brontë's narrative. With a few intelligent exceptions such as Geoffrey Wheatcroft's *Catherine: Her Book* (1983), these vary from the ingenious (such as Lin Haire-Sargeant's *Heathcliff* of 1992, in which Heathcliff's absence is spent helping Mr Rochester to find Jane Eyre) to the downright lazy (such as Emma Tennant's *Heathcliff's Tale*, 2005).

It is refreshing, therefore, to find an original musical version of the novel from an unexpected source. In 2009 the British Asian touring company Tamasha presented a version of *Wuthering Heights* set 'in the scorched desert of Rajasthan'. Actors who mimed and danced to recorded 'fusion' music presented a fast-moving and colourful version of the story recounted by the Heathcliff figure, who has returned after many years with 'Catherine's' ashes. By retaining her ashes, he has ensured that her ghost has walked, but as he finally scatters them in a place precious to them both, they are united as spirits. Emily Brontë's text provides many of the speeches, but some of the dialogue (especially between 'Nelly' and 'Joseph') is in Hindi. In the blending of social structures, the directors have found an 'archetype' based on questioning 'the individual's place in a society steeped in traditional values'.[13]

None of the other Brontë novels has achieved the iconic status of *Jane Eyre* and *Wuthering Heights*, though *Shirley* was filmed, on location near Haworth, as early as the 1920s. *Villette* has, however, inspired a number of creative interpretations, including a fruitful collaboration in 2005 between the adaptor Lisa Evans and the Frantic Assembly theatre company, who rendered the story's inner emotion through choreographed movement. Lisa Evans had already adapted Anne Brontë's *The Tenant of Wildfell Hall* (1995) in the context of married women's property rights. This perspective also shapes David Nokes' influential BBC television version (1996), with Tara Fitzgerald as Helen, which helped to establish the book as a feminist classic.

The attraction of the Brontë novels is not confined to the English-speaking world. Translation, which began within a few years of first publication, now extends to at least forty-three languages.[14] As examples of their popularity, *Jane Eyre* has been translated into fourteen French, fifteen Chinese and forty-seven Korean versions. There are ninety-one Korean translations of *Wuthering Heights*, and Brontë novels have appeared in at least eight German, more than twenty Japanese and thirty-seven Portuguese translations.[15] Ballets, films, musicals and stage plays exist in many different languages;[16] there are, for instance, ten Chinese film versions of *Wuthering Heights*.[17] This worldwide familiarity attests the status of the Brontë novels as international modern archetypes.

NOTES

1 For details see Patsy Stoneman (ed.), *Jane Eyre on Stage, 1848–1898: An Illustrated Edition of Eight Stage Plays with Contextual Notes* (Aldershot: Ashgate, 2007).

2 For details, see Patsy Stoneman, *Brontë Transformations: The Cultural Dissemination of* Jane Eyre *and* Wuthering Heights (Hemel Hempstead: Harvester Wheatsheaf, 1996), chapter 1.

3 [Margaret Oliphant], 'Novels', *Blackwood's Edinburgh Magazine*, 102 (Sept. 1867), 258–9, in Miriam Allott (ed.), *The Brontës: The Critical Heritage* (London: Routledge & Kegan Paul, 1974), pp. 390–1.

4 For details of early film versions, see Patricia Ingham, *The Brontës*, Oxford World's Classics, Authors in Context (Oxford University Press, 2006), pp. 223–8.

5 Germaine Greer, *The Female Eunuch* (1970; St Albans: Granada, 1971), p. 180.

6 Stevi Jackson, 'Women and Heterosexual Love', in Lynne Pearce and Jackie Stacey (eds.), *Romance Revisited* (London: Lawrence and Wishart, 1995), p. 60.

7 Sandra M. Gilbert and Susan Gubar, *The Madwoman in the Attic: The Woman Writer and the Nineteenth-Century Literary Imagination* (New Haven: Yale University Press, 1979; repr. 2000).

8 For details of ballet, film, operatic and musical versions, television and theatre adaptations mentioned throughout this chapter, see Christine Alexander and Margaret Smith (eds.), *The Oxford Companion to the Brontës* (Oxford University Press, 2003).

9 Paula Rego, quoted in T. G. Rosenthal, *Paula Rego: The Complete Graphic Work* (London: Thames and Hudson, 2003), p. 176.

10 In Allott, *The Brontës*, pp. 493 and 443.

11 Lord David Cecil, 'Emily Brontë and Wuthering Heights', in *Early Victorian Novelists: Essays in Revaluation* (London: Constable, 1934), p. 164.

12 Denis de Rougemont, *Love in the Western World* (1940; Princeton University Press, 1983), p. 18.

13 Kristine Landon-Smith and Sudha Bhuchar, prefatory note to Deepak Varma, *Wuthering Heights* (London: Methuen Drama, 2009).

14 See 'Translation', in Alexander and Smith, *Oxford Companion to the Brontës*.

15 I am grateful to Charlotte Borie, Ailee Cho, Barbara Jean Frick, Adelina Gomes, Akiko Higuchi and Guowei Liu for this information.

16 See Stoneman, *Brontë Transformations*.

17 Guowei Liu, personal communication.

PART III

Historical and cultural contexts

CHAPTER 26

Religion

David Jasper

Religion surrounded the Brontë sisters, in Haworth Parsonage and in the wider context of early nineteenth-century England. If Christianity remained rooted in the family, and religion and the Church were still the mainstays of social and moral order, change was in the air. Even in rural Yorkshire, the effects of an often corrupt and divided established Church, the rise of the critical spirit concerning religious thought and practice and the social plight of relatively poor but intelligent young women like Anne, Charlotte and Emily wafted the spectre of secularization closer. Their writings, in different ways, reflect the increasing complexities of their world which, though still saturated in the Bible and belief, saw the beginnings of a religious humanism as critical in spirit as that of George Eliot. In response to this, the reviewer of *Shirley* in the *Church Quarterly Review* wrote (assuming that the novel's author was a man):

The author's acquaintance with religion is of the most superficial description; or, if its truths are in his heart, they do not, from any evidence furnished by the pages before us, find their way to his lips. There is a vagueness about his expressions on religious subjects which leaves us in doubt if he have any defined notions of religion at all.[1]

In the twentieth century, David Lodge identified *Jane Eyre* as 'remarkable for the way it asserts a moral code as rigorous and demanding as anything in the Old Testament in a universe that is not theocentric but centered on the individual consciousness'.[2] It could be said that Charlotte (about whose views on religion we are best informed, largely from letters) was a genuine if unconscious daughter of the Enlightenment, though remaining loyal to her faith and church. She was an admirer of Dr Thomas Arnold, the reforming headmaster of Rugby School, his Broad Churchmanship, his concern for church reform and even his support of Catholic emancipation. Indeed, the case has been made for her similarity to Carlyle in the 'natural supernaturalism' of *Jane Eyre*, with its emphasis on life in this world rather than the next, the link between nature and the truly religious and the alleged capacity of religion to repress natural feelings.[3]

All three sisters were staunchly committed to the idea of sincerity and truth as expressed by S. T. Coleridge in Aphorism xxv of *Aids to Reflection* (1825): 'He, who begins by loving Christianity better than Truth, will proceed by loving his own Sect or Church better than Christianity, and end in loving himself better than all.'[4] Of Miss Ainley in *Shirley*, though old and plain (a 'professor of religion' and a 'saint'), we read: 'Whether truth – be it religious or moral truth – speak eloquently and in well-chosen language or not, its voice should be heard with reverence. Let those who cannot nicely . . . discern the difference between the tones of hypocrisy and those of sincerity, never presume to laugh' (I.x.156). The sisters were educated in the generous theological context of their father's Wesleyan-inspired Arminianism, and despite the relative narrowness of their circumstances, they enjoyed considerable intellectual opportunities and freedom. All of them hated religious intolerance, adhering to the central tenets of the theology that Arminius proposed in the early seventeenth century against Calvin's deterministic legacy: that genuine human free will is compatible with Divine sovereignty and that Christ died not merely for the elect but for all.

In the early nineteenth century, universalism – the belief that finally everyone will be saved – was, albeit condemned as heretical by the early Church, becoming popular, and words spoken by Helen Lawrence/Huntingdon in Anne Brontë's *The Tenant of Wildfell Hall* (1848) are a bold redaction of biblical references from Philippians and Ephesians with one deliberate addition, in its defence:

. . . and He that 'is able to subdue all things to Himself, will have all men to be saved,' and 'will in the fullness of time, gather together in one all things in Jesus Christ, who tasted death for every man, and in whom God will reconcile all things to Himself, whether they be things in earth or things in Heaven.' (I.xx.150)

Anne (or Helen) adds words of her own to Ephesians 1:10 – 'who tasted death for every man, and in whom God will reconcile all things to Himself' – to emphasize her point. In contrast, the extremes of Calvinism – its negations and condemnation of souls to everlasting damnation – are most unfavourably portrayed in the Brontë novels, from the grim Joseph in *Wuthering Heights* with his 'vocation to be where he had plenty of wickedness to reprove' (I.viii.58) to the Revds Brocklehurst and St John Rivers in *Jane Eyre*, who share, though in different ways, a Calvinistic and negative use of the Bible.[5]

Linked with the hatred of such negativity is Charlotte's dislike of Roman Catholicism (shared by her father, despite his support for Catholic emancipation), expressed in a scathingly ironic letter to George Smith written on 31 October 1850 after the consecration of Cardinal Wiseman as Archbishop of Westminster. In her letter, Charlotte pretended to attack Protestantism for

that presumptuous self-reliance – that audacious championship of Reason and Common-Sense which ought to have been crushed out of you all in your cradles – or at least during your school-days – and which perhaps – on the contrary – [were] encouraged and developed – what if these things should induce you madly to oppose the returning Supremacy and advancing victory of the Holy Catholic Church? (Smith, *Letters*, vol. II, pp. 491–2)

At the conclusion to *Villette*, Lucy Snowe, awaiting the return of Paul Emanuel, upholds his virtuous character despite his Catholicism: 'All Rome could not put him into bigotry, nor the Propaganda itself make him a real Jesuit: He was born honest, and not false – artless, and not cunning – a freeman, and not a slave' (xlii.494).

In spite of their immersion in the Church of England – a permanent commitment, at least for Anne and Charlotte – the sisters shared with Coleridge a dislike of priestcraft, sacerdotalism and any assumption that Christianity was simply coterminous with the Church and church attendance. Apart from their suspicion (more social than religious) of Dissenters, Charlotte and Anne dismissed any unthinking reverence given to clergymen. Of Miss Ainley in *Shirley*, it is remarked concerning the clergy (with a passing reference to Isaiah 1:18 – 'though your sins be as scarlet, they shall be as white as snow') that '[n]o matter how clearly their little vices and enormous absurdities were pointed out to her, she could not see them: she was blind to ecclesiastical defects: the white surplice covered a multitude of sins' (II.iii.227). On the other hand, in Anne's first novel, *Agnes Grey*, the Evangelical Mr Weston is almost the perfect cleric, not because of his churchmanship but rather in his assertion that 'the best of happiness ... is mine already ... the power and the will to be useful' (xiii.97). It is Mr Weston's humanity that makes him an effective preacher and reader in church: 'He read the lessons as if he were bent on giving full effect to every passage ... and the prayers, he read as if he were not reading at all, but praying, earnestly and sincerely from his own heart' (x.72). Thus he follows the urging of Charles Simeon to his young clerical friends to '[p]ray the prayers, and don't read them only; adhere sacredly to the directions of the Rubric, except where they have become obsolete, and the resumption of them would clearly do harm'.[6]

Mr Weston's High Church rector Mr Hatfield, however, is quite different. Ambitious and pastorally uncaring, Hatfield was chiefly interested in 'Church discipline, rites and ceremonies, apostolical succession, the duty of reverence and obedience to the clergy, [and] the atrocious criminality of dissent' (x.74). Only a little less pernicious is the Revd Michael Millward in *The Tenant of Wildfell Hall*, whose clerical disposition is characterized by his dislike of dissent and his intolerance of anyone who might contradict him, together with his 'laudable care for his own bodily health' (i.18).

As Marianne Thormählen has pointed out, the quarrelsome, Anglo-Catholic curates who are ridiculed at the beginning of *Shirley* cannot strictly be called Tractarian; but they still expose the absurdities (in Charlotte's eyes) of the debates of the 'shower of curates ... [who] lie very thick on the hills' of northern England, where they had been sent by the aid societies of the day.[7]

What attracts them, it would be difficult to say. It is not friendship; for whenever they meet they quarrel. It is not religion; the thing is never named amongst them: theology they may discuss occasionally, but piety – never. (1.i.7)

[T]hey argued; not on politics, nor on philosophy, nor on literature; these topics were now as ever totally without interest for them; not even on theology, practical or doctrinal; but on minute points of ecclesiastical discipline, frivolities which seemed empty as bubbles to all save themselves. (1.i.8)

What the contentious curates lack is 'religion', that phenomenon which is central to all of the sisters' writings and yet remains contradictory, ambiguous and elusive of definition.

The two key literary influences on *Jane Eyre* are the Bible and *The Pilgrim's Progress*, and both are behind the subtle refigurings of the novel's final synthesis of Romanticism and religion. David Norton has suggested that 'Charlotte Brontë does not just use the King James Bible; her language is in a number of respects shaped by it'.[8] After her broken wedding, Jane's despair is reminiscent of Christian and Hopeful as they wade through the river before entering the Celestial City: 'I heard a flood loosened in remote mountains, and felt the torrent come: to rise I had no will, to flee I had no strength. I lay faint; longing to be dead' (II.xi.296). After she lost her 'idol' Rochester, there remained but 'a remembrance of God', with references to two Psalms (22:11 and 69:1–2), both of which begin in despair and end in comfort. In her wanderings Jane, like the prodigal of Luke 15:16, begs for cold porridge that the pigs refuse (III.ii.329); and, having crossed the marsh, she finds sanctuary through 'a gate – a wicket', like the wicket gate of the Evangelist in *The Pilgrim's Progress* (III.ii.331).

As St John Rivers leaves for the mission field in India at the end of the novel, he is compared to Bunyan's Greatheart: 'His is the exaction of the apostle, who speaks but for Christ, when he says –"Whosoever will come after me, let him deny himself, and take up his cross and follow me"' (III.xii.452; Matthew 16:24). He remains unmarried, joining Christ in the final words of the novel, as of the Bible – 'Amen; even so come, Lord Jesus!' It was St John Rivers' house that had lain beyond the wicket gate for Jane, and in his home she found refuge and ultimately prosperity. But she was to respond to another, more earthly call to 'come', uttered like the 'still small voice' of I Kings 19:12 in 'the moorland loneliness and midnight hush', a 'voice within', but 'it was the voice of a human being – a known, loved, well-remembered voice – that of Edward Fairfax Rochester' (III.ix.419–20). Jane asserts herself against the religious strength of St John Rivers and his denial of emotion:

It was *my* time to assume ascendancy. *My* powers were in play, and in force. I told him to forbear question or remark ... He obeyed at once ... I mounted to my chamber; locked myself in; fell on my knees; and prayed in my way – a different way to St. John's, but effective in its own fashion. I seemed to penetrate very near a Mighty Spirit; and my soul rushed out in gratitude at His feet. (III.ix.420)

These final chapters of *Jane Eyre* are a daring exchange of religion and Romanticism. Who is the Mighty Spirit? Not the 'idol' who had been Rochester, but still not quite the Christian God of St John Rivers, the God who calls him on a self-sacrificial journey which Jane cannot – will not – make. Rochester makes his final act of submission, humbling himself 'with gratitude to the beneficent God of this earth' (III.xi.446); but the final description of their ten years of union is still, like the endings of the Bible and *The Pilgrim's Progress*, a vision of an apocalyptic marriage. A scriptural image, it is nevertheless a condition established by Jane's own decision (made possible, it must be added, by her new wealth).[9] M. H. Abrams has pointed out that in *The Pilgrim's Progress* (the Song of Songs being employed for the purpose), 'the land and the city which [are] the goal [are] represented in a bluff rendering of the language of sexual desire'.[10] In *Jane Eyre* this element is translated into romantic love, returning to one final image of prelapsarian bliss as Jane describes herself as 'ever more absolutely bone of his bone, and flesh of his flesh' (III.xii.450; Genesis 2:23).

In her book *The Religion of the Heart*, Elisabeth Jay compares *Jane Eyre* with the Evangelical Emma Jane Worboise's novel *Thornycroft Hall* (1863), written as a corrective response in the cause of the Gospel. Jay suggests that Mrs Worboise neither could nor would have risked the ambiguities of St John Rivers, nor engaged with the 'transposition of the religious metaphor into the expression of human passion' in Rochester's testimony.[11] Nor would she ever have incurred the censure of the *Christian Observer* as it described Charlotte: '[H]er picture is that of a morbid fancy, mixing up fiction with fact, and traducing, with a random pen, an Institution to which she and her family were wholesale debtors.'[12]

And yet, the Athanasian Creed excluded, Charlotte Brontë, a clergy daughter and later wife, affirmed in a letter of 23 December 1847, 'I love the Church of England' (to W. S. Williams; Smith, *Letters*, vol. I, p. 581). Of Emily less can be said, for she never divulged her religious views. In her most famous poem, she asserts 'No coward soul is mine' in defiance of death and affirmation of her own faith, against which

> Vain are the thousand creeds
> That move men's hearts, unutterably vain,
> Worthless as withered weeds
> Or idlest froth amid the boundless main
> To waken doubt . . . [13]

Certainly in *Wuthering Heights*, the institution of the Church is decaying as represented by the deserted chapel of Gimmerden Sough; and we are left contemplating the graves of Catherine, Edgar Linton and Heathcliff and their 'sleepers in that quiet earth' (II.xx.300). J. Hillis Miller describes the love of Heathcliff and Catherine as another form of 'apocalyptic marriage', for 'their love has brought "the new heaven and the new earth" into this fallen world as a present reality'. This world has no necessity for the Church, and if there is a God, then this 'has been transformed from the transcendent deity of extreme Protestantism . . . to an immanent God, pervading everything, like the soft wind blowing over the heath'.[14] But if by the end of *Wuthering Heights* we have transcended Lockwood's terrible dream of the Revd Jabes Branderham with his vicious congregation, in which 'every man's hand was against his neighbour' (I.iii.20), there still remains the mysterious vision of Emily Brontë, closest to the world of Greek tragedy, a dream of a dark violence in Heathcliff 'which no settlement with organised society can attenuate'.[15]

Charlotte, Anne and Emily express different perspectives on religion: Charlotte – complicated, articulate, devout, rebellious; Anne – gentler in spirit, yet bold and prepared to hold her ground; Emily – mysterious, introverted, turbulent, secretive. And yet they are recognizably sisters, and daughters of the Revd Patrick Brontë. They were deeply religious when Christianity and the Church were changing, for better and for worse, in a world which was evolving in the spirit of the Enlightenment and Kant. In their different ways, they were deeply aware of these changes; and their fictions reflect them, without final resolutions.

NOTES

1 *Church Quarterly Review*, 27 (Jan. 1850), 224–5, easily accessible in Miriam Allott (ed.), *The Brontës: The Critical Heritage* (London: Routledge & Kegan Paul, 1974), pp. 156–7.

2 David Lodge, *Language of Fiction: Essays in Criticism and Verbal Analysis of the English Novel* (New York: Columbia University Press, 1966), p. 135.

3 Barry Qualls, *The Secular Pilgrims of Victorian Fiction* (Cambridge University Press, 1982), chapter 2, pp. 43–84. The phrase 'natural supernaturalism' is from Carlyle's *Sartor Resartus* (1833–4).

4 S. T. Coleridge, *Aids to Reflection* (1825), here quoted from the Bollingen edn, John Beer (ed.), *The Collected Works of Samuel Taylor Coleridge*, vol. XI (London and Princeton: Routledge and Princeton University Press, 1993), p. 107.

5 See Valentine Cunningham, *In the Reading Gaol* (Oxford: Blackwell, 1994), p. 342.

6 Quoted in Horton Davies, *Worship and Theology in England*, vol. III: *From Watts and Wesley to Maurice, 1690–1850* (Princeton University Press, 1961), p. 217.

7 Marianne Thormählen, *The Brontës and Religion* (Cambridge University Press, 1999), p. 195.

8 David Norton, *A History of the Bible as Literature* (Cambridge University Press, 1993), vol. II, p. 173.

9 See Qualls, *Secular Pilgrims*, p. 68 and M. H. Abrams, 'The Shape of Things to Come: The Apocalyptic Marriage', in *Natural Supernaturalism: Tradition and Revolution in Romantic Literature* (New York: W. W. Norton, 1973), pp. 37–46.

10 Abrams, *Natural Supernaturalism*, p. 168.

11 Elisabeth Jay, *The Religion of the Heart: Anglican Evangelicalism and the Nineteenth Century Novel* (Oxford University Press, 1979), pp. 258–9.

12 *Christian Observer* (1857), 428.

13 Quoted from Janet Gezari (ed.), *Emily Jane Brontë: The Collected Poems* (Harmondsworth: Penguin, 1992), p. 182.

14 J. Hillis Miller, *The Disappearance of God: Five Nineteenth-Century Writers* (New York: Schocken Books, 1965), p. 211. Cf. Revelation 21:1.

15 Georges Bataille, 'Emily Brontë', in *Literature and Evil*, trans. Alastair Hamilton (London: Marion Boyars, 1985), p. 24.

CHAPTER 27

The philosophical-intellectual context

Stephen Prickett

Only one generalization can be allowed about nineteenth-century England: *any* generalization about it is probably false – or must, at least, be so carefully qualified as to become useless. As it was arguably the world's first pluralistic society, it would take two or three generations before social and intellectual commentators were able to grasp that diversity and polarization were thenceforth an integral part of any British society, rather than being regrettable aberrations.

Moreover, even 'context' can be a weasel word here. Is the context of past literature that in which authors believed themselves to be writing, or is it rather that which we now, with the benefit of hindsight, attribute to them? One thinks of the ending of Laclos' *Liaisons dangereuses*, where the elderly countess, sorting her pack of cards in 1789, says, 'Well, that was the eighties; I wonder what the nineties will bring?' While not constituting such dramatic irony, context is rarely quite what was imagined at the time. While writing of the 'abundant shower of curates' that had descended on Yorkshire, clearly not presenting it as an altogether favourable phenomenon, did the author of *Shirley* ever imagine that this very period might be seen by later church historians as a key epoch of ecclesiastical reform? And if we think of the 1840s in terms of the growth of Tractarianism in England, should we also consider that the new High Church sensibility hardly exerted any influence at all in the diocese of York at this time?

Stevie Davies has argued that Emily Brontë was aware of most, if not all, of the major intellectual debates of her day: that she knew about new developments in German Higher Criticism, new ideas in philosophy and historiography and recent developments in archaeology, biology, geology and paleontology.[1] Is this simply a case of assuming that because the 1840s were a time of enormous intellectual ferment, the Brontë sisters must have been witnesses to it? What evidence is there, either of ignorance of or of actual engagement with the new ideas? We do, in fact, have highly suggestive evidence for the latter: in late 1849 we find Charlotte Brontë commenting on books sent to her by her publishers, books which included a translation of Goethe's *Conversations with Eckermann* and the Hare brothers' *Guesses at Truth* (Smith, *Letters*, vol. II, pp. 251 and 280). While Charlotte's eager response to the former demonstrates her awareness of current German literature and ideas, her interest in the latter is, in its own way, even more significant.

Studying *Guesses at Truth*, though the work is too little known today, is perhaps one of the best ways to understand the British intellectual world of the second quarter of the nineteenth century. Modelled superficially on sections of the Jena Romantics' journal the *Athenäum* (1798–1800), it was a collection of literary, philosophic and religious fragments composed by two brothers, Julius and Augustus Hare – with some input from a third, Marcus. First published (anonymously) in 1827, it was, despite its distinctly unarresting title, to show astonishing durability. Under Julius it went through a second, much enlarged, edition in 1838 and a third (presumably the edition read by Charlotte) in 1847; it was subsequently reprinted in 1867, 1871 and 1884. The fragmentary form was deliberate; it might even be seen as a realization of the pluralism mentioned above. The first edition carried a prefatory motto from Bacon's *Advancement of Learning*:

As young men, when they knit and shape perfectly, do seldom grow to a further stature; so knowledge, while it is in aphorisms and observations, is in growth; but when once it is comprehended in exact methods, it may perchance be further polished and illustrated, and accommodated for use and practice; but it increaseth no more in bulk and substance.

Or, as Julius Hare was to develop the idea, 'Is not every Grecian temple complete even though it be in ruins? just as the very fragments of [the Greeks'] poems are like the scattered leaves of some unfading flower. Is not every Gothic minster unfinished? and for the best of reasons, because it is infinite.'[2] For Hare, however, the incompleteness of the fragment was not so much an architectural as a biological – and therefore developmental – metaphor. 'Some thoughts are acorns. Would that any in this book were.'[3]

Given this insensible movement from the idea of the fragment to a theory of mental development, it is no surprise that this is the age of the *Bildungsroman*, nor that the Brontës should have been pioneers of the new novel form. A comparison between such eighteenth-century 'histories' as *Tom Jones* – or even the 'autobiographical' *Tristram Shandy* – and, say, *Jane Eyre* illustrates the difference at once. The word *Bildungsroman* was first used by the critic Karl Morgenstern in his 1820s lectures at the University of Dorpat to describe Goethe's *Wilhelm Meister's Apprenticeship*, which, though popular then neither with its translator nor with the wider reading public, was translated by Carlyle in 1824.[4] If *Jane Eyre* was one of the first best-selling English *Bildungsromane*, then *Wuthering Heights* was perhaps, in its own way, a truly dystopian version.

While for much of the British reading public *Guesses at Truth* was probably their main introduction to the ideas and works of Goethe, Herder and the Jena Romantics, the book also contains significant differences from German Romanticism. Hare, himself a clergyman and theologian, had been the tutor of John Sterling and F. D. Maurice at Cambridge, and he had been one of the principal channels by which the theological ideas of Coleridge had been transmitted to a new generation of students: '[S]o frequently have I strengthened my mind with the invigorating waters which stream forth redundantly in Mr Coleridge's works, that, if I mistake not, many of my thoughts will appear to have been impregnated by his spirit.'[5] 'Coleridge', Hare wrote in the 1847 edition, 'had a livelier perception than any other Englishman of the two cardinal ideas of all criticism, – that every work of genius is at once an organic whole in itself, and a part and member of a living, organic universe, of that poetical world in which the spirit of man manifests itself by successive avatars.'[6] Where Hare came to differ from Coleridge was in his belief that a single all-encompassing philosophic 'system' was not merely impossible, but actually undesirable. For him, the more Darwinian notion of ideas as a multiplicity of 'seeds' was part of a wider theory of aesthetics in which the book had become a symbol or surrogate of life itself. But the open-endedness of organicism is already being contrasted with the mechanical metaphors of the steam age: 'Life may be defined to be the power of self-augmentation, or of assimilation, not of self-nurture; for then a steam-engine over a coalpit might be made to live.'[7] Such quotations are sometimes cited as evidence of an inherent anti-mechanical bias among the English Romantics; but as Courtney Salvey's researches show,[8] mid-nineteenth-century metaphors – whether in criticism, literature, philosophy, politics or theology – are so permeated by mechanistic images that it would be more true to say that the differentiation between organism and mechanism expounded by Coleridge and his followers is a subdivision of a branch rather than a fundamental divide of the main stem itself.

Even so, what distinguishes and, in the end, unifies Hare's fragmentary scattering of the seeds of growth is a particular sense of history. Again, there are strong German influences. Hare and Connop Thirlwall (1797–1875) had translated Niebuhr's *History of Rome* in 1827. Barthold Georg Niebuhr (1776–1831) was the first modern historian to attempt to look beyond the accretions of myth and tradition handed down by the Latin authors and to search for documentary evidence. Where that was impossible, he sought explanations in areas not necessarily obvious to contemporary observers, such as institutions, laws, class, culture and even race. Though in retrospect hailed as a watershed in British historiography, the translation was also a 'sign of the times' – a phrase taken up as a title by Thomas Carlyle.

Not all this new emphasis on historical change was progressive. The Gothic novel, for instance, was melodramatic and backward-looking. What had begun with such novels as Walpole's wildly supernatural *Castle of Otranto* and Mrs Radcliffe's barely credible *Mysteries of Udolpho* was an interest in two superficially very different qualities: a sense of the difference of the past, and a language of the unconscious. Both were to become increasingly important in the first half of the nineteenth century. From the first was to grow the historical novel – the literary expression of the new sense of history mentioned above, popularized and made respectable all over Europe by Sir Walter Scott; from the latter, the Gothic's attention to grotesque and abnormal states of mind, was to grow the language of interiority – giving further depth and meaning to the newly invented word 'psychology' which so fascinated Hare. Though *Wuthering Heights* is never exhausted by any one account of it, we forget at our peril that it is probably the finest Gothic novel ever written – with *Jane Eyre*, for all its seductive realism, not that far behind. What for Mary Shelley was to be found in the Romantic forests of Germany, or for Walpole and Radcliffe in an imaginary Italy, is brought home and domesticated by Emily to the bleak Pennine moors of Yorkshire.

As a source of metaphors, however, the Gothic had other uses. Concerned with the production of untimely monsters (in this instance political), Hare was quick to quote *Frankenstein*.[9] In many cases, what had begun as a romantic and often wildly unscholarly interest in largely imaginary Middle Ages became transposed into an idealization of the past in comparison with what was seen as the grime and materialism of the present. Whereas earlier radical attacks on the current state of society, such as Robert Bage's *Hermsprong* (1796), had been forward-looking, *Contrasts* (1836) by A. W. N. Pugin (1812–52) delivers its message of catastrophic moral and aesthetic decline by a series of prints comparing an idealized Roman Catholic medieval England with the civic decay induced by industrialism and the harshness of the Poor Law. Carlyle's pre-Reformation Abbot Samson in *Past and Present* (1843) is a heroic figure who stands in marked contrast to the degeneracy of modern leaders. What Carlyle, with his usual capacity to create memorable compound nouns, called 'the condition-of-England question' was to dominate much writing on contemporary Britain. Similarly, *Sybil* (1845) by Benjamin Disraeli swiftly gives the reader a contrast between the honest communal labour for the common good performed by the monks of old and a dissolute modern aristocracy ('a Venetian oligarchy') whose family fortunes were based on the theft of monastic lands at the Reformation. Carlyle's own titles, from his *Signs of the Times* (1829) to *Past and Present*, hammer home the message of historical flux and transformation – a theme central to his monumental history *The French Revolution* (1837), which explored change not so much as process but as apocalypse. Henceforth, history was to be neither a record of moral exempla nor Gibbon's list of 'crimes, follies, and misfortunes of mankind', but a story of development and change – not merely in politics or social order but, and much more significantly, in terms of aesthetics and human consciousness.

For Hare, society as well as human consciousness and its many literary expressions are in a constant process of change and evolution:

> Goethe in 1800 does not write just as Shakespeare wrote in 1600: but neither would Shakespeare in 1800 have written just as he wrote in 1600. For the frame and aspect of society are different; the world which would act on him, and on which he would have to act, is another world. True poetical genius lives in communion with the world, in a perpetual reciprocation of influences, imbibing feeling and knowledge[.][10]

History matters. Indeed, at the centre of the *Bildungsroman* is the belief that the only way to understand individuals is to understand their story. Whether this new attitude to history, in all the complexity and untidiness of reality, would also explain the notorious 'unreliable narrator' of *Villette* must be a matter of debate; but if, at an individual level, the tangled web of past events may explain the mystery of *The Tenant of Wildfell Hall*, or the even more mysterious events at Wuthering Heights, at another level it also explains the story of humanity itself. Even more significantly, this process of change is not random, but moves in the direction of evergreater self-consciousness.

Owen Barfield has argued that this period is the moment when the long process of individuation, whose beginnings can be traced as far back as Augustine's *Confessions*, reaches its fruition in the English Romantic poets and the Brontë sisters, their natural novelistic successors.[11] Hare himself cites Seneca's late Roman play *Medea*, where the eponymous protagonist can only describe her abandonment by Jason in the third person: *Medea superest* ('Medea remains [i.e. is left behind]'). 'An English poet', writes Hare, 'would hardly say *Medea remains*'. An Italian 'modern opera of little worth' illustrates Hare's point by making Medea reply to the question *Che mi resta* with the simple pronoun, *Io*. 'An ancient poet could not have used the pronoun; a modern poet could hardly use the proper name.'[12] In other words, even as late as the end of the Roman Empire, Seneca's Medea still sees her tragic predicament from the outside – as the abandoned lover, but one still not sufficiently interiorized to be able to speak of herself simply as 'I'.

When Jane Eyre is struggling, almost to the point of breakdown, with her conscience as to whether to become Rochester's mistress, she puts his question to herself: 'Who in the world cares for *you?*' The reply, one of the most deservedly famous statements of personal identity in all nineteenth-century fiction, is a passionate statement of interiority that would have been incomprehensible to Medea or her contemporaries:

I care for myself. The more solitary, the more friendless, the more unsustained I am, the more I will respect myself . . . Laws and principles are not for the times when there is no temptation: they are for such moments as this, when body and soul rise in mutiny against their rigour: stringent are they; inviolate they shall be. If at my individual convenience I might break them, what would be their worth? . . . Preconceived opinions, foregone determinations, are all I have at this hour to stand by: there I plant my foot. (III.i.317)

In a passage that might have been written as a commentary on Jane's predicament, in *Lost Icons*, Rowan Williams cites Walter Davis' comment that '[i]nwardness develops not by escaping or resolving but by deepening *the conflicts that define it*' (Williams' italics).[13] Though the story of Romantic individuation is historically inseparable from the story of Christianity itself (one hardly becomes a martyr without a clear sense of individual identity!), its subsequent evolution was to prove as powerful an impulse towards secularity as towards religion. No surprise, then, that Emily Brontë's best-known poem begins 'No coward soul is mine' and goes on to declare the inability of 'the thousand creeds / That move men's hearts' to make the speaker abandon her pantheistic religion of consciousness and selfhood.

If, on the one hand, *Guesses at Truth* seeks to chart the larger movements of human consciousness, it is, on the other, practical and down-to-earth in its approach to social questions. As a resident clergyman and magistrate in rural Sussex, Hare had a view of society and history which was much more practical and concrete than that of his German mentors. 'It is an odd device', writes Hare, 'when a fellow commits a crime, to send him to the antipodes for it'.[14] Odd indeed, since it had already begun to dawn on concerned observers that criminals transported to Australia had better food, better opportunities and a better life expectancy than their more 'honest' compatriots in England. Throughout the 1840s, the fear of agricultural and industrial disputes spilling over into riots and even outright revolution was never far from middle-class minds, especially after the 1848 revolutions right across Europe. *Shirley* (1849), though not the first 'industrial novel', and despite its ostensible setting in the Luddite riots of forty years before, gains a topical immediacy from the much larger Chartist agitation of the previous year.

One associated political element is, however, decreasingly attractive to the Brontës, and that is imperialism. Whereas it plays a significant part in the childhood stories of Gondal and Glass Town, it always seems to be a negative factor in the adult novels. If, as some critics have suggested, imperialism and the slave trade form a sinister subtext to Heathcliff's Liverpool background, the lurking presence of Bertha, the Caribbean creole and madwoman in the Thornfield attic, can much more clearly be read as a symbol of the damage that imperialism inflicts not only on the colonized, and on the slaves, but also on the imperialists themselves. Slavery, whether in the West Indian plantations or in the factories of England, is always a double-edged sword. In this respect, at least, the Brontës may be best seen not so much as embedded within a particular intellectual and social context as among those who helped to change it.

NOTES

1 Stevie Davies, *Emily Brontë: Heretic* (London: Women's Press, 1994), *passim*.
2 *Guesses at Truth* (London, 1827), vol. ii, p. 250.
3 *Ibid.*, vol. ii, p. 79.
4 See Rosemary Ashton, *The German Idea: Four English Writers and the Reception of German Thought, 1800–1860* (Cambridge University Press, 1980; London: Libris, 1994), p. 82.
5 *Guesses at Truth*, 3rd edn (1847), pp. 279–80.
6 *Ibid.*, pp. 190–1.
7 *Ibid.*, p. 16.
8 Courtney Salvey, unpublished doctoral thesis, University of Kent, forthcoming.
9 *Guesses at Truth*, 3rd edn (1847), p. 77.

10 See *Guesses at Truth* (1827), vol. II, pp. 136–7.
11 See Owen Barfield, 'The Nature of Meaning,' *Seven*, 2 (1981), 38.
12 *Guesses at Truth* (1827), vol. II, pp. 116–17.
13 Walter Davis, *Inwardness and Existence: Subjectivity in/and Hegel, Heidegger, Marx, and Freud* (Madison, WI: University of Wisconsin Press, 1989), p. 105; quoted in Rowan Williams, *Lost Icons* (Edinburgh: T. & T. Clark, 2000), p. 146.
14 *Guesses at Truth*, 3rd edn (1847), p. 82.

CHAPTER 28

Education

Dinah Birch

The long story of the Brontë family's imaginative and professional relations with education begins in eighteenth-century Ireland. 'Pat Prunty', the capable son of a poor farmer in County Down, had known from the first that his aspirations could be realized only through his own labours. For him, as for many of his contemporaries, education was not simply a matter of improving the mind. It was the primary means by which he could further his social and economic ambitions. Writing to Elizabeth Gaskell towards the end of his life, as the respectable elderly Anglican clergyman that he had become, Patrick Brontë recalled his youthful efforts:

> I shew'd an early fondness for books, and continued at school for several years – At the age of sixteen, knowing that my Father could afford me no pecuniary aid I began to think of doing something for myself – I therefore opened a public school – and ⟨?⟩ in this line, I continued five or six years; I was then a Tutor in a gentleman's Family – From which situation I removed to Cambridge, and enter'd St John's College[.][1]

Much that was characteristic of Patrick and his family is implied in this remarkable letter. To have established a profitable school at the age of sixteen, and then to have acquired the Cambridge degree that led to ordination in the Church of England, suggests an extraordinary level of ability and drive. His children were brought up to emulate the independent enterprise that had characterized Patrick's life, and they too saw education as the means both to self-improvement and financial independence. But each of the four siblings who survived into adulthood pursued a different interpretation of Patrick's heroic example. Charlotte shared his ambitions for a public career built on the disciplines of educational achievement, working first as a pupil and then as a teacher, and finally assimilating her experiences as an educator into the substance of her mature fiction. Branwell, caught between his father's 'fondness for books' and a rebellious reluctance to accept the restrictions of Patrick's arduous life, struggled to turn his talents into artistic success. Emily's aspirations were more guardedly private, but still rested on the sense that education would provide her with the means of 'doing something' for herself. Both *Wuthering Heights* and her compelling poetry challenge the values of her family, but neither would have been written without the stimulus of Emily's early pedagogic experiences, in Yorkshire and Brussels. Anne's labours as a governess led her to think deeply about the purposes of education in relation to moral and religious duty, and her distinctive fiction is closely associated with her mixed experiences as pupil and teacher. The family was shaped by the pervasive culture of self-help that drove the English middle classes at a time of opportunity and insecurity, but the extent to which their ambition was defined in relation to the processes of education was exceptional.

The younger Brontës, richer in talent than in money, saw education as the way to adult autonomy: necessary and desirable, but sometimes irksome. The resulting conflicts were grounded in childhood, when the six children began to be schooled at home. Maria Brontë, their mother, died too soon to take much part in the work, but her sister Elizabeth (Aunt Branwell) gave lessons to Anne, the youngest child, and taught all the girls to sew. Patrick, an experienced teacher, assumed a more active role, and took on sole responsibility for the education of young Branwell. Boys' schools were expensive, and Patrick was ideally placed to give his son a gentleman's education himself. Though Branwell's home education was not unusual among boys of his class, it did create an enduring tension in his life. As the only boy in an ambitious family, Branwell was expected to make his mark in the world, but he was given no formal experience of life in communities outside his household. No worldly success other than financial self-sufficiency was expected of the girls. In their case, however, leaving home was a necessity, as no one in the parsonage was in a position to prepare them for the work as governesses and teachers that seemed to offer the best prospect of independence.

The family's experiences of educational institutions for girls reflect a wide diversity in the methods and resources of schools in a period where middle-class education was a matter of private enterprise. Maria and Elizabeth Brontë first attended Crofton Hall, a boarding school near Wakefield, where they flourished. But Crofton Hall was a strain on Patrick's scanty income. His decision to send his four eldest girls to the cheaper Clergy Daughters' School at Cowan Bridge has become the stuff of literary legend, largely because of Charlotte's unforgettable picture of

Lowood School in *Jane Eyre*. Research has qualified the image of the school as a nightmare of callous deprivation and hypocrisy.[2] The Clergy Daughters' School was not a female version of Dotheboys Hall. But it was undoubtedly austere. The pupils were poorly fed and unsympathetically treated, and disease spread easily. Maria and Elizabeth both succumbed to tuberculosis, returning to Haworth to die, and Charlotte and Emily were subsequently removed from the school.

Loss, rather than learning, is what the Clergy Daughters' School came to represent in the Brontë family's history. Later experiences of formal education were more productive. In 1831, the fourteen-year-old Charlotte was sent to Roe Head School, later to be followed by Emily and Anne. Smaller than the Clergy Daughters' School (with no more than ten pupils), more tolerant and with better standards of physical care, Roe Head was a turning-point in the girls' lives (see Figure 18). For the first time, they began to establish a distinct identity outside Haworth. Charlotte, the eldest, spent only eighteen months there as a pupil (she later returned to teach); but she kept the two close friends she made at Roe Head, Mary Taylor and Ellen Nussey, throughout her life. Writing to Elizabeth Gaskell, Mary Taylor recalled that Charlotte was able to command respect through her quick intelligence and wide learning:

> She would confound us by knowing things that were out of our range altogether. She was acquainted with most of the short pieces of poetry that we had to learn by heart; would tell us the authors, the poems they were taken from, and sometimes repeat a page or two, and tell us the plot ... She used to draw much better, and more quickly, than anything we had seen before, and knew much about celebrated pictures and painters ... She made poetry and drawing at least exceedingly interesting to me; and then I got the habit, which I have yet, of referring mentally to her opinion on all matters of that kind[.] (Gaskell, *Life*, pp. 81–2)

Mary's letter makes clear that Charlotte's interests as a schoolgirl were rooted in the vivid creative life that the Brontë siblings had shared in the parsonage. In class, she studied geography, history, grammar and French (coverage of mathematics, science and classics was thin); but what she cared about was literary and visual culture: 'She picked up every scrap of information concerning painting, sculpture, poetry, music, & c., as if it were gold' (Gaskell, *Life*, p. 84). The Brontë sisters were not ignorant of science, thanks to the resources of the circulating library at Keighley and the Keighley Mechanics' Institute, and to their eclectic reading in periodical literature. But their formal education was predominantly in the arts, and in this they were characteristic of girls of their generation.

18 Anne Brontë's drawing of Roe Head School, *c.* 1835–7

Charlotte's sisters had less positive experiences as schoolgirls at Roe Head. Emily spent only three months there at the age of seventeen, and seems to have made no friends. Subdued and homesick, she was glad to return to Haworth. Anne was a dutiful and thoughtful fifteen-year-old when she enrolled; her final months there were complicated by a religious crisis that cast a long shadow over her imaginative life. Neither shared the

academic and social success that had given Charlotte new confidence at
Roe Head. Nevertheless, all three girls encountered the ordered structures
of a world outside the parsonage, as Branwell, ambitious and unruly, did
not. Margaret Wooler, who was 'clever, decent and motherly', according
to Patrick (Barker, p. 171), owned and ran the school together with her
three sisters. She represented a model for independent womanhood that
the Brontë girls did not forget. Miss Wooler also provided Charlotte with
her first paid employment as a teacher. The experience was far from
encouraging, as Charlotte recorded in a particularly bleak moment:
'The thought came over me am I to spend all the best part of my life in
this wretched bondage, forcibly suppressing my rage at the idleness the
apathy and the hyperbolical & most asinine stupidity of these fat-headed
oafs and on compulsion assuming an air of kindness, patience & assiduity?'
('Roe Head Journal', quoted from Barker, p. 254).

Charlotte, Emily and Anne all found the work of teaching toilsome and
depressing. Emily bore it for only six months, working at Law Hill, a
school near Halifax, in a job that Charlotte, writing to Ellen Nussey on
2 October 1838, termed 'slavery' (Smith, *Letters*, vol. 1, p. 182). As a
governess, Anne encountered great difficulty (recalled in *Agnes Grey*) in
establishing authority over her disruptive pupils. Charlotte's impatience
erupted repeatedly throughout her professional experiences in the schoolroom, as both governess and teacher. She struggled with the conflicts
inherent in the work, with its demands that she should exercise strict
control over her pupils while meekly conforming to the requirements of
her employers. Charlotte was happier as a pupil than as a teacher: writing
to Ellen from Brussels in 1842, she said, 'it is natural to me to submit and
very unnatural to command' (Smith, *Letters*, vol. 1, p. 284). But she did
not renounce her longstanding wish to find liberation through establishing a school – perhaps of the kind run by Elizabeth Hastings, a spirited
and independent heroine of Charlotte's Angrian fiction:

She spent her mornings in her drawing room surrounded by her class, not wearily
toiling to impart the dry rudiments of knowledge to yawning, obstinate children,
a thing she hated and for which her sharp, irritable temper rendered her wholly
unfit, but instructing those who had already mastered the rudiments of education; reading, commenting, explaining, leaving it to them to listen; if they failed,
comfortably conscious that the blame would rest on her pupils, not on herself . . .
she was as prosperous as any little woman of five feet high and not twenty years
old need wish to be.[3]

The ambition to establish a school was shared by many young women of
the earlier decades of the nineteenth century. Though the calling was

often precarious, it provided the hope of an income without the notorious subservience and isolation of the life of a domestic governess, or the unrewarding grind of a salaried teacher's position. Emily's diary paper of July 1841, written on her twenty-third birthday, contemplates the prospect with satisfaction: 'we (ie) Charlotte, Anne and I – ⟨will shall⟩ shall be all merrily seated in our own sitting-room in some pleasant ⟨part?⟩ and flourishing seminary having just gathered in for the midsummer holydays our debts will be paid off and we shall have c⟨h⟩ash in hand to a considerable amount' (Barker, p. 358). Anne also spoke optimistically of the plan to found a school: 'I hope we shall' (Barker, p. 359). Thoughts of freedom, rather than servitude, were inviting. But it is noticeable that Emily dwells on the material rewards of the projected school – the money, the sitting-room – rather than the work itself.

It was Charlotte who pursued the scheme with most determination. In 1842, she and Emily embarked on further training in languages at the Pensionnat Heger in Brussels, with the intention of equipping themselves for success in a notoriously competitive market. This was a bold venture, and Charlotte compared herself with her father in undertaking it. 'When he left Ireland to go to Cambridge University, he was as ambitious as I am now. I want us *all* to go on. I know we have talents, and I want them to be turned to account', she wrote to her aunt in the letter of 29 September 1841 where she asked Elizabeth Branwell for financial support (Smith, *Letters*, vol. 1, p. 269). Emily remained detached from the life of the school in Brussels, though she profited from its linguistic training. But for Charlotte the experience was momentous. She fell in love with Constantin Heger, husband of the school's *directrice*. He was neither able nor willing to respond. Charlotte's suffering was profound, but finally creative. Heger's rigorous exercises transformed her habits of composition. She learned to discipline fantasy and desire into the sophisticated structures of her mature narratives, and she did so in the context of the peculiar intensities of pedagogic experience.

For the Brontës, education was not simply an intellectual process, or a professional calling. It could also be a matter of romantic adventure. In this too Patrick had set an example. As a young man, he had as a teacher won the heart of Maria Branwell, the Cornish woman who was to become his wife and the mother of his six children. Maria had been helping to run a boarding school for the sons of Wesleyan Methodist ministers and preachers at Woodhouse Grove in Yorkshire, where Patrick had been invited to act as a visiting examiner in the classics. Authority and tenderness combined to make him an irresistible suitor. Maria had 'deeply felt the want of a guide and instructor'; once she had accepted Patrick's offer of marriage, she felt that 'I shall now no longer feel this want ... It is pleasant to be subject to those we love, especially when they never exert their authority but for the good of the subject.'[4]

The model established by the marriage of Patrick and Maria was fundamental to their children's lives. Patrick was a loving husband and father, and a devoted teacher for his children. But his dominance in the parsonage at Haworth was unrelenting, and his son's defiant struggles to find his own masculine identity proved self-destructive. The consequences of Branwell's reckless emotional entanglements while working as a tutor were disastrous. Charlotte's acquiescent or even masochistic response to her own thwarted situation as a lover cost her much distress, but protected her from disgrace. These conflicts are repeatedly explored in the fiction of the Brontë sisters, where the development of love is often located in the context of pupil–teacher relations. This is particularly true of Charlotte's fiction. William Crimsworth falls in love with his pupil Frances Henri in *The Professor*; Jane Eyre, employed as a governess, marries her master Edward Rochester; Shirley Keeldar marries a tutor ('"Mr Moore," said she, looking up with a sweet, open, earnest countenance, "teach me and help me to be good"'; *Shirley*, III.xiii.523); Lucy Snowe and her fierce teacher Paul Emanuel declare their mutual love in *Villette*.

An interest in romance is in part a reflection of the conventions of mid-Victorian domestic fiction. Six of the seven novels written by the Brontë sisters include a loving partnership in their closing stages; only *Villette* does not. In a pattern that expresses itself in many different ways, the intellectual standing of a teacher shades into the emotional authority of a lover. This is not always a matter of male supremacy. The subtle interplay of dominance in the courtship of Jane Eyre and Edward Rochester is connected with the fact that Jane is both a governess and a poor dependant. She knows how to govern, as well as to submit. One of the few glimpses of romantic happiness in Emily's *Wuthering Heights* takes place in the context of a reading lesson, in which Cathy, as a female teacher, exerts a playfully erotic authority over Hareton: 'His handsome features glowed with pleasure, and his eyes kept impatiently wandering from the page to a small white hand over his shoulder, which recalled him by a smart slap on the cheek, whenever its owner detected such signs of inattention' (*Wuthering Heights*, II.xviii.273). The teacher's power is not confined to men in the Brontës' fiction, where ambivalently gendered perspectives allow for frequent shifts between masculine and feminine identities. Conventions of romantic fulfilment were tested, qualified and complicated in these novels.

Though the Brontë sisters won their success in the field of literature rather than education, their work as teachers and writers was intimately connected. Both kinds of employment were expressions of the drive for self-determination that was the key motive of their lives. Writing on 3 July 1849 to W. S. Williams, the father of daughters who would need to support themselves, Charlotte, as the sole survivor of the younger Brontës, considers the question:

Come what may afterwards, an education secured is an advantage gained – a priceless advantage. Come what may – it is a step towards independency – and one great curse of a single female life is its dependency . . . teachers may be hard-worked, ill-paid and despised – but the girl who stays at home doing nothing is worse off than the hardest-wrought and worst paid drudge of a school. (Smith, *Letters*, vol. II, p. 226)

Charlotte Brontë is here voicing the aspirations of her sex, class and generation as they began to challenge a constraining domestic ideology. Like her sisters, she did so in the context of the opportunities that education provided – prospects which, despite their accompanying difficulties, opened the way to a freer world.

NOTES

1 Dudley Green (ed.), *The Letters of the Reverend Patrick Brontë* (Stroud: Nonsuch, 2005), p. 233.
2 Barker's account of the school (pp. 118–41) is supplemented by Marianne Thormählen in *The Brontës and Education* (Cambridge University Press, 2007), pp. 63–4.
3 Heather Glen (ed.), *Charlotte Brontë: Tales of Angria* (London: Penguin, 2006), pp. 287–8.
4 Green, *Letters*, p. 325; the letter is dated 18 Sept. 1812.

CHAPTER 29

Art and music

Christine Alexander

In their introduction to *The Brontës in the World of the Arts*, Juliette Wells and Sandra Hagan comment on the 'depth, richness and variety' in the Brontë sisters' handling of the arts in their novels. They point out that even without knowledge of the writers' artistic training, an astute reader might discern from the content of their works that the writers had some familiarity with the arts. Scenes depicting drawing, music-making and acting appear frequently in their novels, heroines possess the accomplishment of drawing required of a governess, and Anne's heroine in *The Tenant of Wildfell Hall* is a professional painter.

The Brontës did indeed have close acquaintance with the arts. Their brother Branwell trained and practised for a short time as a portraitist, he played the flute and organ and his sisters learned the piano, and together with their father they enthusiastically followed reviews of local performances and art exhibitions in newspapers and magazines. The writings of all four siblings reveal a knowledge of the arts that was grounded, to use Charlotte's words for her writing, 'in a practice of some years'[1] and in an intense interest in the arts from an early age.

In 1829, when Charlotte was thirteen, she wrote to her father: 'Branwell has taken two sketches from nature, & Emily Anne & myself have likewise each of us drawn a piece from some views of the lakes which Mr Fennell brought with him from Westmoreland' (Smith, *Letters*, vol. 1, p. 105). This is the earliest recorded reference to the Brontës' practice of art and one that encapsulates the gendered education that characterizes their experience of the visual arts. At the age of eleven, Branwell was sketching 'from nature'; and although his sisters eventually followed suit – especially Emily, whose sensitive illustrations of family dogs demonstrate particular skill with her brush – the majority of their surviving works are meticulous copies: pencil drawings of landscape engravings and delicate watercolours of portraits and flowers,[2] works that would typically grace a young lady's album or demonstrate the accomplishment in art that would increase the chance of success in matrimony or as a governess.

The earliest drawings by all four Brontës are pencil sketches of ruins, castles, animals and birds, chiefly copies from Bewick's 1816 edition of *A History of British Birds*, whose 'enchanted page[s]' (as Charlotte referred to them in her 1832 poem 'Lines on the Celebrated Bewick') seized their imaginations as they did that of the young Jane Eyre. They used Bewick's woodcuts, particularly his whimsical vignettes of everyday life, as a copybook, possibly under the direction of John Bradley, a local Keighley painter, who gave a few lessons at the parsonage. Thomas Plummer, son of a schoolmaster friend of Mr Brontë's, may also have given the children lessons at Haworth, lessons Branwell then continued for a short time in Keighley. Branwell, who had a natural talent for 'taking a likeness', was to be the artist in the family, although Charlotte too quietly aspired to a career in art until, at the age of nineteen, it was clear that she must be a governess: there was money for training only one professional artist for entry to the Royal Academy schools in London that Branwell aspired to. He had a series of lessons at the studio of the Royal Academy-trained William Robinson in Leeds to build up a portfolio, but appears never to have submitted his application. His extant paintings of this period include a number of early oils, crudely executed, and no anatomical drawings, suggesting that he may have been impatient with the rudiments of academic training. Nevertheless he set up as a professional portrait painter in Bradford from May 1838 until May 1839, when he was forced to close his studio after exhausting the few local commissions he was able to attract. A number of large oil portraits and pencil sketches of friends and associates, including his fine portraits of John Brown (see Figure 19), Margaret Hartley and the Kirbys, bear witness to his considerable talent; and the two famous portraits of his sisters, painted when he was only seventeen, are prized possessions in the National Portrait Gallery, London. But his vigorous pen-and-ink sketches of himself, his friends and his fictional characters drawn in notebooks near the end of his life are a sad reminder of opportunities and talents lost.

By contrast, his sisters encountered their version of professional art in the conventional education for early nineteenth-century middle-class women that they received at the Misses Wooler's school, Roe Head. Charlotte attended Roe Head alone from 1831 until mid 1832, and on her return home she passed on her newly acquired knowledge to her sisters – the techniques of copying picturesque views, flowers, trees, hands

19 Branwell Brontë's portrait of John Brown, the Haworth sexton, *c*. 1838–9

and facial features in preparation for drawing portraits. Her schoolfellows noted that she was already their superior in drawing, if not in other subjects. She also had a habit of analysing paintings, as Mary Taylor reported in a letter to Elizabeth Gaskell: 'Whenever an opportunity offered of examining a picture or cut of any kind, she went over it piecemeal, with her eyes close to the paper, looking so long that we used

20 'What you please', a pencil drawing by Anne Brontë

to ask her "what she saw in it". She could always see plenty, and explained it very well' (Gaskell, *Life*, p. 82).

When Charlotte returned to Roe Head in 1835 as a teacher, she herself taught art; and first Emily and then Anne, who accompanied her as pupils, learned the same exercises of delineating eyes, ears, noses, lips, profiles and classical heads. Anne's exercises show that she was particularly interested in copying the heads of young children and making meticulous studies of trees, such as those in the Brontës' one surviving art manual, William De la Motte's *Characters of Trees* (1822). But she also sketched from life during periods from home as a governess, recording the land-scape around Thorp Green, and experimented with imaginative compos-itions interpreted variously as symbolically self-expressive and as aesthetic exercises (see Figure 20).[3] Emily too was more venturesome than Charlotte, as is evident in her dramatic *Study of a Fir Tree*, made 'en plein air' during the school holidays in Brussels, where the two girls continued their drawing lessons with the view of eventually teaching in their own school. Charlotte's sketch of the same ruined tree has all the hallmarks of the conventional picturesque engravings she was accustomed to copy, although she had now had the opportunity, in London and in Brussels, of seeing a variety of great pictures and statues.

Like Lucy Snowe in *Villette*, Charlotte worked hard at copying prints, possibly with the intention of being a miniaturist, and two fine pencil drawings of hers were exhibited at the summer exhibition of the Royal Northern Society for the Encouragement of the Fine Arts in Leeds in 1834. However, apart from several later portraits, such as the fictional *Woman in a Leopard Fur*, her work shows little of the imaginative flair that Rochester perceived in several of the drawings in Jane Eyre's portfolio.

The value of Charlotte's experience of art can more readily be discerned in her writing. She not only adapted her many copies of Byron beauties and fashionable plates to represent heroes, heroines and scenes in her Glass Town and Angrian stories and then incorporated them into her writing, but peopled her stories with sculptors and painters modelled on artistic heroes like John Martin, Edward de Lisle, Henry Chantry and William Etty, whom she and Branwell revered. Their juvenilia refer to artistic theories and techniques, and even satirize their own practice of music and art. In 'The Wool is Rising' (1834), Branwell caricaturizes himself and his artistic pretentions as Patrick Benjamin Wiggins, humble colour grinder to the famous painter Sir Edward de Lisle.[4] Charlotte joins in the joke in 'My Angria and the Angrians', ridiculing Wiggins' 'insane devotion to all celebrated characters', his enthusiasm for oil painting, music and boxing, and the boastfulness that masked his unrealistic ambition: 'as a musician he was greater than Bach; as a Poet he surpassed Byron; as a painter, Claude Lorrain yielded to him'.[5] All the Brontës were excited at the time (Wiggins stands on his head for fifteen minutes in sheer delight!) by the installation of the organ in the Haworth Anglican church and the former Keighley organist John Greenwood's return from London for a celebratory performance of Handel's *Messiah* on 23 March 1834.

The Brontës' love of music was nurtured by their father, who was 'passionately fond of oratorio' and who appears to have passed on to his children his view that 'those performances have the most genuine music in them, which make us feel the most'.[6] In relation to his small income, Mr Brontë spent considerable sums on flute and organ lessons for Branwell, and on piano lessons for all his children, given by the Keighley organist Abraham Sunderland in Haworth Church or Sunday School and then at the parsonage from late 1833, when the family acquired a small cabinet piano for the purpose. Mr Brontë also took his family to a number of local concerts, not only in Haworth but also in nearby Keighley, where concerts were frequently sponsored by the Mechanics' Institute and where their music teacher conducted the orchestra and local choir. Further afield was Halifax, which attracted international musicians including Paganini (in 1832), Johann Strauss and Franz Liszt (in 1838) and Mendelssohn (in 1846; see Barker, p. 877 n. 35 and pp. 210–12).

Haworth itself had a surprisingly rich musical life. The local Haworth Choral Society and Haworth Philharmonic Society held regular concerts with varied programmes ranging from sacred music to traditional songs and glees. They specialized in the former, including oratorios such as Haydn's *Seasons* and Handel's *Samson*, which often featured Thomas Parker, a leading Yorkshire tenor who lived in Haworth and whom Branwell painted by commission in November 1838. In November 1831 Branwell began compiling a notebook of his favourite arrangements for flute, comprising hymns, psalms and Scottish ballads – works suggesting that he played in the church orchestra and in local musical groups, as well as assisting with the organ at services.

The girls' experience of music is more likely to have been that of the Rivers sisters and Jane Eyre at Moor Cottage: the enjoyment of mutual industry, encouragement and critique that a shared pursuit of music and drawing afforded them at home. Charlotte was obliged to give up the piano at Roe Head because of her poor eyesight. Her artistic efforts were then concentrated on drawing, but musical references in her writing to songs and performances indicate that she appreciated her sisters' progress and was musically informed.

Emily's and Anne's surviving sheet music and music books indicate that during the 1830s and early 1840s they played popular waltzes, duets and songs, but also arias and choruses from Handel's *Messiah* and works by Purcell, Mozart, Haydn, Beethoven and Weber (see Figure 21). Song settings of the poetry of Thomas Moore, which they knew and quoted in their writing, were particular favourites. Anne copied six of the songs into her manuscript songbook, one from his *Irish Melodies* and five from his *Sacred Songs*.[7] Emily clearly excelled in music beyond the usual level of schoolgirl accomplishment and may well have been obliged to perform before limited audiences at the Pensionnat Heger, where she taught the piano. When she left suddenly to return to Haworth on the death of her aunt, Emily was, according to Constantin Heger writing to Patrick Brontë on 5 November 1842, about to receive music lessons from the best teacher in Belgium (Smith, *Letters*, vol. 1, pp. 299–300).

Barbara Hardy has noted the 'lyricism' of Emily's poetry, and Brontë critics have registered the musical quality of isolated poems,[8] but there has

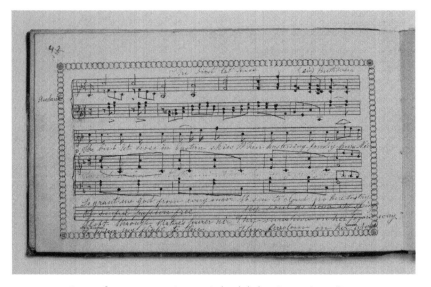

21 A page from a manuscript music book belonging to Anne Brontë.
The book is inscribed 'Anne Brontë, Thorp Green, June, 1843'

been little research done in this fertile area of Brontë studies. Meg Harris
Williams recently picked up this challenge in an adventurous exploration
of Emily's musical imagination and its influence on the structural and
thematic elements in her poetry and *Wuthering Heights*.[9] Building on our
knowledge of Emily's dramatic response to the music of Beethoven,
Robert K. Wallace has suggested that *Wuthering Heights* reveals a sym-
phonic structure akin to those of Beethoven's symphonies.[10]

It is significant that no one in *Wuthering Heights* plays the piano.
Marianne Thormählen has noted that music executed by talented women
is generally represented unfavourably in the Brontë novels.[11] In *The
Tenant*, for example, Arthur Huntingdon's two mistresses are superior
performers of the one art he appreciates; his wife can amuse him only with
her simple songs 'but not delight him thus' (xxvi.194), suggesting that
both his taste and his mistresses' musical skills are contaminated: they lack
sincerity and are associated with ulterior motives. Huntingdon's interpretation of Helen Graham's early 'master-piece' of a girl and a dove that
he admires as a typical fancy piece, drawn to demonstrate accomplishment and display, reveals his gendered values and the passive role he
expects Helen to assume when she becomes his wife. His later confiscation
of her paints and brushes is part of the same attempt to stifle her creativity

and initiative – and rob her of her means to escape. Her resilience as the plot develops and her eventual success as a commercially viable artist are not only a significant victory for self-respect and independence, but also a plea – a radical one at the time – for the professionalization of women.[12]

Charlotte also uses the arts to represent broader cultural and social values. The 'sheer heterogeneity of music-making' in *Shirley* – from Hortense's guitar-playing to the Revd Sweeting's flute displays – is seen by Juliette Wells and Ruth A. Solie as presenting a complex picture of a musical society in transition that reflects the wider concerns and conflicts of the narrative.[13] Akiko Higuchi's *The Brontës' World of Music* provides a detailed compendium of the role of music in the lives and works of all the Brontës. In her novels, however, Charlotte's treatment of music, reflected in that of her narrators, is that of an outsider. At the charity concert in chapter 20 of *Villette*, in the newly opened Salle de la Grande Harmonie in Brussels, it is the festive scene rather than the actual music that Lucy responds to.

Jane Eyre embodies Charlotte's most pervasive use of her experience of the arts, in particular drawing and painting. The novel not only opens with the famous tribute to the illustrations in Bewick's *History of British Birds*, but also explains young Jane's attitude to art as an accomplishment necessary for defining her genteel feminine status, so crucial to establishing the identity and self-respect of a poor orphaned child. She learns the value of artistic skills from the servant Bessie, who regales her with the achievements of her former employer's daughters: 'She boasted of beautiful paintings of landscapes and flowers by them executed; of songs they could sing and pieces they could play, of purses they could net, of French books they could translate; till my spirit was moved to emulation as I listened' (1.iii.25). When, at Lowood, Jane herself has gained proficiency in these skills, she is able to advertise as a governess qualified in 'the usual branches of a good English education, together with French, Drawing, and Music' (1.x.87). She plays 'a waltz or two' and displays 'a landscape in water colours' (1.x.92) for the visiting Bessie, who compliments her as now 'quite a lady'. Rochester, a more seasoned judge, confirms her basic proficiency for teaching music: 'You play a *little,* I see; like any other English school-girl: perhaps rather better than some, but not well' (1.xiii.124). His verdict on her portfolio of paintings has been much discussed by critics, especially his curiosity about the source and production of Jane's three visionary paintings, which allow him to glimpse her fertile imagination but also to conclude that she has 'not enough of the artist's skill and science to give [her ideas] full being' (1.xiii.126).

22 Charlotte Brontë's portrait of 'Zenobia Marchioness Ellrington', 1833

Although the narrator traces her early experience, *Jane Eyre* is not a *Künstlerroman*. The practice of art is used in the novel to confirm the heroine's innate refinement and her cultural equality with Rochester. Her drawing signifies her genteel feminine status; it is a pleasurable occupation and a necessary skill for teaching. Rosamund Oliver, delighted by Jane's portrait of her, declares that she is clever enough to be a governess in a high family (III.vi.369); but Jane is content to remain the schoolmistress at Morton and has no professional ambition.[14] Charlotte's own early aspirations to be a professional artist were transmuted and put to the service of the art in which she excelled: the art of writing.

NOTES

1 Charlotte Brontë, *The Professor*, preface, p. 1.

2 Drawings and paintings by the family have been collected, identified and catalogued in Christine Alexander and Jane Sellars, *The Art of the Brontës* (Cambridge University Press, 1995).

3 See *ibid.*, pp. 141–2, and Antonia Losano, 'Anne Brontë's Aesthetics: Painting in *The Tenant of Wildfell Hall*', in Sandra Hagan and Juliette Wells (eds.), *The Brontës in the World of the Arts* (Aldershot: Ashgate, 2008), p. 55.

4 Victor A. Neufeldt (ed.), *The Works of Patrick Branwell Brontë*, vol. II (New York: Garland, 1999), p. 60.

5 Christine Alexander (ed.), *An Edition of the Early Writings of Charlotte Brontë*, vol. II (Oxford: Blackwell, for the Shakespeare Head Press, 1991), part 2, pp. 250–2.

6 Patrick Brontë, *The Maid of Killarney* (1818), p. 59.

7 Akiko Higuchi, *The Brontës and Music*, vol. II: *The Brontës' World of Music*, 2nd edn (Tokyo: Yushodo Press, 2008), pp. 47–8.

8 Janet Gezari, for example, supplies a useful summary of the effective musical metre and rhyme in Emily's poem 'Remembrance' in her edition *Emily Jane Brontë: The Complete Poems* (Harmondsworth: Penguin, 1992), pp. 228–9. See also Barbara Hardy, 'The Lyricism of Emily Brontë', in Anne Smith (ed.), *The Art of Emily Brontë* (London: Vision, 1976), p. 94.

9 'The Hieroglyphics of Catherine: Emily Brontë and the Musical Matrix', in Hagan and Wells, *The Brontës in the World of the Arts*, pp. 81–99.

10 Robert K. Wallace, *Emily Brontë and Beethoven: Romantic Equilibrium in Fiction and Music* (Athens, GA: University of Georgia Press, 1986).

11 Marianne Thormählen, *The Brontës and Education* (Cambridge University Press, 2007), p. 105.

12 Antonia Losano examines this important aspect of Anne's novel in 'The Professionalization of the Woman Artist in Anne Brontë's *The Tenant of Wildfell Hall*', *Nineteenth-Century Literature*, 58.1 (2003), 1–41.

13 Juliette Wells and Ruth A. Solie, '*Shirley*'s Window on a Musical Society in Transition', in Hagan and Wells, *The Brontës in the World of the Arts*, pp. 101–23.

14 See Juliette Wells, '"Some of Your Accomplishments Are Not Ordinary": The Limits of Artistry in *Jane Eyre*', in Hagan and Wells, *The Brontës in the World of the Arts*, pp. 67–80.

CHAPTER 30

Natural history

Barbara T. Gates

The Brontë children grew up in what has been dubbed 'the heyday of natural history', a time of crazes over collecting everything from birds' eggs to sea cucumbers.[1] It was an active time in the history of science, with biology taking centre stage. As the Brontës carefully copied bird pictures from their father's volumes of Thomas Bewick's 1816 edition of his *History of British Birds*, young Charles Darwin, just six years older than Charlotte Brontë, was setting off for the Galapagos on the HMS *Beagle*. In the first half of the nineteenth century, amateurs were out in the field as frequently as scientists – endlessly observing, cataloguing and recording facts about birds, insects, plants and animals. Such amateurs dominated the study of natural history until the mid century, and they served as some of Darwin's most useful contacts as he assembled the masses of data that would later support his books. In his landmark study of 1976, David Elliston Allen found the naturalists of the 1820s and 1830s both more sensitive and better educated in natural history than their counterparts later in the century, when there were more monied people with more spare time and less seriousness about their science.[2]

Clergymen were among the most active of the earlier amateurs. Often inspired by the Revd Gilbert White's *Natural History and Antiquities of Selborne* (1789), they belonged to local chapters of natural-history societies and sometimes kept records of species and events in their areas. The Revd Patrick Brontë would, for example, keep such a record of the bog eruption on Haworth moor in 1824.[3] The West Riding of Yorkshire, where the Brontës lived, was an especially significant area for natural historians and had one of the most active botanical associations in the British Isles. In his personal library, the father of the Brontës owned not just White and Bewick but Audubon's *Ornithological Autobiography*, the works of William Paley, whose 1802 *Natural Theology* influenced generations of natural historians to think of nature as reflecting divinity, and a copy of *The Garden and Menagerie of the Zoological Society Delineated* – well garnished with sketches by Anne Brontë. He also belonged to the Keighley Mechanics' Institute Library, which held many works of natural history to which his children may have had access. They certainly read *Blackwood's Magazine*, which published essays on the growing popularity of natural history as early as 1818 and encouraged the reading of White's *Selborne* and Knapp's *Journal of a Naturalist*.[4] Impressed by what she gleaned from her early reading, the eighteen-year-old Charlotte Brontë wrote to Ellen Nussey and advised, 'For Natural History read Bewick, and Audubon, and Goldsmith and White of Selborne' (Smith, *Letters*, vol. 1, p. 131). 'Goldsmith' probably refers to Oliver Goldsmith's *History of the Earth and Animated Nature* (1774), a book that went through twenty editions in the Victorian period.

The Brontë sisters were also educated according to the curriculum thought proper for young ladies of their day, which included tuition in natural history, particularly botany, and in sketching and painting subjects from the natural world. Christine Alexander and Jane Sellars believe that trips to the Keighley library yielded them access to books on flower painting,[5] an art in which Charlotte excelled (see Figure 23). In the nineteenth century, young women were so greatly encouraged in the study of botany that by 1887 an essay appeared querying 'Is Botany a Suitable Study for Young Men?'[6] Yet all the Brontës, Branwell included, copied from natural-history books – Charlotte and Anne while at home and at Roe Head, Emily and Branwell from sources like Bewick. Charlotte reproduced Bewick's mountain sparrow, Branwell his goshawk and Emily his ring ousel. Emily seems to have absorbed Bewick's text as well as his drawings. Her *devoirs* for Monsieur Heger suggest a dog-eat-dog natural world, a world-view also in evidence in *Wuthering Heights* and delineated in the introduction to Bewick's *History of British Birds*, where 'from man downwards, to the smallest living creature, all are found to prey upon and devour each other'.[7] This assertion may be compared with Emily Brontë's *devoir* on 'Le Papillon' from August 1842, in which Emily takes note of a creation 'where flies playing above the brook' are '[diminished] every minute' by swallows and fish which will, in turn, become 'the prey of some tyrant of the air or water'. Finally, 'man for his amusement or his needs will kill their murderers. Nature is an inexplicable problem; it exists on a principle of destruction.'[8]

Interestingly, the two elder Brontë sisters diverge distinctly in their views of nature, generated by their powers of observation and interest in natural history. Alexander and Sellars cite as an example similar drawings of a fir tree made 'from nature', a common nineteenth-century term for

23 Charlotte Brontë's watercolour study of a blue convolvulus, *c.* December 1832

24 A pencil drawing by Charlotte Brontë of a landscape with fallen trees, *c.* August 1842

painting *en plein air*, made by Charlotte and Emily during a school holiday in Belgium. Charlotte's drawing shows an entire scene, a picturesque view of the tree in the context of rocks and fallen trees, done in a fine pencil stroke (see Figure 24). Emily's is of the tree itself, and it is bolder and more rugged in character (see Figure 25). The two trees show different aspects of the same scene, the dissimilarities being characteristic of the two sisters' different takes on the natural world. The distinction between them is also seen in their chosen subjects for their art. Charlotte, who had more training in drawing and painting than Emily, produced many flower paintings. Her sister tended to draw wilder things, including the now-famous pictures of parsonage animals like the mastiff Keeper and the injured merlin Nero (see Figure 26).

Similar divergences may be discerned in the sisters' novels. When Jane Eyre turns to nature to mother her after leaving Rochester, she finds herself marooned on the moors. Entirely without funds, she harbours a romantic hope that nature will somehow be sufficiently nurturing, though soon enough she becomes fearful:

25 A study of a fir tree by Emily Brontë, c. 1842

I struck straight into the heath; I held on to a hollow I saw deeply furrowing the brown moor-side; I waded, knee-deep in its dark growth; I turned with its turnings, and finding a moss-blackened granite crag in a hidden angle, I sat down under it. High banks of moor were about me; the crag protected my head . . . Some

26 A watercolour painting by Emily Brontë, believed to be of her pet merlin Nero

time passed before I felt tranquil even here: I had a vague dread that wild cattle might be near . . . If a gust of wind swept the waste, I looked up, fearing it was the rush of a bull; if a plover whistled, I imagined it a man. (III.ii.323)

The language here is dark throughout, emphasizing Jane's aloneness and the upcoming rejections both by nature and by the local population. Not until she is ill and completely forlorn does Jane Eyre awake to the safety of other people at Moor House. This attitude may be contrasted with Emily

Brontë's love of areas similar to the one that Jane Eyre fears, a love evident
in *Wuthering Heights* and in ecstatic poems like 'High Waving Heather':

> High waving heather 'neath stormy blasts bending
> Midnight and moonlight and bright shining stars
> Darkness and glory rejoicingly blending
> Earth rising to heaven and heaven descending
> Man's spirit away from its drear dungeon sending
> Bursting the fetters and breaking the bars[9]

These lines express not fear but jubilation, not dread but freedom, the free
movement of the language of participles reflecting the fleeting, windswept
landscape.

Petrels (Brontë favourites from Bewick) too are not frightening in
Emily Brontë's work but beautiful, as in the haunting image from
the poem 'Stars', where the narrator 'was at peace, and drank [the stars']
beams / As they were life to me; / And revelled in my changeful dreams, /
Like petrel on the sea.'[10] 'My sister Emily loved the moors', Charlotte
Brontë tells the readers of her 'Prefatory Note' to 'Selections from Poems
by Ellis Bell'. 'Flowers brighter than the rose bloomed in the blackest of
the heath for her ... She found in the bleak solitude many and dear
delights' (Smith, *Letters*, vol. II, p. 753). And indeed, petrels, wild deer,
linnets in rocky dells, moor-larks, briars and bees all populate Emily's
writing. Again to quote Charlotte Brontë, this time on *Wuthering Heights*,
Emily's work 'is moorish, and wild, and knotty as a root of heath'.[11]
Ferocity, wildness and solitude beckoned to Emily Brontë and to the
strong characters in her poetry, fiction and juvenilia.

This is certainly not to suggest that Charlotte Brontë's own poems and
books are without appreciation for nature or natural history. At the age of
seventeen, Charlotte dedicated a poem to Bewick and his birds. In its
third stanza, the narrator goes so far as to equate Bewick's hand with
nature's: 'How many winged inhabitants of air, / How many plume-clad
floaters of the deep, / The mighty artist drew in forms as fair / As those
that now the skies and waters sweep.'[12] Moreover, Charlotte Brontë's
characters Jane Eyre and Paulina Home are, like herself, fascinated by
natural history – Jane with Bewick as she sits in her window seat at the
book's outset, and Polly with turning the pages of 'some illustrated work of
natural history' (*Villette*, xxv.289). Each finds comfort in these works. Like
the Brontës themselves, through illustrated natural history Polly also feels a
link with her past. And in *Shirley*, there is a governess/mother who, like
many a nineteenth-century counterpart, is an amateur natural historian.

As Shirley's governess, Mrs Pryor talked 'about the various birds singing in the trees, discriminated their species, and said something about their habits and peculiarities. English natural history seemed familiar to her. All the wild flowers round their path were recognised by her' (II.x.314). Another kindred spirit of the heroines of this novel is the labourer William Farren, who befriends Caroline in part because '[t]hey took a similar interest in animals, birds, insects, and plants: they held similar doctrines about humanity to the lower creation and had a similar turn for minute observation on points of natural history' (III.ii.371).

Shirley evokes other important concerns in the Brontës' time – land preservation, for example. As the Brontës were growing up, writers like Mary Russell Mitford in *Our Village* (1826) were advocating the protection of rural environments and trees, as well as of animals and birds. By the end of Charlotte's complex novel, a servant looks back nostalgically at a time before the men in *Shirley* have had a chance to destroy the landscape. At the book's conclusion, Robert Moore's dreams of a new industrialized heaven and earth have come true. The copse has been rooted up, and there are no more fairies in Fieldhead Hollow – nor are there places for young girls like its heroines, and fanciful boys like Martin Yorke, to daydream in edenic spaces. The author tells us not to look for a moral in all of this; but a sensitive reader cannot help but discern the loss of freedom and beauty described in the book's penultimate paragraph with its 'lonesome' and 'bonnie spot – full of oak trees and nut trees' that 'is altered now' (III.xiv.542).

Mrs Pryor is not the only good governess or mother with a fondness for plants and animals in the Brontë canon. Anne Brontë's heroines in both *Agnes Grey* and *The Tenant of Wildfell Hall* display similar interests. The youngest of the Brontës belonged to a long line of female natural-history writers who inculcated decent behaviour towards all living creatures in their charges. Mary Wollstonecraft's *Original Stories from Real Life* (1783) had recommended gentle behaviour towards animals, placing their rights alongside those of women; Sara Trimmer's *Fabulous Animals* (1786) offered an early example of the teaching of morality to youngsters through discussion of kindness towards animals; and Mary Sherwood, in a number of books from the 1820s, suggested that beneficence towards animals ought to reflect beneficence towards one's own species. The Royal Society for the Prevention of Cruelty to Animals was established when Anne was just two (1822–4) and reflected the growing interest in compassionate treatment of non-human creatures in the early decades of the nineteenth century.

In *Agnes Grey*, Agnes is appalled when she discovers young birds tortured by her first boy pupil, and she finds the blood sports of her second set of pupils repulsive. 'When Master Bloomfield's amusements consist in injuring sentient creatures', Agnes responds to her employer, 'I think it my duty to interfere' (v.44). She is shocked when Mrs Bloomfield replies that the 'do-unto-others' maxim refers only to people and is wholly misplaced with regard to torturing animals. Other characters in the novel are also judged by their behaviour towards animals. After the cottager Nancy's beloved cat is kicked across the floor by the callous rector, Mr Hatfield, Mr Weston, the novel's curate-hero, strokes it and later saves it from a gamekeeper's clutches. Similarly, he rescues the dog that later discovers Agnes on the beach and is one cause of the final reunion between hero and heroine. In her introduction to *Agnes Grey*, Anne Brontë reminds us that 'all true histories contain instruction'. One kind of instruction that both of her novels contain is tutelage in the interconnectedness of all living things. A moralist, the youngest Brontë wanted to make sure that creatures count in the larger scheme of things, and that people who are sensitive to this are people worth knowing.

Similar teachings are conveyed in *The Tenant of Wildfell Hall*. In its last pages, Gilbert Markham spends time with the child Arthur, studying his new book, 'a natural history with all kinds of birds and beasts in it, and the reading as nice as the pictures!' (liii.414). At this point in their lives, both Helen and Gilbert have learned about trying too hard to please or rescue other people. False ideas and precepts have fallen by the wayside, and simple things with simple messages, like the illustrated natural history given to a little boy, assert their value.

Anne Brontë is of course a very different novelist from her two elder sisters. Wild passion, like wild nature, has no redeeming features in her books. A slow understanding of self through trial and error is what brings a modicum of maturity and love into one's life. In both her novels, characters cannot understand what they do not see clearly. One way for Anne Brontë to point this out is through the language of flowers. Another feminine pursuit that touches upon the nineteenth-century vogue for natural history, the language of flowers held a strong fascination in the Brontës' Britain. Brought over from France, this language entailed understanding a code signalled by gifts of flowers. In *Agnes Grey*, Mr Weston sends signals to Agnes through this medium. Early in their acquaintance, he reaches out to pick primroses, which Agnes desires but which are just beyond her grasp, asking her what her favourite flowers are. She responds that she loves primroses, bluebells and heath-blossoms. Weston replies,

'Not violets?' (xiii.96). In the language of flowers, primroses suggest early youth, first love and 'I cannot live without you', though Agnes seems unaware of this. Bluebells symbolize humility, constancy and gratitude, whereas violets betoken something similar, modesty and faithfulness. Weston appears to take careful note, and before long he brings Agnes a gift of bluebells, an indication of his gratitude for her and of his own constancy of character. Weston has guessed correctly with respect to Agnes, for the very first primroses he presents to her are cherished and kept in a glass until withered and then further preserved, pressed between the leaves of Agnes' Bible.

In *The Tenant*, Helen Huntingdon too resorts to the language of flowers after she becomes an heiress and is in a superior station to Gilbert Markham, but wishes to marry him. She presents him with a Christmas rose just emerging from the snow. Gilbert, like Agnes, seems unaware of any deeper implications. Disappointed, Helen snatches the flower from him and tosses it back into the snow. She is then forced to tell him that it was an emblem of her heart, which anyone in the know would realize meant 'tranquillize my anxiety'. These simple actions in the Anne Brontë novels are a far cry from visions of ghosts on the heath in *Wuthering Heights* or riven trees in gardens during the prospectively bigamous midsummer love-scene in *Jane Eyre*. Less dramatic and elemental, they are nevertheless deeply embedded in nature as it was understood in the nineteenth century. Each in her distinctive way, through art, poetry and novels, the famous Brontë sisters owned the heritage of natural history alive at Haworth Parsonage in Darwin's century.

NOTES

1 See in particular Lynn Barber's *The Heyday of Natural History, 1820–1870* (London: Jonathan Cape, 1980) and Lynn L. Merrill's *The Romance of Victorian Natural History* (Oxford University Press, 1989).

2 David Elliston Allen, *The Naturalist in Britain: A Social History* (London: Allen Lane, 1976), p. 137.

3 For this information I am indebted to Christine Alexander and Margaret Smith, 'Natural History and the Brontës', in their *Oxford Companion to the Brontës* (Oxford University Press, 2003), pp. 339–40.

4 Allen, *The Naturalist*, p. 99.

5 Christine Alexander and Jane Sellars, *The Art of the Brontës* (Cambridge University Press, 1995).

6 J. F. A. Adams, *Science*, 9 (1887), 116–17.

7 Thomas Bewick, *The History of British Birds* (Newcastle, 1816), vol. II, p. xviii.
8 Quoted from Sue Lonoff (ed. and trans.), *Charlotte Brontë and Emily Brontë, the Belgian Essays: A Critical Edition* (New Haven: Yale University Press, 1996), p. 176.
9 Quoted from Janet Gezari (ed.), *Emily Jane Brontë: The Complete Poems* (Harmondsworth: Penguin, 1992), p. 34.
10 *Ibid.*, p. 5.
11 Editor's preface to the 1850 edn of *Wuthering Heights*, quoted from Smith, *Letters*, vol. II, p. 748.
12 Tom Winnifrith (ed.), *The Poems of Charlotte Brontë* (Oxford: Blackwell, 1984), p. 138.

CHAPTER 31

Politics

Simon Avery

Writing to Elizabeth Gaskell in 1856, Charlotte Brontë's long-term friend Mary Taylor told Charlotte's biographer that the recently deceased writer 'had taken [an] interest in politics ever since she was five years old' (Gaskell, *Life*, p. 83). In fact, all the Brontës maintained a lively interest in political debates across the course of their lives – an interest which is frequently dealt with, overtly or covertly, in their extensive body of writing. Nevertheless, this area of concern has often been elided in criticism, which has tended to emphasize the Brontës as somehow *a*-political and, to use Terry Eagleton's apposite phrasing, seemingly 'deposited on the Yorkshire moors from some metaphysical outer space'.[1]

Even a cursory examination of the Brontës' lives and works shows how far this is from the truth. The family lived through some of the most politically volatile decades of modern history, and traces of those turbulent times are everywhere in their writings. Patrick, with his roots in Ireland, was twelve when the French Revolution broke out, its ideals of liberty, equality and fraternity soon leading to the Terror and to the Napoleonic Wars, which Charlotte would later use as the setting for *Shirley*. The Brontë children themselves were born in the tense years of widespread economic depression which immediately followed the cessation of hostilities with France, and they would live to see the passing of major Reform Acts, European uprisings and, in Charlotte's case, the Crimean War.

In terms of political stance, Patrick Brontë was a staunch Tory, a position most obviously adopted by Charlotte and one which encompassed a lively concern for the poor and the marginalized in society. Like Patrick's religion, which brought together both Tory-aligned Church of England commitment and Dissenting structures of thought, his politics, and those of his offspring, were never straightforward. The family read both the Whig *Leeds Mercury* and the Tory *Leeds Intelligencer*, and their position at Haworth Parsonage placed them in the midst of political ferment on all sides. As one of the major industrial centres of the West Riding of Yorkshire, Haworth and nearby Keighley witnessed fierce class conflict, political turmoil and call for legislative and parliamentary reform. Such political concerns were continually to inflect the Brontës' writings throughout their careers.

From the outset, the children's commitment to writing was firmly rooted in politics, initiated by the wooden soldiers which Patrick brought home for Branwell in 1826 and which the siblings named after prominent political figures (Wellington and Bonaparte) and great explorers (Parry and Ross). This notion of hero-worship would always be crucial to the family's engagement in politics. The children subsequently developed the fantasy world of Glass Town, which was based on European colonization of an African state, massacre of the native race, revolution and aristocratic figures fighting for political control, before Charlotte and Branwell jointly created Angria and began composing the extant Angrian tales.

Overall, the Angrian tales raise issues to do with nationality and the nation state, leadership and heroism, civil unrest and parliamentary debate, and strategies of war and seemingly 'legitimate' violence. Indeed, there often seems to be a fascinating parallel between the Angrian narratives and contemporary political issues concerning liberty and reform. In 1829, for example, the Catholic Emancipation Bill was passed – a Bill which, despite Charlotte's fierce criticism of Roman Catholicism in her later fiction, was supported by her and all the family because of its promotion by the Tories and Wellington as Prime Minister. Then, in 1831–2, the family avidly followed the slippery progress of that great piece of Whig legislation, the First Reform Bill, which sought to extend the franchise and yield a better representation in the Commons. Despite her father's support for the Bill, Charlotte was fervently opposed, writing to Branwell in May 1832 of her joy at its being thrown out of the Lords (Smith, *Letters*, vol. 1, p. 112). The Act initiated a decade of reform, not least with regard to the plight of factory workers and the poor. Paralleling the call for increased rights in France and other European countries, this offers an intriguing context for reading the Brontës' intellectual and creative development at the time.

During the year of agitation that preceded the passing of the First Reform Bill, Emily and Anne broke away from the Glass Town and Angria saga to establish the alternative world of Gondal with its increased focus on female power figures. As Stevie Davies highlights, however, Gondal was still 'a brutally anarchic universe' characterized by warfare and mutiny – concerns which formed the framework for the extensive poetry and prose which Emily continued to produce until her late twenties.[2] Although the prose has been lost, references to Gondal characters and politics still remain in a number of Emily's poems which constitute part of that body of work that Charlotte characterized as 'not at all like the poetry women generally write'.[3] Emily's poetry, with its terse, elliptical language, philosophical and metaphysical depth and refusal to conform to any established belief system, is indeed far from the writings of contemporary women poets like Felicia Hemans and Laetitia Landon.

The dominant critical reading of works such as 'High Waving Heather', 'Stars', 'To Imagination' and 'No Coward Soul Is Mine' as celebrating a transcendent, apolitical state would benefit from a wider analysis of the poems in relation to their moment of production. In his important study *Romantic Ideology*, for example, Jerome McGann argues that Wordsworth, a major influence on the Brontës, turned to writing about nature as a reaction against industrialization and the failure of the political ideals associated with the French Revolution.[4] McGann's thesis could also be applied to Emily's poetry, which can be seen to celebrate nature as a sustaining alternative to the problems of industrialization and political upheaval on the Brontës' doorstep. Moreover, Emily's poetry on imagination, mystical experience and death, written across the late 1830s and the 'Hungry 40s', highlights oppressive structures of power and a proto-Darwinian notion of the survival of the fittest, as well as offering models of liberation from quotidian 'reality'. In their focus on entrapment and escape, the right to a voice and resistance to identities associated with imposed social roles, the poems can be read as highly political. Such an interpretative approach would lend weight to Edward Chitham's and Stevie Davies' assertion that in her last poem, 'Why ask to know what date what clime' – composed in 1846 and reworked in the revolutionary year of 1848 – Emily sought to write a new poetry of radical political theory and war.[5]

The poetry of Anne and Charlotte which was published alongside Emily's in the ill-fated *Poems by Currer, Ellis and Acton Bell* in 1846 also speaks of freedom, either through nature (as in Anne's 'Lines Composed in a Wood on a Windy Day' and 'The Captive Dove') or social/religious relations (as in Anne's 'A Word to the "Elect"' and Charlotte's intriguing dramatic monologue on the ideology of colonialism, 'The Missionary'). Throughout, the language of slavery is repeatedly employed, drawing upon the political reality of a British slave trade that had been finally dismantled only in 1834.

A similar stance is evident in Charlotte's first novel, *The Professor*, which, despite its critical marginalization in the Brontë canon, is more consistent with the politics of the other, more famous texts than is often acknowledged. Written in a self-consciously 'plain and homely' style, as Charlotte terms it in the preface, *The Professor* charts the professional, social and emotional development of William Crimsworth in the 1830s, a time before 'trains and railroads' (vii.50). Rejecting the industrial north associated with his brother's mill in Yorkshire, a world condemned as being founded upon mammon-worship and systems of oppression that eradicate nature and liberty, Crimsworth instead becomes a teacher in Brussels. Initially teaching in Pelet's boys' school, he constructs himself as akin to the Dutch colonizers of Belgium (the country achieved independence only in 1830) in his attempt to maintain order in the classroom. Thus the school becomes 'merely an epitome of the Belgian Nation' (vii.61). In Mlle Reuter's school, however, this stance becomes tempered as Crimsworth balances his resistance to Reuter's system of surveillance and control – as he notes, 'it was ... the power of the politician to which she aspired' (x.80) – with his growing affection for the Anglo-Swiss Frances. His rejection of the duplicitous Catholic Reuter in favour of the honest Protestant Frances opens up debates regarding nationality, patriotism and religion which would resonate throughout Charlotte's later work. Indeed, Crimsworth's final home back in Yorkshire affords him access to the estate where Yorke Hunsden entertains both English visitors who debate free trade and European guests who 'take a wider theme– European progress–the spread of liberal sentiments over the Continent' (xxv.238), a range of topics which effectively mirrors Charlotte's own political concerns.

If *The Professor* is a neglected participant in that strong group of 1840s social-problem novels, it was the Brontë novels published in the following year – *Jane Eyre*, *Wuthering Heights*, *Agnes Grey* – that threw down the sisters' greatest challenge to the dominant political and social ideologies of the day. As Lord John Russell's Whig government passed the Ten Hours Factory Act – a major piece of legislation which recognized the pressures of employment on individuals – and as political fervour and call for reform bubbled in Europe, Charlotte, Emily and Anne entered the literary marketplace with texts which question class relations, structures of power and authority, and established gender roles. Between them they shook the very foundations of early to mid Victorian society by framing, through angry and frustrated individuals, dysfunctional families and in-fighting communities, a vision of the wider world on the brink of political revolution.

It is little wonder that Elizabeth Rigby famously said that *Jane Eyre* emerged from the anarchic politics which she located in Chartism: the narrative of the 'disconnected, poor, and plain' heroine (II.i.161), who claims equality with the gentry and who forcefully challenges the authoritarian embodiments of patriarchal education and religion, represents Chartist thinking on multiple levels.[6] Interrogating the social displacement of the governess, the sexual exploitation of women and manifestations of British imperialism, *Jane Eyre* asserts the right of the marginalized figure to social and psychological integrity, an independent voice and a meaningful place in the world. Moreover, the construction of Bertha Mason continues, albeit not unproblematically, Charlotte's fascination with national identity and colonization (geographical, personal and sexual), as well as the clash between competing cultural ideologies.

Emily's *Wuthering Heights* interrogates a similar political culture clash in terms of an intricate layering of concerns with gender, sexuality, class and race. Its multiple narratives enact the tensions and conflicts underlying a fictional world which repeatedly foregrounds the power politics and artificial notions of the 'civilized' in the world at large. In doing so, the novel employs an alienated outsider – the orphan Heathcliff, who may be read, as Eagleton suggests, as a refugee from Ireland, ravaged by famine at the time of the Brontës' first venture into book-publishing[7] – in order to explore the fate of those whom the structures of dominant society cannot or will not accommodate. Throughout, the power of those in control is shown to be grounded in violence as represented variously by the bulldog and guns at the Grange, Joseph's psychologically destructive manipulation of religion, and the processes of socialization which effectively kill Catherine first in spirit and then in body. Indeed, Heathcliff can become a political player in this world only by mimicking it, mysteriously acquiring capital and status and then utilizing the violence associated with them to enact his revenge and break the socio-economic structures of both the Lintons and the Earnshaws. Dante Gabriel Rossetti said that *Wuthering Heights* is a text whose action is 'laid in Hell',[8] but it is also laid in the challenge to political orthodoxies which was sweeping Europe in the mid to late 1840s.

Anne's novel of 1847, *Agnes Grey*, has repeatedly suffered in comparison with the seemingly more rebellious texts by her sisters, although in its own quietly forceful way it too stakes a claim for the refashioning of the socio-political world. Modelling dominant systems of exploitation in stark detail, the text constructs Agnes as the type of the individual standing firm against the establishment, rejecting the 'naturalized' associations of power with privilege which *Wuthering Heights* interrogates, and effectively re-aligning dignity, morality and social responsibility with the political underdog. Anne's second novel, *The Tenant of Wildfell Hall* (1848), then extends and deepens these concerns in the figure of Helen Huntingdon, whose commitment to her own integrity, her son's welfare and her professional vocation makes possible a radical critique of established social structures and class- and gender-based power games, as well as of the abuse and humiliation embedded in that idealized central unit of the Victorian political system, the family. In the year when revolutions swept Europe, as country after country rose up to overthrow oppression and claim self-agency – Charlotte, in a letter to Miss Wooler, acknowledged the fascination of the revolutions while also seeing them as 'moral earthquakes' which 'put back the world in all that is good, check civilis-ation, [and] bring the dregs of society to its surface' (Smith, *Letters*, vol. ii, p. 48) – Anne created a work of fiction imbued with the spirit of reform. Though her own preface rejects the idea that the author might consider herself 'competent to reform the errors and abuses of society' (*The Tenant of Wildfell Hall*, p. 3), the book suggests that an independent woman may be able to achieve nothing less than a reconfiguring of the socio-political order around her.

Charlotte's next novel, *Shirley*, which was written through both the period of revolution and the deaths of her siblings, foregrounds political concerns by dealing with the last stages of the Napoleonic Wars and the Luddite riots in Yorkshire. Patrick had witnessed such rioting, but Charlotte sought historical accuracy for her novel by drawing on reports in the *Leeds Mercury* for 1811–12. The result is a text which brings together the politics of the 'Condition of England' with the politics of the 'woman question' in ways which align the fate of the mill-workers with the seemingly alienated figure of Caroline. In the clashes between the French-Anversois, Whig-sympathizing Moore, the ardent radical Yorke and the English arch-Tory Helstone, and in the revolt of disaffected workers against the new technology which robs them of their livelihood, Charlotte explores issues such as the history of Napoleonic expansionism, nationality, party politics and the effects of the Orders in Council on trade and competition. As Charlotte's most obviously political novel, *Shirley* has significant parallels with Elizabeth Gaskell's *Mary Barton* (1848) and *North and South* (1855), particularly in its dependence on women (Caroline and Shirley) to engender that greater empathy between opposing groups which will bring about positive socio-political trans-formation. Typically for Charlotte, however, the closure is left disturbingly ambiguous with the sense of industrialization despoiling the Hollow and eradicating the Romantic-political associations of imaginative and physical freedom.

By this stage in her career Charlotte was a lionized writer, and when she visited London in 1851, she was keen to see politics in action by visiting the Ladies' Gallery of the House of Commons and the Chapel Royal to glimpse her hero, Wellington. She also visited the Great Exhibition several times and recorded her admiration for Trafalgar Square, with its monument celebrating Nelson's victory over the combined French and Spanish fleet in 1805, in a letter to Elizabeth Gaskell dated 6 August 1851 (Smith, *Letters*, vol. II, p. 676). As the Second French Republic fell and Napoleon III became Emperor, Charlotte returned to dealing with European politics in that strange and fascinating 'heretic narrative' (xv.163), *Villette*. Reworking several of the political concerns of *The Professor*, *Villette* follows Lucy Snowe as she battles with her perception of the opposing constructions of England and Continental Europe (Protestant/Catholic, liberty/entrapment, 'reality'/illusion) and refashions her position from 'nobody's daughter' (xiv.146) into an independent woman with her own home and career. It is particularly significant that this transformation occurs at the annual fête to celebrate Belgium's liberation from the Netherlands, as Lucy decisively resists her own oppressors in the form of Père Silas, Mme Beck and Mme Walravens. In this, her final completed novel, Charlotte aligns personal and political histories in a way which enables Lucy to claim the foreign space as her adopted homeland.

In 1852, Charlotte wrote to Gaskell about Harriet Beecher Stowe's major novel on American slavery, *Uncle Tom's Cabin*, suggesting that '[t]o manage these great matters rightly they must be long and practically studied' (Smith, *Letters*, vol. III, p. 75). Through their own writings, the Brontës themselves 'long studied' the effects of politics in terms of war, revolution, colonialism, nation, class antagonism, gender relations and the push for equality. Indeed, as Mary Taylor noted, the Brontës were nothing less than 'furious politicians' (Gaskell, *Life*, p. 82) whose lives were intricately bound up with one of the most fascinating periods of modern political history.

NOTES

1 Terry Eagleton, *Myths of Power: A Marxist Study of the Brontës* (1975), 30th anniversary edn (Basingstoke: Palgrave Macmillan, 2005), p. 3.
2 Stevie Davies, *Emily Brontë* (Manchester: Carcanet, 1983), p. 11.

3 'Biographical Notice of Ellis and Acton Bell' (1850), quoted from Smith, *Letters*, vol. II, p. 742.

4 Jerome McGann, *The Romantic Ideology* (University of Chicago Press, 1983).

5 Stevie Davies, *Emily Brontë: Heretic* (London: Women's Press, 1994), pp. 240–6; Edward Chitham, *A Life of Emily Brontë* (Oxford: Blackwell, 1987), p. 220.

6 Elizabeth Rigby, in an unsigned review of *Jane Eyre* in the *Quarterly Review* (1848), available, in abridged form, in Miriam Allott (ed.), *The Brontës: The Critical Heritage* (London: Routledge & Kegan Paul, 1974), pp. 109–10.

7 Terry Eagleton, *Heathcliff and the Great Hunger* (London: Verso, 1995).

8 Dante Gabriel Rossetti, letter to William Allingham of 19 Sept. 1854, quoted in Allott, *The Critical Heritage*, p. 300.

CHAPTER 32

Newspapers and magazines

Joanne Shattock

Papa and Branwell are gone for the newspaper, the *Leeds Intelligencer*; a most excellent Tory paper edited by Mr Wood [for] the proprietor Mr Henneman. We take 2 and see three newspapers a week. We take the *Leeds Intelligencer*, party Tory, and the *Leeds Mercury*, Whig, edited by Mr Baines and his brother, son-in-law and his 2 sons, Edward and Talbot. We see the *John Bull*; it is a High Tory, very violent. Mr Driver lends us it, as likewise *Blackwood's Magazine*, the most able periodical there is. The editor is Mr Christopher North, an old man, 74 years of age; the lst of April is his birthday. His company are Timothy Tickler, Morgan O'Doherty, Macrabin Mordecai, Mullion, Warrell, and James Hogg, a man of most extraordinary genius, a Scottish shepherd.[1]

Charlotte Brontë's 'The History of the Year', dated 12 March 1829 and written when she was twelve, provides an accurate guide to the newspapers and periodicals which were available to the Brontë children at a formative period in their writing lives. Early in 1829 Charlotte and Branwell embarked on what would become the Glass Town saga, which included a series of miniature magazines modelled on *Blackwood's Edinburgh Magazine*, the original of which was on loan to the parsonage from a neighbour. The reading of newspapers had been part of the children's daily lives from an early period. Elizabeth Gaskell records the recollection of a local woman who nursed Mrs Brontë that Maria, the eldest, at the age of seven would 'shut herself up ... in the children's study with a newspaper and be able to tell one everything when she came out; debates in parliament, and I don't know what all' (Gaskell, *Life*, p. 43). Patrick Brontë, we learn from Gaskell's biography, was in the habit of discussing political events and issues both national and local with his children, prompted and informed by his reading of the newspapers. He was a regular contributor of letters to both Leeds papers, on issues ranging from Catholic emancipation and the reform of criminal justice through to church rates.

Charlotte's accolade 'the most able periodical there is' was a testimony to the place that *Blackwood's* occupied in the Brontë household. The children embraced its Tory politics and adopted real-life characters like the Duke of Wellington and Byron, who featured prominently in the magazine, as their heroes. The magazine expanded their knowledge of current publications on a range of subjects – history, geography, politics and travel – through its reviews, which were accompanied by extensive quotations. Its influence on Branwell, in particular, was profound. Christine Alexander has argued that it was as a reader of *Blackwood's* that he found his voice as a writer.[2] It was Branwell who devised the miniature 'Branwell's Blackwood's Magazine' in January 1829, its format and layout modelled on the original, complete with advertisements, and its articles reflecting the contents of the Edinburgh monthly.

Founded in 1817 by the bookseller William Blackwood as a Tory rival to the Whig-affiliated *Edinburgh Review*, *Blackwood's* was one of the first magazines to combine serialized fiction with the contents of a miscellany. John Galt, Samuel Warren and Susan Ferrier were serialized in the magazine's first decade, but its main impact in the early years was through its political satire and often savage literary reviewing. Dominated by John Wilson and John Gibson Lockhart, the magazine's Tory politics were obvious from the start. The 'Translation from an Ancient Chaldee Manuscript' in the first number for October 1817 was a satire on local Edinburgh figures. 'The Cockney School of Poetry', an infamous attack on Keats, Leigh Hunt and Hazlitt, set the tone for the magazine's reviewing. The 'Noctes Ambrosianae' or 'Nights at Ambrose's [tavern]', which ran from 1822 to 1835, was an innovative series of dialogues or conversations in which the magazine's anonymous contributors adopted pseudonyms: 'Christopher North' (Wilson), 'the Scorpion' (Lockhart), 'the Ettrick Shepherd' (James Hogg), 'Timothy Tickler' (William Maginn) and 'Ebony' (Blackwood). The 'Noctes' held a special appeal for Branwell and Charlotte, and they imitated the series in their own magazines.

The children's careful reading of *Blackwood's* is reflected in their admiration for its principals, Wilson, Lockhart, Hogg and Maginn. Gaskell's *Life* contains Charlotte's account of the genesis of their Islanders' Play, in which each sibling chose an island and peopled it with his or her 'chief men'. Emily's choices were Walter Scott, 'Mr Lockhart' and 'Johnny Lockhart', Scott's grandson, for whom he had written *Tales of a Grandfather*. Charlotte's included the Duke of Wellington and his two sons, who would figure later in her Angrian stories, and, significantly, 'Christopher North and Co.' (Gaskell, *Life*, p. 68).

'Branwell's Blackwood's Magazine', designed for circulation among the Islanders, began in January 1829 and ran for six months. The title changed to 'Blackwood's Young Men's Magazine' when Charlotte took over the editorship in August 1829 and changed again to 'The Young Men's Magazine' when she began the second series in July 1830. The tiny magazines were written on sheets of paper measuring five by three centimetres, the minute script designed to imitate the typeface of *Blackwood's*.

Juliet Barker suggests that some of the items on dreams, apparitions and fairy transformations were influenced by articles in *Blackwood's*, including an 1821 article 'Buried Alive'. Articles on the expedition to discover the North-West Passage under Sir William Edward Parry and his colleague Sir James Clarke Ross gave Anne and Emily the names of two of the main characters in what was to become the Gondal saga (Barker, pp. 159 and 155). Alexander speculates that an article in the June 1826 number, 'Geography of Central Africa: Denham and Clapperton's Journals', may have influenced the actual setting of Glass Town.[3] Echoes of the 'Noctes' occur in 'Military Conversations' and 'Nights', published in 'Branwell's Blackwood's Magazine' in June and July 1829.

The impact of *Blackwood's Magazine* on all four Brontës was far-reaching, both as a source of knowledge about politics, history and geography and as a stimulus to their own writing. Yet none of them became a *Blackwood's* contributor. The magazine in the 1850s, transformed from its early satirical days, would have been a very congenial environment. The new editor John Blackwood used it to attract promising novelists to the firm. Anthony Trollope, Charles Lever, R. D. Blackmore, Edward Bulwer Lytton, Charles Reade, Margaret Oliphant and George Eliot all became *Blackwood's* contributors, the last dominating the firm's fiction list for a quarter of a century.

In 1831, the regular loan of *Blackwood's* to the parsonage ceased. Whether the 'Mr Driver' who had provided it was the Revd Jonas Driver of Haworth, who died in December 1831, or a local tradesman, it was no longer forthcoming (see Smith, *Letters*, vol. 1, p. 114 n.). Aunt Branwell, possibly in anticipation of Charlotte's return from Roe Head, subscribed to *Fraser's Magazine* as a replacement. The substitution was well judged. *Fraser's*, like *Blackwood's*, was a monthly, Tory in politics although more progressive, and sharing many of the same contributors, including its first editor, William Maginn. *Blackwood's* was its main competitor. The proprietor of *Fraser's*, James Fraser, was a London bookseller, and the magazine's readership was more metropolitan than that of *Blackwood's* (its full title was *Fraser's Magazine for Town and*

Country). Like *Blackwood's* it sold for two shillings and sixpence, a substantial outlay for a middle-class household with limited means.

Again like *Blackwood's*, *Fraser's* was a miscellany that serialized fiction. Thackeray's *The Yellowplush Correspondence, Catherine* and *The Luck of Barry Lyndon* were published in the magazine, along with a number of his short stories. Maginn dominated the periodical, impressing his personality on every issue until 1836 and famously commissioning the artist Daniel Maclise to produce illustrations for the 'Gallery of Illustrious Literary Characters', for which he supplied the text. The young Brontës would have found *Fraser's* under Maginn a palatable substitute for *Blackwood's*. Carol Bock suggests that its representation of authorship and its increasing professionalization, through the portraits of writers included in the 'Gallery' and elsewhere, would have found a receptive audience in the four siblings as they contemplated writing as a possible career.[4] It was later, in 1848, when the magazine had entered what is acknowledged to be its 'Victorian' phase under the proprietorship of J. W. Parker, that *Fraser's* published two of Anne Brontë's poems. The year before, in December 1847, *Fraser's* published G. H. Lewes' discerning review of *Jane Eyre*.

Whereas the reading of *Blackwood's* and *Fraser's* seems to have been undertaken either singly or collectively and independently of their father, the domestic consumption of the two newspapers, the Whig *Leeds Mercury* and its Tory rival the *Leeds Intelligencer*, is more likely to have been mediated by Patrick Brontë's interests and enthusiasms, at least in the children's early years. Established in the eighteenth century, the *Mercury* became one of the most distinguished and influential provincial papers in the country after it was purchased by Edward Baines in 1801. A Dissenter and a Liberal, Baines was a pioneering editor and proprietor who supported free trade, parliamentary reform, Catholic emancipation and the extension of civil liberties. One of Baines' sons, also Edward, became editor in the 1820s. Charlotte satirized all three of Baines' sons in 'Tales of the Islanders' because of the paper's attacks on the Duke of Wellington's Tory government.[5]

The *Mercury* had the support of Yorkshire mill-owners, and Baines himself had close connections with the industry. The paper campaigned vigorously for the revocation of the Orders in Council, which had stopped trade with Europe and North America during the Napoleonic Wars and as a result had blighted Yorkshire manufacturing. It also endorsed general education for the working classes and was sympathetic to the distress caused by the downturn in trade, but it was against the Factory Acts and the Charter and anti-Poor Law reform. As a result it had little influence among the working class. Its extensive coverage of the outbreak of violence against mill-owners by the Luddites in 1811–12 – which Charlotte may have been reminded of by her father, whose curacy at Hartshead had been close to the scene – led her to send to Leeds 'for a file of the "Mercuries" of 1812, '13 and '14' when she was writing *Shirley* (Gaskell, *Life*, p. 314). Herbert Rosengarten and Patrick Collier have shown how extensively she drew on the *Mercury* for material while still subtly critiquing Baines' unqualified support of the manufacturing interests and what Charlotte saw as the latter's narrowness, selfishness and hypocrisy.[6]

Although he is generally regarded as a Tory, Patrick Brontë's politics would have been accommodated by both Leeds papers. The *Leeds Intelligencer and Yorkshire General Advertiser*, like the *Mercury*, was initially a weekly, established in the eighteenth century and from 1790 recognized as the leading Yorkshire Tory paper. It was supportive of the landed interests, anti-Catholic, opposed to the Chartists and, in the 1840s, critical of the Anti-Corn Law League. Patrick wrote to the paper on a number of occasions. In January and February of 1818, it published three of his letters in support of Catholic emancipation. He wrote to the *Mercury* in 1828 proposing a liberalization of the criminal code, and he wrote again in late 1829 proposing the abolition of the death penalty for everything apart from murder, following this with a similar letter to the *Leeds Intelligencer* in May 1830. His letter to the *Intelligencer* early in 1834 – in opposition to proposals to remove bishops from the House of Lords, abolish church rates and admit Dissenters to the universities, signed with his initials – prompted responses in letters to the *Mercury*. As Barker points out, the younger Brontës would have become used to seeing their father's name in both of the Leeds papers (Barker, pp. 131, 157, 158 and 167–8).

John Bull, the third of the newspapers named by Charlotte, was a pugnacious ultra-conservative weekly with a strong anti-Catholic bias, edited and mainly written by Theodore Hook. Established in 1820, it supported the King in his divorce from Queen Caroline and then focused on attacking prominent Whigs and radicals. It was at its most vituperative, and its circulation at its most buoyant, in its first decade, justifying Charlotte's description of it as 'very violent'. According to Barker, Branwell regularly read *Bell's Life in London* (established in 1822), a weekly metropolitan paper which featured sport and for which he sent to the Shake Hands public house near Keighley (Barker, p. 229). Barker also makes the point that local circulating libraries, particularly those in Keighley, furnished some of the books and periodicals read by the Brontës, so that not all of their reading of serials can be traced to subscriptions or loans from friends and neighbours (Barker, pp. 148–9).

A letter written by Charlotte to Hartley Coleridge in 1840 suggests another source for her childhood reading of magazines:

You see Sir I have read the Lady's Magazine and know something of its contents – ... I read them before I knew how to criticize or object – they were old books belonging to my mother or my Aunt; they had crossed the Sea, had suffered ship-wreck and were discoloured with brine – I read them as a treat on holiday afternoons or by stealth when I should have been minding my lessons[.] (Smith, *Letters*, vol. I, p. 240)

A link is often made between this account and Caroline Helstone's reading in the rectory of *Shirley* of 'some venerable Lady's Magazines, that had once performed a sea-voyage with their owner, and undergone a storm, and whose pages were stained with salt water; some mad Methodist Magazines, full of miracles and apparitions, of preternatural warnings, ominous dreams, and frenzied fanaticism' (II.xi.327–8). The *Lady's Magazine* would have been appropriate reading material for Aunt Branwell and Mrs Brontë. Established in 1770, it was a monthly selling for two shillings and sixpence, aimed at upper-class women and including fiction, biography, poetry, pieces on dress and fashion and articles of a generally didactic kind, some of which would become standard features of the 'woman's magazine' of the next century. Methodist magazines would also have been likely reading for the Branwells, given their Methodist background. The *Methodist Magazine*, originally titled the *Arminian Magazine* and then the *Wesleyan Methodist Magazine*, was established by John Wesley in 1778 as part of a plan to control the theological material issued to the faithful.

Charlotte's account of the pleasures of illicit and holiday reading is of a piece with the reading undertaken by all the Brontë siblings in their formative years. During her professional writing life she acquired a more extensive knowledge of the mid-century periodical press, particularly the weeklies, monthlies and quarterlies which reviewed current publications and circulated literary gossip. It was Charlotte who drew up, for the publishers Aylott and Jones, the list of periodicals to which the 1846 volume of *Poems* was to be sent for review (see Smith, *Letters*, vol. I, p. 470). The disappointing response to that volume was soon over-shadowed by the controversial review of *Jane Eyre* and *Vanity Fair* by Elizabeth Rigby in the *Quarterly Review* in 1848, and the explosion of reviews of *Jane Eyre*, *Wuthering Heights* and *The Tenant of Wildfell Hall*, making her all too aware of the power of reviewers in the current climate. She regularly read *The Athenaeum*, one of the publications sent to her in the box of books from her publishers Smith, Elder & Co., its contents chosen by George Smith's colleague W. S. Williams. Her developing relationship with G. H. Lewes, who once boasted that he had contributed to every existing periodical 'except the d___d old Quarterly',[7] made her aware of a professional literary life dependent on the periodical press. She took a keen interest in the radical weekly *The Leader*, founded in 1850 by Lewes and Thornton Hunt, which was also sent to Haworth in the Smith, Elder & Co. box, noting in particular its review of *Henry Esmond*. She discussed two articles in the *Westminster Review* in letters to Elizabeth Gaskell, one a review of Sarah Lewis' *Woman's Mission* in the January 1850 issue and the other Harriet Taylor's article on the 'Enfranchisement of Women' in July 1851 (Smith, *Letters*, vol. II, pp. 457 and 695 and vol. III, p. 82).

For the surviving Brontë, the world of nineteenth-century newspapers and periodicals, which had once been determined by subscriptions from Haworth Parsonage, the holdings of the local circulating library and the offerings of neighbours, became a textual world in which she and her sisters were central figures, and one in which she battled to protect their reputations. It was also an element of her professional writing life. One tantalizing question remains: had she lived until 1860, would she have been persuaded by the lavish rewards offered by its proprietor, George Smith, and the blandishments of the editor, W. M. Thackeray, to contribute to the *Cornhill Magazine*?

NOTES

1 Christine Alexander (ed.), *An Edition of the Early Writings of Charlotte Brontë*, vol. I: *The Glass Town Saga, 1826–1832* (Oxford: Blackwell, for the Shakespeare Head Press, 1987), p. 4.

2 Christine Alexander, 'Readers and Writers: *Blackwood's* and the Brontës', *Gaskell Society Journal*, 8 (1994), 54–69.

3 Alexander, *An Edition of the Early Writings of Charlotte Brontë*, vol. I, p. II n. 8.

4 Carol A. Bock, 'Authorship, the Brontës, and *Fraser's Magazine*: "Coming Forward" as an Author in Early Victorian England', *Victorian Literature and Culture*, 29 (2001), 241–66.

5 Alexander, *An Edition of the Early Writings of Charlotte Brontë*, vol. I, p. 26 n.

6 Herbert J. Rosengarten, 'Charlotte Brontë and the *Leeds Mercury*', *Studies in English Literature 1500–1900*, 16 (1976), 591–600; Patrick Collier, '"The lawless by force ... the peaceable by kindness": Strategies of Social Control in Charlotte Brontë's *Shirley* and the *Leeds Mercury*', *Victorian Periodicals Review*, 32.4 (1999), 279–98.

7 Quoted by Francis Espinasse, *Literary Recollections and Sketches* (London: Hodder and Stoughton, 1893), p. 276.

CHAPTER 33

Agriculture and industry

Marianne Thormählen with Steven Wood

The second quarter of the nineteenth century is usually represented as a period when the industrial and agricultural revolutions proceeded in parallel, feeding off and into each other as the population of England and Wales rose dramatically, from about 9 million in 1800 to nearly 18 million in 1851.[1] Recent historians have qualified the picture of extreme and comprehensive change, pointing out that much industrial labour was still carried out in the home in the early nineteenth century, that the advent of agricultural machinery was a slow, uneven process and that radical improvements in agriculture had in fact begun as far back as the seventeenth century. Nevertheless, it is safe to say that the youth and brief adulthood of the Brontë siblings coincided with a period in the life of their country which witnessed transformations on an exceptional scale, not least with regard to the ways in which people earned their living.

Up until the mid nineteenth century, by far the largest proportion of the working population in Britain laboured on the land.[2] In the realm of industry, textiles reigned supreme in the lifetime of the Brontës, the cotton industry alone employing about 450,000 'hands' around 1830.[3] While cotton manufacture was certainly known to the Brontës – the early failure of Ponden Mill to spin cotton profitably was a financial burden on the Heaton family for generations – it was woollen and worsted that dominated the textile industry in and around Haworth.[4]

In west Yorkshire where the Brontë children grew up, a large part of the population worked in both these sectors of the economy at once. Among the people who lived on farms in the township of Haworth, only a limited number were able to rely entirely on agriculture for their subsistence: about 40 per cent of farmers had a second occupation in 1841, nearly all in textile production. This dual economy had been a feature of the region long before the era of the industrial revolution; in *A Tour through the*

The material on Haworth is written by Wood and the remainder of the chapter by Thormählen.

Whole Island of Great Britain (1724–6), Daniel Defoe described the area around Halifax as one where diligent domestic workers – men, women and children of all ages – relied more on various elements of cloth manufacture than on anything the soil might yield.[5] As textile production gradually moved out of the home and into the factory, farming households around Haworth continued to depend on the income brought by children who left their homes to work in mills.

It is not surprising that agricultural activity alone could not feed more than a small part of the population in and around Haworth. There was little cultivation in the area, where the acidic soil required the application of lime to be productive (in this context it might be noted that one of Joseph's farm jobs is 'loading lime on the farther side of Pennistow Crag'; *Wuthering Heights*, I.viii.60). The township of Haworth, which includes Stanbury and Oxenhope, only contained 120 acres of arable land in 1851, to be compared with over 5,000 acres of meadow and pasture and 2,400 acres of uncultivated land. Such cultivated land as there was would be devoted to the growing of oats, potatoes and other root vegetables.

Cattle-raising was more profitable than the growing of crops of any kind. Then as now, sheep dotted the hills around Haworth; but the laithe or barn seen beside nearly every farm today bears witness to the importance of dairy farming at an earlier point in time, when cows spent the winter in the laithe subsisting on laboriously mown and transported hay.

It is while she is helping with the hay-making that Nelly Dean in *Wuthering Heights* hears about the birth of Hareton (I.viii.56), and the Earnshaw farm is clearly one where cattle-raising plays an important role. Some grain is grown even on this upland property; the farm employs a plough-boy, there are references to working 'in the field', and Catherine's pony tramples through ridges of corn. However, the sale of cattle at the local market generates the only visible income from the farm in the book (II.xviii.280). Another source is indicated in passing: Joseph is said to 'hector over tenants and labourers' (I.viii.58), the reference to tenants supporting the idea of Wuthering Heights as a sizable property.

Thrushcross Grange outranks it, of course, and its situation on lower ground makes it a more profitable agricultural estate. The library may be Edgar Linton's natural habitat; but he is aware of his duties as a landowner and oversees the harvest, moving among the reapers with his daughter and staying until the last sheaves are done, at a cost to his health (II.viii.202). Even so, the fact that Gimmerton harvests are a full three weeks later than elsewhere (II.xviii.271) implies that whatever income the Grange can be expected to yield as an agricultural estate is modest, and the Gimmerton crop Lockwood sees is oats and not wheat, which demands good soil.

The farm managed by Gilbert Markham in *The Tenant of Wildfell Hall* is an entirely different concern. His very name may be taken as an indication of his respectability as an agriculturist, recalling that of the best-known agricultural authority of the seventeenth century, Gervase Markham, whose works – including *The First Book of the English Husbandman* (1635) – were still referred to in nineteenth-century periodicals known to the Brontës.[6] For anyone familiar with early nineteenth-century developments in agriculture, Anne Brontë's novel supplies a portrait of a typical progressive farmer: Gilbert pledges his commitment to 'the improvement of agriculture in general' (i.11), the classic early nineteenth-century watchword 'improvement' being a never-ending refrain in works about farming from the period; he proudly informs his mother – in words that sound like a quotation from eighteenth- and nineteenth-century literature on farming, in which the importance of draining is constantly emphasized – that he has been 'carrying out a plan for the extensive and efficient draining of the low meadow-lands' (i.12); he studies the *Farmer's Magazine*, which has, among other things, pictures of model farms, a prominent feature in progressive agriculture;[7] and he works among his labourers in order to set them an example of leadership, as recommended in contemporaneous works on farming (viii.61–2; his abandonment of this worthy intention when a reason to visit Helen suddenly materializes reveals the intensity of his infatuation with her).[8]

Socially inferior to Helen, Gilbert is still a representative of a respectable class: the gentleman farmer who owns and serves his own land. In a rural economy where most prosperous farmers were content to extract comfortable incomes from land they held as tenants of big landowners, the undisputed possessor of well-tended 'paternal acres' was a person of some social consequence (the Earnshaw family is another Brontë example of the prestige that came with such a position). Nor did being a farmer exclude educational attainments and cultural refinement, though prejudice against the wit and manners of country folk among urban intellectuals, common in any age, was certainly in evidence in the Brontës' time. William Howitt, whose tastes coincided with those of the Brontë family in several respects, did his best to persuade his readers not only that farming was a noble occupation in itself, but also that there was no need for its practitioners to 'forgo the refined pleasures of society'. On the contrary, Howitt argued, farming called for 'a first-rate education' and could coexist with enjoyment of 'the arts, the elegancies, the news and knowledge of civilized life'.[9]

Gilbert answers to that description as well as being a model farmer and steward: the Markham–Huntingdon marriage may be a 'mésalliance' for Helen, but the reader may expect the good husbandman to make a good husband, unlike Helen's late spouse.[10] Arthur Huntingdon's worthlessness as a person becomes apparent when he fails to take an interest in the running of his estate. 'If he would play the country gentleman, and attend to the [home] farm – but that he knows nothing about, and won't give his mind to consider', sighs his wife (xxv.191), who has to take care of 'the welfare and comfort of [his] poor tenants and labourers' herself (xxix.208). Being a landowner might enable a man to live a life of leisure off the exertions of others; but he was expected to take an informed interest in agricultural advancements, fund repairs and improvements where needed and extend charity towards his workfolk in bad times. Failure to honour these duties is tantamount to betrayal of a sacred trust, and this early revelation of Arthur Huntingdon's inadequacy is ominous indeed. Conversely, the contemporary reader of *Jane Eyre* had reason to hope for good things when learning of Mrs Fairfax's impression that her master, and Jane's, 'is considered a just and liberal landlord by his tenants' (i.xi.105).

While the manufacture of woollen cloth is the branch of the British economy that dominates *Shirley*, the owner of Hollow's Mill knows where her main responsibilities lie. The chief landowner of the district, Shirley Keeldar is aware that although she has some income from the mill, 'a larger share comes from the landed estate around it', and '[i]t would not do to take any measures injurious to the farmers' (ii.vii.276). In supporting the charitable schemes of poorer and wiser people, she proves her worth as a landlord.

Shirley can, of course, afford to be 'just and liberal'; the man who rents the mill from her does not have her economic resources. But the trouble with Robert Gérard Moore is that he does not have any charitable instincts either: his sole preoccupation is to make enough money to pay off his father's debts and gain sufficient solvency to realize his own projects. It is of him, not of herself, that Shirley is really speaking when saying to the foreman Joe, tongue in cheek, 'clothier and mill-owner as I am, besides farmer, I cannot get out of my head a certain idea that we manufacturers and persons of business are sometimes a little – a *very little* selfish and short-sighted in our views, and rather *too* regardless of human suffering, rather heartless in our pursuit of gain' (ii.vii.277). Visits to city slums teach the previously unfeeling Moore compassion for the poor (III.vii.453–4), and marriage to the virtuous Caroline, who has concrete experience of charitable work, seals his transformation into a model mill-owner. The simultaneous marriage of his studious brother Louis to the local 'squire', Shirley Keeldar, completes the rise of the Moore brothers to joint community leaders where they were once struggling outsiders additionally handicapped by foreign blood.

The two Moore marriages are interesting for the way in which they establish a coalition of landowner and manufacturer perspectives. To members of the aristocracy, as *The Professor* reminds us, anyone in 'Trade' was excluded from their circles (i.4–6); but day-to-day rural life was less strongly affected by that class boundary than one might have expected. While manufacturers were rarely recruited from the ranks of the upper class, they were a tough, new breed of men whose activities changed their environments in ways not even the possessors of 'old money' could afford to ignore;[11] the transformation of the Hollow in *Shirley* forms a graphic example. Besides, successful industrialists – many of whom had begun, like Robert Moore, with a mill rented from a rich landowner – occasionally purchased country estates, 'gentrifying' their families in consequence.[12] Among the reasons why landowners could not afford to be aloof from manufacturing and trade was the fact that their properties might not possess value as generators of agrarian earnings only: there was income to be had from allowing land to be used for mining, quarrying, canals, railways and so on.[13]

A prosperous manufacturer was thus a person of consequence in all walks of life, but the population category on which his activities had the greatest impact was of course his employees and their families. Neither *Shirley* nor *The Professor* supplies pictures of day-to-day labour in the mills owned by Robert Moore and Edward Crimsworth; but the former's responsibility for the welfare of his workforce, a responsibility he shoulders only towards the end of the book, is emphasized throughout. The narrator's stance is clear: the necessity of rationalization through machinery is acknowledged, but indifference to the plight of those who lose their livelihood as a result is blameworthy.[14]

What both *Shirley* and *The Professor* bring home to the reader is the vulnerability of the manufacturer to sudden changes in the terms of trade and production. The Crimsworth industrialists, father and son, both suffer sudden financial ruin for reasons that are never made clear; but the reason for Robert Moore's financial straits is found in political decisions at high levels, and he is as powerless to fight the consequences as his workpeople are to oppose the innovations that take the bread out of their mouths. The Brontë family were well aware of the vicissitudes of textile manufacturers: in addition to the shifting fortunes of the Nussey and Taylor families, they knew about Haworth people whose efforts in that trade had failed.[15] At a lower social level, local families suffered hardship when mechanization robbed them of much-needed income from handloom weaving (and, later, combing; see Chapter 1).[16]

The progress of the industrial and agricultural revolutions thus entailed changes, gradual and abrupt, with which all classes struggled to cope as best they could. Like Thomas Hardy's fiction, the Brontë novels accommodate a measure of nostalgia for the rural life of bygone days while making it clear that the future belongs to those who embrace the improvements of the new era.[17] The backward glance at the end of *Shirley* is both rueful and ironic: the manufacturer's realized dream, a mighty mill with 'a chimney, ambitious as the tower of Babel' and model cottages clustered around it, spelled the end of the old Hollow where the last of the fairies was allegedly seen 'fifty years syne' among oaks and nut trees (III.xiv.541–2). In the words of another nineteenth-century advocate of progress, William Howitt, civilization – 'the spirit of man' – had become 'too strong for them'.[18]

NOTES

1 Figures quoted in Tom Williamson, *The Transformation of Rural England: Farming and the Landscape 1700–1870* (University of Exeter Press, 2002), p. 4.

2 For exact figures, see G. E. Mingay, *Rural Life in Victorian England* (London: Heinemann, 1976), p. 26.

3 The figure is supplied by Norman McCord in *British History 1815–1906* (Oxford University Press, 1991), p. 83.

4 On Ponden Mill, see John Hodgson, *Textile Manufacture, and Other Industries, in Keighley* (Keighley, 1879), pp. 232–3.

5 See M. J. Daunton, *Progress and Poverty: An Economic and Social History of Britain 1700–1850* (Oxford University Press, 1995), pp. 148–52.

6 Including the *Chambers' Edinburgh Journal*, which Charlotte Brontë mentions in *Shirley*, III.ii.372 (e.g. 14 Mar. 1846 and 5 June 1847).

7 As editors of the novel have noted, it is not clear to which periodical with that title Anne was referring. On model farms, see Susanna Wade Martins, *The English Model Farm: Building the Architectural Ideal, 1700–1914* (Macclesfield: Windgather Press, 2002).

8 See, for instance, Clark Tillyard, *Practical Farming and Grazing* [etc.], 2nd edn (n.p., 1837), pp. 103–4.

9 William Howitt, *The Rural Life of England* ([London], 1838), pp. 74–5.

10 On Gilbert as the good steward Helen has stood in such great need of, see Marianne Thormählen, 'Aspects of Love in *The Tenant of Wildfell Hall*', in Julie Nash and Barbara A. Suess (eds.), *New Approaches to the Literary Art of Anne Brontë* (Aldershot: Ashgate, 2001), pp. 166–8.

11 On the social origins of industrialists see, for instance, Daunton, *Progress and Poverty*, pp. 196–8.

12 According to Lawrence Stone and Jeanne C. Fawtier Stone, this aspect of social mobility was much less significant than historians used to think; see *An Open Elite? England 1540–1880* (Oxford University Press, 1984).

13 See Mingay, *Rural Life*, p. 29, and B. A. Holderness, 'Agriculture and Industrialization in the Victorian Economy', in G. E. Mingay (ed.), *The Victorian Countryside* (London: Routledge & Kegan Paul, 1981), vol. I, pp. 183–4.

14 On class conflict in *Shirley*, see Patricia Ingham, *The Brontës*, Oxford World's Classics, Authors in Context (Oxford University Press, 2006), pp. 110–20.

15 One such failure took place during the writing of *Shirley*; see Steven Wood, *Haworth: 'A strange uncivilized little place'* (Stroud: Tempus, 2005), p. 27, and Robin Greenwood, 'Who was Who in Haworth during the Brontë Era 1820–61', unpublished typescript, 4th edn (2005), pp. 25–6; copy in the library of the Brontë Parsonage Museum, Haworth.

16 On the various stages of textile manufacturing, see James Bischoff, *A Comprehensive History of the Woollen and Worsted Manufactures* (London: Smith, Elder & Co., 1842; repr. 1968), vol. II, pp. 388–421, and W. B. Crump and Gertrude Ghorbal, *History of the Huddersfield Woollen Industry* (Huddersfield, 1935; repr. Kirklees Historical Reprints, 1988), vol. II. The latter contains an illustrated description of the sort of frames that Robert Moore introduced (pp. 95–100).

17 Hardy's position is brought out in Jane Mattisson, *Knowledge and Survival in the Novels of Thomas Hardy*, Lund Studies in English, 101 (Lund, 2002).

18 Howitt, *Rural Life*, p. 227.

CHAPTER 34

Transport and travel

Edward Chitham

Modes of transport developed out of all recognition during the lifetime of Patrick Brontë. In his native Ireland, walking was the obvious way of getting from one place to another, and his father Hugh covered long distances on foot. In bad weather even well-off coach passengers had to walk, using porters to carry their luggage. Patrick braved the sea to go to England in 1802, despite such attitudes as that of Lord Darnley, who wrote, 'I cannot think of a sea voyage without horror.' Patrick visited Ireland in 1812, the year in which an English traveller wrote, 'I have all my life had a dread of the passage from Liverpool to [Ireland]. I went on board ... bound for Newry ... and sailed immediately afterwards. I was hardly on board before I wished myself back again: the evening was lowering, the wind every moment becoming more unfavourable and the Captain evidently intoxicated.'[1]

It is uncertain how Patrick travelled on to Cambridge from Liverpool. Much later, Emily Brontë wrote of old Mr Earnshaw as having walked to Liverpool and back, a distance of about 150 miles from the Halifax area, in three days, though he says he would not have another such walk (with the child Heathcliff under his greatcoat) 'for the three kingdoms' (*Wuthering Heights*, I.iv.31). Patrick usually walked all over his curacy. For freight, which in the countryside usually meant agricultural produce, carts with rounded covers on top were used. Moving from Thornton near Bradford to Haworth in 1820, Patrick hired eight carts for the furniture and a covered wagon for his wife and children; their slow progress as they ground up the hill to Denholme was recorded by William Scruton.[2] Nevertheless, for most people walking remained the main way of travelling over quite considerable distances.

It is well known that the Brontës as children went for long walks across the moors, doubtless making use of the maze of field paths and moorland tracks. These walks sometimes had an object, such as delivering messages from Mr Brontë to a parishioner or a church official. On the day in 1824, when Crow Hill bog burst, the young family had already walked the three miles to the hill and would have to walk three miles back with the maid Sarah Garrs to escort them. Later, we hear frequently of walks to and from Keighley, a distance of four miles. Two well-known instances are the late-night return from William Weightman's classical lecture in early 1840 (see Smith, *Letters*, vol. I, p. 213 n.) and the dash through a thunderstorm on 7 July 1848, when Charlotte and Anne began their journey to London to confront their publishers (letter to Mary Taylor of 4 September 1848; Smith, *Letters*, vol. II, p. 112); they sent their luggage on ahead. By 1850 there were horse-drawn omnibus services from Haworth to meet trains at Keighley, and a number of carriers' carts were in operation.[3]

If walking was impossible, the Brontës hired a 'gig'. There was one in Haworth itself. In the view of Charlotte's friend Ellen Nussey, who went to Bolton Abbey with them in 1833, the vehicle was 'no handsome carriage, but a rickety dogcart, unmistakably betraying its neighbourhood to the carts and ploughs of some rural farmyard. The horse [was] taken directly from the fields[.]'[4] Elsewhere, Ellen described the conveyance as 'a small double gig or phaeton'.[5] Eight years earlier, Patrick had travelled by coach to fetch his ailing daughter Maria home from Cowan Bridge school. The route from Keighley to Cowan Bridge was via the Keighley to Kendal toll road, called a 'turnpike', which had been opened in 1753 and followed much the same course as the modern A65. In *Jane Eyre*, the heroine leaves Gateshead at 6.00 a.m. to travel to Lowood in a coach which stops at the Gateshead porter's lodge. There was a halt for food on the way. The journey was fifty miles altogether, much the same as that from Keighley to Cowan Bridge. It is not entirely clear to what extent the Brontës were aware of, or attentive to, historical accuracy in their narratives; but most of England had such turnpike roads suitable for coaches by 1750, and the transport arrangements in *Jane Eyre* seem to reflect those of Charlotte's childhood.

During the nineteenth century there was constant upgrading of roads both large and small. Even the little lane leading from Thorp Green to Little Ouseburn was straightened during Anne Brontë's last few months as governess there, the hedges on both sides being grubbed up and new hawthorn hedges planted in the early spring of 1845.[6] Despite such improvements in the smaller roads, journeys were still 'formidable'. This was especially the case in winter, as Anne emphasizes when her character Agnes Grey arrives at Horton Lodge in a snowstorm, travelling in a phaeton – a small private carriage – sent to meet her by her employers. The drive inside the mansion gates is actually 'smoother' than the road.

Anne's employers, the Robinsons, kept their own coach, their coachman, William Allison, paying a dubious visit to Branwell after his disgrace.[7] There is no firm evidence about the mode of horse-drawn transport employed by the Robinson sisters when they visited Anne early in December 1848. Some nuanced class distinctions can be perceived in the modes of travel in *Agnes Grey*. The upper-class clergyman Mr Hatfield arrives via Moss Lane on horseback, while his curate Mr Weston generally walks. Agnes herself, as a governess, does not merit a seat in the family carriage until, in chapter 17, Rosalie and Matilda have specious reasons for wanting to walk.

An enormous change in land transport was heralded by the opening, in 1838, of the London to Birmingham Railway, part of which line members of the Brontë family would later use. Its effect was immense and immediate. During the next decade this exciting new method of transport made and destroyed fortunes, deeply affecting many families including the Brontës. Charlotte wrote to her friend Ellen Nussey, probably in September 1840, that Branwell was to take up a post in the 'wild, wandering, adventurous, romantic, knight-errant-like capacity' of clerk on the Manchester & Leeds Railway at Sowerby Bridge near Halifax (Smith, *Letters*, vol. 1, p. 228). This ebullience is only partially feigned. 'Railway clerk' then had the kind of ring that 'air traffic controller' might have now. The new stretch of line from Hebden Bridge to Leeds was opened on 5 October. Trains took fifteen minutes from Hebden Bridge to Sowerby Bridge, and passengers could be in Leeds in one hour and thirty-five minutes. A few months later, the through route to Manchester was opened, making trade between the commercial centres of Yorkshire and Lancashire much easier.

The Brontë family embraced this new form of transport wholeheartedly, buying railway shares and travelling by rail as soon as it became available. It would be many years before the Keighley and Worth Valley line reached Haworth itself; but the Leeds to Shipley line, opened in 1846, was extended on 16 March 1847 to Keighley, where handsome station buildings had been erected. Subsequently the Brontës made use of this route. However, Emily recorded in her largely destroyed account book four shillings spent on rail tickets for Leeds on the first part of her journey with Anne to York in July 1845. (In the same fragment, she records a shilling spent on '2 omnibuses'.[8]) She and Charlotte travelled to London by rail with Patrick in 1842, on their way to school in Belgium. Anne accompanied Charlotte to London in July 1848 to visit their publishers, travelling from Leeds via Rugby, where the train joined the London to Birmingham line.

On 1 April 1841 Branwell took up a post as clerk-in-chief at Luddenden Foot, a mile north-west of Sowerby Bridge. The accommodation at small stations at that time could be primitive, and Branwell had only a small office; by the time proper facilities with living quarters were built, he had left.[9] Traffic on the line was mainly freight, including coal and wool. Branwell took his job seriously, writing to the company with suggestions for improvements to the station, which were finally approved. Rail safety in those days was very haphazard. Trains were regulated on a timing system, with signals provided by the railway police by means of flags and lamps. It was not until 1841 that the first semaphore signal was erected, and a considerable time later that the 'block' system was devised by which only one train at a time could be in a block.[10]

The process of 'booking' passengers in the early days was just as it had been for coaches: paper forms with counterfoils were used until the spread of the pasteboard ticket, which reached the Lancashire and Yorkshire lines in 1839. Engine maintenance and driving skills were primitive. Engine drivers were paid seven shillings a day in the mid 1840s, a relatively high wage for working men at the time.[11] Sometimes firemen (earning four shillings and sixpence a week) had to carry out repairs as the train was moving, lubricating cylinders with tallow after running along the running board of the engine. Fortunately the passengers knew little about these incidents, nor about the system by which the railway police would run back along the track to stop a following train after an accident in the manner of E. Nesbit's *Railway Children*. Charles Dickens' short story 'The Signalman' (though perhaps inaccurate in detail) gives a flavour of the portentousness of early railway accidents.

By the time Charlotte, Emily and Patrick travelled across the English Channel to Belgium in 1842, great changes had taken place in sea transport. In 1819, the 350 ton steamer *Savannah* had completed the trans-Atlantic voyage from New York to Liverpool in twenty-six days; by 1838, the number of days required for the crossing was reduced to seventeen.[12] After 1862, the North Sea and cross-Channel trade was largely in the hands of the railway companies, but in 1842 the service was operated by the Steamship Company. That company's wharf was just below London Bridge, with other wharves catering for boats to other parts of the Thames as well as the Continent. Near the wharf the Brontës would see the fine Custom House, built in 1817 as a successor to a series of buildings, the first of which dated from 1304. The means of propulsion used on steam boats at this time was huge side paddles, adapted from the same principles as the mill wheel. Charlotte used her experiences in travelling down the Thames in *Villette*, chapter 6, from her initial reaction that the Thames at night was like the infernal river Styx to the sea breezes as she passed Margate, and the resultant seasickness.

There were two steamer routes between England and Belgium, one arriving at Ostend and one at Antwerp. The Brontës chose the Ostend route, arriving late after a fourteen-hour voyage.[13] Here, on 13 February 1842, Patrick's passport was endorsed, but there is little external evidence for this part of the journey, and it is usual to extrapolate from *The Professor* and *Villette*. This should be done with great caution, however, remembering that Charlotte was writing fiction; as Professor D'Arcy Thompson first noticed in 1931, she was 'intentionally mixing things up'.[14] Returning to England in great trouble because of their aunt's death in November 1842, Charlotte and Emily travelled via Antwerp, possibly because this was the only passage available in an emergency. They sailed on the steam packet *Wilberforce*, arriving in London on 7 November. However, Charlotte chose Ostend again when she finally returned home from Brussels on 1 January 1844.

Charlotte's 'Belgian' novels describe her fictional characters as travelling to the scenes of their adventures by 'Diligence', a fast-moving horse-drawn vehicle available for public use. That this, and not the recently opened railway line, was the choice of the Brontës in February 1842 is strongly suggested by their choice of hotel, the Hôtel de la Hollande near the diligence terminus in Brussels' Rue de la Madeleine. After taking leave of his daughters the next day, Patrick visited Calais, Lille and Dunkirk, noting that the cost of travel in Belgium and northern France was similar to that in England.[15] He also visited the battlefield at Waterloo, perhaps walking from Brussels, as apparently did Charlotte on a later occasion. On her second journey to Belgium on 28 January 1843, Charlotte varied her previous plan by catching the train from Ostend to Brussels. She had crossed in *The Earl of Liverpool* and stayed in Ostend before catching the midday train, arriving at the Pensionnat Heger at 7.00 p.m. Most of the rest of Charlotte's visits in Belgium seem to have taken place on foot.

When she had become famous Charlotte made many journeys by train, but on one further occasion she travelled by sea. This was on her honeymoon in 1854, when she went as Mrs Arthur Nicholls to visit Arthur's relatives in Banagher, Ireland. In Dublin she met one of Arthur's brothers, Alan, described as 'manager' of the Grand Canal, which had begun to be built in 1756 and linked Dublin's Liffey to the Shannon, the major Irish river which flows westwards. Canals were a form of transport with which the Brontës had little to do, though the Leeds and Liverpool

Canal Co. had once considered a branch from Stockbridge to Keighley. Charlotte and her husband could have made the whole journey from Dublin to Banagher by the Grand Canal, but the train was much quicker, and so won the day.

The first part of the honeymoon had been by carriage and pair, to Keighley station, then by train to Conway in North Wales. The Nichollses crossed an almost calm Irish Sea by paddle steamer to Dun Laoghaire, then called Kingstown, on the outskirts of Dublin. On 7 July they left Dublin for Banagher, departing from Kingsbridge station (now Heuston). The railway did not go as far as Banagher, however, so the last stage of the journey to Charlotte's husband's former home will, like the first, have been by horse-drawn carriage. There is little information about the methods of transport that the newlyweds used for the rest of their stay in Ireland; but the Irish honeymoon included Charlotte's falling off an unruly pony on a path near Killarney, a frightening incident whose happy outcome – she claimed not to have suffered any bruises, nor kicks from the mare's hoofs – left her, as she wrote to her friend Catherine Winkworth, feeling 'gratitude for more sakes than [her] own' (Smith, *Letters*, vol. III, p. 280).

NOTES

1 John Stevenson, *Two Centuries of Life in Down, 1600–1800* (Belfast: McCaw, Stevenson & Orr, 1920; Belfast: White Row Press, 1990), pp. 475–6.

2 William Scruton, *Thornton and the Brontës* (Bradford: J. Dale & Co., 1898), p. 79.

3 Ian Dewhirst, *A History of Keighley* (Keighley Corporation, 1974), p. 59.

4 From an account given to T. Wemyss Reid; see Reid's *Charlotte Brontë: A Monograph* (London, 1877), pp. 29–33.

5 In her 'Reminiscences'; see Smith, *Letters*, vol. I, p. 602.

6 See George Whitehead, *Journal*, ed. Helier Hibbs (Ouseburn: privately printed, 1990), p. 13.

7 The information is supplied by the Robinson papers in the Brontë Parsonage Museum, Haworth, Robinson account book, 93/2.

8 Transcription in Edward Chitham, *A Life of Emily Brontë* (Oxford: Blackwell, 1987), pp. 270–2.

9 On Branwell's career as a railway employee, see Winifred Gérin, *Branwell Brontë* (London: Nelson, 1961), chapter 14.

10 G. M. Kitchenside, *British Railway Signalling* (London: Ian Allan, 1963), pp. 5–8.

11 Michael Robbins, *The Railway Age* (London: Routledge & Kegan Paul, 1962), pp. 84–5.

12 Francis Miltoun [pseud.], *All about Ships and Shipping*, 10th edn, ed. Edwin P. Harnack (London: Faber and Faber, 1959), p. 105.

13 The most recent research concerning the Brussels journey and stay is that of Eric Ruijssenaars in *Charlotte Brontë's Promised Land: The Pensionnat Heger and Other Brontë Places in Brussels* (Haworth: Brontë Society, 2000).

14 *Ibid.*, p. 36.

15 John Lock and W. T. Dixon, *A Man of Sorrow: The Life, Letters and Times of the Rev. Patrick Brontë 1777–1861* (London: Nelson, 1965), p. 303 (including quotations from Patrick's diary).

CHAPTER 35

Law

Ian Ward

At a first glance, it might be thought that among all the things which the novels of the Brontë sisters might seem to be about, law is not really one of them. To a certain extent, it is a perception that might be extended across much of nineteenth-century English literature.[1] The revitalized interdisciplinary engagement of law and literature rather appears to have left the nineteenth century behind. Shakespeare and Milton are much in evidence; so are Dostoevsky, Kafka and Camus. But critical essays on law or jurisprudence in the Victorian literary canon are rare. There is, of course, one very obvious exception to this, the critical literature on Charles Dickens' *Bleak House*.[2] In addition, there are scattered essays on the presence of law in works such as Robert Browning's *The Ring and the Book* and Hardy's *Tess of the D'Urbervilles*. Otherwise, however, there is not much. In this, then, the apparent absence of legal matters in the fiction of the Brontës is not exceptional.

And yet initial impressions can be deceptive. Certainly law does not appear to dominate in any Brontë text, as it might be said to do in *Bleak House* or even *Tess*. But it is there all the same. It could not really be otherwise. In the nineteenth century as in the twenty-first, lives are lived, by and large, within the bounds that law defines. On closer inspection, the law is everywhere in the Brontë novels. For example, the passage in *The Tenant of Wildfell Hall* where Helen Huntingdon berates Hattersley for his failure to comprehend the wider implications of his rough treatment of his wife carries a resonance down the generations (xxxiii.245–7).[3] Spousal abuse occurs in *Wuthering Heights* as well. Both novels also engage issues of child-abuse – a subject of considerable contemporary concern, partly generated by proposals to amend existing child-custody law. Equally, it is difficult to read *Jane Eyre* outside the immediate context of serial 'wrongful confinement' scares which ran through much of the 1830s and 1840s.[4] In all these instances, it was less the force of law that the novels revealed, and rather more the absence of law: the failure to protect spouses, children and the mad. Little wonder that Frances Power Cobbe entitled her famous 1869 essay on female subjugation 'Criminals, Idiots, Women and Minors'.[5] Little wonder, too, that she identified the law, in its absence as much as in its presence, as the root cause of the subjugation.[6]

Aside from the experiences of domestic abuse, there was one further area of law in which female subjugation was instantiated. This was the law of real property. Of course, the holding of estates does not capture the literary imagination in the way that spousal abuse might do. No one thought of writing a sensation novel about strict settlements.[7] Accordingly, Brontë criticism has tended to eschew matters of property. C. P. Sanger's classic essay on the 'structure' of *Wuthering Heights* is a notable exception; but it remains an exception.[8] Even so, the abuse which the laws of property inflicted upon married women was very real. In *The Subjection of Women*, John Stuart Mill argued that the statutory and common laws of marriage and property made the mid-Victorian wife 'the actual bond-servant of her husband: no less, as legal obligation goes, than slaves are commonly called'. There were, he confirmed, post-emancipation, 'no legal slaves' in England, 'except the mistress of every house'.[9]

This jurisprudence of exclusion was founded in the principle of coverture, famously defined by William Blackstone in these terms:

In marriage the husband and wife are one person in law: that is, the very being or legal existence of the woman is suspended during the marriage, or at least is incorporated and consolidated into that of the husband under whose wing, protection, and cover, she performs everything ... For this reason, a man cannot grant anything to his wife, or enter into covenant with her: for the grant would suppose her separate existence; and to covenant with her, would be only to covenant with himself.[10]

No married woman could independently contract, sue, bequeath or alienate property. It can be noted, of course, that coverture applied only to married women. But then, few middle-class women in nineteenth-century England sought to do other than marry, a circumstance that is not contradicted in the novels of the Brontës.

Moreover, when a mid-Victorian novelist wrote about marriage, he or she engaged, however implicitly, with a set of larger debates regarding the reform of matrimonial property law and indeed the reform of Chancery jurisdiction. In both senses, the debates moved around the nature of equity. At a simpler level, coverture was increasingly perceived to be unfair and demeaning. As late as 1886, Chief Justice Coleridge noted the underlying cultural prejudice which presumed in law that a wife was akin to some 'kind of inferior dog or horse'.[11] On presenting a petition to Parliament in support of divorce-law reform in 1856, Lord Brougham pointedly identified the precarious financial dependence of married women, the 'manifold evils occasioned by the present law, by which the property and earnings of the wife are thrown into the absolute power of the husband'.[12]

There is, as Sanger noted, a settlement written into *Wuthering Heights*.[13] The precise nature of the Linton settlement remains elusive, though it appears to be distinguished as carrying a tail general (that is, the estate can descend to heirs of both sexes) rather than the more customary tail male (where the estate descends to a specific male heir and then to male descendants). Nelly recalls that she 'mentally abused' old Linton for securing the settlement in this way (II.ii.145). Heathcliff is later troubled by the possibility that his son's death in advance of Edgar Linton might divert the entail to Catherine Linton. He is thus inclined to force the marriage of Catherine and his son Linton in order to 'prevent disputes' (II.vii.190). What is perhaps most notable about the Linton settlement, however, is its strength. Heathcliff is able to dismiss other legal provisions, whether they relate to assault or false imprisonment or trespass, with scarcely veiled contempt, and conversely is able to employ other legal instruments, such as the legal mortgage, to further his 'diabolical prudence'. But he is unable to disrupt the settlement. While Linton can bequeath his and his wife's moveable property to Heathcliff, the lands, Nelly confirms, 'being a minor, he could not meddle with' (II.xvi.261). In the end, the happier prospect that Emily implies at the close of the novel is to a large extent based on the supposition that Hareton will be able to finance the re-conveyance of the mortgaged fee of the Earnshaw estate by virtue of the capital likely to accrue from the Linton estate, the equitable interest in which has come into his possession through his wife.

The supposition that instruments of Chancery law, such as the strict settlement, imported a distinctive gender resonance is rather more obviously apparent in two other Brontë novels, *The Tenant of Wildfell Hall* and *Jane Eyre*. In both, equitable principles are used to mitigate the rigours of settled estates otherwise bound by common law to neglect the interests of female protagonists.

The Huntingdon estate in *The Tenant of Wildfell Hall* is mostly bound by a strict settlement trust, though there are a 'few mortgages on the rest' (xx.146). Such trusts were designed to preserve the integrity of inherited estates against possible alienation. The settlement created a fiction of possession, where property is held as a life 'interest' and then settled on male progeny successively in tail. The Huntingdon estate, it is later confirmed, is 'entailed upon little Arthur' (lii.400). Following her husband's death, Helen is described as 'nursing a fine estate' for her son (lii.403) – an allusion to the trust which would anyway have existed to manage the estate, but which would have been further expected to deal with the eventuality of little Arthur's minority. The fact that Helen inherits the Staningley estate from her uncle adds a further dimension. During the eighteenth century, Chancery courts had continued to recognize interests in 'separate' trusts for the female spouse's 'use'. Such estates were chiefly intended to reassure anxious fathers against the hazards of potentially wanton sons-in-law.[14] It is interesting to note, in passing, that Charlotte Brontë's pre-marital settlement included provision for such an estate.

With regard to Helen's inheritance, it is reported that her aunt 'advised her husband to it . . . she'd brought most of the property, and it was her wish that this lady should have it' (lii.403). The couple had no extant children, and clearly the aunt was happy to accept 'an annuity'. Nonetheless, Gilbert Markham's fellow passenger would not have been alone in thinking it 'strange' (lii.403): such trusts were not common. Interestingly, just a few moments earlier Markham had heard report of the recent Hargrave marriage. Hargrave, it appears, had earlier refused the proposed terms of an alternative marriage precisely because they included, by inference, the establishment of a trust for the wife's separate use. His new bride, apparently more desperate, has proved to be less demanding. Ominously, it is suggested that she will soon have reason to regret her bargain (lii.399). Although the Staningley estate provides Helen with a 'fortune of her own', the precise nature of its settlement is not clear. Given her niece's earlier experience, it is reasonable to suppose that her aunt might have asked the family lawyer to establish a trust for separate use. If not, then much will depend on Helen's judgement; and the reader is left to hope that she makes a better choice with her second husband than she did with her first.[15]

In his confession to Jane at the beginning of volume III of *Jane Eyre*, Rochester states that his father, an 'avaricious, grasping man', was determined to keep the property together and hence withheld 'a fair portion' from his younger son Edward (the reader has already been informed that the Rochester family have owned Thornfield and surrounding lands 'time out of mind'; 1.xi.104). The life interest in the estate, accordingly, passed to the elder son, Rowland. Rochester was to be consoled with a £30,000 dowry brought by marriage to Bertha Mason. The consolation, of course, was scant. After his brother dies, Rochester inherits the entail of the estate, and Bertha burns the house down. So much, it might be thought, could be attributed to misfortune. But it is not just ill-luck: Charlotte Brontë clearly wanted her readers to ponder rather longer the iniquities and inefficacies of the Rochester settlement.

This inference is confirmed in Jane's intended disbursement of the £20,000 she receives in her uncle's bequest.[16] Contrary to the principle of primogeniture, upon which the strict settlement was founded, Jane undertakes to share the inheritance equally between herself and her three cousins. In that way 'justice would be done, – mutual happiness secured' (III.vii.385). Her cousin St John Rivers, though one of the intended beneficiaries, is clearly taken aback. When asked if he sees the 'justice' in her proposal, Rivers responds:

I *do* see a certain justice; but it is contrary to all custom. Besides the entire fortune is your right: my uncle gained it by his own efforts; he was free to leave it to whom he would: he left it to you. After all, justice permits you to keep it: you may, with a clear conscience, consider it absolutely your own. (III.vii.387)

Rivers conjectures that time and experience will change Jane's mind. They do not. After many 'further struggles', Jane persuades all of the 'equity of the intention' and '[carries her] point' (III.vii.388). While there is no firm evidence either way, it seems likely that Jane's inheritance is not part of a settled or separate estate. If not, she would, once married to Rochester, find that the financial 'independence' she has come to cherish would be compromised by the harsher realities of the common law (III.xi.434–5). The novel does close with the reassurance of at least ten years of happy marriage (III.xii.450). But, as with the Markham–Huntingdon marriage in *The Tenant of Wildfell Hall*, there is no lasting certainty. In nineteenth-century fiction, as in nineteenth-century life, the possibilities of domestic bliss, and financial security, rested in very large part upon the benevolence of husbands. It was the way that those who wrote the law preferred it to be. While Anne and Charlotte Brontë may not have intended their readers to focus too long on the law of property, they could not do other than leave their readers with this sobering thought.

NOTES

1 See Margaret Finn, 'Victorian Law, Literature and History: Three Ships Passing in the Night', *Journal of Victorian Culture*, 7 (2002), 134–46, and Stephen Petch, 'Law, Literature, and Victorian Studies', *Victorian Literature and Culture*, 35 (2007), 361–84.

2 See, for instance, Kieran Dolin, *Fiction and the Law: Legal Discourse in Victorian and Modernist Literature* (Cambridge University Press, 1999), pp. 71–96, and Richard Weisberg, *Poethics and Other Strategies of Law and Literature* (New York: Columbia University Press, 1992), pp. 67–73.

3 For a discussion of this exchange within the broader context of divorce-law reform, see Ian Ward, 'The Case of Helen Huntingdon', *Criticism*, 49 (2007), 156–9.

4 See Ian Ward, 'The Rochester Wives', *Law and Humanities*, 2 (2008), 99–130.

5 Repr. in Susan Hamilton (ed.), *Criminals, Idiots, Women, and Minors: Victorian Writing by Women on Women* (Peterborough, Ont.: Broadview, 1995), pp. 108–28.

6 See Kieran Dolin, *A Critical Introduction to Law and Literature* (Cambridge University Press, 2007), pp. 128–9.

7 A strict settlement means that land is settled on a person for life, with the stipulation that it will then pass to a first son and then to other descendants in tail. Trustees are appointed to preserve contingent remainders. The settlement would be renegotiated as necessary on the successive marriages of elder sons.

8 First published by the Hogarth Press of London in 1926 as Hogarth Essays, 19, it has frequently been reprinted, wholly or partly, for instance in Ian Gregor (ed.), *The Brontës: A Collection of Critical Essays* (Englewood Cliffs: Prentice-Hall, 1970), pp. 7–18.

9 John Stuart Mill, *The Subjection of Women* (1869); quoted from the 1988 edn published by Hackett (London), pp. 5–6, 32–5 and 86.

10 William Blackstone, *Commentaries on the Laws of England* (London: William Walker, 1826), vol. i, p. 430.

11 In *R. v. Little* (1886), quoted in Martin Wiener, *Men of Blood: Violence, Manliness, and Criminal Justice in Victorian England* (Cambridge University Press, 2004), p. 16.

12 Quoted in Ann Chedzoy, *A Scandalous Woman: The Story of Caroline Norton* (London: Allison and Busby, 1992), p. 248.

13 Gregor, *The Brontës*, pp. 13–14.

14 For a broader discussion of separate estates, and their often uncertain status, see Lee Holcombe, *Wives and Property: Reform of Married Women's Property Law in Nineteenth Century England* (Toronto University Press, 1983), pp. 37–47; Susan Moller Okin, 'Patriarchy and Married Women's Property in England: Questions on Some Current Views', *Eighteenth-Century Studies*, 17 (1983–4), 124–6, 134–5; and Mary Shanley, *Feminism, Marriage and the Law in Victorian England 1850–1895* (Princeton University Press, 1989), pp. 58–60.

15 Critics have long pondered this. See, for example, Nicole Diederich, 'The Art of Comparison: Remarriage in Anne Brontë's *The Tenant of Wildfell Hall*', *Rocky Mountain Review of Language and Literature*, 57 (2003), 25–41.

16 A not inconsiderable sum, worth in the region of £1.5 million today, a calculation based on the Retail Prices Index (RPI).

CHAPTER 36

Class

Elizabeth Langland

The father of Charlotte, Emily and Anne Brontë was born Patrick Brunty or Prunty on 17 March 1777 into a humble family of farm labourers in County Down, Ireland. One of ten children, he was apprenticed to several jobs. Through the fortuitous interest of the Revd Andrew Harshaw, who offered to tutor and then sponsored the promising lad, he became a teacher – a career that led him to St John's College, Cambridge, as a 'sizar' or poor scholar, where he earned his bachelor of arts degree on 10 August 1806. That simply described trajectory masks the enormous determination and energy represented in what was an extraordinary achievement for someone from his background. Patrick's success enabled him to secure a series of Anglican curacies and finally, at the age of forty-three, the desirable position of perpetual curate of Haworth parish, thereby establishing his family firmly within the middle classes. His marriage, at the age of thirty-five, to Maria Branwell, from a well-to-do Cornish middle-class family, further solidified that status. At some point, Patrick changed the spelling of his last name, adding the diaeresis over the final 'e' to indicate that the name had two syllables. We do not know why he chose to introduce it, but we may speculate that it was part of his transformation from the labouring to the middle classes.

In the family situations of both Patrick and Maria, we see the enormous fluidity in class status that was transforming Britain in the nineteenth century. The roots of that change may be traced to England's agricultural revolution in the eighteenth century, which set the stage for the country's industrial revolution. The result of a series of Enclosure Acts, the agricultural revolution saw common lands gradually aggregated into larger estates, with the result that a populace that had subsisted on those common lands was increasingly forced to become tenant farmers and labourers on individual estates. In effect, the agricultural revolution disrupted the old place-bound cottage industries and guilds (in which a son was apprenticed to his father's trade) and created a class of labourers prepared to move to wherever there was work. England was thus ripe for the industrial revolution, having already created a mobile work-force ready to leave their homes to seek their fortunes in the emerging cities and factories.

The new wealth generated by industrialization and the rise of new occupations created unprecedented class mobility, which is exemplified not only in Patrick's rise but also in that of his father-in-law. Maria Branwell's father owned a prosperous grocery store and accumulated sufficient wealth in trade to move his family into the middle classes. We may recollect the Bingley family in Jane Austen's *Pride and Prejudice*, whose father had similarly acquired such wealth in trade that the family was able to leave the commercial life, purchase a country estate and 'retire' to its management – fitting employment for a gentleman. In only one generation, the Bingley sisters learned to be contemptuous of Elizabeth Bennet's uncle, Mr Gardiner, a prosperous tradesman who lives in Cheapside, 'within view of his own warehouses'.[1] Middle-class status, of course, exists on a broad continuum and encompasses a wide range, from those in trade or professions living off their wages to those who live on income produced by their estates or investments. Many who joined the middle classes aspired to purchase an estate and became part of the landed gentry; the estate would normally be passed to the next generation, the eldest son inheriting and any younger sons taking up employments deemed fitting for a gentleman, typically in the military or clergy. For many in the middle classes, as would be true for the Brontë children, suitable employment would be necessary for their support.

As a clergyman, Patrick Brontë had entered the middle classes, the signature of which was employing at least one servant, who, if a sole servant, was typically a maid of all work.[2] At the parsonage, the Brontës initially employed two house servants. After Mrs Brontë's death, Tabitha Aykroyd joined the family as servant and cook, influencing the talented children with her local tales and lore; she also helped raise them under the supervision of their aunt Elizabeth Branwell.

Although servants do not play prominent roles in the Brontë fiction, their presence always serves as a marker of the protagonists' middle-class status. For example, when Jane Eyre accepts the very modest post of village schoolmistress at Morton, she is granted the services of a little orphan girl who functions as a 'handmaid' (III.v.358). The exception to this lack of prominence is, of course, the servant Nelly Dean in *Wuthering Heights*. Nelly narrates most of the actual story and figures in the evolution of the plot. Her pragmatic, commonsensical approach to events lends credibility to an unworldly tale, even as that same conventional approach also seriously limits her ability to understand the tale she tells. Further, her servant status allows her both unique access to all the characters (a necessity for the narrative) and the ability to illuminate the class tensions that exist in it, particularly Heathcliff's status as an outsider in relation to the landed gentry: the Earnshaws of Wuthering Heights and the Lintons of Thrushcross Grange. Yet, because Nelly is a servant and peripheral to the action, the novel's events leave her own situation essentially untransformed.

Although the Brontë family had achieved middle-class status and Patrick was in the fortunate situation of having procured the Haworth curacy – fortunate because, as he wrote, '[t]his Living . . . is mine for life, no-one can take it from me . . . My salary is not large, it is only about two hundred a year. But in addition to this two hundred a year I have a good House, which is mine for life also, and is rent free'[3] – his children faced the sure necessity of finding not only work, but appropriate employment for the middle-class children of a clergyman. The three sisters anticipated with no pleasure the usual route for genteel, educated women: teaching – either as a mistress in a school or as a governess in a private home. Branwell, as a man, had more options, and his talents initially seemed to promise a distinguished career. His father dedicated both his own time and his scarce funds to his son's education, hiring, for example, a painting instructor. The early attempt to launch Branwell as an artist failed, however. This debacle presaged the future, in which his conduct in various employments, as a clerk on the railway and a tutor in private families, ultimately led to dismissal. Certainly, he was not prepared to apply himself to consolidating the middle-class status that his father had secured with such effort.

Although the class conventions that shaped the Brontës' lives figure in all their novels, a focus on two – Emily's *Wuthering Heights* and Charlotte's *Shirley* – illuminates the ways in which class affects events and characters. Class is at once central and incidental to the plot of *Wuthering Heights*. While it is important not to reduce the complex relationship between Heathcliff and the worlds of Wuthering Heights and Thrushcross Grange to one of class differences only, nonetheless those differences motivate the plot and play a significant role in the development of Catherine and Heathcliff's relationship.

We see Heathcliff first through Lockwood's eyes, 'a dark-skinned gypsy in aspect, in dress and manners a gentleman' (1.i.3), and soon, through Nelly's narrative, learn of his alleged origin as a 'gipsy brat' (1.iv.31). Heathcliff's arrival at the Heights as a young boy of indeterminate age allows the normal constraints of class to be erased in the easy childhood companionship he forges with Catherine. However, Hindley, the Earnshaw son and heir, quickly comes to regard Heathcliff as a 'usurper of his parent's affections and his privileges' (1.iv.33). On his father's death, Hindley sets about Heathcliff's degradation, starving him of education and reducing him to a common stable-boy. Unsurprisingly, Heathcliff's revenge is to take over Hindley's property, replace him as master of Wuthering Heights and relegate Hindley's son Hareton to the same role that he had himself occupied as a boy under Hindley's rule.

Catherine understands Heathcliff in both otherworldly and class-orientated terms: on the one hand, she describes Heathcliff as 'more myself than I am'; on the other, she anticipates that by marrying Linton she will be rich and able to 'aid Heathcliff to rise, and place him out of [her] brother's power' (1.ix.71–2). She argues that her relationship with Heathcliff transcends social considerations; but those considerations are fundamental to her decision to marry Linton, as she recognizes that '[i]t would degrade [her] to marry Heathcliff now' (1.ix.71).

Heathcliff responds to the class barrier by disappearing from the Heights, returning only when he has the wealth and bearing of a gentleman. He uses class to seek revenge on Hindley Earnshaw and the Lintons, first seducing Isabella Linton and provoking Edgar Linton's dismay at 'the degradation of an alliance with a nameless man' and concern that 'in default of heirs male', his own property 'might pass into such a one's power' (1.x.89), and then reducing Hindley's son, Hareton, who 'should now be the first gentleman in the neighbourhood ... to a state of complete dependence ... [so that he now] lives in his own house as [an unpaid] servant' (II.iii.166). When Heathcliff forces his sickly son Linton to marry Catherine and Edgar Linton's daughter, he gleefully anticipates the 'triumph of seeing *my* descendent fairly lord of their estates; my child hiring their children, to till their fathers' lands for wages' (II.iv.184).

This classic revenge plot based on social-class reversals is, however, finally irrelevant to the fulfilment Heathcliff seeks, a consummation with Catherine. As he senses its approach – 'Today, I am within sight of my heaven' – he relinquishes his pursuit of Hareton's and young Cathy's degradation. At his death, the order on which he had wreaked his anger quietly re-establishes itself in the marriage of the cousins Catherine Linton and Hareton Earnshaw. Heathcliff's lineage is extinguished, but the 'frightful, life-like gaze of exultation' (II.xx.298) on his face suggests that his real goal has been achieved.

Charlotte's story of class conflict differs markedly from Emily's tale. Despite talk of fairies, *Shirley* is solidly grounded in the pain and suffering that class expectations and conventions can inflict. The class conventions that proscribe meaningful work and confine middle-class women to the domestic sphere are detailed in Caroline Helstone's anguished existence in her uncle's rectory. Caroline is wasting away for want of meaningful work: 'a funereal inward cry haunted and harassed her: the heaviness of a broken spirit, and of pining and palsying faculties, settled slow on her buoyant youth. Winter seemed conquering her spring: the mind's soil and its treasures were freezing gradually to barren stagnation' (I.x.158). The only project she can frame that holds out any prospect of relief is to 'take a situation, to be a governess – she could do nothing else' (I.xi.159). However, her uncle's wealth is sufficient to sustain her in idleness, so that even her impassioned request to be able to pursue the one respectable avenue for employment open to her is emphatically denied: 'I will not have it said that my niece is a governess' (I.xi.163). But the topic does not die there. In response to Shirley's query regarding the impossible – 'don't you wish you had a profession – a trade?' – Caroline responds, 'I wish it fifty times a day. As it is, I often wonder what I came into the world for ... successful labour has its recompense; a vacant, weary, lonely, hopeless life has none' (II.i.193).

The narrator's passionate appeal to the 'Men of England' to create occupations for their daughters testifies to the dire effects of idleness imposed by social proprieties: '[L]ook at your poor girls, many of them fading around you ... Fathers! Cannot you alter these things? ... seek for them an interest and an occupation which shall raise them above the flirt, the manoeuvrer, the mischief-making tale-bearer' (II.xi.330).

Caroline's profound ennui plunges her into a wasting illness from which she is rescued only by the timely discovery of her mother. Tellingly, however, the full restoration of her health and spirits depends on quiet companionable moments in the garden with the working man William Farren. Her mother, Mrs Pryor, 'wondered how her daughter could be so much at ease with a "man of the people"' (III.ii.372); but in fact the two share experiences of debilitating constrictions on their abilities due to social conventions.

Although less circumscribed than those of women, men's lives are also blighted by the pressures of social custom. The Gérard Moore brothers, Robert and Louis, come from a family of wealthy merchants – the Gérards of Antwerp – that has suffered total ruin in the 'shock of the French Revolution'. That fall encompasses the Yorkshire firm of Moore, allied with the Antwerp house by marriage; Robert has inherited the liabilities of the firm and a relentless determination to rebuild it. The less mercantile Louis, educated in England, has 'adopted the very arduous and very modest career of a teacher' (I.v.55) – a tutor in a private family – and he suffers a loss of caste comparable to what a governess would have to submit to. Although Robert is in trade – and like the Gardiners in *Pride and Prejudice* also lives within sight of his warehouses – he enjoys a higher social cachet than Louis, because he may prosper and build wealth. Energetic and talented tradesmen could amass riches and purchase all the trappings of a gentleman, including a socially superior wife. It was not inappropriate for a prosperous tradesman to seek a higher-born woman's hand in marriage; the historians Lawrence and Jeanne Stone note 'the relatively early acceptance of self-made men, as companions or marriage partners, by persons of genteel birth and elite status'.[4] Thus it is natural for Robert to aspire to marrying the wealthy heiress Shirley Keeldar. In his conceit, he interprets Shirley's interest in him as love; and even though he does not love her – 'never felt as if nature meant her to be my other and better self' – he flings off his doubts, 'saying brutally, I should be rich with her, and ruined without her' (III.vii.446). Shirley rejects him, not for his class presumptions but for his lack of love: 'You spoke like a brigand who demanded my purse, rather than like a lover who asked my heart' (III.vii.447).

In contrast, the tutor Louis, who truly loves Shirley, feels he cannot declare his passion. In the Sympsons' household, where he lives, Louis is a 'satellite . . . connected, yet apart. . . . the daughters saw in him an abstraction, not a man' (III.iii.379). Unlike the Sympson daughters, Shirley has perceived Louis' worth and learned to love him; but since she is a woman and his social superior, convention dictates that she cannot take the initiative. Speaking to each other and of each other in the third person, Louis and Shirley detail the social constraints that keep them apart. Louis' complaint that '[s]he received me haughtily: she meted out a wide space between us and kept me aloof' is met by Shirley's riposte: 'She was an excellent pupil! Having seen you distant, she at once learned to withdraw.' To Louis' response that '[c]onscience, and honour . . . kept me sundered with ponderous fetters. She was free', Shirley answers simply: 'Never free to compromise her self-respect: to seek where she had been shunned' (III.v.432). Ultimately, enabled by her independent fortune, Shirley defies convention, first by refusing the highly eligible baronet Sir Philip Nunnely and then by claiming Louis as her husband. However, the irony with which Charlotte concludes this novel suggests that this happy resolution is a 'romance', not the 'real, cool, and solid' substance that the narrator promised at the outset (1.i.5).

This ironic acknowledgement of the harsh realities of social-class expectations confirms the strictures under which the genius of the three gifted sisters had to emerge. Their seemingly preordained fates to grind out their lives teaching gave way, with Charlotte's serendipitous discovery of Emily's poetry, to the possibility that they might profitably pursue that other profession available to middle-class women: writing. Sadly, there remained but a short period in which their extraordinary talents could blossom.

NOTES

1 Jane Austen, *Pride and Prejudice*, II.ii; Oxford World's Classics (Oxford University Press, 2004), p. 108.

2 Pamela Horn, *The Rise and Fall of the Victorian Servant* (New York: St Martin's Press, 1975), p. 17, notes that 'when Seebohm Rowntree conducted his survey of York in 1888, he took "the keeping or not keeping of domestic servants" as the dividing line between "the working classes and those of a higher social scale"', a practice that had long been in effect.

3 In a letter of 21 Apr. 1823 to Mary Burder's mother; Dudley Green (ed.), *The Letters of the Reverend Patrick Brontë* (Stroud: Nonsuch, 2005), p. 46.

4 Lawrence Stone and Jeanne C. Fawtier Stone, *An Open Elite? England 1540–1880* (Oxford University Press, 1984), p. 20.

CHAPTER 37

Careers for middle-class women

Elizabeth Langland

Opportunities for employment in early Victorian England, especially for women, were shaped by class considerations. For middle-class women those possibilities were slim, being limited by the expectation that a respectable woman would pursue a career in what was designated the 'private' sphere – that is, do work that could be carried out in the home or in home-like settings, such as private academies and schools for girls. Naturally, those careers were precious few: teaching and writing were the primary avenues for women's employment, although options such as painting, sketching and pursuing other fine arts were also possible. Opportunities for a middle-class woman to engage in any retail enterprise were hedged about with special qualifications, as we shall see.

This insistence on respectable women remaining in the private sphere obviously excluded them from a vast array of careers that depended on everyday interactions in public contexts. There are some exceptions, of course; but whenever boundaries were transgressed, they were typically breached in ways that still preserved a stereotype of womanly nature as self-sacrificing rather than self-serving or self-assertive. Thus it is not surprising that when a genteel woman fought convention, as Florence Nightingale did, she chose a service occupation, nursing.

WOMEN AND EDUCATION

Middle-class women who needed to work typically became governesses in private families or schoolmistresses in academies for girls. The sphere of women's teaching was circumscribed partly because women's education was so limited. The goal of that education in early nineteenth-century England did not extend far beyond providing a finishing polish to a girl's manners by means of, to quote Anne Brontë's Agnes Grey, the acquisition of 'showy accomplishments . . . French, German, music, singing, dancing, fancy-work, and a little drawing' (*Agnes Grey*, vii.58). It was almost impossible for a woman to secure a good education except by dint of self-application and discipline, yet there, too, she was inevitably limited. The universities were barred to her; women could not attend Oxford and Cambridge until the 1860s and were unable to earn degrees until several decades later. Even a woman as distinguished as George Eliot was ambivalent about the effects of a rigorous course of education on woman's nature.

Governessing usually entailed physical drudgery and emotional battery. The governess had no constituency within the household: she was marooned as on an island, neither the equal of the family nor clearly beneath them, as were the other servants. Unless a governess was very fortunate in her family, she could expect to find that she would be given entire responsibility for the children without any significant power to exercise control. She often experienced great loneliness and the humiliation of finding her frequently substantial talents ignored or despised, a situation Charlotte captured in a letter to Emily in June 1839: 'I see now more clearly than I have ever done before that a private governess has no existence, is not considered as a living rational being except as connected with the wearisome duties she has to fulfil' (Smith, *Letters*, vol. 1, p. 191).

Given Charlotte's experiences, it is somewhat ironic that Anne's *Agnes Grey* more realistically details the loneliness and mortifications of being a governess than does Charlotte's *Jane Eyre*, whose protagonist has one pliable child to instruct and a master quickly captivated by her. Anne was ultimately much more successful than Charlotte as a teacher, and her pupils in the second family with whom she resided, the Robinsons, remained friends for her lifetime.

Difficult as a governess's situation was, being a schoolmistress proved no better for Emily and Charlotte. Emily taught briefly, a position Charlotte described in a letter to Ellen Nussey as 'slavery' (Smith, *Letters*, vol. 1, p. 182). Charlotte held two teaching positions, first at Roe Head and later in Brussels, both places where she had been a happy pupil. She loathed teaching, however, and felt only a sense of 'Duty – Necessity . . . stern Misstresses [*sic*] who will not be disobeyed' (in an earlier letter to Ellen of 2 July 1835; Smith, *Letters*, vol. 1, p. 140). Charlotte's experience was not Jane Eyre's more positive one of finding affection and reward through teaching 'rustics' in a village school, work procured by St John Rivers to enable her to provide for herself (*Jane Eyre*, III.vi.365–6). Despite Jane's contentment with her school, she nonetheless experiences substantial relief on receiving her uncle's inheritance of £20,000: the legacy liberates her and her cousins, the Riverses, from the burden of uncongenial employments very similar to those of the Brontë sisters.

Because opening one's own school freed one from the social subjection of working for others, many young women strove to amass the resources to start their own educational establishments. The Brontë sisters initially planned to open a school in Haworth Parsonage until their own failure to gain pupils, and their brother Branwell's increasing degradation and drunkenness, made the dream impossible. At this time of near-paralysis for the family, Charlotte happened to discover some of Emily's poetry, and the door opened for the three sisters to the possibility of writing as a profession. As previous chapters have shown, they soon turned their talents from poetry to novels.

WOMEN AND WRITING

From the eighteenth century onwards, the readers of novels came from all the literate strata in society. They included both men and women, though there were frequently expressed concerns about the advisability of making novels too readily available to young girls, who might be adversely influenced by them. Generally speaking, however, novel-reading was an established activity for women by the dawn of the Victorian age, not least because domestic ideology discouraged women's 'work' and the increasing wealth generated by the industrial revolution produced leisure hours which middle-class women needed to fill.

Jane Eyre sounds an early clarion call for freedom from the constraints of enforced leisure:

Women are supposed to be very calm generally: but women feel just as men feel; they need exercise for their faculties, and a field for their efforts as much as their brothers do; they suffer from too rigid a restraint, too absolute a stagnation, precisely as men would suffer; and it is narrow-minded in their more privileged fellow-creatures to say that they ought to confine themselves to making puddings and knitting stockings, to playing on the piano and embroidering bags. It is thoughtless to condemn them, or laugh at them, if they seek to do more or learn more than custom has pronounced necessary for their sex. (*Jane Eyre*, I.xii.109)

This cry is echoed in the description of Caroline Helstone's circumscribed lady's existence as 'a long, slow death' (*Shirley*, II.xii.335). *Villette* recalls these images of immobilization in Lucy Snowe's restlessness on finding that 'a great many women and girls' are expected to pass their lives 'as a bark slumbering through halcyon weather, in a harbour still as glass' (iv.35).

From the perspective of the early twentieth century, Virginia Woolf captured the challenges facing Victorian women writers in her depiction of that avatar of the Victorian home, the 'Angel in the House' – basically the social expectation that a middle-class wife, mother or daughter would sublimate all of her own needs and desires to the well-being of her family, sacrificing time and privacy to her domestic responsibilities. Woolf claims that she had to kill her domestic predecessor to prevent her from destroying her own career: 'Had I not killed her she would have killed me. She would have plucked the heart out of my writing.'[1]

Inspired by the prospect of employing her talents as a writer, the twenty-year-old Charlotte Brontë sought support from England's Poet Laureate, Robert Southey. His reply (which he referred to elsewhere as a 'cooling admonition') was characteristically disheartening. In answering his letter, Charlotte revealed the inner conflicts it provoked:

> You do not forbid me to write ... You only warn me against the folly of neglecting real duties, for the sake of imaginative pleasures ... I have endeavoured not only attentively to observe all the duties a woman ought to fulfil, but to feel deeply interested in them. I don't always succeed, for sometimes when I'm teaching or sewing I would rather be reading or writing; but I try to deny myself[.] (Smith, *Letters*, vol. 1, pp. 168–9)[2]

Despite the fact that middle-class women lacked the time and the proverbial 'room of one's own' that made Woolf's fiction possible and 'were possessed only of a single sitting-room between them', many women wrested an advantage from their situation by dint of sheer determination. The social nexus that structured their existence encouraged 'all the literary training that a woman had in the early nineteenth century ... training in the observation of character, in the analysis of emotion'.[3] Middle-class women at home began writing prolifically.

Jane Austen helped usher in the century. To Virginia Woolf, she was unusual because her literary gifts were perfectly matched to her constricted circumstances. The compatibility Jane Austen felt with her conditions, 'glad that a hinge creaked, so that she might hide her manuscript before any one came in', was not enjoyed by most of her successors, especially if they were wives with children and large households to manage.[4]

Elizabeth Gaskell and Margaret Oliphant, who both spoke eloquently about the many challenges facing them, were more typical of women writing within the domestic sphere, coping with a multitude of responsibilities for husbands, children and complicated households. Like several other professionally successful women, Gaskell made a point of her capabilities as a housekeeper.[5] Her felicitous circumstances, however, cannot be taken as normative for women writers in the nineteenth century. That most women with literary aspirations were distracted by the multiple claims on their time is apparent in Gaskell's response to a woman who had sent her a manuscript and expressed frustration with her lot:

I dare say you already know how much time may be saved, by beginning any kind of work in good time, and not driving all in a hurry to the last moment ... try hard to arrange your work well. That is a regular piece of headwork and taxes a woman's powers of organization; but the reward is immediate and great.[6]

Even writers who shared Gaskell's talent for organization often found themselves less happily situated within their households. Margaret Oliphant, for example, became the primary breadwinner for her extended family: husband, children, mother, brothers, nieces and nephews. The pressures she faced in struggling to produce an adequate income to support her establishment led her to adopt a more pragmatic tone. She claimed, 'I have written because it gave me pleasure, because it came natural to me, because it was like talking or breathing, besides the big fact that it was necessary for me to work for my children.' Like Jane Austen, Oliphant wrote in the family drawing room, 'where all the (feminine) life of the house [went] on'; she doubted that she 'ever had two hours undisturbed (except at night, when everybody [was] in bed) during [her] whole literary life'.[7]

In her *Life of Charlotte Brontë*, Gaskell succinctly captured the tension for a woman writer:

When a man becomes an author, it is probably merely a change of employment to him ... But no other can take up the quiet regular duties of the daughter, the wife, or the mother ... a woman's principal work in life is hardly left to her own choice; nor can she drop the domestic charges devolving on her as an individual, for the exercise of the most splendid talents that were ever bestowed. (Gaskell, *Life*, pp. 271–2)

At the same time as women picked up pens, they adopted male or masculine-sounding pseudonyms. As is well known, Charlotte, Emily and Anne Brontë published their novels as Currer, Ellis and Acton Bell. Charlotte explained the rationale of their pseudonyms: '[T]he ambiguous choice [was] dictated by a sort of conscientious scruple at assuming Christian names positively masculine, while we did not like to declare ourselves women, because ... we had a vague impression that authoresses are liable to be looked on with prejudice'

('Biographical Notice', in Smith, *Letters*, vol. II, p. 743). Perhaps this same concern with how her works would be perceived if known to be from the hand of a woman motivated Mary Ann Evans to adopt the pseudonym George Eliot. In Evans' case, there was also concern that the reception of her work would suffer from her reputation as a woman who had eloped to the Continent with a married man. Still, even women of impeccable reputations had to worry that they might be accused of having lived the lives they merely imagined.

Charlotte's first published novel, *Jane Eyre*, enjoyed an immediate popular success, and it set the stage for the fortunes of her subsequent novels. Complicating that early popular reception, however, was the critical concern about her book's immorality and confusion between her sisters and herself. As previous chapters have described, the Bells' common surname allowed the unscrupulous Thomas Newby to attempt to boost sales by claiming that Ellis/Emily's *Wuthering Heights* and Acton/Anne's *Agnes Grey* were from the same hand that wrote the popular *Jane Eyre*. Charlotte and Anne rushed to London to set matters straight with Charlotte's publishers Smith, Elder & Co.; they also visited Newby, to confront him with his lie (see Charlotte's letter to Mary Taylor of 4 September 1848; Smith, *Letters*, vol. II, p. 112). Nonetheless, the confusion about the three writers' identities persisted; and when Anne published *The Tenant of Wildfell Hall*, which chronicles one man's drunken, immoral and brutal career, critics were quick to recollect the tendency of earlier 'Bell' novels to focus on depraved and dissolute behaviour. Charges of impropriety continued to dog the Brontës once their identities as women were discovered. Charlotte's 'Biographical Notice of Ellis and Acton Bell', written after the deaths of her sisters, was motivated in part by a desire to redeem their reputations: 'to wipe the dust off their gravestones, and leave their dear names free from soil' (Smith, *Letters*, vol. II, p. 747).

ALTERNATIVE WORK FOR MIDDLE-CLASS WOMEN

Although teaching and writing dominated career paths for middle-class women throughout early and mid Victorian England, occasionally a woman from the middle classes could push the boundaries a little further, adapting the home to other genteel pursuits. While many women dabbled in drawing and painting, a few pursued the visual arts for the same reasons that their sisters cultivated their literary abilities: they needed the money. Anne presents such a figure in *The Tenant of*

Wildfell Hall, a mother who has left her husband and who forthrightly declares, when asked about keeping and displaying her paintings: 'No, I cannot afford to paint for my own amusement.' Her son adds, 'Mamma sends all her pictures to London ... and somebody sells them for her there, and sends us the money' (v.41). Women artists often used men as their agents. Part of the reason for this was a desire to secure their anonymity and procure less partial judgements of their work, but the practice also kept middle-class women out of the public marketplace.

Although women did sometimes operate as merchants in Victorian Britain, being 'in trade' would usually have branded them firmly as lower-middle or servant class. *Shirley*'s Caroline longs for a profession or trade 'fifty times a day' because 'successful labour has its recompense; a vacant, weary, lonely, hopeless life has none'. The damaging taint of trade for a lady is dramatized in Gaskell's *Cranford* when Miss Matty's social status is threatened by the collapse of the Town and County Bank, in which most of her funds are invested. She is persuaded to adopt the expedient of selling choice teas from her home (not, we note, from a shop); but first, she must be rescued from any potential loss of standing by Mrs Jamieson, the reigning arbiter of social class, who must consider 'whether by [selling tea] Miss Matty would forfeit her right to the privileges of society in Cranford'. Mrs Jamieson pronounces that 'whereas a married woman takes her husband's rank by the strict laws of precedence, an unmarried woman retains the station her father occupied'.[8] Of course, the amusing arbitrariness of this decision points to the flexibility of class boundaries in nineteenth-century Britain, a topic for another chapter (see Chapter 36).

Despite the fluidity of class in Victorian England, there were strong social pressures that effectively limited middle-class women's work to the domestic sphere and to caring or 'feminine' professions, such as teaching, writing and nursing. To be a middle-class woman meant that one was ensconced, whether comfortably or not, at home, where women's remunerated work could be circumscribed within a legitimized sphere of private activity, subordinate to selfless concern for the needs of others.

Given the restrictive expectations and conventions that circumscribed their activities, middle-class women used the tools available to them, particularly the pen, with striking effectiveness. Questioning their status and advancing their standing, they paved the way for expanded opportunities for the women who followed them.

NOTES

1 Virginia Woolf, 'Professions for Women', a speech delivered in 1931; easily accessible in Sandra Gilbert and Susan Gubar (eds.), *The Norton Anthology of Literature by Women* (New York: Norton, 1985), where the relevant passage is quoted on p. 1385.

2 The correspondence between Southey and Charlotte took place in March 1837, a short time before Charlotte's twenty-first birthday.

3 Virginia Woolf, *A Room of One's Own* (1929); references here are to the 1957 Harcourt, Brace & World edn (New York and Burlingame), p. 70.

4 *Ibid.*, pp. 71 and 70, in that order.

5 The Brontë sisters also took pride in executing housework well; see, for instance, Micael M. Clarke, 'Brontë's *Jane Eyre* and the Grimms' Cinderella', *Studies in English Literature 1500–1900*, 40.4 (2000), 695–710.

6 J. A. V. Chapple and Arthur Pollard (eds.), *The Letters of Mrs Gaskell* (Manchester University Press, 1966), pp. 694–5.

7 Margaret Oliphant, *The Autobiography*, arranged and ed. 'Mrs Harry Coghill' (*née* Annie Louisa Walker) (1899; University of Chicago Press, 1988), pp. 4, 24.

8 Elizabeth Gaskell, *Cranford*, ed. Elizabeth Porges Watson with an introduction and notes by Dinah Birch, Oxford World's Classics (Oxford University Press, 2011), chapter 15, p. 143.

CHAPTER 38

Marriage and family life

Marianne Thormählen

The uniqueness of the Brontë family is often asserted, but in some ways the Brontës were very typical of their time. Like most middle-class English couples, Patrick Brontë and Maria Branwell were no longer young when they married (thirty-five and twenty-nine respectively); in spite of this they had a large number of children, contributing to the sharp rise in the population of the British Isles in the beginning of the nineteenth century (at her death, after almost nine years of marriage, Maria had spent most of her married life being pregnant); the widowed father attempted to remarry, partly to secure a good home-maker for his children; and as that project failed, the dead wife's sister exercised the role of domestic manager until her death.[1]

Other aspects of family life at Haworth Parsonage were also in agreement with dominant values and views in early nineteenth-century Britain. Above all, family members were bound together by intense affection. The parents' marriage had been a love match freely entered into on both sides, again in the best English tradition.[2] The children it produced were the beneficiaries of that love, although motherless from an early age: Patrick Brontë may have had his faults, but he was a devoted father whose dedication to his children's welfare and happiness was never in doubt among those who knew the family. Besides, as a clergyman, whose home was part of his professional sphere, he was in a particularly good position to embody the early nineteenth-century ideal of the domesticated husband.[3]

Typically, too, the Brontë children loved their home, like so many of their contemporaries. In the early nineteenth century, the idea of the loving home as a sacred temple where virtue was cultivated, security guaranteed, and warm affection kept inmates emotionally strong and pure became extraordinarily powerful;[4] and volumes of verse were filled with poetical effusions on childhood paradises, now often lost to or distant from speakers nostalgic for the perfect place that was home. Although the parsonage lacked that figure who should have kept it all together, a wife and mother, it was the north to which every Brontë compass pointed.

It is the more noteworthy that so much of the Brontës' fiction is set in unhappy, sometimes hellish, homes. Wuthering Heights, Gateshead in *Jane Eyre* and Grassdale Manor in *The Tenant of Wildfell Hall* are places of such suffering that even an uncertain fate away from them is preferable to residence there for Isabella Heathcliff, the child Jane Eyre and Helen Huntingdon. The latter two houses are presided over by mothers; but one is cruel to the childish outsider, and the other is forced to realize how helpless even the most resilient woman is when her efforts to create a good home run counter to the inclinations of her husband.

The position of married women under the legal principle known as coverture is described in Chapter 35. Put simply, the legal situation of a married woman in the early and mid nineteenth century amounted to total subjugation under her husband's authority. She did not exist as a separate subject in the eyes of the law, and her husband – whatever his failings – was entitled to any income she might earn by her own efforts. Divorce was impossible for a woman except in extreme circumstances (such as the husband's incestuous adultery), and then only at considerable expense. Until the first Infant Custody Act (the Custody of Children Act) of 1839, a woman who lived separated from her husband had to face the fact that it was up to him whether she could even see her children, to say nothing of having them to live with her. Even after the passing of that Act, in the wake of the Caroline Norton case, a separated wife's expectation to have a child under seven live with her could be foiled by the Lord Chancellor. Besides, she would have to lead an entirely blameless life, which meant that any comfort derived from more congenial male companionship was denied her.[5]

Clearly, then, a woman in Helen Huntingdon's situation could not have lived apart from her husband without renouncing her child. A man in Heathcliff's position would have been entitled to insist on his son's being sent to live with him (that threat is expressed in *Wuthering Heights* long before Isabella's death; II.iii.161–2 and 165). And a husband in Huntingdon's or Heathcliff's situation could have asserted his right to have his wife returned to him for the purpose of sexual intercourse if he had wanted to.

In view of the indissoluble nature of the marriage bond, it was not unnatural for writers of conduct books for married women to encourage their readers to do whatever they could to keep their husbands in a good temper, however offensive such advice seems to a later age. The Brontë fiction does not supply any instance of long-term success along these lines, however; Helen Huntingdon's early efforts to soothe and cheer her errant husband are of no avail, and her friend Milicent Hattersley's meekness does not abate her husband's tyranny – if anything, it provokes him to additional cruelty. The only example of a paragon whose constant endeavour to raise her spouse's spirits succeeds in creating a happy home is Mrs Grey in *Agnes Grey*, and in that case husband and wife are devoted to each other, though the former is of a rather morbid disposition.

When loving marriages occur in the Brontë novels, they usually do so as part of happily-ever-after conclusions. Even the marriage of William and Frances Crimsworth, the only happy union to be dwelt on at any length, only takes up one chapter, the last in *The Professor*. Occasionally, winding-up words of reassurance to readers are decidedly hasty; for instance, a brief paragraph must suffice with regard to Diana and Mary Rivers' marriages (*Jane Eyre*, III.xii.452). Indeed, married unhappiness is far more prevalent than domestic bliss in the Brontë fiction: the Yorkes in *Shirley* are fundamentally incompatible, which makes for an interestingly dysfunctional family; the Bloomfields and Ashbys in *Agnes Grey* and the Edward Crimsworths of *The Professor* are unions of silly but harmless women with nasty bullies; and the enormities of Emily Brontë's Heathcliff and Anne's Arthur Huntingdon have a counterpart in Charlotte's James Helstone (in *Shirley*), the memory of whose infernal cruelty causes his wife to shudder even after twenty years.

Whenever the reader of a Brontë novel encounters a particularly happy domestic environment, it is more likely to be run by a widow or a spinster than by a wife. For example, the warm, cheerful and sensible home-maker Mrs Bretton in *Villette* is a widow of many years' standing, and the clergyman who enjoys the most comfortable home life of all the clerics in *Shirley* is Mr Hall, whose sister Margaret, 'spectacled and learned like himself, made him happy in his single state' (II.iii.228–9).[6]

Even so, a good marriage is desired by all the main Brontë protagonists. Jane Eyre's description of her union with Mr Rochester is a paean to the ideal of the companionate marriage, enhanced by its insistence on physical closeness and by the incorporation of the word 'free': 'To be together is for us to be at once as free as in solitude, as gay as in company' (*Jane Eyre*, III.xii.450–1). Life as an 'old maid' is never presented as preferable to a happy marriage, only as a state which does not preclude the achievement of something worthwhile (see *Shirley*, I.x and *The Professor*, xxv.236, the latter passage coming after Frances' resounding call for freedom from marital oppression). When a Brontë character talks about lifelong spinsterhood, the implication is that there are better things in life. Charlotte Brontë's letters convey the same impression.

In view of the perils of matrimony – in the Brontë fiction, *Jane Eyre* supplies a powerful reminder of its dangers for men – one may wonder why people were so eager to enter into it.[7] For women, it offered the prestige of the married woman and the chance to run their own establishments as mature adults. For men, a large part of the answer was of course sex; and the nineteenth-century pattern of swiftly repeated pregnancies even when lactation offered some protection against conceiving – and even at a stage in life when a woman's fertility had begun to decrease – suggests a high degree of sexual activity. Victorian women were not supposed to possess much knowledge about reproduction (let alone harbour any sexual appetite), but the Brontë sisters' much-criticized 'coarseness' places them in the category of women who knew something of the subject. A telling detail is Jane Eyre's observation that St John Rivers would be sure to have sex with her if she married him, in spite of not having the slightest desire for her ('Can I receive from him the bridal ring, endure all the forms of love (which I doubt not he would scrupulously observe) and know that the spirit was quite absent?' *Jane Eyre*, III.viii.405). The Anglican Church regarded sexual intercourse between spouses as an obligation;[8] and being a good son of the Church, St John would, in Jane's words, 'scrupulously observe' that injunction. Jane's qualms at the prospect – the word 'endure' is significant – are understandable in terms of the importance that the nineteenth century placed on love as the cornerstone of marriage; but they also imply that the author was quite aware of what 'all the forms of love' entailed.

What the unmarried state witholds is not only sexual satisfaction and the comfort of a companion but also the result of sexual union, children. Despite the dangers and suffering that maternity involved, nineteenth-century women were expected to yearn for motherhood. The desire for offspring was also supposed to be a strong incentive for men to marry; 'Children – (if it please God)' was the first 'pro' item on Charles Darwin's famous list of the arguments for and against matrimony.[9]

Historians of childhood have moved away from the idea, chiefly associated with Philippe Ariès, that pre-Enlightenment societies did not recognize the child as essentially different from the adult and that parental love of the kind we know today came in only with the age of sentiment in the eighteenth century.[10] Another notion that has not stood the test of time is that parents in the past did not allow themselves to become emotionally involved with infants they were as likely as not to lose, and that the death of a child, being such a common occurrence, did not cause distress.[11] Such records as can be consulted – the issue of sources is a notoriously difficult one here – suggest that parents have always loved their children, agonized over their young ones' pain when ill or injured and mourned for any child they lost.

This is a point that needs making in respect of the nineteenth century as well, as so many children did not live to adulthood. It is hard for a present-day student of the period to understand how loving parents could bear the bereavements that afflicted them. Letters and journals from the time speak of attempts to think of the dead child as an angel in heaven (see Chapter 4 on Patrick Brontë's letter of comfort to Eliza Brown). Without the hope of reunion in eternal bliss, such losses must have been unendurable; as it was, that hope coexisted with heartbreak articulated in the most harrowing terms.[12]

Some nineteenth-century representations of children depict them as angels on earth. Scholars who discuss conceptions of the child in the nineteenth century often present a dichotomy between the Romantic view of the child as the bearer of radiant innocence and the Puritan idea of children as tainted with original sin and hence in need of constant surveillance and strict correction.[13] As so often, such dichotomies are more helpful as models of thought patterns frequently articulated at a certain period than as characterizations of what most people actually thought, felt and practised.

Certainly, the Brontë novels do not contain a single angelic child, with the exception of the intellectually and morally precocious Helen Burns, in whom 'childness' is not a predominant characteristic. Naughty, even evil, children are more in evidence, for example John Reed in *Jane Eyre* and the Bloomfield brood in *Agnes Grey*. However, even they are not represented as congenitally wicked: the blame for their warped characters is laid on parents whose over-indulgence, stupidity and lack of moral fibre are seen to ruin their offspring.[14] Anne Brontë's description of young Agnes Grey's fond thoughts of guiding trusting little ones on the basis of her own memories of a happy childhood (chapter 1) is heavily overlaid with irony; and Charlotte satirized the Romantic idea of the angelic child in Mr Brocklehurst's greedy little hypocrite of a son, who was clever enough to know that the way to parental favour, and to the biscuit-tin, consisted in posing as 'a little angel here below' (*Jane Eyre*, I.iv.33).

The controversy between 'Helen Graham' and the inhabitants of Linden-Car, especially Gilbert Markham, in chapter 3 of *The Tenant of Wildfell Hall* is a particularly interesting example of how the fiction of the Brontës interacts with the debates of the time. The vulnerability of the child in combination with his impressionability places a heavy burden of responsibility on the parent who is his sole educator in every sense; and Helen's desperate seriousness, the reasons for which only become apparent halfway through the book, underlines the dimension of parenthood that engaged many commentators in the lifetime of the Brontës: the idea that parents' chief duty to their children was to make them fit for Heaven.[15] Two things make Helen's stance particularly remarkable: to twenty-first-century readers, her conviction that her darling's death would be preferable to his growing up 'a man of the world' seems strange to the point of repulsiveness; and a mid-nineteenth-century audience would query her resistance to the notion that while a girl should be shielded from temptation and danger, a boy must face them unprotected by the parental solicitude that would envelop any sister of his.

As children and adolescents at Wuthering Heights, Heathcliff and Catherine are neglected by their elders – apart from the occasional imposition of blows and pious reading – and respond by withdrawing into a world of their own creation, a world where their childish alliance forms the fundament that would ordinarily have been made up of parental care. When Catherine rejects this alliance, attracted by the splendours of the Grange and the adoration she receives there, that childhood world is shattered; Heathcliff is rendered permanently homeless and two naughty children become tormented adults, without any sense of development into maturity. As a study of childhood – an aspect of the novel often commented on by critics – *Wuthering Heights* deserves the epithet which was the highest praise that Charlotte Brontë could bestow, 'original'.

However typical the home life of the Brontës may appear when seen in relation to common family fortunes, patterns and conceptions in early nineteenth-century England, it was original in one particular respect: the freedom of thought and movement that allowed Patrick Brontë's children to evolve their imaginative worlds, stimulated by unrestricted reading and untrammelled by rules of propriety. Some of that freedom will simply have been due to their elders' lack of time to supervise them and interfere in their activities; Patrick Brontë was an extremely busy man, and running the household was no sinecure for Aunt Branwell. For the three Brontë girls, the liberty they enjoyed in their home fed their creativity and fostered their genius.[16] One may well wonder how Charlotte Nicholls, who found – somewhat to her surprise – that being married to a clergyman was a full-time job (a theme in letters to Miss Wooler and Ellen Nussey in late 1854; see Smith, *Letters*, vol. III, pp. 290–1 and 306–7), would have coped with the loss of her freedom in the long term.

Unfortunately, that struggle never had a chance to materialize and contribute to the massive engagement of nineteenth-century English literature with the problems of the domestic sphere.

NOTES

1 How typical all these characteristics are may be seen from part 3 of Leonore Davidoff and Catherine Hall's classic study *Family Fortunes: Men and Women of the English Middle Class, 1780–1850* (University of Chicago Press, 1987).

2 On the fundamental importance of mutual love and consent as the basis for marriage, see Alan Macfarlane, *Marriage and Love in England: Modes of Reproduction 1300–1840* (Oxford: Blackwell, 1986), *passim*, esp. pp. 127–9, 154–8 and 174–208.

3 On clerics as ideal husbands, see A. James Hammerton, *Cruelty and Companionship: Conflict in Nineteenth-Century Married Life* (London: Routledge, 1992), p. 79.

4 See, for instance, Walter E. Houghton, *The Victorian Frame of Mind, 1830–1870* (New Haven: Yale University Press, 1957), chapter 13.

5 See Lawrence Stone, *Road to Divorce: England 1530–1987* (Oxford University Press, 1990), *passim*, esp. pp. 169–79 and 361–2, and Macfarlane, *Marriage and Love*, pp. 225–31.

6 On sisters as housekeepers for unmarried brothers, see Davidoff and Hall, *Family Fortunes*, p. 350.

7 Insanity in a wife precluded divorce, a circumstance which Rochester refers to in a way that presupposes Jane's acquaintance with that fact (*Jane Eyre*, III. i.306).

8 See Macfarlane, *Marriage and Love*, pp. 304 and 315.

9 *Ibid.*, pp. 3–5.

10 For a comprehensive attack on the ideas of earlier scholars, including Ariès, see Linda A. Pollock, *Forgotten Children: Parent–Child Relations from 1500 to 1900* (Cambridge University Press, 1983), chapters 1 and 2.

11 *Ibid.*, pp. 51–2 and 127–8.

12 For examples, see Pollock, *Forgotten Children*, pp. 127–8, 130–4 and 140.

13 See, for instance, David Grylls, *Guardians and Angels: Parents and Children in Nineteenth-Century Literature* (London: Faber and Faber, 1978), *passim*, and Penny Kane, *Victorian Families in Fact and Fiction* (Basingstoke: Macmillan, 1995), pp. 46–9.

14 On parental responsibility for children's character development in relation to the Brontës, see Marianne Thormählen, *The Brontës and Education* (Cambridge University Press, 2007), chapter 4.

15 Cf. Davidoff and Hall, *Family Fortunes*, pp. 340–1.

16 For their brother, on the other hand, it was destructive; see Thormählen, *The Brontës and Education*, p. 46.

CHAPTER 39

Dress

Birgitta Berglund

Between the birth of the first of the Brontë siblings (Maria) in 1814 and the death of the last survivor (Charlotte) in 1855, both men's and women's fashions changed considerably, though women's certainly more than men's.

The first and perhaps greatest change in men's clothing was the disappearance of breeches. These knee-long garments, which showed off men's calves, had been universally worn during previous centuries; but during the first few decades of the nineteenth century, they were gradually replaced by long trousers. By the time of Queen Victoria's accession to the throne in 1837, breeches had all but disappeared, and a gentleman's costume consisted of trousers, coat and waistcoat – although before the 1860s, these were usually not of the same colour or material. The second important change in men's dress was the gradual disappearance of colour. The bright colours of the eighteenth century grew more and more sombre, via white, fawn and pale grey for trousers and brown, dark green and burgundy for coats, until by around 1860 black had become the standard for evening wear. The garment where bright colours remained for longest was the waistcoat; all through the 1850s, it was made of the same colourful silks, satins and brocades as women's dresses, and it was often brightly patterned or embroidered. Later in the century, however, the waistcoat also dwindled into obscurity, and men's dress more or less took on the appearance it has today, with three-piece suits of all black for the city and brown or dark green tweeds for the country.

The costume for women went through more, and more dramatic, changes. At the beginning of the century, the 'Empire' style of dress dominated. Gowns were made of thin, gauzy materials, low-cut and short-sleeved, with a straight and narrow skirt falling from below the bust and worn without petticoats. White was by far the most fashionable colour, although the snowiness of the white gown could be offset by strong colours for accessories and shawls. Large cashmere shawls, first imported from Kashmir in India and then increasingly manufactured in Britain, became coveted status symbols for women to wrap themselves in. They remained so for the whole of the century – so much so, in fact, that in *Villette*, published in 1853, the mere ownership of such a garment is enough to secure employment for the ignorant and tipsy Mrs Sweeny as nursery-governess to Madame Beck's children. 'I feel quite sure that without this "Cachemire" she would not have kept her footing in the pensionnat for two days', says Lucy Snowe. '[B]y virtue of it, and it only, she maintained the same a month' (viii.70).

The Empire style remained until about 1820, when the silhouette started to change. Skirts grew wider and started to sprout flounces at the hems which made them flare out rather than fall straight down, and big collars and puff sleeves widened the shoulder part of the dress. The waist, which had been just below the bust for almost thirty years, gradually dropped until it reached its natural position around 1840. At the same time it grew tighter, so that a slim waist accentuated by puffy sleeves and a wide skirt was the fashionable silhouette in the 1830s. Materials were sturdier than before, satins and silks having replaced thin cotton muslins, and bright colours had become popular as a reaction against the predominance of white for so many years. In the 1840s colours grew more sombre, dark greens and browns and dusky mauves now being in vogue – generally offset by white in the form of plain collars and cuffs, lace fichus or muslin frills at the neck and sleeves. Shoulders and sleeves grew tighter and narrower while skirts grew even wider, necessitating a large number of starched petticoats to support them. The introduction of the lightweight steel hoop crinoline was a relief to women, as it freed their legs from the layers of heavy and cumbersome petticoats; but that did not happen until 1856, the year after Charlotte's death.

The main point of difference between women's underwear then and now, however, was the corset. Virtually all nineteenth-century women were severely restricted in their movements and respiration by wearing tightly laced corsets virtually all the time. There were several reasons for wearing a corset. To begin with, there was a medical aspect to it: stays were considered essential for back support and good posture and could be compared to the practice of swaddling babies tightly to make them grow up straight. Then there was the moral aspect: a woman who did not wear a corset was considered indecent, 'loose', as if the structural firmness of the corseted body equalled a moral firmness. Finally, there was the aesthetic aspect: fat women laced themselves to look slimmer, and slim women used corsets to accentuate their slimness and to mould their

27 Charlotte's 'going away' dress, believed to have been worn by Charlotte Nicholls, *née* Brontë, on her honeymoon tour in Ireland

28 Whalebone corset belonging to Charlotte Brontë

bodies into the desired 'wasp-waist' shape. In this connection it should be pointed out that the corset not only compressed the waist and supported the back; it also worked as a push-up bra which emphasized the bust. Some corsets also contained padding for the small-busted. But the emphasis was on the waist. The ideal was an 18- to 19-inch waist, something very few, if any, women could boast naturally. The only solution was to use a corset to mould the body, and nineteenth-century steel and whalebone corsets were much more efficient in doing so than the simpler stays of earlier periods.

To what extent did women in the nineteenth century actually form or deform their bodies with their corsets? According to Valerie Steele's standard work on the subject, corset sizes normally varied from 18 to 30 inches.[1] As they were not intended to be laced fully closed, this means that the sizes of most women's waists when corseted would range between 20 and 32 inches. This tallies with the statement of a writer on the subject in 1866, who claimed that although a normal healthy woman usually had a natural waist of 28 to 29 inches, a fashionable young woman would not permit herself when corseted to exceed 24 inches, and many laced themselves down to 22 or even 20.[2] However, doctors and moralists were unanimous in condemning 'tight-lacing', that is, the extreme moulding of the body to a desired form. Tight-lacers were regarded as vain and wilful young women who endangered their present health and risked their future reproductive capacity in order to satisfy their vanity. When told that eighteen-year-old Aurelia, an unusually obnoxious schoolgirl in *The Professor*, has a 'waist disproportionally compressed by an inhumanly braced corset' (xii.89), Victorian readers would thus not have been surprised to learn that the girl is vain and flirtatious as well as stupid and lazy.

Just as a slim waist was admired while tight-lacing to achieve it was criticized, conduct books and manuals for young girls sent out similarly mixed messages about beauty and dress in general. On the one hand they impressed on their readers that it was part of woman's duty to be decorative, and on the other hand girls were warned not to take too much interest in their appearance, as this was a sign of vanity. The ambiguous attitude is commented on in *Agnes Grey*, when the heroine muses on how, as a child, she had been taught that beauty is not important, whereas experience has taught her otherwise: 'If a woman is fair and amiable, she is praised for both qualities, but especially the former, by the bulk of mankind: if, on the other hand, she is disagreeable in person and character, her plainness is commonly inveighed against as her greatest crime' (xvii.122).

Novels of the time reflect this ambivalent attitude in that the pretty heroine is almost invariably artless, whereas the girl who is overly concerned with her own appearance usually comes to grief in one way or another. The Brontës are no exception to this rule. From Agnes Grey to

Lucy Snowe, the Brontë heroine is either a small, plain and obscure young woman who dresses neatly but unobtrusively, or, as in the case of Catherine Earnshaw and Shirley Keeldar, beautiful but careless and downright neglectful of her clothes. Caroline Helstone and Helen Huntingdon are the only Brontë heroines who are described as both pretty and prettily dressed – but they never express any interest in clothes either.

Fashionable women are never depicted in a positive light in the Brontë novels. They are invariably vain, shallow and frivolous, although the degree of their worthlessness varies. At one end of the scale, these women are depicted as being so superficial as to have no personality at all, as when William Crimsworth in *The Professor* refers to 'the band of young ladies ... enveloped in silvery clouds of white gauze and muslin' whom he encounters at a ball (iii.19). These nameless and anonymous young women are just a 'band' of beautiful materials with as little individuality as they would have if they were dressmakers' dummies, an impression stressed when Yorke Hunsden comments on aristocratic women that 'they cultivate beauty from childhood upwards, and may by care and training attain to a certain degree of excellence in that point – just like the oriental odalisques' (iii.21–2). Rosalie Murray in *Agnes Grey*, who seems to live for parties, flirtation and pretty dresses, is just such a young woman, who at the end of the novel is unhappy in her loveless marriage to a rich but debauched and callous man. These girls are silly but pathetic, as is Isabella Linton in *Wuthering Heights*, who runs away from her abusive marriage on a cold and wet winter night 'dressed in the girlish dress she commonly wore, befitting her age more than her position; a low frock, with short sleeves, and nothing on either head or neck. The frock was of light silk, and clung to her with wet, and her feet were protected merely by thin slippers' (II.iii.150). Here, the lack of judgement which made Isabella marry Heathcliff in the first place is illustrated in her pretty and expensive but entirely inadequate dress.

At the far end of the scale of well-dressed ladies are women like Céline Varens in *Jane Eyre*, who sells herself to Mr Rochester for diamonds, silks and cashmeres while entertaining another lover behind his back; Blanche Ingram, who also feigns an attachment to Rochester while really only coveting his wealth and social status; Rosalie's mother Mrs Murray in *Agnes Grey*, who encourages her daughter's marriage for social prestige; and Arabella Lowborough in *The Tenant of Wildfell Hall*, who marries one man for his money and title while first carrying on a flirtation and then entering into an illicit relationship with another. All of these are handsome as well as exquisitely dressed women, who deliberately use their beauty and their knowledge of how to dress to advantage in order to dazzle the men around them; and all of them are worldly to the point of mercenary, as well as deceitful, cruel and cold.

So far, the three Brontë sisters have been seen to be fairly similar in their manner of picturing beauty and fashion. However, there is a difference between Charlotte and her sisters in that dress is a subject that carries more significance in Charlotte's novels than in Anne's and Emily's. It is also a somewhat more complex issue in Charlotte's fiction.

Growing up in Haworth, the sisters were obviously not exposed to high fashion, nor do they seem to have taken much interest in the subject. When Charlotte and Emily arrived in Brussels in 1842, they were unfashionably dressed in the styles of the previous decade. Charlotte quickly adapted to the sartorial habits of the neatly and fashionably dressed Belgian girls, but Emily refused to change, and when mocked for her unfashionably straight skirts and wide sleeves she angrily retorted: 'I wish to be as God made me' (Barker, p. 393). This difference in their attitudes is reflected in their novels. In *Wuthering Heights*, pretty clothes have no positive connotations at all. Not only is Isabella's lack of character and judgement reflected in her dress, but what Nelly Dean scornfully calls 'fine clothes and flattery' are also the means by which the adolescent Catherine Earnshaw is turned away from her playfellow Heathcliff. When Catherine returns to Wuthering Heights after her prolonged visit to Thrushcross Grange, she is splendidly dressed in a feathered hat, a silk frock and a long cloak which she has to hold up with both hands in order to cross the dirty farmyard (1.vii.46). Here the artificiality of the extravagant clothes (which are ridiculously unsuitable for a working farm) is in direct opposition to genuine feeling, as the naturally passionate Catherine can neither embrace her friends nor stroke her dogs for fear of crumpling or soiling her dress; and there is no doubt that the authorial sympathy is with the 'hatless little savage' that Catherine used to be rather than with the elegant young lady she has been transformed into.

Conversely, Charlotte's delight in pretty clothes and her annoyance with badly dressed people are noticeable in all her novels. Her Brussels experience is expressed in William Crimsworth's comments on the badly dressed British in *The Professor*:

[G]racious Goodness! why don't they dress better? My eye is yet filled with visions of the high-flounced, slovenly and tumbled dresses in costly silk and satin, of the large, unbecoming collars in expensive lace, of the ill-cut coats and strangely-fashioned pantaloons which every Sunday, at the English service, filled the chairs of the Chapel royal and after it, issuing forth into the square, came into disadvantageous contrast with freshly and trimly attired foreign figures[.](xix.152)

The pain at seeing a beloved relative ridiculously dressed which Charlotte experienced when Emily was mocked for her old-fashioned clothes also seems to be reflected in *Shirley*, written while Charlotte was mourning the deaths of her sisters. In this novel Caroline Helstone – herself a neat dresser who knows exactly what colours and fits suit her best – exclaims to her mother, Mrs Pryor: 'Mama, I am determined you shall not wear that old gown any more; its fashion is not becoming: it is too strait in the skirt ... Why do you wear such dresses and bonnets, mama, such as nobody else ever wears?' (iii.ii.373–4).[3]

That Charlotte also differs from Anne in this respect can be seen in the ways in which they depict men's clothing. In *Agnes Grey* Anne ridicules the vain and sycophantic rector Mr Hatfield, whose ecclesiastic gown is made of costly silk and who flaunts his lavender gloves and sparkling rings in church, whereas the curate Mr Weston is praised for his simple dress and charity to the poor – qualities that seem to go hand in hand. In *Shirley*, on the other hand, Charlotte makes fun of the clumsy and badly dressed curates whose unfashionable clothes reflect their general stupidity and vulgarity. She also tells us that another clergyman, St John Rivers in *Jane Eyre*, who is certainly neither superficial nor worldly, nevertheless dresses well – as does the saintly Miss Temple, whose elegance of dress is described in loving detail by Jane.

The pleasure that Charlotte obviously took in nice clothes creates certain tensions in her texts, as contempt for fashionable ladies is combined with admiration for good dress sense. This tension is resolved in two ways. First, the virtuous character's dress sense is connected with a general habit of neatness and cleanliness. The pleasure which Jane takes in Miss Temple's beauty of person and dress is akin to that which both Jane and Helen Burns take in her pleasant room, and Jane later emulates these qualities in her own life: 'All about me was spotless and bright – scoured floor, polished grate, and well-rubbed chairs. I had also made myself neat' is how she describes herself on a day off from her duties as a schoolmistress (iii.vi.370). When William Crimsworth first visits Frances Henri, he likewise notes approvingly: '[W]ell-arranged was her simple attire, smooth her dark hair, orderly her tranquil room' (*The Professor*, xxiii.200). Presented in this way, the heroine's ability to dress well seems not like vanity but like an embodiment of her domesticity – a cardinal Victorian female virtue.

Second, the extreme simplicity and frugality of the protagonist's dress are stressed. The only Brontë heroine who is allowed brilliant colours without having her integrity compromised is Shirley Keeldar, who is so singularly uninterested in clothes that she hardly seems to be aware of them at all. All the others are depicted in simple dresses in sombre colours: Frances Henri always wears black, as does Jane Eyre, who owns two black dresses and one grey when she arrives at Thornfield. Caroline Helstone generally wears brown and Lucy Snowe grey. Their elegance primarily consists in perfect fit and exquisite cleanliness. The latter is particularly important. Since cleanliness came at a cost – sending away your laundry was expensive, and doing it yourself was extremely cumbersome – the heroine's spotless collars and cuffs are both a class-marker and a sign of morality. The partiality for dark colours is in accordance with the fashions of the 1840s, but together with the lack of ornaments of any kind it also stresses the Puritan aspect of these characters, in contrast to the flamboyance and self-gratification of the fashionable women with their colourful dresses and beautiful jewellery.

Consequently, Charlotte Brontë's heroines react strongly against any attempt to make them dress more colourfully. When Mr Rochester wants to buy his fiancée silk frocks and jewels, she forcefully opposes his plans and in the end accepts only a string of pearls, symbols of purity. The 'brilliant amethyst' and 'superb pink' frocks she manages to change for a black and a grey – the latter meant for her wedding dress (ii.ix.268). (In this connection it should be pointed out that although Frances Henri in *The Professor* is married in a white dress, this was by no means the rule at the time. A wedding dress could be of any colour. It was only towards the end of the century that white became the predominant colour for fashionable brides.) Jane is more successful in her resistance than Lucy Snowe in *Villette*, who is presented with a pink silk dress by her godmother Mrs Bretton. 'I thought no human force should avail to put me into it. A pink dress! I knew it not. It knew not me', Lucy exclaims (xx.207). After she has been persuaded into the dress by Mrs Bretton and experienced John Graham's appreciative smile, however, she becomes reconciled to it; and six months later Lucy is comfortable enough with the idea to buy herself a new pink dress for a May Day picnic with Paul Emanuel, the man she is now more than half in love with.

That colour and ornaments are connected with sexuality in a woman is also shown by the fact that Frances Henri, who has never been seen wearing anything but the severest black with no ornaments, puts on 'a pretty lilac gown ... a piquant black silk apron, and a lace collar with some finishing decoration of lilac ribbon' only a couple of hours after her wedding (xxv.227). Similarly, during her brief period of happiness and bloom while first engaged to Mr Rochester, Jane is sufficiently relaxed to don a light summer dress. After the aborted wedding, however, she changes back into black, and only when she is happily married do we see her in a colour again, when as a beloved young wife she wears a pale blue dress and a glittering gold chain (*Jane Eyre*, III.xii.451). There is obviously nothing wrong with colours or decorations as such, only with a young woman's wearing them for her own gratification. The protagonist's sexuality has to be awakened by the man she loves – and even then she will wear pale, girlish pastels. Only in this way, it seems, can a love of pretty clothes be indulged without compromising the protagonist's purity.

NOTES

1 Valerie Steele, *The Corset* (New Haven: Yale University Press, 2001), p. 44.
2 *Ibid.*, p. 52. However, stories of Victorian women surgically removing their lower ribs in order to achieve the desired silhouette are as much of a fiction as the persistent myth that the Victorians put skirts on legs of furniture out of exaggerated modesty.
3 Incidentally, Charlotte gets her historical references wrong here. Since the events in *Shirley* are supposed to take place in 1811–12, Mrs Pryor would be quite fashionable wearing straight skirts.

CHAPTER 40

Sexuality

Jill L. Matus

What could three young women, daughters of a country parson and coming of age in the 1830s, know and write about sex? Were we to go by the persistent stereotypes of the Victorian age as one of prudishness, ignorance and sexual repression, this chapter would be a very short one indeed. This was the age in which piano legs were allegedly draped lest they provoke association with naked limbs. Literature was never to bring a blush to a maiden's cheek, and the Queen's advice to women on their marital duty in the bedroom was supposedly to lie back and think of England. These popular myths have defined the Victorian moment in the history of sexuality as a kind of aberration, book-ended on the one hand by a more congenial era of revolution and romanticism and on the other by the modern. The label 'Victorian' became a disparaging synonym for all things prudish only after Victoria's reign had ended, as the next generation reacted against what they saw as the stifling respectability and sexual moralism of their predecessors. But as Michael Mason has argued, even though the idea of a pendulum of sexual moralism swinging back and forth has some plausibility, the censorious attitudes that are now the clichés of Victorian attitudes to sex grew directly from aspects of late eighteenth-century and early nineteenth-century culture.[1] The relationship between early and later nineteenth-century attitudes is better described in terms of continuities and overlap than in those of a sharp break. As the historian K. Theodore Hoppen notes, 'Victorian sexual relationships were varied and complex . . . crude caricatures will not do.'[2]

The family was the centre of Victorian life, and although size varied greatly, 'anything less than seven born alive would have been considered "small"' in the 1840s.[3] Middle-class women were supposed to marry and have families; working-class women worked as well as bore children. Contraceptive methods were widely used, but were not as effective as they might have been because key facts about ovulation and conception were not scientifically known until the twentieth century. There was a great deal of lore about how to deal with unwanted pregnancies, and 'abortifacients' were widely advertised in the Victorian popular press. Until 1870 there were no laws to protect the property of women when they married. Given that the law bestowed everything a wife owned on her husband, it was all the more important to keep a watchful eye out for unscrupulous and inappropriate suitors. A complex marriage market with elaborate courtship etiquettes developed, extending from the upper to the middle classes. Those who did not marry – old maids – were thought to have failed in the business of life, and the problem of 'surplus' women occasioned much debate. Even as female chastity and fidelity were lauded, the infamous male double standard meant that the number of prostitutes in large urban centres swelled – there were 80,000 in London alone, wrote Henry Mayhew.[4] (There were very wide disparities in the reporting of this figure, however.) While the question of female desire was much debated, with Dr William Acton pronouncing that most women are happily not much troubled by sexual desire, it is clear that his views were not universally held; for instance, older views linking female orgasm to successful conception persisted. Attitudes to sexuality were hence by no means monolithic during the period, and it is misleading to position the Victorians as simply the 'other' of our own enlightened and permissive selves.

Furthermore, since Michel Foucault's work on the history of sexuality, we have had to entertain the notion that the nineteenth and twentieth centuries may be more alike in their interest in sex than different – that it is not a question of repressive and anti-repressive waves, but one of different ways in which social control is exercised through intense scrutiny of and discourse about sexuality.[5] By 'discourse' is meant a practice that sets out to *form* the objects which it purports merely to *describe*.[6] It has long been argued that gender is a discursive production; but how is it to be differentiated from sex? While it was once customary to delineate the latter as having to do with differential anatomy and the former with social identity, the stability of that opposition has been unsettled for some time. Not only was 'sex' meant to refer to the physical and anatomical aspects of a person, and 'gender' used to refer to the socially constructed (masculine and feminine elements); the realm of sex was understood to be natural and primary, while gender was secondary and socially constructed. 'The grand function of a woman, it must always be recollected, is, and ever must be, Maternity', wrote G. H. Lewes in a review of Charlotte Brontë's *Shirley*.[7] Earlier, in March 1837, the poet Robert Southey had written to Charlotte Brontë saying that literature could never be the business of a woman's life (Smith, *Letters*, vol. 1, pp. 166–7). Both men were invoking a common assumption in which the social roles of women (gender) were based on assertions about 'natural' female reproductive function (sex). Judith Butler, among others, has complicated the distinction between sex and gender by arguing that they are not ontologically different, belonging to different realms, a primary independent realm (sex) and a secondary dependent cultural realm (gender). Rather, according to Butler, both sex and gender are socially constructed and form mutually reinforcing categories.[8]

Sexuality in a variety of forms, not least in its illicit social expressions such as bigamy, adultery and illegitimacy, appears throughout the Brontës' work, suggesting their acquaintance at some level with the 'facts of life' and their consequences. In *Jane Eyre*, the heroine almost contracts a bigamous marriage; incarcerated in Thornfield's attic is a lunatic who has gone mad at least in part because of sexual excess – her 'giant propensities' (III.i.306); Mr Rochester provides a frank account of his mistresses and courtesans; and the ward in his home is possibly his illegitimate child. In *Wuthering Heights*, the quasi-incestuous passion of Catherine and Heathcliff threatens and overwhelms conventional family structures and marriage bonds, though many readers and critics over the years have questioned the extent to which that passion is sexual.[9] *The Tenant of Wildfell Hall* depicts the consequences of dissolution, debauchery and extra-marital affairs, daring to expose the injustice of early nineteenth-century divorce and child-custody laws. Even *Agnes Grey*, the most apparently dispassionate of the novels, turns on the passage from puberty to sexual maturity, its governess narrator observing her charge Rosalie 'coming out' on the marriage market. Sexual competition, jealousy, desire and attraction animate her narrative even as she struggles to disguise her feelings.

Of course, we do not find the graphic and explicit descriptions of sexual relations that a reader of twentieth- and twenty-first-century novels might expect to encounter. But from the point of view of their first critics, the Brontës knew and wrote far too much about sex. Early reviewers of works by Acton, Ellis and Currer Bell criticized their coarseness of tone and subject matter. G. H. Lewes summed it up: 'Coarse even for men, coarse in language and coarse in conception'.[10] What that meant, among other things, was that the Brontë sisters wrote books with sexual content, books that would fail the proverbial Victorian litmus test: the blushing maiden cheek. Once it became known that the authors were themselves maidens, readers were all the more shocked by the implied sexual knowledge of the novels, some to the point of wondering what sinister pasts were concealed by their ostensibly respectable country parsonage existence.[11]

The implication that the Brontës wrote 'naughty books' occasioned vigorous defence. It accounts in part for the apologetic tone of Charlotte's 'Biographical Notice' excusing her sister Emily's rough-hewn genius in *Wuthering Heights*; it also explains the sanitizing work of Elizabeth Gaskell's *Life of Charlotte Brontë*, which attempts to locate the 'coarseness' in the Brontës' surroundings, the moorland town of harsh and strange realities. Isolated from the world around Haworth, these three young women were faithfully representing the only reality they knew, more inadvertent than blameworthy in capturing its coarseness. But by the mid nineteenth century, Haworth had in fact become a bustling commercial town: Gaskell's representation of it was about one hundred years out of date.

Even if Haworth had been as Gaskell represented it, the myth of Brontë isolation can be dispelled on other grounds. None of the Brontës was a naïve realist, mimetically transcribing her local context. On the contrary, they were, as previous chapters in this book have shown, precocious *writers* and highly literate, sophisticated *readers*. Avid consumers of nineteenth-century print culture, the Brontë children read *Blackwood's Magazine* and *Fraser's*, newspapers such as the *Leeds Intelligencer* and the books in their father's library. The family also borrowed books from local libraries. They were conversant with a wide range of contemporary publications, and their extant juvenilia provide evidence of creative experimentation with literary genres and subjects, as well as sophisticated awareness of forms of authorship and publishing.

Voracious reading appetites account in part for the Brontë sisters' knowledge of sexuality. In addition to the Bible, Shakespeare, the *Arabian Nights* and Scott, they were familiar with the Romantic poets. Growing up when the cult of Byron was still in full swing, they would have soaked up from his works, and from Thomas Moore's *Letters and Journals of Lord Byron, with Notices of his Life* (1830), much about Regency society with its rakes, debauchery and scandals. The elaborate tales of Gondal (penned by Emily and Anne) and Angria (Charlotte and Branwell) took up many tiny volumes, though only some of the Angrian sagas have survived. Charlotte continued well into her twenties to write Angrian stories, full of amoral heroes and passionate heroines, the last of which racy tales have recently been collected and published.[12] Scandal and sexual licence are not untypical in the novelettes with their society courtesans, meetings between wives and mistresses and, in 'Caroline Vernon', a duke who seduces his not entirely innocent ward.

Familiar as they were with literary representations of illicit liaisons, the Brontës actually lived through a mortifying sexual scandal of their own in 1845 when their brother Branwell brought disgrace upon himself by being dismissed from his post as tutor apparently because of his relationship with Mrs Robinson, the wife of his employer. Gaskell's account in the first edition of her biography of Charlotte (1857) does not skirt the issue of sexual misconduct:

All the disgraceful details came out. Branwell was in no state to conceal his agony of remorse ... from any dread of shame. He gave passionate way to his feelings; he shocked and distressed those loving sisters inexpressibly; the blind father sat stunned, sorely tempted to curse the profligate woman, who had tempted his boy – his only son – into the deep disgrace of deadly crime.[13]

Gaskell continues: 'The case presents the reverse of the usual features; the man became the victim; the man's life was blighted, and crushed out of him by suffering ... the man's family were stung by keenest shame' (Gaskell, *Life*, p. 523).

Gaskell's comment on the 'usual features' implies the conventional script of attraction and seduction in which men act and women suffer. The interrelations of sex and power informing this script are subjected to keen scrutiny in most of the Brontë novels. The narrators of *Villette*, *Jane Eyre* and *Agnes Grey* observe the dynamics of attraction and desire in others and directly or indirectly criticize social constructions of beauty and desirability. Lucy Snowe monitors male response to a painting of a voluptuous and orientalized female subject; Jane observes Rochester's apparent courtship of Blanche Ingram. On occasion, these heroines enter the fray of sexual competition themselves: acting in the school play, Lucy inserts herself in a triangle of desire, as she recognizes Dr John's fascination with Ginevra Fanshawe (chapter 14), and Agnes Grey finds herself competing with her charge Rosalie for the attention of the local curate. Challenging the conventional piety that inner beauty trumps external attractiveness, she wonders how, without beauty, a poor, plain governess can attract a mate. As Agnes considers the spectre of doomed female passivity and the agony of possibly unrequited attraction, she draws on the image of the glow-worm, an example invoked by naturalists and Victorian writers on sexuality and reproduction to show how 'Nature' manages the business of sexual attraction.[14]

As was noted above, *Wuthering Heights* presents an unusual case in the dynamics of desire because the connection between Catherine and Heathcliff, though passionate, seems asexual. Nor is Heathcliff's seduction of Isabella much more than an elaborate revenge scheme; he sees Isabella as a pawn in a game, and also manipulates marriage ties between his sickly son and his niece in order to amass property and title. Styled in Nellie's narrative at times as a cuckoo in the nest, he is the outsider who usurps all. In the second generation, Emily Brontë explores a more muted and socially manageable form of relationship, in which the teasing, chastising banter of Cathy and Hareton signals the domestication of the Heights. Hareton, we recall, is not only the presaged heir of the Heights, but the product of Hindley and Frances' marriage, which is portrayed as a rarity in the world of this novel – a genuinely happy union. Readers must think carefully about relationship and attraction or they will err, as does the narrator Lockwood when he misinterprets family ties and misreads signals of attraction on first entering the Heights and encountering Heathcliff, Catherine and Hareton. The story he tells of his own flirtation with a young woman at a fashionable resort indicates both his effete social timidity and his familiarity with a mode of polite social interaction very different from the violent and passionate world of the Heights which he finds himself dragged into.

Though *Wuthering Heights* is certainly the novel that springs to mind when readers think about violence and passion, it is not alone in representing these forces. In contrast to the finely calibrated sexual competition depicted in *Agnes Grey*, Anne Brontë offers readers a glimpse into the violence of sexual jealousy in *The Tenant of Wildfell Hall*, where Gilbert Markham savagely beats his imagined rival. If not quite so explosive, men in Charlotte Brontë's novels frequently assume the commanding characteristics of the Duke of Wellington, whom she much admired. They are imperious and irascible, but redeemed by stimulating and witty conversation and well-disguised goodness and decency. Rochester has sinned, no doubt, but he has also been sinned against by his family, who contracted his marriage to Bertha. Though he certainly has to pay for his past as well as for his illicit attempt to enlist Jane as the agent of his salvation, he is granted survival. As much as the finale of *Jane Eyre* emphasizes harmony and equality, readers have not failed to notice that it is in many respects a fantasy of dominance – Jane is now the stronger of the two, and the incapacitated Rochester must rely on her for everything. Similarly, many readers have found Monsieur Paul in *Villette* to be an odious little man, but Lucy Snowe comes to love his dictatorial ways and the tenderness they conceal.

Sexuality in the Brontë novels is largely heterosexuality, though critics have read Lucy Snowe's donning of male costume and wooing of Ginevra in the school play as an interesting intervention into the dynamics of heterosexuality. Similarly, the novels draw on prevailing nineteenth-century assumptions about sexuality and race, in which the Orient, the Caribbean and Africa are associated with excessive sexuality. But even as they reflect many of their culture's normative views of sexuality, the Brontë novels are also more venturesome than much fiction of the period. This is the more remarkable in that they were penned by three young women, two of whom died unmarried around the age of thirty.

NOTES

1 See Michael Mason, *The Making of Victorian Sexuality* (Oxford University Press, 1995), pp. 4, 9–10 and 18–20.

2 K. Theodore Hoppen, *The Mid-Victorian Generation: 1846–1888* (Oxford University Press, 1998), p. 324.

3 *Ibid.*, p. 317. On unwanted pregnancies, see p. 318.

4 Henry Mayhew, *London Labour and the London Poor*, vol. IV (London: Charles Griffin, 1861), p. 215.

5 Michel Foucault, *The History of Sexuality*, trans. R. Hurley (Harmondsworth: Penguin, 1981), vol. I.

6 See Susan Speer's discussion of discourse and the sex–gender distinction in *Gender Talk: Feminism, Discourse and Conversation Analysis* (London and New York: Routledge, 2005), p. 48.

7 See Miriam Allott (ed.), *The Brontës: The Critical Heritage* (London: Routledge & Kegan Paul, 1974), p. 161.

8 See Judith Butler, *Gender Trouble: Feminism and the Subversion of Identity* (London and New York: Routledge, 1990).

9 See also Chapter 42 in this volume. Sandra M. Gilbert and Susan Gubar have viewed the attraction between the two in terms of power, interpreting Catherine's need for Heathcliff as a substitute for the whip she had asked her father to bring her from Liverpool; see *The Madwoman in the Attic: The Woman Writer and the Nineteenth-Century Imagination* (New Haven: Yale University Press, 1979; repr. 2000), pp. 263–7.

10 Quoted in Allott, *Critical Heritage*, p. 292.

11 See Juliet Barker, 'The Haworth Context', in Heather Glen (ed.), *The Cambridge Companion to the Brontës* (Cambridge University Press, 2002), p. 14.

12 Heather Glen (ed.), *Charlotte Brontë: Tales of Angria* (London: Penguin, 2006), p. xi.

13 Under threat of law, Gaskell revised this account in the third edition. See the explanatory notes and text of the first edition provided in Gaskell, *Life*, p. 523.

14 See Jill L. Matus, *Unstable Bodies: Victorian Representations of Sexuality and Maternity* (Manchester University Press, 1995), pp. 105–7.

CHAPTER 41

Physical health

Janis McLarren Caldwell

The imaginary worlds of the Brontës were profoundly shaped by the chronic ill-health and early deaths that plagued the family. It is impossible to furnish precise diagnoses of their maladies, given differences in medical theory and in cultural understanding; but in what follows, I have tried to be as specific as Brontë biography allows, translating nineteenth-century disease categories into our (approximate) terminology. The six children were left motherless at an early age when Maria Brontë died of cancer, probably of the uterus. The eldest children, Maria and Elizabeth, died of consumption at the ages of eleven and ten respectively. Now called pulmonary tuberculosis, consumption was endemic throughout Britain, and it was certainly well established in the Brontë household. Characterized by a bloody cough, intermittent fever and weight loss, tuberculosis was also later to ravage the remaining children in early adulthood. Consumption claimed the lives of Emily and Anne, and it was a major contributing factor to Branwell's death, which was complicated in addition by drunkenness (or what we would call alcoholism) and delirium tremens, or withdrawal from alcohol intoxication. Like those of her siblings, Charlotte's death certificate cited 'phthisis', or the lung inflammation caused by consumption. For Charlotte, the wasting of tuberculosis was compounded by intractable vomiting, probably due to prolonged and violent morning sickness (the condition current doctors would call *hyperemesis gravidarum*) in early pregnancy (see Barker, pp. 772 and 967–8 n. 96). Patrick senior, although he suffered from poor digestion and had surgery for cataracts, was healthy enough to survive all his children – a sorrowful piece of good fortune.

It is of course part of the Brontë mythology to picture the gloomy location of the parsonage, overlooking the gravestone-encrusted churchyard, and to marvel at the tragic multiplication of loss so unfortunately visited on one family. It is the degree of devastation suffered by the Brontë family, however, rather than the kind, that is remarkable. Orphanhood, maternal death, epidemic diseases and consumption were common enough in Victorian families. Most Brontëan narratives, from the juvenilia onwards, feature an orphan, which we should attribute not only to the authors' particular experience but also to the harsh realities beyond the parsonage. Maternal death figures show that throughout England and Wales, nine mothers died in childbirth every day. Of infants, 15 to 20 per cent died in their first year. Many more children and adults were killed by the cholera epidemics that swept the country in 1831–2, 1848–9 and 1853–4. Typhus and typhoid were both endemic in Great Britain, and poor sanitation contributed to their spread, especially in prisons and urban slums.

Even rural locations suffered from contaminated water supplies, and the Brontës had more than their share of exposure to poor sanitation. The Babbage report of 1850 (see Chapters 1 and 2) rated the annual average mortality in Haworth at 25.4 in 1,000, compared with 17.6 in a nearby village – worse than most neighbourhoods in London. For the children, leaving home was even more dangerous. The four eldest sisters were exposed to typhus at Cowan Bridge school, the original for *Jane Eyre*'s Lowood School, where kitchen sanitation was very poor. Already suffering from tuberculosis and in a weakened condition, Maria and Elizabeth expired soon after being brought home. All of these common Victorian medical realities – poor sanitation, epidemic disease, maternal and childhood death and consumption – appear in the Brontës' novels, signalling attention to actual material circumstances but also shaping plots, furnishing metaphors and offering opportunities for revenge or reconciliation.

All of the Brontë sisters demonstrate a firm conviction of the intimate interrelationship between the mind and the body, but they vary in the extent to which they assign to the individual a moral responsibility for his or her own disease. In *Agnes Grey*, for instance, Agnes' father Richard Grey declines and dies from a melancholy arising from the loss of his fortune. For this 'ingenious self-tormentor', full of 'morbid imagination', 'the mind preyed upon the body, and disordered the system of the nerves, and they in turn increased the troubles of the mind, till by action, and re-action, his health was seriously impaired' (i.9). Here Anne describes the 'action and re-action' of mind and body in a two-way interrelation that results in a fatal imbalance of the body's elements. Anne is the only Brontë sister who occasionally seems to invoke the language of older, humoral medicine, which advises tempering the body's constituents and carefully balancing mental exertion and physical propensities.

Anne Brontë's principal discourse of temperance in *The Tenant of Wildfell Hall* wrestles subtextually with the problem of Branwell's drunkenness and the degree to which this beloved brother was responsible for his own decline. There is evidence that the Brontë family wondered about inherited tendencies to drink, as Patrick Brontë had underlined a pertinent passage to that effect in their household medical volume (of which more below). Some medical literature of the time suggested that temperance, or moderation, may not be enough in cases where family tendencies are strong. Thus Helen Huntingdon worries that her son, young Arthur, might be vulnerable, and she imposes aversive treatment on him.[1] Similarly, Anne depicts Lord Lowborough as the kind of drunkard who cannot tolerate any drink and must resort to abstinence rather than moderation. Even so, Anne is a long way from treating drunkenness as a purely physical disease. Arthur Huntingdon senior invites his disease throughout his long career of poor moral choices, so endangering his constitution that a fall from his horse proves fatal.[2] And Lord Lowborough exercises his will towards recovery, receiving Helen's highest moral approbation for making the difficult choices that lead to his reformation.

Emily Brontë gives us an even darker view of drunkenness in her portrayal of *Wuthering Heights*'s Hindley. Emily seems much less interested than Anne in moral explanations of disease. Hindley's decline is relentless, and the narrative grants him neither compassion, nor blame, nor any hope of healing. The medical view of Hindley is that he is incurable and that death would be a mercy; Heathcliff reports that Kenneth, the gruff country surgeon, wagers that Hindley will 'outlive any man on this side Gimmerton, and go to the grave a hoary sinner; unless some happy chance out of the common course befall him' (1.ix.67).

Of the sisters, Emily reflects most fully the naturalist domestic medical theory of the period. The Brontës lived in a time when British medical theory was changing course, becoming more sceptical about the traditional interventions of humoral medicine (such as bloodletting or purging) which were meant to temper the body's internal economy, and encouraging what we might see as more natural or preventative cures which were closely connected with the external environment. Domestic medical manuals advocated natural cures emphasizing freedom, a healthy diet and outdoor exercise. As a clergyman, Patrick Brontë visited the sick and was concerned with the physical as well as spiritual welfare of his parishioners; he thus considered himself a sort of lay medical practitioner. The source and impetus for much of the Brontë family's medical theorizing was Thomas John Graham's tome *Modern Domestic Medicine* (1826).

The family's copy, now in the Brontë Parsonage Museum library, is freely annotated in Patrick Brontë's handwriting. Patrick's annotations demonstrate a strain of self-help in medicine as well as a lay empowerment in the reading of the body (see Figure 29).

More than any member of the family, Emily demonstrates her grounding in this lay medical self-empowerment. Famously, when she was bitten by a dog believed to be rabid, she took matters into her own hands, seizing a red-hot iron and performing self-cautery (Barker, p. 198). When she was dying, she repeatedly refused medical assistance, much to Charlotte's distress, until she was beyond any help. Her habit of striding across the moors in all weathers reflects the pleasure in exposure to the elements prescribed by current domestic medicine, as well as the confidence that Nature batters her devotees into strength. Young Cathy, the 'wild, hatless' (and intermittently shoeless) little 'savage' (*Wuthering Heights*, 1.vii.46), develops a strong constitution, so that Kenneth suspects mental more than physical disturbance when he hears about her final illness. 'A stout, hearty lass like Catherine does not fall ill for a trifle', he comments (1.xii.114). In fact, Emily moves beyond a doctrine of medical self-help to the view that individuals will themselves to health – or to illness. Nelly's narrative leaves us in doubt as to whether Catherine and Heathcliff die more of illness visited upon them or of ill-health determined by their own headstrong will. 'I'll cry myself sick', says Catherine when her desire is thwarted (1.viii.63).[3] And during Heathcliff's final self-willed decline, even his involuntary nervous system seems to be under his conscious control: 'I have to remind myself to breathe – almost to remind my heart to beat!' (11.xix.289). Strong bodies, for Emily Brontë, signify strong wills, and for these individuals both health and illness seem to obey personal volition. Because Catherine and Heathcliff are particularly adept at controlling their environments via restriction of food, some critics have suggested that Emily was portraying the disease *anorexia nervosa* before it was formally named in 1873.[4] Certainly all the sisters depicted wasting women; but they mostly suffer from the nineteenth-century disease 'lovesickness' rather than from what we call anorexia, with its overt concern for body image.

Charlotte's treatment of illness has much in common with the dominant cultural figurations of her time – indeed, her own writing serves to establish such stereotypes more firmly. It is not difficult to find instances of what Susan Sontag has called 'illness as metaphor' in Charlotte's works. For Charlotte, the wasting body does not signal a wasting soul; rather, as in many nineteenth-century depictions of consumptives, the fever burns

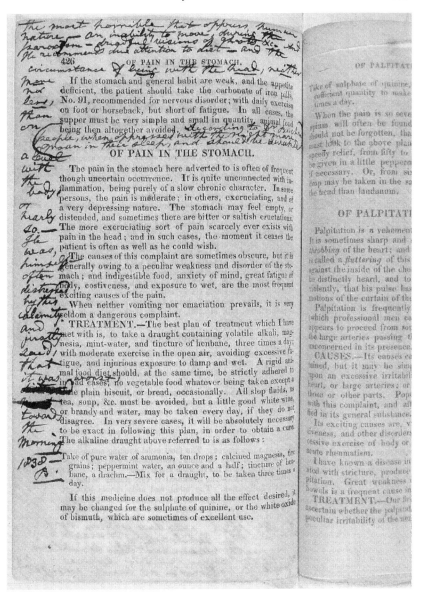

29 A page from Thomas John Graham's *Modern Domestic Medicine* (1826), heavily annotated by Patrick Brontë

away the sufferer's investment in the physical world, leaving behind a purified soul. Helen Burns' brave and saintly death is, of course, the classic example, her name signalling her martyrdom at the stake of her febrile disease. Later, in *Villette*, Charlotte used an alternative version of the Romantic tubercular metaphor: the actress Vashti, whom Lucy admires, embodies the metaphor of the passionate and supersexual artist, whose very strength of spirit rends the fabric of the body.

Charlotte Brontë also clearly demonstrates Miriam Bailin's thesis that the Victorian sickroom often functions as a space for redemption. We find Jane Eyre twice bedridden, and during each episode her life undergoes a major transformation. After her trauma in the red room, she finds a friend in Bessie and in Mr Lloyd the apothecary, who recommends a change of scene and departure from Gateshead. Later, when she recovers from her illness at Moor House, she finds a family in the Rivers household. The plot of *Shirley* in particular has turning-points in sickroom scenes, which unite child with parent and lover with lover. Caroline Helstone is nursed by Mrs Pryor, thereby discovering that Mrs Pryor is her mother. Louis' fever brings Shirley to his bedside and revives their old teacher–pupil relationship. As Robert Moore recovers from his wound, he experiences a depression which assists in his reconciliation with Caroline. Even Shirley's pride is humbled after she is bitten by a possibly rabid dog, and her worry about impending illness allows an understanding to develop more fully between Louis and herself. Illness in Charlotte's pre-*Villette* fiction seems equally an infliction and an opportunity; its fictional moral and spiritual possibilities are fully mined.

Like Emily, Charlotte wandered the moors and was familiar with the domestic medical teaching which entrusted healing to the embrace of the external environment. In her works, Charlotte represented the interaction between the body and the environment mainly through the doctrine of miasmatism. Miasmatism, the reigning explanation for contagious disease before the acceptance of Koch's germ theory in the 1880s, held that poisonous vapours from decaying organic matter cause disease. The very name of Lowood, for instance, signals its unhealthy location, as miasmas were thought to gather in low-lying places. 'That forest-dell, where Lowood lay', writes Charlotte, 'was the cradle of fog-bound pestilence, which ... breathed typhus' through the school (*Jane Eyre*, 1.ix.76). Because of this attention to diseased locations, miasmatism is sometimes credited with inspiring early sanitary reform. But as Alan Bewell has argued, miasmatism also contained the seeds of nationalist and racist explanations of disease.[5] Caroline Helstone thus succumbs to a miasmatic fever, 'the breath of Indian plague' which arises from 'the poisoned exhalations of the East' (*Shirley*, III.i.351). Similarly, in *Jane Eyre*, Jamaica is repeatedly represented as a tropical hell which accelerates Bertha's madness, Rochester's suicidal despair and Richard Mason's sallow ill-health. Even so, Bewell interprets the ending of *Jane Eyre* as a critique of the poor state of sanitation in Britain. Jane has escaped grilling in India with St John, but she and Rochester retire to the 'insalubrious site' of Ferndean (III.xi.430).

For Charlotte, bodies, perhaps even more than places, are insistently significant, and her narrators and characters are often adept readers of bodily meaning, as demonstrated by the frequent use of the language of phrenology, in which bumps and indentations of the skull were thought to mark qualities of character (see Chapter 42). And yet illness was an unstable metaphor, not only throughout the course of the nineteenth century but also over the course of Charlotte's writing life.

As Charlotte strove increasingly to discipline herself into a sober realism – and as she experienced her siblings' deaths in rapid succession – she turned towards some of the patterns characteristic of mid-nineteenth-century realist fiction. One marker of this is the rising status of the doctor as fictional hero, which reflects the increasing authority of the medical profession in a more scientific culture. Before *Villette*, Charlotte had toyed with the older caricatures of the swearing surgeon and the dram-drinking, 'dragon' nurse in her portrayal of MacTurk and Mrs Horsfall of *Shirley* (III. ix.473). But Dr John Graham Bretton (who takes his name in part from the author of *Modern Domestic Medicine*) gets serious treatment as an enduring love interest of Lucy's, held in the temple of her heart even after she meets M. Paul. Bretton is thought to have been modelled after Charlotte's publisher George Smith, young, handsome, intelligent and of an optimistic temperament.[6] If this traditional parallel is accepted, it is interesting that she cast Smith as a doctor, as if the professional is on par with the urbane man of letters, both members of a new meritocratic upper-middle class. Perhaps the characteristic she was most interested in capturing is an über-masculine self-confident sunny temperament, grounded in scientific positivism as well as in positive thinking. Dr John has a 'fund of deep and healthy strength', shedding around him a 'fostering sunshine' – he is a foil in many ways to the small, dark, stormy M. Paul. After Lucy confesses her encounter with the spectral nun, Dr John, in his 'dry material[ism]', diagnoses 'a highly nervous state' and recommends that she 'cultivate happiness' (*Villette*, xxiii.257, xxii.248 and xxii.250). Dr John reflects the changing status of materialists and medical practitioners in the Brontës' time, as well as the attractiveness of those who find a response to a sunny temperament in the material world.

More than any of Charlotte's other novels, *Villette* depicts physical and mental illness as inexplicably visited upon people who have done nothing to deserve it. Yet she did not entirely relinquish the possibility of meaning-making in illness. After she had watched her siblings endure their final illnesses, it is the endurance of suffering itself that takes on moral power in Charlotte's last novel. Her persistent metaphor of the storm, and her final literalization of that metaphor in M. Paul's homeward voyage, acknowledges her full severance from romance and her embrace of the realist world as a force that subdues even the strongest of wills. In *Villette* illness is no longer a metaphor for purification, and the sickroom is not redemptive. Rather, as Terry Eagleton has argued, the sufferer has become the *pharmakos*, the scapegoat who may advance healing for the community.[7] As Lucy Snowe writes of herself, 'I concluded it to be a part of [God's] great plan that some must deeply suffer while they live, and I thrilled in the certainty that of this number, I was one' (xv.157). Lest we conclude, however, that Charlotte's mature version of endurance resembles that of the saintly Helen Burns, she leaves us with that striking vision of Vashti on stage, understood by some critics as a tribute to Emily's wrestling with tuberculosis:[8] 'Pain, for her, has no result in good; tears water no harvest of wisdom: on sickness, on death itself, she looks with the eye of a rebel ... [H]er strength has conquered Beauty' (xxiii.258). One of the legacies of the Brontë family's accumulated suffering is this dramatic representation of physical illness as at once horrifically ugly and mysteriously, profoundly meaningful.

NOTES

1 See Josephine McDonagh's introduction to the Oxford World's Classics edition of *The Tenant of Wildfell Hall* (2008), pp. xx–xxii.

2 See Marianne Thormählen, 'The Villain of *Wildfell Hall*: Aspects and Prospects of Arthur Huntingdon', *The Modern Language Review*, 88.4 (Oct. 1993), 837–8.

3 See Susan Rubinow Gorsky, '"I'll Cry Myself Sick": Illness in *Wuthering Heights*', *Literature and Medicine*, 182 (1999), 173–91.

4 See *ibid.*, pp. 174–6, and Katherine Frank, *A Chainless Soul: A Life of Emily Brontë* (Boston: Houghton Mifflin, 1990), pp. 2, 98–9, 100, 125–6.

5 See Alan Bewell's 'Jane Eyre and Victorial Medical Geography', *ELH*, 63.3 (Fall 1996), 797–804.

6 See, for instance, Winifred Gérin, *Charlotte Brontë: The Evolution of Genius* (Oxford University Press, 1967; frequently reprinted), pp. 482, 493 and 519.

7 See the introduction to the thirtieth anniversary edition of Terry Eagleton's *Myths of Power: A Marxist Study of the Brontës* (Basingstoke: Palgrave Macmillan, 2005), p. xvi.

8 See, for instance, Janet Gezari, *Charlotte Brontë and Defensive Conduct: The Author and the Body at Risk* (Philadelphia: University of Pennsylvania Press, 1992), p. 142.

CHAPTER 42

Mental health

Janis McLarren Caldwell

We might think of the Brontë sisters as exhibiting rather robust mental health, given that they weathered the loss of so many intimate family members; though grieving normally, they seemingly remained both functional and productive. But Patrick Brontë, and all of his children who survived into adulthood, suffered forms of what we would call neurosis. Each experienced a different kind, attributing his or her distress to one of the multiple types of mental illness described in the Victorian period. Patrick acknowledged a tendency to melancholy, often associated with stress in his job as a clergyman combined with the task of supporting his motherless children. Branwell, disappointed in love, consumed alcohol and opium at a suicidal rate. Under the stress of leaving home for school at Roe Head, Emily suffered a homesickness expressed as wasting and weakness, which frightened Charlotte enough to have her sent home. When Anne was sent to Roe Head instead, she also experienced a form of depression, in her case identified as religious melancholy. Anne's worries about her spiritual salvation were accompanied by such severe symptoms that Charlotte became extremely alarmed, eventually accompanying her sister back to Haworth. And Charlotte herself often classified her various depressions as hypochondria – meaning not, as in our definition, proneness to imagine physical ailments but rather, as for other Victorians, a specific physical and mental illness characterized by pain under the ribs and low spirits. The whole family, then, experienced mental suffering; but like most in their culture, they drew no clear line between physical and mental health, often experiencing a specific somatic correlate for a particular kind of mental ailment.

Most medical developments of the Victorian period involved designating bodily locations of disease, a tendency borne out in the psychology of the period. While neurology was busy establishing the cerebrospinal locations of various nervous functions, psychology, especially in its early pseudo-scientific offshoot phrenology, was bent on identifying locations for various mental faculties and propensities. The Brontë family was intrigued by and well read in phrenology, which posited that well-developed brain 'organs' of psychological faculties such as 'amativeness' or 'philanthropy' could cause elevations in the skull, and that lack of such qualities could result in cranial dents or depressions. By feeling the skull, a trained phrenologist would thus read the subject's character and even predict behaviour, so that some job applicants, like Lucy Snowe in *Villette*, found themselves under phrenologic scrutiny. As Sally Shuttleworth has written, phrenology was attractive to a meritocratic rising middle class because it theorized that the brain organs could be exercised and enlarged, thus permitting those with certain innate mental talents to raise themselves through self-help.[1] Phrenology also posited a mind of multiple competing faculties vying for prominence, all under the control of the individual will. This belief may have undermined the idea of a unified self, but it also stressed the necessity of strong executive self-control.

This phrenologic vision of a divided and warring mind subject to an iron will is one we see often in Brontëan fiction and poetry. But perhaps even more attractive to the Brontës was the notion that the reading of character is a special science, requiring a particularly trained reader. The older art of physiognomy, or interpretation of facial features, had become quite conventional in fiction, whereas phrenology provided new terminology and knowledge, arming the adept phrenologic practitioner with an advantage in interpersonal power skirmishes. Although we can find the phrenologic jargon of 'organs' and 'faculties' in all the Brontës' fiction, Charlotte most thoroughly incorporates phrenology into her instances of character reading. In *Jane Eyre*, for example, Rochester reverses the usual power differential by inviting his new governess to assess the structure of her master's forehead. Jane seizes the advantage, noting a 'solid enough mass of intellectual organs ... but an abrupt deficiency where the suave sign of benevolence should have risen' (1.xiv.131). Rochester sounds out Jane's capacity as a body-reader, and he finds her dangerously adept. Although phrenology in this instance serves ends that might nowadays be thought of as 'progressive', it also supports racist readings of the body, as demonstrated by William Crimsworth's virulent readings of his Belgian pupils in *The Professor*. As Charlotte Brontë matured as a writer, however, her use of phrenology became more nuanced. From Yorke Hunsden to Lucy Snowe, Charlotte is interested in the unreadable character, the person with too many different, conflicting traits to provide a predictive face; but in *The Professor*, the chameleon Hunsden is part of the supporting cast, whereas in *Villette*, the unreadable Lucy Snowe takes centre stage. When M. Paul is asked to read Lucy's 'indefinite' face, he finds 'bien des choses', or many things, and can only advise his cousin to risk employing her for the sake of charity (vii.67). Thus, although Charlotte is often thought to be a phrenologic enthusiast, she by no means accepted the reductionist implications of doctrines of cerebral localization.

The most important development in early Victorian psychiatry was the concept of 'moral madness', or the idea that madness could affect temper and moral inclinations without disturbing the intellect or reason. Moral madness by this definition was partial, and also curable. Physicians championing the idea of moral madness, such as J. C. Pritchard and John Conolly, were influential in reforming the British madhouse as an institution. Partial or potentially curable madness might be 'morally' managed – that is, treated behaviourally, if possible, rather than through punishment and physical restraint. Moral management, however, was a two-edged sword: if madness could be treated and cured, then the patient also bore greater individual responsibility for his or her condition and could be expected to undergo discipline in order to internalize institutional control. The boundaries between sanity and insanity were consequently blurred, creating the anxiety that everyone was potentially susceptible to forms of mental derangement. Mental health, like so many things in the Victorian self-help culture, required a strong degree of individual self-control.

Most histories of mental illness place a further shift towards theories of inherited madness later in the century, after the publication of Darwin's *On the Origin of Species* in 1859. But of course concern with inheritance preceded Darwin, and it is very visible in the Brontës' lives and fiction. Under the causes of insanity in his copy of the family medical reference work, Thomas John Graham's *Modern Domestic Medicine* of 1826, Patrick underlined 'hereditary disposition'. Because he also entered notes about delirium tremens on those pages, biographers deduce that he was thinking especially about Branwell, attributing his drunkenness not only to moral failings but also to inherited physical susceptibility. Similarly, Charlotte Brontë gives us a complex aetiology of madness in her representation of Bertha Mason. Bertha inherits the propensity for madness from her mother, so that Jane does not consider her responsible for her illness: 'Sir', she pleads with Rochester, 'you are inexorable for that unfortunate lady: you speak of her with hate – with vindictive antipathy. It is cruel – she cannot help being mad' (*Jane Eyre*, III.i.301). But Rochester vilifies

Bertha for her unchastity and intemperance, claiming that 'her excesses had prematurely developed the germs of insanity' (III.i.306). The causes of madness, by mid century, were already being represented as an intermixture of inheritance and moral choices, which complicated the issue of individual responsibility. Still, Jane's momentary compassion is arguably bypassed in a novel which so neatly disposes of Bertha, whom postcolonial critics have regarded as a demonized representative of the racial Other.

For feminist criticism, Bertha has of course also become Gilbert and Gubar's 'Madwoman in the Attic', expressing what Jane manages to suppress: the rage of women at their constrained role in Victorian culture. Furthermore, although we never know her specific diagnosis, Bertha is often taken to be a fictional example of that Victorian diagnostic category, the hysteric. The origin of hysteria was thought to be, as the etymology suggests, the female reproductive system (*huster* is Greek for 'womb'). The cause of hysteria was supposedly an excess of passion overcoming weak female reason, and its symptoms were various, including weakness, fainting, seizures, paralysis and dumbness. As Elaine Showalter has famously argued, hysteria was primarily defined as a 'female malady' by doctors who pathologized female reproductive functions, associating menstrual cycles with mental and emotional instability.[2] For Showalter, Bertha becomes symbolic of Victorian women wrongly confined, female hysterics whose madness consisted of self-assertion and resistance to a culture in which normality was defined by medical men. More recent criticism has emphasized the multiplicity of personal motives and cultural forces operating in the psychiatry of the period, but histories of hysteria still rightly acknowledge Showalter's impact on our understanding of hysteria as a gendered disease category which shaped gendered treatments.

The Brontës, however, experienced and represented male as well as female maladies, an assortment of mental illnesses they seldom categorized as hysteria. One of the challenges for the present-day reader consists of peeling away our Freudian assumptions about madness. As Freud's successors, we tend to allow hysteria to stand in for many kinds of mental distress, to assume the erotic origins of hysteria and to interpret hysteria as the body expressing unconscious sexual desire. The Brontës, however, wrote not so much about hysteria as about religious melancholy, monomania and hypochondria.[3] While lovesickness may be a precipitating cause for both male and female characters, isolation from any human companionship seems more important; and desires are not repressed into the unconscious mind, but are rather fiercely debated in the conscious mind and amplified by the body.

Anne Brontë's own suffering from religious melancholy, as well as her fictional representation of it, probably strikes most contemporary readers as an unfamiliar kind of mental suffering. With the stress of being away from home at Roe Head, Anne came to fear that she was among the damned. Her anxiety was expressed somatically, as serious breathing trouble according to Charlotte and, as a visiting clergyman thought, 'gastric fever' so serious that 'her life hung on a slender thread'. That clergyman, James La Trobe, was able to reassure her as to her salvation, but only a return to Haworth helped her recover completely.[4] Although she eventually accepted the comforting if heterodox doctrine of universal salvation, which she had Helen Huntingdon express in *The Tenant of Wildfell Hall*, Anne continued throughout her life to experience feelings of religious unworthiness. Interestingly, her novelistic depiction of religious melancholy in *Agnes Grey* rests on a peasant character, Nancy Brown. Nancy, a woman of a 'serious, thoughtful turn of mind', gets highly sympathetic treatment as a woman who, doubting her salvation, has searched the Scriptures and sought assistance from the unhelpful rector (xi.78). The new curate Mr Weston visits her and is able to reassure her. Anne Brontë devotes a number of pages to narrating this episode, virtually allowing Weston to preach a homily on the subject. Nancy is to some degree a character witness for the newly introduced Weston, as well as a plot vehicle to allow Agnes and Weston to meet; but it is clear that Brontë also speaks through her and Weston to readers who may have experienced a similar melancholy. The irony that Anne registers through the character of Nancy is that the pious and conscientious suffer most severely from this type of mental distress, so that an external adviser becomes necessary, as well as a supportive community. The physical aspect of the disease is considered real and life-threatening, but the cure is relational.

Emily Brontë's depiction of mental illness is also highly somatic – so much so, indeed, that it may be difficult to tease out physical and mental illnesses in *Wuthering Heights*. Is Hindley's drunkenness entirely caused by his grief at the loss of his wife? Is Catherine's brain fever after Heathcliff's departure, and again after Heathcliff and Linton fight, a destabilizing factor which ultimately sends a congenitally vulnerable young woman across the border between sanity and insanity?[5] Is Heathcliff's self-starvation a result of monomania? Because all these illnesses involve the loss of a partner, we could consider them in the tradition of lovesickness, although not specifically in the tradition of the female hysteric. Hindley and Heathcliff are of course male sufferers, which should be no surprise because in the Brontë family's own experience, it was Branwell who became seriously ill when his love was thwarted. And, as Helen Small has argued, by the nineteenth century lovesickness was so thoroughly conventionalized that novelists were challenged to represent it with originality.[6] Emily could be said entirely to remake the lovesickness convention, especially as neither Catherine nor Heathcliff wastes away with traditional passivity; rather, they starve themselves with shocking energy. Neither is a traditional victim; both are perpetrators of their own unhappiness. And, as many have argued, their desire for each other, although embodied and possessive, is surprisingly unerotic.[7] In these several ways, Emily creates her own myth of loss in which both male and female are equally engulfed, and in which longing for home, deep companionship and implicit, absolute understanding seem more important than sexual fulfilment.

Charlotte Brontë, throughout her fiction, thinks through the mental distress incurred by solitude, and also by the shock of long-desired union after prolonged isolation. As in Emily's fiction, her sufferers are both male and female. Furthermore, they may be rejected lovers or, by contrast, those momentarily unhinged by unexpected fulfilment. In *The Professor*, William Crimsworth experiences hypochondria twice, in his 'lonely, parentless' boyhood and, later, just after his engagement to Frances. He explains this second depression as a 'reaction', in which 'the soul, of late rushing headlong to an aim, had overstrained the body's comparative weakness' (xxiii.211). Frances, too, suffers low spirits on her wedding day, but her reasons are not narrated – we simply know that she weeps briefly and trembles, uttering 'something like a checked sob' (xxv.226). Jane Eyre's troubled dreams before the planned marriage may be a foreshadowing of Rochester's intended bigamy, but they may also be about the loss of her independent identity. The depressions accompanying the illnesses of *Shirley* – Caroline's brain fever, Louis' miasmatic fever, Shirley's worries about rabies and Robert's mental weakness following his gunshot wound – are all exacerbated by love concerns, and all are to some extent cured by companionship. Notably, the sick Caroline is nursed by and cured in the presence of her mother rather than her lover. In *Villette*, Lucy Snowe's depression is brought on by what Dr John terms 'solitary confinement', or her isolation at Madame Beck's school during eight weeks of the long vacation (xvii.185). The penal language is significant. On visits to Pentonville prison and Bethlem asylum,

Charlotte had witnessed the devastating effects of solitary confinement, which was being used during this time as an experiment in supposedly humane and 'moral' treatment. Although Lucy is at the time secretly in love with Dr John, she identifies her ailment as more basic: 'I wanted companionship, I wanted friendship, I wanted counsel' (xvii.185). Lucy insists that the need for human companionship is as distinctly real as any essential physiologic process; it is 'a feeling that would make its way, rush out, or kill me – like ... the current which passes through the heart, and which, if aneurism or any other morbid cause obstructs its natural channels, impetuously seeks abnormal outlet' (xvii.185). If Lucy demonstrates some elements of the hysteric female, she also enlarges the category. Lucy is fully conscious of her need, which she claims as universally human. The role of the body, then, is not to speak the repressed erotic desire, but socially to amplify the human deprivation, even when that amplification threatens the individual life.

It is no longer fashionable to think of the Brontës as isolated geniuses; rather, we emphasize their embeddedness, through wide reading of books and periodicals, in a larger culture. But it is perhaps time, in examining their psychological insights, to take seriously their sense of social isolation, the ways in which social mediation through books and literature was insufficient to their experience of mental health. Their contribution to psychological realism in particular is seen in their somatic amplification of mental illness, where the body is used as a dramatic marker of the importance of social intercourse for men as well as for women. This seems to be the Brontës' way, fictionally, of taking social isolation seriously, as a matter of life and death.

NOTES

1 Sally Shuttleworth, *Charlotte Brontë and Victorian Psychology* (Cambridge University Press, 1996), p. 69.

2 See Elaine Showalter, *The Female Malady: Women, Madness, and English Culture, 1830–1980* (New York: Penguin, 1987), esp. pp. 1–20.

3 This chapter focuses on the Brontës' own categories of mental illness. There is, however, an important strand of work which maps our category of post-traumatic stress disorder on to the Victorians. See Jill L. Matus, *Shock, Memory and the Unconscious in Victorian Fiction* (Cambridge University Press, 2009), pp. 1–19. Also moving beyond the Brontës' own categories of pathology, Sally Shuttleworth reads the passionate children Jane Eyre and Catherine Earnshaw as possible psychiatric subjects in *The Mind of the Child: Child Development in Literature, Science, and Medicine* (Oxford University Press, 2010).

4 See Edward Chitham, *A Life of Anne Brontë* (Oxford: Blackwell, 1991), pp. 52–5, and Barker, pp. 280–2 and 285.

5 See Marianne Thormählen, 'The Lunatic and the Devil's Disciple: The "Lovers" in *Wuthering Heights*', *The Review of English Studies*, 48.190 (1997), 187–9.

6 See Helen Small, *Love's Madness: Medicine, the Novel, and Female Insanity, 1800–1865* (Oxford: Clarendon Press, 1996), *passim*.

7 For an early and influential example of this view, see Dorothy Van Ghent, *The English Novel: Form and Function* (New York: Rinehart & Co., 1953), p. 158.

Further reading

Some of the scholarly works listed below recur under different headings, as they are relevant to more than one topic. Three sources form a special case, however, in that they are indispensable to anyone who seeks further information about any aspect of the Brontës' lives and works: Juliet Barker's biography of the family, Margaret Smith's edition of Charlotte Brontë's letters and Christine Alexander and Margaret Smith's Brontë encyclopaedia. The titles of these three works are stated in full here and are not repeated under the individual headings:

Barker, Juliet. *The Brontës.* London: Weidenfeld & Nicolson, 1994; new edn 2011.
Smith, Margaret, ed. *The Letters of Charlotte Brontë with a Selection of Letters by Family and Friends.* Oxford: Clarendon Press, vol. I: *1829–1847*, 1995, with corrections 1996; vol. II: *1848–1851*, 2000; vol. III: *1852–1855*, 2004.
Alexander, Christine, and Margaret Smith, eds. *The Oxford Companion to the Brontës.* Oxford University Press, 2003.

For a student of the Brontës in their time who lacks expert knowledge of the period, the following general works, some of which have already served generations of scholars, will supply excellent and wide-ranging guidance:

Altick, Richard D. *The English Common Reader: A Social History of the Mass Reading Public, 1800–1900.* University of Chicago Press, 1957; subsequently reissued.
Briggs, Asa. *The Age of Improvement 1783–1867.* 1959; new edn Harlow: Longman, 2000.
Davis, Philip. *The Victorians.* The Oxford English Literary History, 8. Oxford University Press, 2002.
Gash, Norman. *Aristocracy and People: Britain 1815–1865.* The New History of England, 8. London: Edward Arnold, 1979.

Gilmour, Robin. *The Victorian Period: The Intellectual and Cultural Context of English Literature, 1830–1890*. Harlow: Longman, 1993.

Harrison, J. F. C. *The Early Victorians, 1832–1851*. London: Weidenfeld & Nicolson, 1971.

Houghton, Walter E. *The Victorian Frame of Mind, 1830–1870*. New Haven: Yale University Press, 1957; subsequently reissued.

McCord, Norman. *British History 1815–1906*. Oxford University Press, 1991.

Woodward, Llewellyn. *The Age of Reform 1815–1870*. London: Oxford University Press, 1962.

Young, G. M. *Victorian England: Portrait of an Age*. Oxford University Press, 1936.

Young, G. M., ed. *Early Victorian Britain 1830–1865*. 2 vols. Oxford University Press, 1934.

1. HAWORTH IN THE TIME OF THE BRONTËS

Baumber, Michael. *A History of Haworth*. Lancaster: Carnegie Publishing, 2009.

Dinsdale, Ann. *The Brontës at Haworth*. London: Frances Lincoln, 2006.

Lemon, Charles, ed. *Early Visitors to Haworth*. Haworth: Brontë Society, 1996.

Whitehead, S. R. *The Brontës' Haworth: The Place and the People the Brontës Knew*. Haworth: Ashmount Press, 2006.

Wood, Steven. *Haworth: 'A strange uncivilized little place'*. Stroud: Tempus, 2005.

2. DOMESTIC LIFE AT HAWORTH PARSONAGE

Alexander, Christine. 'Myth and Memory: Reading the Brontë Parsonage'. In Harald Hendrix, ed., *Writers' Houses and the Making of Memory*. London: Routledge, 2008, pp. 93–110.

Burton, Elizabeth. *The Early Victorians at Home 1837–1861*. Newton Abbot: Victorian & Modern History Book Club, 1973.

Cohen, Monica F. *Professional Domesticity in the Victorian Novel: Women, Work and Home*. Cambridge University Press, 1998.

Dinsdale, Ann. *The Brontës at Haworth*. London: Frances Lincoln, 2006.

Edgerley, C. Mabel. 'The Structure of Haworth Parsonage: Domestic Arrangements of the Brontës' Home'. *BST*, 9.46 (1936), 27–31.

Harland, Marion. *Charlotte Brontë at Home*. New York: G. P. Putnam's Sons, 1899.

Harling, Robert. *Home: A Victorian Vignette*. London: Constable, 1938.

Hesketh, Sally. 'Needlework in the Lives and Novels of the Brontës'. *BST*, 22 (1997), 72–85.

Kellett, Jocelyn. *Haworth Parsonage: The Home of the Brontës*. Haworth: Brontë Society, 1977.

Logan, Thad. *The Victorian Parlour*. Cambridge University Press, 2001.

Parker, Rozsika. *The Subversive Stitch: Embroidery and the Making of the Feminine*. London: Women's Press, 1984.

3. LOCATIONS IN NORTHERN ENGLAND ASSOCIATED WITH THE BRONTËS' LIVES AND WORKS

Dinsdale, Ann. *The Brontës at Haworth*. London: Frances Lincoln, 2006.

Marsden, Hilda. 'The Scenic Background of *Wuthering Heights*'. *BST*, 13.67 (1957), 111–30.

Raymond, Ernest. *In the Steps of the Brontës*. London: Rich and Cowan, 1948.

Stead, J. J. 'Hathersage and Jane Eyre'. *BST*, 1.4 (1896), 26–8.

Stuart, J. A. Erskine. *The Brontë Country: Its Topography, Antiquities, and History*. London: Longmans, Green & Co., 1888.

Watson, Nicola J. *The Literary Tourist: Readers and Places in Romantic & Victorian Britain*. Basingstoke: Palgrave, 2006.

Wroot, Herbert E. 'Sources of Charlotte Brontë's Novels: Persons and Places'. *BST*, 8.45 (1935), 5–214.

4. THE FATHER OF THE BRONTËS

Alexander, Christine. 'Father of the Brontës: Romantic or Victorian?' In Natalie McKnight, ed., *Victorian Fathers*. Cambridge: Cambridge Scholars, 2011, pp. 13–33.

Green, Dudley. *Patrick Brontë: Father of Genius*. Stroud: Nonsuch, 2008.

Green, Dudley, ed. *The Letters of the Reverend Patrick Brontë*. Stroud: Nonsuch, 2005.

Lock, John, and W. T. Dixon. *A Man of Sorrow: The Life, Letters and Times of the Rev. Patrick Brontë 1777–1861*. London: Nelson, 1965.

Turner, J. Horsfall, ed. *Brontëana: The Rev. Patrick Brontë, A.B.: His Collected Works and Life*. Bingley: T. Harrison & Sons, 1898.

5. A MOTHER AND HER SUBSTITUTES

Edgerley, C. Mabel. 'Elizabeth Branwell: The "small, antiquated lady"'. *BST*, 9.47 (1937), 103–14.

Grylls, Richard G. *Branwell & Bramble: A Brief History of a West Cornwall Clan*. Tring, Herts.: Richard G. Grylls, 2006.

Lane, Margaret. 'Maria Branwell'. *BST*, 18.93 (1983), 208–16.

Newbold, Margaret. 'The Branwell Saga'. *Brontë Studies*, 27.1 (Mar. 2002), 15–26.

6. PATRICK BRANWELL BRONTË

Alexander, Christine, and Jane Sellars. *The Art of the Brontës*. Cambridge University Press, 1995.

Conover, Robin St John. 'Creating Angria: Charlotte and Branwell Brontë's Collaboration'. *BST*, 24.1 (1999), 16–32.

Gérin, Winifred. *Branwell Brontë: A Biography*. London: Hutchinson & Co., 1967.

Grundy, F. H. *Pictures of the Past*. London: Griffith and Farrar, 1879.

Leyland, Francis A. *The Brontë Family with Special Reference to Patrick Branwell Brontë.* 2 vols. London: Hurst and Blackett, 1886.

Neufeldt, Victor A., ed. *The Poems of Patrick Branwell Brontë.* New York: Garland, 1990.

The Works of Patrick Branwell Brontë. 3 vols. New York: Garland, 1997–9.

Symington, J. Alexander, and C. W. Hatfield, eds. *Patrick Branwell Brontë: A Complete Transcript of the Leyland Manuscripts Showing the Unpublished Portions from the Original Manuscripts.* Privately printed, 1925.

Winnifrith, Tom. 'The Life of Patrick Branwell Brontë'. *BST*, 24.1 (1999), 1–10.

7. CHARLOTTE BRONTË

Alexander, Christine. *The Early Writings of Charlotte Brontë.* Oxford: Blackwell, 1983.

Fraser, Rebecca. *Charlotte Brontë.* London: Methuen, 1988.

Gérin, Winifred. *Charlotte Bronte: The Evolution of Genius.* Oxford University Press, 1967; frequently reprinted.

Glen, Heather. *Charlotte Brontë: The Imagination in History.* Oxford University Press, 2002.

Moglen, Helene. *Charlotte Brontë: The Self Conceived.* New York: Norton, 1976.

Shuttleworth, Sally. *Charlotte Brontë and Victorian Psychology.* Cambridge University Press, 1996.

8. EMILY BRONTË

Chitham, Edward. *The Birth of* Wuthering Heights*: Emily Brontë at Work.* Basingstoke: Macmillan, 1998.

Davies, Stevie. *Emily Brontë: Heretic.* London: Women's Press, 1994.

Gérin, Winifred. *Emily Brontë: A Biography.* Oxford University Press, 1971.

Pykett, Lyn. *Emily Brontë.* Basingstoke: Macmillan, 1989.

9. ANNE BRONTË

Berry, Elizabeth Hollis. *Anne Brontë's Radical Vision: Structures of Consciousness.* ELS Monograph Series, 62. University of Victoria, Canada, 1994.

Chitham, Edward. *A Life of Anne Brontë.* Oxford: Blackwell, 1991.

Frawley, Maria. *Anne Brontë.* Twayne English Authors Series. New York: Twayne, 1996.

Hagan, Sandra, and Juliette Wells, eds. *The Brontës in the World of the Arts.* Aldershot: Ashgate, 2008.

Langland, Elizabeth. *Anne Brontë: The Other One.* Totowa, NJ: Barnes and Noble, 1989.

Nash, Julie, and Barbara A. Suess, eds. *New Approaches to the Art of Anne Brontë.* Aldershot: Ashgate, 2001.

10. FRIENDS, SERVANTS AND A HUSBAND

Bellamy, Joan. *'More Precious than Rubies': Mary Taylor, Friend of Charlotte Brontë, Strong-Minded Woman*. Beverley: Highgate Publications, 2002.

Palmer, Geoffrey, ed. *Dear Martha: The Letters of Arthur Bell Nicholls to Martha Brown*. Haworth: Brontë Society, 2004.

Whitehead, Barbara. *Charlotte Brontë and her 'Dearest Nell': The Story of a Friendship*. Otley: Smith Settle, 1993.

Whitehead, Stephen. 'Arthur Bell Nicholls: A Reassessment'. *Brontë Studies*, 33.2 (July 2008), 97–108.

11. THE BRONTËS' SIBLING BONDS

Adams, Maurianne. 'Family Disintegration and Creative Regeneration: The Case of Charlotte Brontë and Jane Eyre'. In Anthony S. Wohl, ed., *The Victorian Family: Structure and Stresses*. New York: St Martin's Press, 1978, pp. 148–79.

Elfenbein, Andrew. 'Byron at the Margins: Emily Brontë and the Fate of Milo'. In *Byron and the Victorians*. Cambridge University Press, 1995, pp. 126–68.

Lamonica, Drew. *'We are Three Sisters': Self and Family in the Writing of the Brontës*. Columbia: University of Missouri Press, 2003.

Tayler, Irene. *Holy Ghosts: The Male Muses of Emily and Charlotte Brontë*. New York: Columbia University Press, 1990.

12. JUVENILIA

Alexander, Christine. *The Early Writings of Charlotte Brontë*. Oxford: Blackwell, 1983.

Alexander, Christine, ed. *An Edition of the Early Writings of Charlotte Brontë*. Oxford: Blackwell, for the Shakespeare Head Press, vol. I: *The Glass Town Saga, 1826–1832*, 1987; vol. II: *The Rise of Angria, 1833–1835*, 1991; vol. III: *The Angrian Legend, 1836–1839*, forthcoming.

   The Brontës: Tales of Glass Town, Angria, and Gondal. Oxford World's Classics. Oxford University Press, 2010.

Chitham, Edward, ed. *The Poems of Anne Brontë: A New Text and Commentary*. London: Macmillan, 1979; repr. 1987.

Gezari, Janet. *Last Things: Emily Brontë's Poems*. Oxford University Press, 2007.

Gezari, Janet, ed. *Emily Jane Brontë: The Complete Poems*. Harmondsworth: Penguin, 1992.

Glen, Heather. 'Configuring a World: Some Childhood Writings of Charlotte Brontë'. In Mary Hilton, Morag Styles and Victor Watson, eds., *Opening the Nursery Door: Reading, Writing and Childhood 1600–1900*. London and New York: Routledge, 1997, pp. 215–34.

Glen, Heather, ed. *Charlotte Brontë: Tales of Angria*. London: Penguin, 2006.

Neufeldt, Victor A., ed. *The Works of Patrick Branwell Brontë*. 3 vols. New York: Garland, 1997–9.

13. THE BRUSSELS EXPERIENCE

Duthie, Enid. *The Foreign Vision of Charlotte Brontë*. London: Macmillan, 1975.
Lonoff, Sue, ed. and trans. *Charlotte Brontë and Emily Brontë, the Belgian Essays: A Critical Edition*. New Haven: Yale University Press, 1996.
Ruijssenaars, Eric. *Charlotte Brontë's Promised Land: The Pensionnat Heger and Other Brontë Places in Brussels*. Haworth: Brontë Society, 2000.

14. THE BRONTË CORRESPONDENCE

Green, Dudley, ed. *The Letters of the Reverend Patrick Brontë*. Stroud: Nonsuch, 2005.
Smith, Margaret, ed. *The Letters of Charlotte Brontë with a Selection of Letters by Family and Friends*. Oxford: Clarendon Press, vol. I: *1829–1847*, 1995, with corrections 1996; vol. II: *1848–1851*, 2000; vol. III: *1852–1855*, 2004.
Symington, J. Alexander, and Thomas J. Wise, eds. *The Brontës: Their Lives, Friendships and Correspondence*. 4 vols. Oxford: Blackwell, for the Shakespeare Head Press, 1932.

15. PORTRAITS OF THE BRONTËS

Alexander, Christine, and Jane Sellars. *The Art of the Brontës*. Cambridge University Press, 1995.
Barker, Juliet. 'The Brontë Portraits: A Mystery Solved'. *BST*, 20.1 (1990), 3–11.
Lister, Raymond. *George Richmond: A Critical Biography*. London: Robin Garton, 1981.
Maas, Jeremy. *The Victorian Art World in Photographs*. London: Barrie and Jenkins, 1984.

16. THE POETRY OF THE BRONTËS

Birch, Dinah. 'Emily Brontë'. In Claude Rawson, ed., *The Cambridge Companion to English Poets*. Cambridge University Press, 2011, pp. 408–21.
Chitham, Edward, ed. *The Poems of Anne Brontë: A New Text and Commentary*. London: Macmillan, 1979; repr. 1987.
Gezari, Janet. *Last Things: Emily Brontë's Poems*. Oxford University Press, 2007.
Gezari, Janet, ed. *Emily Jane Brontë: The Complete Poems*. Harmondsworth: Penguin, 1992.
Homans, Margaret. *Women Writers and Poetic Identity*. Princeton University Press, 1980, pp. 104–61.
Leighton, Angela. *Victorian Women Poets: Writing against the Heart*. London: Harvester Wheatsheaf, 1992.
'The Poetry'. In Heather Glen, ed., *The Cambridge Companion to the Brontës*. Cambridge University Press, 2002, pp. 53–71.
Neufeldt, Victor A., ed. *The Poems of Charlotte Brontë*. New York: Garland, 1985.
The Works of Patrick Branwell Brontë. 3 vols. New York: Garland, 1997–9.

Roper, Derek, with Edward Chitham, eds. *The Poems of Emily Brontë*. Oxford University Press, 1995.

Tayler, Irene. *Holy Ghosts: The Male Muses of Emily and Charlotte Brontë*. New York: Columbia University Press, 1990.

17. LITERARY INFLUENCES ON THE BRONTËS

Alexander, Christine. '"That kingdom of gloom": Charlotte Brontë, the Annuals and the Gothic'. *Nineteenth-Century Literature*, 47.4 (Mar. 1993), 409–36.

Alton, Anne Hiebert. 'Books in the Novels of Charlotte Brontë'. *BST*, 21.7 (1996), 265–74.

Glen, Heather. *Charlotte Brontë: The Imagination in History*. Oxford University Press, 2002.

Glen, Heather, ed. *The Cambridge Companion to the Brontës*. Cambridge University Press, 2002 (see especially the contributions by Glen, Juliet Barker and Carol Bock).

Thormählen, Marianne. *The Brontës and Education*. Cambridge University Press, 2007.

Wheat, Patricia H. *The Adytum of the Heart: The Literary Criticism of Charlotte Brontë*. Rutherford: Fairleigh Dickinson University Press, 1992.

Winnifrith, Tom. *The Brontës and their Background: Romance and Reality*. London: Macmillan, 1973.

18. THE BRONTËS' WAY INTO PRINT

AND

19. READING THE BRONTËS: THEIR FIRST AUDIENCES

Allott, Miriam, ed. *The Brontës: The Critical Heritage*. London: Routledge & Kegan Paul, 1974.

Altick, Richard D. *The English Common Reader: A Social History of the Mass Reading Public 1800–1900*. University of Chicago Press, 1957; subsequently reissued.

Beetham, Margaret. 'Women and the Consumption of Print'. In Joanne Shattock, ed., *Women and Literature in Britain 1800–1900*. Cambridge University Press, 2001, pp. 55–77.

Black, Alistair. *A New History of the English Public Library: Social and Intellectual Contexts, 1850–1914*. London: Leicester University Press, 1996.

Black, Alistair, and Peter Hoare, eds. *The Cambridge History of Libraries in Britain and Ireland*, vol. III: *1850–2000*. Cambridge University Press, 2006.

Bock, Carol. *Charlotte Brontë and the Storyteller's Audience*. Iowa City: University of Iowa Press, 1992.

'Authorship, the Brontës, and *Fraser's Magazine*: "Coming Forward" as an Author in Early Victorian England'. *Victorian Literature and Culture*, 29 (2001), 241–66.

Duckett, Bob. 'Where Did the Brontës Get Their Books?' *Brontë Studies*, 32.3 (Nov. 2007), 193–206.

Eliot, Simon. "'Never Mind the Value, What about the Price?'" *Nineteenth-Century Literature*, 56.2 (2001), 160–97.

Flint, Kate. *The Woman Reader 1837–1914*. Oxford: Clarendon Press, 1993.

Griest, Guinevere L. *Mudie's Circulating Library and the Victorian Novel*. Bloomington: Indiana University Press, 1970.

Jordan, John O., and Robert L. Pattern, eds. *Literature in the Market-Place: Nineteenth-Century British Publishing and Reading Practices*. Cambridge University Press, 1995.

McKitterick, David, ed. *The Cambridge History of the Book in Britain*, vol. VI: *1830–1914*. Cambridge University Press, 2009.

Sutherland, J. A. *Victorian Novelists and Publishers*. University of Chicago Press, 1976.

20. BRONTË BIOGRAPHY: A SURVEY OF A GENRE

Adamson, Alan. *Mr Charlotte Brontë: The Life of Arthur Bell Nicholls*. Montreal: McGill-Queens University Press, 2008.

Bellamy, Joan. *'More Precious than Rubies': Mary Taylor, Friend of Charlotte Brontë, Strong-Minded Woman*. Beverley: Highgate Publications, 2002.

Bentley, Phyllis. *The Brontës*. London: Home and Van Thal, 1947.

Blondel, Jacques. *Emily Brontë: Expérience spirituelle et création poétique*. Paris: Presses Universitaires de France, 1955.

Brontë family. *The Life and Works of Charlotte Brontë and her Sisters*. Haworth edn. 7 vols. London: Smith, Elder & Co., 1899–1900.

Chitham, Edward. *A Life of Emily Brontë*. Oxford: Blackwell, 1987; 2nd edn Stroud: Amberley Press, 2010.

Cochrane, Margaret and Robert. *My Dear Boy: The Life of Arthur Bell Nicholls B.A., Husband of Charlotte Brontë*. Beverley: Highgate Publications, 1999.

Franks, Kathleen. *A Chainless Soul: A Life of Emily Brontë*. Boston: Houghton Mifflin, 1990.

Fraser, Rebecca. *Charlotte Brontë*. London: Methuen, 1988.

Gérin, Winifred. *Anne Brontë*. London: Nelson, 1959.

  Branwell Brontë. London: Nelson, 1961.

  Charlotte Brontë: The Evolution of Genius. Oxford University Press, 1967; frequently reprinted.

  Emily Brontë. Oxford University Press, 1971.

Gordon, Lyndall. *Charlotte Brontë: A Passionate Life*. London: Chatto & Windus, 1994.

Green, Dudley. *Patrick Brontë: Father of Genius*. Stroud: Nonsuch, 2008.

Hanson, L. and E. M. *The Four Brontës*. Oxford University Press, 1949.

Harrison, Grace Elizabeth. *The Clue to the Brontës*. London: Methuen, 1948.

Hewish, John. *Emily Brontë: A Critical and Biographical Study*. London: Macmillan, 1969.

Lane, Margaret. *The Brontë Story: A Reconsideration of Mrs Gaskell's* Life of Charlotte Brontë. London: Heinemann, 1953.

Law, Alice. *Emily Jane Brontë and the Authorship of* Wuthering Heights. Altham: Old Parsonage Press, 1925.

Lemon, Charles. *A Centenary History of the Brontë Society.* Haworth: Brontë Society, 1993.

Leyland, Francis. *The Brontë Family with Special Reference to Patrick Branwell Brontë.* 2 vols. London: Hurst and Blackett, 1886.

Lock, John, and W. T. Dixon. *A Man of Sorrow: The Life, Letters and Times of the Rev. Patrick Brontë 1777–1861.* London: Nelson, 1965.

Maurier, Daphne du. *The Infernal World of Branwell Brontë.* London: Gollancz, 1960.

Miller, Lucasta. *The Brontë Myth.* London: Jonathan Cape, 2001.

Moglen, Helene. *Charlotte Brontë: The Self Conceived.* New York: Norton, 1976.

Moore, Virginia. *The Life and Eager Death of Emily Brontë: A Biography.* London: Rich and Cowan, 1936.

Myer, Valerie Grosvenor. *Charlotte Brontë: Truculent Spirit.* London: Vision Press, 1987.

Peters, Margaret. *Unquiet Soul: A Biography of Charlotte Brontë.* New York: Simon & Schuster, 1975.

Ratchford, Fannie. *Gondal's Queen: A Novel in Verse by Emily Jane Brontë.* Austin: University of Texas Press, 1955.

Robinson, Mary F. *Emily Brontë.* London: W. H. Allen, 1883.

Shorter, Clement. *Charlotte Brontë and her Circle.* London: Hodder and Stoughton, 1896.

The Brontës: Life and Letters. 2 vols. London: Hodder and Stoughton, 1908.

Simpson, Charles. *Emily Brontë.* London: Country Life, 1929.

Smith, Margaret. *The Letters of Charlotte Brontë with a Selection of Letters by Family and Friends.* 3 vols. Oxford: Clarendon Press, 1995–2004.

Smurthwaite, John. *The Life of John Alexander Symington, Bibliographer and Librarian.* New York: Edward Mellen Press, 1985.

Symington, John A., and Thomas J. Wise. *The Brontës: Their Lives, Friendships and Correspondence.* 4 vols. Oxford: Blackwell, for the Shakespeare Head Press, 1932.

Whitehead, Barbara. *Charlotte Brontë and her 'Dearest Nell': The Story of a Friendship.* Otley: Smith Settle, 1993.

Wilson, Romer. *All Alone: The Life and Private History of Emily Jane Brontë.* London: Chatto & Windus, 1928.

Winnifrith, Tom. *The Brontës and their Background: Romance and Reality.* London: Macmillan, 1973.

Wright, William. *The Brontës in Ireland.* London: Hodder and Stoughton, 1893.

Yates, W. W. *The Father of the Brontës: His Life and Work at Dewsbury and Hartshead.* Leeds: Spack and Son, 1897; repr. Mirfield: Imelda Marsden, 2006.

21. MID-NINETEENTH-CENTURY CRITICAL RESPONSES TO THE BRONTËS

Allott, Miriam, ed. *Emily Brontë,* Wuthering Heights: *A Casebook.* Basingstoke: Macmillan, 1970.

The Brontës: The Critical Heritage. London: Routledge & Kegan Paul, 1974.

Lodge, Sara. Jane Eyre: *A Reader's Guide to Essential Criticism.* Basingstoke: Palgrave Macmillan, 2009, chapter 1.

Miller, Lucasta. *The Brontë Myth.* London: Jonathan Cape, 2001.

Stoneman, Patsy. Wuthering Heights: *A Reader's Guide to Essential Criticism.* Basingstoke: Palgrave Macmillan, 1993; Duxford: Icon, 2000.

Brontë Transformations: The Cultural Dissemination of Jane Eyre *and* Wuthering Heights. Hemel Hempstead: Harvester Wheatsheaf, 1996.

Stoneman, Patsy, ed. *Jane Eyre on Stage, 1848–1898: An Illustrated Edition of Eight Plays with Contextual Notes.* Aldershot: Ashgate, 2007.

22. BRONTË SCHOLARSHIP AND CRITICISM, 1920–1970

Allott, Miriam, ed. *Emily Brontë,* Wuthering Heights: *A Casebook.* Basingstoke: Macmillan, 1970.

Charlotte Brontë, Jane Eyre *and* Villette: *A Casebook.* Basingstoke: Macmillan, 1973.

Cecil, David. *Early Victorian Novelists: Essays in Revaluation.* London: Constable, 1934.

Craik, W. A. *The Brontë Novels.* London: Methuen, 1968.

Ewbank, Inga-Stina. *Their Proper Sphere: A Study of the Brontë Sisters as Early-Victorian Female Novelists.* London: Edward Arnold, 1966.

Hafley, James. 'The Villain in *Wuthering Heights*'. *Nineteenth-Century Fiction,* 13.3 (Dec. 1958), 199–215.

Heilman, Robert. 'Charlotte Brontë, Reason, and the Moon'. *Nineteenth-Century Fiction,* 14.4 (Mar. 1960), 283–302.

Knies, Earl A. *The Art of Charlotte Brontë.* Athens: Ohio University Press, 1969.

Lodge, David. 'Fire and Eyre: Charlotte Brontë's War of Earthly Elements'. In *Language of Fiction: Essays in Criticism and Verbal Analysis of the English Novel.* London: Routledge & Kegan Paul, 1966, pp. 114–43.

Martin, Robert Bernard. *The Accents of Persuasion: Charlotte Brontë's Novels.* London: Faber and Faber, 1966.

Ratchford, Fannie Elizabeth. *The Brontës' Web of Childhood.* New York: Columbia University Press, 1941.

Sanger, Charles P. *The Structure of* Wuthering Heights. Hogarth Essays, 19. London: Hogarth Press, 1926; frequently reprinted, e.g. in Ian Gregor, ed., *The Brontës: A Collection of Critical Essays.* Englewood Cliffs: Prentice-Hall, 1970, pp. 7–18.

Thompson, Wade. 'Infanticide and Sadism in Wuthering Heights'. *PMLA,* 78.1 (Mar. 1963), 69–74.

Van Ghent, Dorothy. 'The Window-Figure and the Two-Children Figure in Wuthering Heights'. *Nineteenth-Century Fiction,* 7.3 (Dec. 1952), 189–97.

Walker, Arthur D., and R. J. Duckett, eds. *The Brontë Society Transactions 1895–2001: An Index and History.* Haworth: Brontë Society, 2005.

23. BRONTË SCHOLARSHIP AND CRITICISM, *c.* 1970–2000

Some entries below are from the first decade of the twenty-first century. For a survey of post-2000 work on the Brontës, with bibliographical information, see Chapter 24 in its entirety.

Armstrong, Nancy. *Desire and Domestic Fiction: A Political History of the Novel.* Oxford University Press, 1987.

Berry, Laura C. 'Acts of Custody and Incarceration in *Wuthering Heights* and *The Tenant of Wildfell Hall'. Novel,* 30.1 (Fall 1996), 32–55.

Boumelha, Penny. *Charlotte Brontë.* London: Harvester, 1990.

Eagleton, Terry. *Myths of Power: A Marxist Study of the Brontës.* London: Macmillan, 1975; 30th anniversary edn 2005.

Heathcliff and the Great Hunger. London: Verso, 1995.

Frawley, Maria. *Anne Brontë.* Twayne English Authors Series. New York: Twayne, 1996.

Gezari, Janet. *Last Things: Emily Brontë's Poems.* Oxford University Press, 2007.

Gilbert, Sandra, and Susan Gubar, *The Madwoman in the Attic: The Woman Writer and the Nineteenth-Century Literary Imagination.* New Haven: Yale University Press, 1979; repr. 2000.

Glen, Heather. *Charlotte Brontë: The Imagination in History.* Oxford University Press, 2002.

Glen, Heather, ed. Jane Eyre: *A New Casebook.* Basingstoke: Macmillan, 1997.

Homans, Margaret. *Bearing the Word: Language and Female Experience in Nineteenth-Century Women's Writing.* University of Chicago Press, 1986.

Langland, Elizabeth. *Anne Brontë: The Other One.* Basingstoke: Macmillan, 1989.

Lodge, Sara. Jane Eyre: *A Reader's Guide to Essential Criticism.* Basingstoke: Palgrave Macmillan, 2009.

Longmuir, Anne. '"Reader, perhaps you were never in Belgium?": Negotiating British Identity in Charlotte Brontë's *The Professor* and *Villette'. Nineteenth-Century Literature,* 64.2 (2009), 163–88.

McMaster, Juliet. '"Imbecile Laughter" and "Desperate Earnest" in *The Tenant of Wildfell Hall'. Modern Language Quarterly,* 43.3 (1982), 352–68.

Meyer, Susan. *Imperialism at Home: Race and Victorian Women's Fiction.* Ithaca: Cornell University Press, 1996.

Michie, Elsie. 'White Chimpanzees and Oriental Despots: Racial Stereotyping and Edward Rochester'. In Beth Newman, ed., *Case Studies in Contemporary Criticism:* Jane Eyre. New York: St Martin's Press, 1996, pp. 584–98.

Nash, Julie, and Barbara A. Suess, eds. *New Approaches to the Literary Art of Anne Brontë*. Aldershot: Ashgate, 2001.

Shuttleworth, Sally. *Charlotte Brontë and Victorian Psychology*. Cambridge University Press, 1996.

Spivak, Gayatri. 'Three Women's Texts and a Critique of Imperialism'. *Critical Inquiry*, 12.1 (Autumn 1985), 243–61.

Stoneman, Patsy. Wuthering Heights: *A Reader's Guide to Essential Criticism*. Basingstoke: Palgrave Macmillan, 1993; Duxford: Icon, 2000.

    Brontë Transformations: The Cultural Dissemination of Jane Eyre *and* Wuthering Heights. Hemel Hempstead: Harvester Wheatsheaf, 1996.

Stoneman, Patsy, ed. Wuthering Heights: *A New Casebook*. Basingstoke: Macmillan, 1993.

Thormählen, Marianne. 'The Villain of Wildfell Hall: Aspects and Prospects of Arthur Huntingdon'. *The Modern Language Review*, 88.4 (Oct. 1993), 831–41.

Winnifrith, Tom, ed. *Critical Essays on Emily Brontë*. New York: Simon & Schuster, 1997.

25. ADAPTATIONS, PREQUELS, SEQUELS, TRANSLATIONS

Ingham, Patricia. *The Brontës*. Oxford World's Classics, Authors in Context. Oxford University Press, 2006.

Pyrhönen, Heta. *Bluebeard Gothic:* Jane Eyre *and its Progeny*. University of Toronto Press, 2010.

Rubik, Margarete, and Elke Mettinger-Schartmann, eds. *A Breath of Fresh Eyre: Intertextual and Intermedial Reworkings of* Jane Eyre. Amsterdam: Rodopi, 2007.

Stoneman, Patsy. *Brontë Transformations: The Cultural Dissemination of* Jane Eyre *and* Wuthering Heights. Hemel Hempstead: Harvester Wheatsheaf, 1996.

Stoneman, Patsy, ed. *Jane Eyre on Stage, 1848–1898: An Illustrated Edition of Eight Plays with Contextual Notes*. Aldershot: Ashgate, 2007.

26. RELIGION

Bebbington, D.W. *Evangelicalism in Modern Britain: A History from the 1730s to the 1980s*. London: Unwin Hyman, 1989.

Bradley, Ian. *The Call to Seriousness: The Evangelical Impact on the Victorians*. London: Jonathan Cape, 1976.

Chadwick, Owen. *The Victorian Church*, part I: *1829–1859*. London: A. and C. Black, 1966; repr. London: SCM Press, 1987.

Cunningham, Valentine. *Everywhere Spoken Against: Dissent in the Victorian Novel*. Oxford: Clarendon Press, 1975.

Davies, Horton. *Worship and Theology in England*, vol. III: *From Watts and Wesley to Maurice, 1690–1850*. Princeton University Press, 1961.

Jay, Elisabeth. *The Religion of the Heart: Anglican Evangelicalism and the Nineteenth Century Novel*. Oxford: Clarendon Press, 1979.

Qualls, Barry. *The Secular Pilgrims of Victorian Fiction.* Cambridge University Press, 1982.

Reardon, Bernard M. G. *From Coleridge to Gore: A Century of Religious Thought in Britain.* London: Longman, 1971.

Storr, Vernon. *The Development of English Theology in the Nineteenth Century 1800–1860.* London: Longman, Green & Co., 1913.

Thormählen, Marianne. *The Brontës and Religion.* Cambridge University Press, 1999.

'The Brontës'. In Rebecca Lemon, Emma Mason, Jonathan Roberts and Christopher Rowland, eds., *The Blackwell Companion to the Bible in English Literature.* Oxford: Wiley-Blackwell, 2009, pp. 512–24.

Wheeler, Michael. *Death and the Future Life in Victorian Literature and Theology.* Cambridge University Press, 1990.

Wolff, Robert Lee. *Gains and Losses: Novels of Faith and Doubt in Victorian England.* London: John Murray, 1977.

27. THE PHILOSOPHICAL-INTELLECTUAL CONTEXT

Ashton, Rosemary. *The German Idea: Four English Writers and the Reception of German Thought, 1800–1860.* Cambridge University Press, 1980; London: Libris, 1994.

Barfield, Owen. *Saving the Appearances: A Study in Idolatry.* New York: Harcourt Brace, 1957.

Bowie, Andrew. *Aesthetics and Subjectivity: From Kant to Nietzsche.* Manchester University Press, 1990.

Carlyle, Thomas. *Past and Present.* London: Chapman and Hall, 1843.

Coleridge, Samuel Taylor. *Aids to Reflection.* 1825, many subsequent edns; in John Beer, ed., *The Collected Works of Samuel Taylor Coleridge,* Bollingen edn, vol. XI, London and Princeton: Routledge and Princeton University Press, 1993.

Confessions of an Inquiring Spirit, ed. H. N. Coleridge. London: Pickering, 1840.

Davies, Stevie. *Emily Brontë: Heretic.* London: Women's Press, 1994.

Goethe, J. W. von. *Wilhelm Meister's Apprenticeship,* trans. Thomas Carlyle. Edinburgh: Oliver & Boyd, 1824.

Hare, Augustus and Julius. *Guesses at Truth.* 1st edn, London, 1827, and 3rd edn, London, 1847.

Prickett, Stephen. *Origins of Narrative: The Romantic Appropriation of the Bible.* Cambridge University Press, 1996.

Modernity and the Reinvention of Tradition: Backing into the Future. Cambridge University Press, 2009.

Pugin, A. W. N. *Contrasts.* 1836; repr. Leicester University Press, 1969.

Thormählen, Marianne. *The Brontës and Religion.* Cambridge University Press, 1999.

28. EDUCATION

Birch, Dinah. *Our Victorian Education.* Oxford: Blackwell, 2008.
Lawson, John, and Harold Silver. *A Social History of Education in England.* London: Methuen, 1973.
Lecaros, Cecilia Wadsö. *The Victorian Governess Novel.* Lund Studies in English, 100. Lund University Press, 2001.
Rauch, Alan. *Useful Knowledge: The Victorians, Morality, and the March of Intellect.* Durham, NC: Duke University Press, 2001.
Shuttleworth, Sally. *The Mind of the Child: Child Development in Literature, Science, and Medicine, 1840–1900.* Oxford University Press, 2010.
Silver, Harold. *Education as History: Interpreting Nineteenth- and Twentieth-Century History.* London: Methuen, 1983.
Stephens, W. B. *Education in Britain, 1750–1914.* New York: St Martin's Press, 1998.
Stewart, W. A. C., and W. P. McCann. *The Educational Innovators: 1750–1880.* London: Macmillan, 1967.
Thormählen, Marianne. *The Brontës and Education.* Cambridge University Press, 2007.
Tropp, Asher. *The School Teachers: The Growth of the Teaching Profession in England and Wales from 1800 to the Present Day.* London: Heinemann, 1957.

29. ART AND MUSIC

Alexander, Christine. *The Early Writings of Charlotte Brontë.* Oxford: Blackwell, 1983. '"The burning clime": Charlotte Brontë and John Martin'. *Nineteenth-Century Literature,* 50.3 (Dec. 1995), 285–316.
Alexander, Christine, ed. *An Edition of the Early Writings of Charlotte Brontë.* Oxford: Blackwell, for the Shakespeare Head Press, vol. I: *The Glass Town Saga, 1826–1832,* 1987; vol. II: *The Rise of Angria, 1833–1835,* 1991; vol III: *The Angrian Legend, 1836–1839,* forthcoming.
Alexander, Christine, and Jane Sellars. *The Art of the Brontës.* Cambridge University Press, 1995.
Hagan, Sandra, and Juliette Wells, eds. *The Brontës in the World of the Arts.* Aldershot: Ashgate, 2008.
Higuchi, Akiko. *The Brontës and Music,* vol. I: *Anne Brontë's Song Book and Branwell Brontë's Flute Book;* vol. II: *The Brontës' World of Music.* 2nd edn. Tokyo: Yushodo Press, 2008.
Kromm, Jane. 'Visual Culture and Scopic Custom in *Jane Eyre* and *Villette*'. *Victorian Literature and Culture,* 26.2 (1998), 369–94.
Leyland, Francis A. *The Brontë Family with Special Reference to Patrick Branwell Brontë.* 2 vols. London: Hurst and Blackett, 1886.
Losano, Antonia. 'The Professionalization of the Woman Artist in Anne Brontë's *The Tenant of Wildfell Hall*'. *Nineteenth-Century Literature,* 58.1 (2003), 1–41.
Rastall, Richard, ed. *Anne Brontë's Song Book and Branwell Brontë's Flute Book.* Leeds: Boethius Press, 1980.

Smith, Anne, ed. *The Art of Emily Brontë*. London: Vision, 1976.

Thormählen, Marianne. *The Brontës and Education*. Cambridge University Press, 2007.

Wallace, Robert K. *Emily Brontë and Beethoven: Romantic Equilibrium in Fiction and Music*. Athens, GA: Georgia University Press, 1986.

30. NATURAL HISTORY

Alexander, Christine, and Jane Sellars. *The Art of the Brontës*. Cambridge University Press, 1995.

Allen, David Elliston. *The Naturalist in Britain: A Social History*. London: Allen Lane, 1976.

Barber, Lynn. *The Heyday of Natural History, 1820–1870*. London: Jonathan Cape, 1980.

Berman, Ronald. 'Charlotte Brontë's Natural History'. *BST*, 18.94 (1984), 271–8.

Duthie, Enid L. *The Brontës and Nature*. London: Macmillan, 1986.

Gates, Barbara T. *Kindred Nature: Victorian and Edwardian Women Embrace the Living World*. University of Chicago Press, 1998.

Gates, Barbara T., ed. *In Nature's Name: An Anthology of Women's Writing and Illustration, 1780–1930*. University of Chicago Press, 2002.

Merrill, Lynn L. *The Romance of Victorian Natural History*. Oxford University Press, 1989.

Stedman, Jane W. 'Charlotte Brontë and Bewick's British Birds'. *BST*, 15.76 (1966), 36–40.

Thormählen, Marianne. *The Brontës and Education*. Cambridge University Press, 2007.

31. POLITICS

Brantlinger, Patrick. *The Spirit of Reform: British Literature and Politics, 1832–1867*. Cambridge, MA: Harvard University Press, 1977.

Briggs, Asa. *The Age of Improvement 1783–1867*. First published 1959; new edn Harlow: Longman, 2000.

Dinwiddy, J.R. *From Luddism to the First Reform Bill*. Oxford: Blackwell, 1986.

Ingham, Patricia. *The Brontës*. Oxford World's Classics, Authors in Context. Oxford University Press, 2006.

Matthew, Colin. *The Nineteenth Century*. Oxford University Press, 2000.

Morris, Pam. 'Heroes and Hero-Worship in Charlotte Brontë's *Shirley*'. *Nineteenth-Century Literature*, 54.3 (Dec. 1999), 285–307.

Offor, Richard. 'The Brontës – Their Relation to the History and Politics of their Time'. *BST*, 10.53 (1943), 150–60.

Plasa, Carl. *Charlotte Brontë*. Basingstoke: Palgrave, 1994.

Poovey, Mary. *Making a Social Body: British Cultural Formation, 1830–1864*. University of Chicago Press, 1995.

Rogers, Philip. 'Tory Brontë: Shirley and the "MAN"'. *Nineteenth-Century Literature*, 58.2 (Sept. 2003), 141–75.

Tucker, Herbert F., ed. *A Companion to Victorian Literature and Culture.* Oxford: Blackwell, 1999.

Wilson, A. N. *The Victorians.* London: Hutchinson, 2002.

32. NEWSPAPERS AND MAGAZINES

Alexander, Christine. 'Readers and Writers: *Blackwood's* and the Brontës'. *Gaskell Society Journal,* 8 (1994), 54–69.

Alexander, Christine, ed. *An Edition of the Early Writings of Charlotte Brontë,* vol. 1: *The Glass Town Saga, 1826–1832.* Oxford: Blackwell, for the Shakespeare Head Press, 1987.

Bock, Carol A. 'Authorship, the Brontës, and *Fraser's Magazine*: "Coming Forward" as an Author in Early Victorian England'. *Victorian Literature and Culture,* 29 (2001), 241–66.

Brake, Laurel, and Marysa Demoor, eds. *Dictionary of Nineteenth Century Journalism.* London: British Library, 2009.

Collier, Patrick. '"The lawless by force ... the peaceable by kindness": Strategies of Social Control in Charlotte Brontë's *Shirley* and the *Leeds Mercury*'. *Victorian Periodicals Review,* 32.4 (1999), 279–98.

Leeds Mercury. Full text in *19th Century British Library Newspapers.* http://newspapers.bl.uk/blcs (accessed 17 May 2012).

Rosengarten, Herbert J. 'Charlotte Brontë and the *Leeds Mercury*'. *Studies in English Literature 1500–1900,* 16 (1976), 591–600.

33. AGRICULTURE AND INDUSTRY

Baumber, Michael. *A History of Haworth.* Lancaster: Carnegie Publishing, 2009.

Crump, W. B. *The Little Hill Farm.* Rev. edn London: Scrivener Press, 1951.

Daunton, M. J. *Progress and Poverty: An Economic and Social History of Britain 1700–1850.* Oxford University Press, 1995.

Hartwell, R. M. 'The Yorkshire Woollen and Worsted Industry, 1800–1850'. Unpublished doctoral thesis, University of Oxford, 1955.

Heaton, Herbert. *The Yorkshire Woollen and Worsted Industries: From the Earliest Times up to the Industrial Revolution.* Oxford University Press, 1920.

Loudon, J. C. *An Encyclopaedia of Agriculture [etc.].* London, 1831; several edns during the nineteenth century.

Martins, Susanna Wade. *Farmers, Landlords and Landscapes.* Macclesfield: Windgather Press, 2004.

Mingay, G. E. *Rural Life in Victorian England.* London: Heinemann, 1976.

Mingay, G.E., ed. *The Victorian Countryside.* 2 vols. London: Routledge & Kegan Paul, 1981.

Williamson, Tom. *The Transformation of Rural England: Farming and the Landscape 1700–1870.* University of Exeter Press, 2002.

Wood, Steven. *Haworth: 'A strange uncivilized little place'.* Stroud: Tempus, 2005.

34. TRANSPORT AND TRAVEL

Buzard, James. *The Beaten Track: European Tourism, Literature, and the Ways to 'Culture', 1800–1918*. Oxford: Clarendon Press, 1993.

Dewhirst, Ian. *A History of Keighley*. Keighley Corporation, 1974.

Emsley, Kenneth. *Historic Haworth Today*. Bradford Libraries, 1995.

Felton, William. *A Treatise on Carriages*. 2 vols. London, 1794–5. Partly repr. as *Felton's Carriages: Being a Selection of Coaches, Chariots, Phaetons & C. from A Treatise on Carriages, Illustrated by Alan Osbahr*. London: Hugh Evelyn, 1962.

Jenkinson, David. *The London and Birmingham: A Railway of Consequence*. Harrow Weald: Capital Transport, 1988.

Miltoun, Francis [pseud.]. *All about Ships and Shipping*. 10th edn, ed. Edwin P. Harnack. London: Faber and Faber, 1959.

Robbins, Michael. *The Railway Age*. London: Routledge & Kegan Paul, 1962.

Ruijssenaars, Eric. *Charlotte Brontë's Promised Land: The Pensionnat Heger and Other Brontë Places in Brussels*. Haworth: Brontë Society, 2000.

Schivelbusch, Wolfgang. *The Railway Journey: Trains and Travel in the 19th Century*, trans. Anselm Hollo. Oxford: Blackwell, 1980.

35. LAW

Chedzoy, Ann. *A Scandalous Woman: The Story of Caroline Norton*. London: Allison and Busby, 1992.

Diederich, Nicole. 'The Art of Comparison: Remarriage in Anne Brontë's *The Tenant of Wildfell Hall*'. *Rocky Mountain Review of Language and Literature*, 57 (2003), 25–41.

Doggett, Maeve E. *Marriage, Wife-Beating and the Law in Victorian England*. London: Weidenfeld & Nicolson, 1992.

Dolin, Kieran. *Fiction and the Law: Legal Discourse in Victorian and Modernist Literature*. Cambridge University Press, 1999.

  A Critical Introduction to Law and Literature. Cambridge University Press, 2007.

Finn, Margaret. 'Victorian Law, Literature and History: Three Ships Passing in the Night'. *Journal of Victorian Culture*, 7 (2002), 134–46.

Holcombe, Lee. *Wives and Property: Reform of Married Women's Property Law in Nineteenth Century England*. Toronto University Press, 1983.

Petch, Stephen. 'Identity and Responsibility in Victorian England'. In Michael Freeman and Andrew D. E. Lewis, eds., *Law and Literature*. Current Legal Issues, 2. Oxford University Press, 1999, pp. 397–415.

  'Law, Literature, and Victorian Studies'. *Victorian Literature and Culture*, 35 (2007), 361–84.

Sanger, Charles P. *The Structure of* Wuthering Heights. London: Hogarth Press, 1926; frequently reprinted, e.g. in Ian Gregor, ed., *The Brontës: A Collection of Critical Essays*. Englewood Cliffs: Prentice-Hall, 1970, pp. 7–18.

Schramm, Jan-Melissa. *Testimony and Advocacy in Victorian Law, Literature and Theology*. Cambridge University Press, 2000.
Shanley, Mary. *Feminism, Marriage and the Law in Victorian England 1850–1895*. Princeton University Press, 1989.
Spring, Eileen. *Law, Land and Family: Aristocratic Inheritance in England 1300 to 1800*. Chapel Hill: University of North Carolina Press, 1993.
Ward, Ian. 'The Case of Helen Huntingdon'. *Criticism*, 49 (2007), 151–82.
'The Rochester Wives'. *Law and Humanities*, 2 (2008), 99–130.
Weisberg, Richard. *Poethics and Other Strategies of Law and Literature*. New York: Columbia University Press, 1992.
Wiener, Martin. *Men of Blood: Violence, Manliness, and Criminal Justice in Victorian England*. Cambridge University Press, 2004.
Williams, Melanie. *Empty Justice: One Hundred Years of Law, Literature and Philosophy*. London: Cavendish, 2002.

36. CLASS

Cohen, Monica F. *Professional Domesticity in the Victorian Novel: Women, Work and Home*. Cambridge University Press, 1998.
Davidoff, Leonore, and Catherine Hall. *Family Fortunes: Men and Women of the English Middle Class, 1780–1850*. University of Chicago Press, 1987.
Gallagher, Catherine. *The Industrial Reformation of English Fiction: Social Discourse and Narrative Form, 1832–1867*. University of Chicago Press, 1985.
Ingham, Patricia. *The Language of Gender and Class: Transformation in the Victorian Novel*. London and New York: Routledge, 1996.
The Brontës. Oxford World's Classics, Authors in Context. Oxford University Press, 2006.
Langland, Elizabeth. *Nobody's Angels: Middle-Class Women and Domestic Ideology in Victorian Culture*. Ithaca: Cornell University Press, 1995.
Levy, Anita. *Other Women: The Writing of Class, Race and Gender, 1832–1989*. Princeton University Press, 1994.
Poovey, Mary. *Uneven Developments: The Ideological Work of Gender in Mid-Victorian England*. University of Chicago Press, 1988.

37. CAREERS FOR MIDDLE-CLASS WOMEN

Davis, Tracy C., and Ellen Donkin, eds. *Women and Playwriting in Nineteenth-Century Britain*. Cambridge University Press, 1999.
Ewbank, Inga-Stina. *Their Proper Sphere: A Study of the Brontë Sisters as Early-Victorian Female Novelists*. London: Edward Arnold, 1966.
Gates, Barbara T., and Ann B. Shteir, eds. *Natural Eloquence: Women Reinscribe Science*. Madison: University of Wisconsin Press, 1997.
Hughes, Kathryn. *The Victorian Governess*. London: Rio Grande, 1993.
Shattock, Joanne, ed. *Women and Literature in Britain 1800–1900*. Cambridge University Press, 2001.

Swindells, Julia. *Victorian Writing and Working Women: The Other Side of Silence*. Cambridge: Polity, 1985.

Thompson, Nicola Diane, ed. *Victorian Women Writers and the Woman Question*. Cambridge University Press, 1999.

Thormählen, Marianne. *The Brontës and Education*. Cambridge University Press, 2007.

Vicinus, Martha, ed. *A Widening Sphere: Changing Roles of Victorian Women*. Bloomington: Indiana University Press, 1977.

38. MARRIAGE AND FAMILY LIFE

Davidoff, Leonore, and Catherine Hall. *Family Fortunes: Men and Women of the English Middle Class, 1780–1850*. University of Chicago Press, 1987.

Foster, Shirley. *Victorian Women's Fiction: Marriage, Freedom and the Individual*. London: Croom Helm, 1985.

Gillis, John R. *For Better, for Worse: British Marriages, 1600 to the Present*. New York: Oxford University Press, 1985.

Gleadle, Kathryn. *British Women in the Nineteenth Century*. Basingstoke: Palgrave, 2001.

Grylls, David. *Guardians and Angels: Parents and Children in Nineteenth-Century Literature*. London: Faber and Faber, 1978.

Houghton, Walter E. *The Victorian Frame of Mind, 1830–1870*. New Haven: Yale University Press, 1957; subsequently reissued.

Jalland, Pat. *Death in the Victorian Family*. London: Oxford University Press, 1997.

Kane, Penny. *Victorian Families in Fact and Fiction*. Basingstoke: Macmillan, 1995.

Lamonica, Drew. *'We Are Three Sisters': Self and Family in the Writing of the Brontës*. Columbia: University of Missouri Press, 2003.

Lerner, Laurence. *Love and Marriage: Literature and its Social Context*. London: Edward Arnold, 1979.

Macfarlane, Alan. *Marriage and Love in England: Modes of Reproduction 1300–1840*. Oxford: Blackwell, 1986.

Perkin, Joan. *Women and Marriage in Nineteenth-Century England*. Chicago: Lyceum, 1989.

Pollock, Linda A. *Forgotten Children: Parent–Child Relations from 1500 to 1900*. Cambridge University Press, 1983.

Stone, Lawrence. *Road to Divorce: England 1530–1987*. Oxford University Press, 1990.

Thormählen, Marianne. *The Brontës and Education*. Cambridge University Press, 2007.

39. DRESS

Ashelford, Jane. *The Art of Dress: Clothes and Society 1500–1914*. London: National Trust, 1996.

Berglund, Birgitta. 'In Defence of Madame Beck'. *Brontë Studies*, 30.3 (Nov. 2005), 185–211.

Bernstein, Sara T. '"In this same gown of shadow": Functions of Fashion in *Villette*'. In Sandra Hagan and Juliette Wells, eds., *The Brontës in the World of the Arts*. Aldershot: Ashgate, 2008, pp. 149–67.

Buck, Anne. *Victorian Costume and Costume Accessories*. New York: Thomas Nelson & Sons, 1961.

Foster, Vanda. *A Visual History of Costume: The Nineteenth Century*. London: B. T. Batsford, 1984.

Foster, Vanda, and Christina Walkley. *Crinolines and Crimping Irons: Victorian Clothes: How They Were Cleaned and Cared For*. London: Peter Owen, 1978.

Hughes, Clair. *Dressed in Fiction*. Oxford and New York: Berg, 2006.

Laver, James. *Costume and Fashion: A Concise History*. London: Thames and Hudson, 1982.

Lescart, Alain. 'All Women Are Grisettes in *Villette*'. *Brontë Studies*, 30.2 (July 2005), 103–11.

Newton, Stella Mary. *Health, Art and Reason: Dress Reformers of the 19th Century*. London: John Murray, 1974.

Steele, Valerie. *The Corset*. New Haven: Yale University Press, 2001.

40. SEXUALITY

Hoppen, K. Theodore. *The Mid-Victorian Generation: 1846–1888*. Oxford University Press, 1998.

Marcus, Steven. *The Other Victorians: A Study of Sexuality and Pornography in Mid-Nineteenth-Century England*. London: Weidenfeld & Nicolson, 1966.

Mason, Michael. *The Making of Victorian Sexuality*. Oxford University Press, 1995.

Matus, Jill L. *Unstable Bodies: Victorian Representations of Sexuality and Maternity*. Manchester University Press, 1995.

Maynard, John. *Charlotte Brontë and Sexuality*. Cambridge University Press, 1984.

Porter, Roy, and Lesley Hall. *The Facts of Life: The Creation of Sexual Knowledge in Britain 1650–1950*. New Haven: Yale University Press, 1985.

41. PHYSICAL HEALTH

Bailin, Miriam. *The Sickroom in Victorian Fiction: The Art of Being Ill*. Cambridge University Press, 1994.

Bewell, Alan. 'Jane Eyre and Victorian Medical Geography', *ELH*, 63.3 (Fall 1996), 773–808.

Caldwell, Janis McLarren. *Literature and Medicine in Nineteenth-Century Britain: From Mary Shelley to George Eliot*. Cambridge University Press, 2004.

Gezari, Janet. *Charlotte Brontë and Defensive Conduct: The Author and the Body at Risk*. Philadelphia: University of Pennsylvania Press, 1992.

Gorsky, Susan Rubinow. '"I'll Cry Myself Sick": Illness in Wuthering Heights'. *Literature and Medicine*, 18.2 (1999), 173–91.

McDonagh, Josephine. Introduction to Anne Brontë, *The Tenant of Wildfell Hall*. Oxford World's Classics. Oxford University Press, 2008.

Smith, F. B. *The People's Health, 1830–1910*. London: Croom Helm, 1979.

Sontag, Susan. *Illness as Metaphor*. New York: Farrar, Straus and Giroux, 1978.

Torgerson, Beth. *Reading the Brontë Body: Disease, Desire and the Constraints of Culture*. Basingstoke and New York: Palgrave Macmillan, 2005.

Wohl, Anthony. *Endangered Lives: Public Health in Victorian Britain*. Cambridge, MA: Harvard University Press, 1983.

42. MENTAL HEALTH

Cooter, Roger. *The Cultural Meaning of Popular Science: Phrenology and the Organization of Consent in Nineteenth-Century Britain*. Cambridge University Press, 1984.

Dames, Nicholas. *Amnesiac Selves: Nostalgia, Forgetting, and British Fiction, 1810–1870*. Oxford University Press, 2001.

Gilbert, Sandra M., and Susan Gubar. *The Madwoman in the Attic: The Woman Writer and the Nineteenth-Century Literary Imagination*. New Haven: Yale University Press, 1979; repr. 2000.

Logan, Peter Melville. *Nerves and Narratives: A Cultural History of Hysteria in Nineteenth-Century British Prose*. Berkeley: University of California Press, 1997.

Scull, Andrew. *The Most Solitary of Afflictions: Madness and Society in Britain 1700–1900*. New Haven: Yale University Press, 1993.

Showalter, Elaine. *The Female Malady: Women, Madness, and English Culture, 1830–1980*. New York: Penguin, 1987.

Shuttleworth, Sally. *Charlotte Brontë and Victorian Psychology*. Cambridge University Press, 1996.

Small, Helen. *Love's Madness: Medicine, the Novel, and Female Insanity, 1800–1865*. Oxford: Clarendon Press, 1996.

Taylor, Jenny Bourne, and Sally Shuttleworth, eds. *Embodied Selves: An Anthology of Psychological Texts 1830–1890*. Oxford: Clarendon Press, 1998.

Torgerson, Beth. *Reading the Brontë Body: Disease, Desire and the Constraints of Culture*. Basingstoke and New York: Palgrave Macmillan, 2005.

van Wyhe, John. *Phrenology and the Origins of Victorian Scientific Naturalism*. Aldershot: Ashgate, 2004.

Vrettos, Athena. *Somatic Fictions: Imagining Illness in Victorian Culture*. Stanford University Press, 1995.

Wood, Jane. *Passion and Pathology in Victorian Fiction*. Oxford University Press, 2001.

Index

Recipients of letters are not indexed in that capacity. Nor are names and titles in notes when indexed as occurring in the running text. Titles of works by authors other than the Brontës are indexed (under their authors' names) only when the primary reference in the running text is to the relevant work and not to its author.

Printed in Great Britain
by Amazon.co.uk, Ltd.,
Marston Gate.